What People S
The Literary Er

"The Literary Enneagram *is a groundbrea.* ⎯ ⎯⎯ ⎯⎯⎯ *aemonstrates the universality of the Enneagram. Rightly understood, the nine types are more than psychological styles, they are worldviews—and out of these emerge literature, theater, music—all of the arts—to hold up a mirror to human nature. This book is an important resource in a growing field. It will be valuable to anyone seeking a more profound understanding of literary characters."*

—Don Richard Riso & Russ Hudson, authors, *The Wisdom of the Enneagram, Personality Types, Understanding the Enneagram*

"*In this fascinating book, Judith Searle explores the essences of characters, giving us insights into ourselves and the people we know and create. I strongly recommend the book for writers and actors, as well as all who are intrigued with the complexity, diversity, and dimensionality of our humanity."*

—Dr. Linda Seger, author, *Creating Unforgettable Characters*

"*By seeing her characters through the lens of type, Judith skillfully reveals an unexpected inner coherence, an illuminating consistency that propels the human condition. Now we know a lot more about it."*

—Helen Palmer, teacher and author, *The Enneagram, The Enneagram in Love and Work, The Pocket Enneagram, The Enneagram Advantage*

"*Two-thirds of the way through this book, I realized that by understanding it I would know which actors would like which book or screenplay, and thus I would waste less time pursuing the 'wrong' people. In Hollywood you hear a lot about 'character arc' and odd claims like 'character is story.' With this book, you'll understand character basics, completely. It's really a crystal lens of understanding, and I'm grateful Judith wrote it."*

—Skip Press, author, *The Complete Idiot's Guide to Screenwriting*

"*Both scholarly and compassionate,* The Literary Enneagram *is enriched by many examples from literature along with Searle's insightful commentary and analysis. This book makes a definitive contribution the Enneagram by applying it to the realm of literature. It is not necessary to agree with all of Judith's point of view and analyses to benefit from her work. This is one of the fortunate aspects of literature: there are many ways to experience authors' meanings."*

—David Daniels, M.D., co-author of *The Essential Enneagram*

"*This book is the first synthesis of the Enneagram in literature. An enjoyable read both for someone familiar with the Enneagram and for a newcomer, this book is lucid, exciting and poignant, and shows Judith Searle to be a leading thinker and articulate writer who knows how to bring theories to life through the vehicle of some of our favorite literary characters."*

—Andrea Isaacs, Co-Editor, *Enneagram Monthly*

THE
LITERARY
ENNEAGRAM

Characters from
the Inside Out

JUDITH SEARLE

Ignudo Press

Santa Monica, California

First Ignudo Edition, August 2011

Copyright © 2001, 2011 by Judith Searle

Published by
Ignudo Press
855 10th Street #208
Santa Monica, California
310-393-5372
www.judithsearle.com

Previously published: Portland, OR
Metamorphous Press, © 2001

All rights reserved. No part of this book may be reproduced in any form or by any means, electronic or mechanical, including photocopying, recording, or by any information storage and retrieval system, without permission in writing from the author. Sole exception is in the case of brief quotations embodied in critical articles and reviews.
The opinions expressed in this book are those of the author and do not represent the teachings of any institution or school. Sources are credited whenever possible. Although this book is exhaustively researched the author and publisher can assume no responsibility for errors, in accuracies, omissions, or any other inconsistency herein. Any slights against people or organizations are unintentional.

Cover design by Steven J. Slomkowski
Printed in the United States of America

ISBN: 978-1-55552-107-3

Library of Congress Cataloging-in-Publication Data

Searle, Judith.
    The literary enneagram : characters from the inside out / Judith Searle
    p. cm.
    Includes bibliographical references and index.

    1.   Characters and characteristics in literature. 2. Enneagram. I. Title.

    PN56.5 .S43 2001
    809'.927—dc21

                                                                                    20010266603

For Basil

Acknowledgements

This book would not exist without the help of many people:

First, it would not have been conceivable without Oscar Ichazo's brilliant and innovative delineation of the Enneagram of Personality. My four years of research into literary examples of the types have only increased my respect for his monumental contribution to our understanding of the human condition.

I owe a great debt of gratitude to Claudio Naranjo, whose development of Enneagram theory and practice has enriched the lives and work of all students of the system. Not only have his writings and workshops been an invaluable source of understanding for me, he has also been generous in his suggestions of literary examples.

I also owe much to Tom Condon, Russ Hudson, Helen Palmer, and Don Richard Riso, whose writings and workshops have deepened my understanding of the nine Enneagram styles. Their encouragement about this book has meant a great deal to me.

Andrea Isaacs and Jack Labanauskas, the editors of *Enneagram Monthly*, have been helpful and supportive throughout my work on this project, and their decision to publish portions of this book has been important to me.

David Balding, my publisher, deserves much credit for his wise counsel about the final shaping of the manuscript. I am also grateful to Tom Condon for his invaluable editorial advice in the last stages of this book. I appreciate Clarence Thomson's support at a crucial juncture in the publishing process.

Mary Bast, Barbara Babcock, Mona Coates, Ed Jacobs, Bruce Love, Virginia Mullin, Liz Rich, Carolyn See, and Bert Somers read and commented on the manuscript at various stages. Many of their suggestions for literary examples are included here, and their sage advice has allowed me to eliminate many mistakes. I accept full responsibility for whatever errors remain.

Others who have made helpful suggestions of examples include Becky Malecki, Ed McInnis, Mary Porter-Chase, Gayle Scott, Mary Jo Shane, and Anne Silver.

I am grateful to the IEA/SoCal board for their support and encouragement of my work: Katie Atherton, Barbara Brandt, Stephanie Davis, Kathryn Grant, Laurie Cook Johnson, Richard Long, Gayle Scott, and Mary Jo Shane.

Members of the Women's Lunch Group have expressed interest and encouragement from the beginning of this project: Linda Phillips Ashour, Susan Chehak, Jo Giese, Yasmin Kafai, Rae Lewis, Dale Pring MacSweeney, Jo Ann Matyas, Luchita Mullican, Virginia Mullin, Maria Munroe, Doreen Nelson, Nancy Nimoy, Amanda Pope, Carolyn See, Janet Sternburg, and Susan Suntree.

Finally, Basil Langton has been a rock of support throughout my work on this book, offering astute editorial suggestions as well as loving encouragement.

Contents

Introduction

When I was a graduate student at Harvard in the 1960s I took a class called "Theories of Personality." My professor, the humanist psychologist Gordon Allport, assigned a final paper in which each of us was to describe someone we knew well, using the various typologies we'd just spent the semester studying.

I chose as my subject my college roommate, a lively, quirky young woman who resembled no one I'd ever met. Dutifully, I applied the theories of Freud, Jung, Adler, Sheldon, and the others to her and discussed how, according to Freud's theory, she clearly had a strong id; how Jung would classify her as an extroverted sensing type; how Sheldon would see her as a combination meso-morph-ectomorph.

I hated doing the paper and found it a useless, even fraudulent way of capturing my friend's distinctive qualities. The guidelines for the paper included a request from Professor Allport that we discuss in the final section what we had learned from this exercise. I expressed my outrage over the assignment, aware that I was probably killing my chances for a decent grade but so angry about being forced to participate in this academic charade that I didn't care. To my amazement, my paper was returned with an "A" and a friendly note from the Professor explaining that the hidden purpose of the exercise had been to help me see exactly what I had seen: the limitations of any theory of personality for capturing the essence of a live human being.

For years afterward I resisted any theory that tried to pigeonhole people into types. As a college teacher of writing and literature, a professional actress, and a published novelist, I maintained a wary distance from such psychological typologies. When a friend suggested I might find the Enneagram—a system based on nine personality types—a valuable tool for my acting, writing, and teaching, I expressed polite interest but felt privately skeptical.

When a second friend made the same recommendation, I finally bought Helen Palmer's *The Enneagram*, although the nine-pointed diagram on the cover looked forbidding, even faintly occult. A psychotherapist friend who saw the book on my living room table remarked that she'd found the Enneagram useful in her work. When I got around to reading Palmer's book, the system struck me as more true-to-life than the theories I'd studied at Harvard. Also more complex, though from what I read, I immediately guessed that I was probably a One: perfectionistic, concerned with issues of right and wrong, irritable with others who seemed unconcerned about these issues.

I went to a lecture about the system at a local bookstore, where I learned that the best way to understand the nine basic styles was to attend workshops that included panels of exemplars. The first panels I attended, given by Helen Palmer and Richard Rohr, worked this way: Five people—a mix of genders and ages, but all having the same Enneagram point—were interviewed by Palmer about their lives. Out of their responses a pattern emerged that was characteristic of their particular style. By watching all nine panels you could get a picture of each style and decide which was closest to your own.

The members of the One panel struck me as humorless, self-righteous, nit-picking bores. Was I really like that? Rohr had said in his introduction to the workshop that when you encounter your own Enneagram type for the first time, a common reaction is to feel horrified and humiliated. But Rohr had a delightful sense of humor—and hadn't he admitted to being a One? In the midst of my distress over being a One, I found a shred of hope.

Was it possible I was wrong about my type? I decided to attend more Enneagram panels, to see other living examples. Several workshops later, I realized I truly was a One and that Ones, like all the other Enneagram styles, have both splendid and horrifying qualities. Hard for a Perfectionist to stomach, but by now I was thoroughly hooked on this game. I was already beginning to recognize Enneagram patterns in people I knew.

Now, basic Enneagram etiquette is *not* to go around telling your family and friends their type and, for the most part, I resisted this temptation. Several Enneagram authors have commented that Ones tend to be obsessive-compulsive, and I was no exception. I read everything I could get my hands on and attended even more workshops, sometimes appearing as an exemplar on panels.

My hunger for more on the Enneagram led me to the Training Programs offered by Don Richard Riso and Russ Hudson. During my two Trainings with them, Don and Russ expanded my consciousness about many aspects of the system, including the stress and security points (the arrows), the wings, the Instincts (commonly called the "subtypes"), childhood patterns, the Levels of Development, and the Hornevian Triads.

Realizing that there were at least eight ways of seeing the universe that were fundamentally different from my own was a major shock and produced a huge shift in awareness for me. I was also impressed by the Enneagram's complete-ness: there are no loose ends, no basic human temperaments or faculties unaccounted for. Possibly the most important revelation about the system for me was its usefulness in the real world.

Practical Uses of the Enneagram

In the 1970s, the modern version of the Enneagram outlined by Bolivian psychologist Oscar Ichazo, and rooted in centuries of spiritual tradition, was first introduced to the United States by Chilean psychiatrist Claudio Naranjo. Since that time a few of Naranjo's students have applied his teachings to their own contexts and developed the material further. Knowledge of the Enneagram has spread widely and found a variety of practical applications.

Every system of knowledge has the potential for both positive and negative applications, and the Enneagram is no exception. So far it has been adapted to purposes ranging from spiritual growth, improving relationships, and increasing tolerance for human diversity to cynically manipulating people for personal, political, legal, and economic advantage.

Psychotherapists and career counselors use the Enneagram to deepen their work with their clients. Lawyers use it in jury selection. Businesses apply it to team building, conflict resolution and leadership development. Teachers find the system helpful to better understand different learning and teaching styles. Religious communities use it to help their members develop spiritually. Writers and actors use the Enneagram for character development. Parents use it to gain insight into their children's needs and problems. Other people use it in their daily lives to simply understand themselves better and become more compassionate.

Why Literary Examples?

In *The Politics of Experience*, R.D. Laing writes: "We can see other people's behavior, but not their experience. This has led some people to insist that psychology has nothing to do with the other person's experience, but only with his behavior."

In all Enneagram styles there is a gulf between outer behavior and inner experience. Although two people may behave the same way, their actions may arise from different, even opposite, motivations. For example, Fives and Nines are both known for avoiding conflict, but Fives do so because they are afraid of being engulfed by others, while Nines avoid conflict in the service of merging with others.

To fully understand an Enneagram style, it is necessary to grasp the inner subjective tensions that drive it. Enneagram students have sought to understand the inner process of the styles through various means—interviews with exemplars, analysis of therapy sessions, self-reports of insightful individuals, analysis of film and television characters—and all these approaches have greatly enriched our understanding of the system. Some writers have offered literary characters as examples of Enneagram styles, but this extraordinary resource has generally been underexplored.

Great fiction offers us a unique opportunity to examine the raw material of subjective experience before it crystallizes into behavior. Through the technique of interior monologue—which shows a character's thoughts, feelings, and instincts—fiction writers offer us a dramatic and intimate way to experience individuals as they experience themselves. Interior monologue reveals the texture of consciousness, the moment-to-moment life process, and is a powerful way of exploring psychology in depth.

T.S. Eliot once wrote: "If we learn to read poetry properly, the poet never persuades us to believe anything. . . . What we learn from Dante or the Bhagavadgita or any other religious poetry is what it *feels* like to believe that religion." In a similar sense, literary exemplars offer us a glimpse of what it feels like to have a particular Enneagram style.

Novels, short stories, and even some plays allow us to trace a character's development through *both inner experience and outer behavior* giving us a deeper understanding of his or her Enncagram style as a whole. These insights are far more profound than those available through simply watching the actions of a character in a film.

During the four years I have worked on this book, I have been continually stunned by the way literary examples—from authors who could have had no knowledge of the Enneagram—validate the system. My research has given me a fresh awareness of the power of this elegant, subtle, and insightful way of looking at human personality.

Part One:
How the Enneagram Works

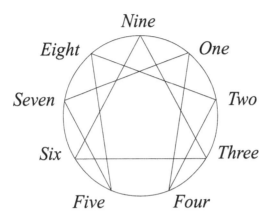

While the Enneagram describes nine basic temperaments, the system's variations allow for a wide spectrum of human characteristics and expression. The numbers assigned to the nine styles do not represent a hierarchy: no Enneagram style is better than any other. As you'll see in the literary examples I present in later chapters, every type can be a hero or a villain.

Our personal Enneagram style is defined by what Helen Palmer has called our "habitual focus of attention." This is something like the default position on a computer: when no counter instructions are specifically given, the computer defaults to the procedure that it knows best. So our "home" Enneagram style simply represents our usual way of perceiving the world. Through this perspective we focus more strongly on some aspects of our experience and are oblivious to others.

I'll discuss the variations within the styles in detail later, but let's begin with a thumbnail sketch of the Enneagram's nine styles:

• One (The Critic): "I perfect, therefore I am."
Ones are principled, orderly, self-doubting, irritable.
• Two (The Lover): "I love, therefore I am."
Twos are nurturing, seductive, emotional, proud.
• Three (The Achiever): "I succeed, therefore I am."
Threes are energetic, competitive, driven, vain.
• Four (The Aesthete): "I suffer, therefore I am."
Fours are authentic, passionate, depressed, envious.

- Five (The Analyst): "I think, therefore I am."
Fives are observant, independent, withdrawn, stingy.
- Six (The Pessimist): "I doubt, therefore I am."
Sixes are loyal, authority conscious, suspicious, fearful.
- Seven (The Optimist): "I enjoy, therefore I am."
Sevens are optimistic, egalitarian, self-indulgent, dilettantish.
- Eight (The Trail-Blazer): "I dominate, therefore I am."
 Eights are forceful, impulsive, excessive, vengeful.
- Nine (The Connector): "I connect, therefore I am."
Nines are accepting, generous, distractible, indolent.

A Few Examples

Famous fictional characters often have distinct and identifiable Enneagram styles. For instance, Blanche DuBois in Tennessee Williams's *A Streetcar Named Desire* is a Four (The Aesthete). Her emotional sensitivity, fastidiousness, and ostentatious refinement are especially characteristic of that Enneagram style, as is her abhorrence of her sister Stella's boorish husband, Stanley:

> "Thousands and thousands of years have passed him right by, and there he is—Stanley Kowalski—survivor of the stone age! . . . *God!* Maybe we are a long way from being made in God's image, but Stella— my sister—there has been *some* progress since then! Such things as art—as poetry and music—such kinds of new light have come into the world since then! In some kinds of people some tenderer feelings have had some little beginning! That we have got to make *grow!* and *cling* to, and hold as our flag! In this dark march toward whatever it is we're approaching. . . . *Don't—don't hang back with the brutes!*" (Scene 4, p. 83)

Stanley Kowalski, the "brute" that Blanche describes, also has a distinct style: Eight (The Trail Blazer), someone who is typically aggressive and crude, especially as perceived by a sensitive Four.

In an interior monologue from James Jones's *From Here to Eternity* we see another Enneagram style. Here we are inside the mind of Sergeant Milton Warden:

> Oh, Milton, Warden thought, what a son of a bitch you are, what a fine lyin son of a bitch. You'd sell your own mother to Lucky Luciano if it would secure the hatches on this outfit. You'll lie and cajole poor old Niccolo into staying, just to make your supply efficient. You've lied so much now, he told himself, you don't know whats true and what aint. And all because you want to make your company *Superior.* You mean Holmes's company, he thought . . . Its his company, not yours. Why dont you let him do it? Why dont you let him sacrifice his soul upon the altar

of efficiency? Yes, he thought, why dont you? Why dont you get out of it? When *are* you going to get out of it and save your self-respect? Never, he told himself. Because its been so long now you're afraid to find out if you've still got the self-respect to save. Have you got it? he asked himself. No, Milton, no, I dont think you have. (pp. 27-28)

Warden's mental process indicates that he's a One—self-critical, obsessed with perfection, continually flogging himself to be a better person. Contrast him with Bowman, the main character in Eudora Welty's story "Death of a Traveling Salesman." A shoe salesman traveling through rural Mississippi, Bowman has a car accident and approaches an isolated farmhouse. Exhausted, sick, and discouraged, he is met at the door by a suspicious old woman who invites him in:

"I have a nice line of women's low priced shoes . . . " he said.
But the woman answered, "Sonny'll be here. He's strong. Sonny'll move your car."
"Where is he now?"
"Farms for Mr. Redmond."
Mr. Redmond. Mr. Redmond. That was someone he would never have to encounter, and he was glad. Somehow the name did not appeal to him . . . In a flare of touchiness and anxiety, Bowman wished to avoid even mention of unknown men and their unknown farms.
"Do you live here alone?" He was surprised to hear his old voice chatty, confidential, inflected for selling shoes, asking a question like that—a thing he did not even want to know.
"Yes. We are alone." (p. 239)

Bowman is a Three (The Achiever), a man who pays little attention to his personal feelings and automatically shapes his behavior according to what will bring him success in work. Even on the verge of death, Bowman is driven to present an attractive and successful image.

The Enneagram also accounts for complex, seemingly contradictory characters. Shakespeare's Hamlet, for instance, is readily identifiable as a Six (The Pessimist), preoccupied with worst-case scenarios, mistrustful, continually testing the loyalties of friends and family, often immobilized by fear and conflicted about action. Hamlet's most famous soliloquy reflects all these themes:

To be, or not to be: that is the question:
Whether 'tis nobler in the mind to suffer
The slings and arrows of outrageous fortune,
Or to take arms against a sea of troubles,
And by opposing end them. To die: to sleep. . . .
To sleep: perchance to dream: ay, there's the rub,

For in that sleep of death what dreams may come
When we have shuffled off this mortal coil,
Must give us pause. . . .
Thus conscience does make cowards of us all,
And thus the native hue of resolution
Is sicklied o'er with the pale cast of thought,
And enterprises of great pitch and moment,
With this regard their currents turn awry,
And lose the name of action. (III, i, 56-88)

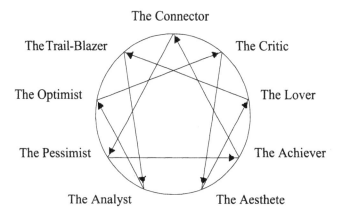

The Connector
The Trail-Blazer   The Critic
The Optimist   The Lover
The Pessimist   The Achiever
        The Analyst   The Aesthete

About the Diagram

The Enneagram diagram has ancient roots; it was known as early as 2500 B.C. in Babylon or the Middle East. The symbol was also familiar to the Greek mathematician/philosopher Pythagoras (ca 582 - ca 507 B.C.).

Spiritual teacher George Ivanovich Gurdjieff, a Greek-Armenian probably born in 1866, is responsible for introducing the Enneagram symbol to the modern world. Although Gurdjieff was interested in human growth and transformation, he mainly used the diagram to illustrate natural laws and processes of spiritual development.

The modern Enneagram, with its emphasis on psychology and personality styles, was created by Oscar Ichazo, a Bolivian-born psychologist who as a child had access to many esoteric books and who later traveled extensively in the Middle East and elsewhere. In the 1950s he discovered the connections between the Enneagram symbol and the nine personality styles, which he placed in order on the diagram, an extraordinary stroke of insight. He also assigned each style a name and described its basic qualities. Ichazo's sources for the Enneagram may include ancient Greek philosophy and the mystical traditions of Christianity, Buddhism, Judaism, and Islam, but the exact origins of his work are unknown.

Psychiatrist Claudio Naranjo is responsible for developing many significant aspects of the Enneagram as we currently know it. It was Naranjo who correlated the nine styles with familiar psychiatric diagnostic categories and devised the panel method of interviewing people who share the same style. He also augmented the basic diagram with arrows that describe the personality dynamics of each style.

Later in the book, I'll show how these dynamics work in practice. For now it is enough to emphasize that the Enneagram does not describe fixed types but rather active character dynamics. These are especially evident when an individual feels stressed and temporarily shifts into the attitudes and behavior of a different Enneagram style, followed by other times when he or she feels secure, which usually prompts a shift to another style.

The arrows in the Enneagram diagram indicate the consistent directions that each style shifts towards. The arrow that points *away* from the home style leads to what is called the "stress" point. Thus a One under stress often behaves like a Four, while a Four under stress behaves in ways commonly associated with a Two, and so forth. Movement against the direction of the arrows is towards the direction of "security." Thus a One when feeling secure behaves more like a Seven, while a Seven behaves in ways commonly associated with a Five, and so on.

Range and Arc in Literary Characters

These movements are the key to both the *range* and the *arc* of literary characters. A character's *range* is defined by the variety of responses he or she is capable of at any point in time. For example, the range of Hamlet, a Six, is visible in the many moods he exhibits in the soliloquy below, delivered after he watches a troupe of actors rehearsing a play. Reacting to the intense emotion he sees in one of the actors, Hamlet suddenly feels guilty over his own failure to avenge his father's murder. Then he realizes that fear is the root cause of his inaction, grows angry at the uncle who murdered his father, and shifts into sarcastic self-laceration. Next he hatches a detailed plan of action, justifies his previous failure to act, and then finally becomes resolute:

What's Hecuba to him, or he to Hecuba,
That he should weep for her? What would he do
Had he the motive and the cue for passion
That I have? . . .
But I am pigeon-livered and lack gall
To make oppression bitter, or ere this
I should have fatted all the region kites
With this slave's offal. Bloody, bawdy villain!
Remorseless, treacherous, lecherous, kindless villain!
O, vengeance!
Why, what an ass am I! This is most brave,

That I, the son of a dear father murdered,
Prompted to my revenge by heaven and hell,
Must, like a whore, unpack my heart with words
And fall a-cursing like a very drab,
A scullion!
Fie upon't! foh! About, my brain! I have heard
That guilty creatures sitting at a play
Have by the very cunning of the scene
Been struck so to the soul that presently
They have proclaimed their malefactions.
For murder, though it have no tongue, will speak
With most miraculous organ. I'll have these players
Play something like the murder of my father
Before mine uncle. I'll observe his looks,
I'll tent him to the quick. If he but blench,
I know my course. The spirit that I have seen
May be the devil, and the devil hath power
To assume a pleasing shape, yea, and perhaps
Out of my weakness and my melancholy,
As he is very potent with such spirits,
Abuses me to damn me. I'll have grounds
More relative than this. The play's the thing
Wherein I'll catch the conscience of the King. (II, ii, 585-634)

The amazing range of Hamlet's responses in this soliloquy shows the basic
complexity of his character. It is also consistent with a Six's primary focus on
fear and worst-case scenarios and the style's tendency towards contradictory
impulses.

Skillfully written literary characters also allow us to watch an individual
psychologically change over the course of the story—what is called the *arc* of
a character. Hamlet's character arc begins with his initial state of psychological
disintegration and is complete at the play's end when he has grown significantly.

At the beginning of Shakespeare's play, after he learns from his father's
Ghost that the father was murdered, Hamlet feels a personal responsibility to
settle the score with the murderer:

The time is out of joint. O cursèd spite,
That ever I was born to set it right! (I, v, 188-189)

His melancholy and pretended madness alternate with attempts to flog
himself into action. The direction of stress for a Six is toward Three, who finds
action easy because he is able to ignore his feelings. The Six moving to Three
exhibits the negative aspects of the stress point, and Hamlet's action of killing
Polonius is rash and counterproductive:

HAMLET: [*Draws*] How now? A rat? Dead for a ducat, dead!
[*Makes a pass through the arras and*] kills Polonius.
POLONIUS. [*Behind*] O, I am slain!
QUEEN: O me, what has thou done?
HAMLET: Nay, I know not. Is it the King?
QUEEN: O, what a rash and bloody deed is this!
HAMLET: A bloody deed—almost as bad, good Mother,
As kill a king, and marry with his brother.
QUEEN: As kill a king?
HAMLET: Ay, lady, it was my word.
[*Lifts up the arras and sees Polonius*]
Thou wretched, rash, intruding fool, farewell!
I took thee for thy better. . . . (III, iv, 23-32)

After Polonius's murder, Hamlet is forced to leave Denmark and sail to England. On the ship, in order to save his own life, he takes further action, which results in the deaths of his schoolmates Rosencrantz and Guildenstern. Observing a land battle from the deck of the ship, he takes it as a personal call to vengeance on his uncle for the murder of his father:

O, from this time forth,
My thoughts be bloody, or be nothing worth! (IV, iv, 65-66)

By the end of the play, however, Hamlet has changed, arriving at a distinctly different view of mortality, a calm acceptance of his personal fate, and a simple spirituality he never showed in the first half of the play. When his villainous uncle invites him to take part in a fencing match with Polonius's son, Hamlet's friend Horatio suspects a trick and urges him to refuse the invitation. But Hamlet says:

Not a whit, we defy augury. There is special providence in the fall
of a sparrow. If it be now, 'tis not to come; if it be not to come, it will be
now; if it be not now, yet it will come. The readiness is all. . . . Let be.
(V, ii, 230-235)

The Hamlet who dies at the end of the play is vastly different from the one who was so ambivalent about both life and death at the beginning. And his character arc is predicted by the Enneagram: the arrows show the Six under stress moving to the negative side of Three—becoming so bent on action that he ignores its destructive consequences, then finally coming to rest in his security space, on the positive side of Nine—accepting and merging with the will of providence, no longer concerned with personal danger.

As we shall see, combining the concepts of range and arc with the Enneagram's stress and security points will help us appreciate how the subjective depths of literary characters—and ourselves—are continually in motion.

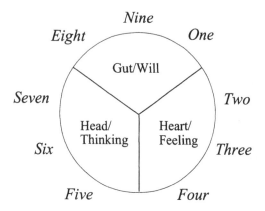

The Three Centers

The Enneagram diagram traditionally divides the nine styles into three groups of three. Each of these triads is associated with a different human faculty and thought to be located in a different part of the body. For many people, identifying their primary center is the first step toward discovering their dominant Enneagram style.

The Gut or Will Centered Types

Located at the top of the diagram, Eight, Nine and One are the Ennegram styles centered in the faculty of will. People with these styles are often extra conscious of the boundaries between themselves and others, and make strong efforts to defend their autonomy. Because anger is often a major problem for them, Eights, Nines and Ones are sometimes called "anger" styles.

• Eights (The Trail Blazer) use their anger directly to impose their will on other people and to dominate situations. Their working hypothesis is: "If I can intimidate and dominate others, then I will be safe."

• Nines (The Connector) see themselves as easygoing and are often unaware of their anger. However, their passive-aggressive behavior betrays their strong and stubborn will. "If I can keep an open mind about all possible strategies, then I will be safe."

• Ones (The Critic) turn their anger inward to self-criticism and their will to fierce self-discipline. Their irritability reveals their resentment at what they see as the ethical lapses of others. "If I can make myself and everything around me perfect, then I will be safe."

The Heart or Feeling Centered Types

Ennegram styles Two, Three and Four, clustered on the right-hand side of the diagram, are most aware of emotions and interpersonal connections. People with these styles seek approval from others and are especially conscious of the image they present to the world. This triad's focus is on "feelings," especially sad or painful ones:

• Twos (The Lover) focus so strongly on the feelings of others that they often lack awareness of their own feelings and desires. They seek to present the image of a loving and helpful person. Their working hypothesis is: "If I can make others love me and depend on me, then I will be safe."

• Threes (The Achiever) are so concerned about presenting the image of a successful person that they are often out of touch with their own feelings and the feelings of others. "If I can establish a public image of myself as a successful person, then I will be safe."

• Fours (The Aesthete) often grow deeply absorbed with their own feelings and concerned with presenting an image that is beautiful, authentic, and original. "If I can make friends with the darkness and become a connoisseur of my own pain, then I will be safe."

The Head or Thinking Centered Types

Fives, Sixes and Sevens, grouped on the left side of the diagram, are most aware of life's dangers. People with these styles tend to use their minds to cope with their anxieties about being at risk in the world and are sometimes called "fear" styles.

• Fives (The Analyst) often fear being engulfed by other people. They shore up their boundaries by amassing knowledge, which they use as a buffer to keep others at a distance. "If I can keep my mind focused on grasping the world's complexities, then I will be safe."

• Sixes (The Pessimist) are usually preoccupied with worst-case scenarios. Ever on the lookout for danger, they manage their fear by forming solid relationships with reliable people and having a clear understanding of lines of authority. Some people with this style seek the protection of authority, while others rebel against it. "If I can stay alert to all possible dangers and find trustworthy allies, then I will be safe."

• Sevens (The Optimist) deny their fears and concentrate instead on enjoyable activities, maintaining a positive attitude and staying continually in motion. "If I can distract myself with pleasure and avoid thinking about any dangers, then I will be safe."

The Hornevian Triads

Karen Horney, a psychoanalyst trained by Freud, observed from her clinical work that individuals choose one of three neurotic "solutions": "moving away from people," "moving against people," or "moving toward people."

It is interesting to note that in each of the three centers we find one Enneagram point from each of Horney's three categories: In the Gut/Will triad, the Eight style is aggressive — "moving against people," the Nine withdrawn— "moving away from people," and the One compliant/dependent—"moving toward people." In the Heart/Feeling triad, Two is compliant/dependent, Three aggressive, and Four withdrawn. In the Head/Thinking triad, Five is withdrawn, Six compliant/dependent, and Seven aggressive. I'll have more to say about the implications of these correlations in later chapters.

Stress and Security Points

As I mentioned, each Enneagram style has characteristic ways of moving and changing when stressed or when feeling secure. For instance, Ones under stress frequently resemble Fours in that they can become self-absorbed, depressed, masochistic, mired in suffering. When feeling secure, however, the same One could seem and act like a Seven: imaginative, confident, fun-loving, appreciative of life's pleasures. Four—following the arrow on the diagram— would be called the One's "stress point" and Seven—against the direction of the arrow—is the One's "security point."

Remember Warden, the self-critical One in *From Here to Eternity* who was so obsessed with efficiency? When he feels secure and outside the constraints of his normal work environment, he sees the world quite differently. Here, for instance, he is on the verge of making love to Karen, his commanding officer's wife:

> Warden set his glass down carefully. He moved toward her on the chair, seeing the nipples wrinkled tightly like flowers closed for night, seeing the feminine grossness that he loved, that was always there, that he always knew was there, hidden maybe behind perfume, unmentioned, unacknowledged, even denied, but still always there, existing, the beautiful lovely grossness of the lioness and the honest bitch dog, that no matter how much, shrinking, they tried to say it wasn't so, in the end always had to be admitted. (p. 119)

This passage sounds more like a Seven than a One. Sevens are strongly connected to the physical world and often indulge their sensual appetites, even to the point of sexual promiscuity. Though this side of Warden's character is in distinct contrast to the one we saw earlier, it is accounted for in the Enneagram. Ones experience a consistent pattern of tension between the extremes of Four and Seven. Thus the poles of Four and Seven define the One's emotional compass, which can swing from depression to euphoria.

A predictable emotional continuum exists for the other styles, as well. For some it is wide, while for other styles it is narrow. Self-dramatizing Fours, for example, have a narrower range than Ones. Returning to Blanche DuBois, we see that when she feels secure she displays some of the self-aware clarity and cogency of a One—for instance as she describes her first meeting with Stanley:

> Oh, I guess he's just not the type that goes for jasmine perfume, but maybe he's what we need to mix with our blood now that we've lost Belle Reve. We thrashed it out. I feel a bit shaky, but I think I handled

it nicely, I laughed and treated it all as a joke. . . . (Scene 2, p. 45)

Under stress, however, Fours frequently take on negative characteristics of Twos. Late in the play, as Blanche feels more beleaguered, she becomes hysterical and obsessed with pleasing people like an unhealthy Two:

STELLA: Why did you scream like that?

BLANCHE: I don't know why I screamed! [*continuing nervously*] Mitch—Mitch is coming at seven. I guess I am just feeling nervous about our relations. [*She begins to talk rapidly and breathlessly*] He hasn't gotten a thing but a goodnight kiss, that's all I have given him, Stella. I want his respect. And men don't want anything they get too easy. But on the other hand men lose interest quickly. Especially when the girl is over—thirty. They think a girl over thirty ought to—the vulgar term is—"put out.". . . And I—I'm not "putting out." Of course he—he doesn't know—I mean I haven't informed him—of my real age!

STELLA: Why are you sensitive about your age?

BLANCHE: Because of hard knocks my vanity's been given. What I mean is—he thinks I'm sort of—prim and proper, you know! [*She laughs out sharply*] I want to *deceive* him enough to make him—want me. . ." (Scene 5, pp. 94-95)

Here we see Blanche—her pride wounded, her position in her sister's household precarious—scheming to manipulate Stanley's friend Mitch into marrying her. After Stanley tells Mitch about her sordid past and he rejects her, she spirals downward through pathological levels of the Two style into her final madness.

The contrast between Blanche's behavior at her One security point and her Two stress point is expressed in her ambivalence about people. Are others to be indiscriminately courted out of her fear of being totally isolated—as she does when feeling insecure, at Two? Or are they to be evaluated with a cool and intelligent eye—as she does when secure, at One?

Each Enneagram style has a characteristic emotional compass, which I'll detail in the chapters on the individual points. For now it's enough to recognize that each style copes with conflicting emotional tendencies. The struggle to resolve them or at least find a livable compromise is part of what shapes the point's characteristic "flavor" and prompts its habitual behaviors.

Stress and security points can also be a significant source of conflict and bonding between literary characters—and between individuals in life—especially when one style's stress point is another's security point. For example, Four—the One's stress point—has as its security point One, while One—the Seven's stress point—has as its security point Seven. Thus types linked this way may find themselves feeling a mixture of attraction and repulsion for each other.

Wings

Another source of variation within Enneagram styles is due to what are called *wings*. Wings are the Enneagram styles located on either side of a person's "home" Enneagram style. The wings of Nine, for example, are Eight and One, while the wings of One are Nine and Two and so on. The wings, to some degree, influence the experience and expression of someone's home style and produce a mixture of qualities and defenses.

Generally, people favor one wing over the other. A Three, for example, might be said to have a "Four wing," meaning that his Three personality has an additional flavor of Four. Some individuals experience their dominant wing only slightly, while others lean strongly on it, and so we say that a person has a "slight," "moderate" or "strong" wing. Although it is less common, some people are equally influenced by both wings.

In the chapters on the styles, I will offer literary examples that illustrate the qualities of each wing connection.

Subtypes

People and fictional characters with the same Enneagram style can also vary because of their *subtype*. Each Enneagram style has three subtypes that further modify the style's primary focus of attention:

• Self-Preservation subtypes are generally preoccupied with personal survival and driven by a need for material security and self-sufficiency.

• Social subtypes focus on their relationships with the community and are driven by a need to be effective in the wider world and accepted by their "tribe."

• Sexual subtypes are concerned primarily with one-to-one relationships and may be driven by their need to make and preserve a close connection with a partner. People with this subtype are often intense and energetic.

An individual is thought to have a dominant subtype, a secondary subtype, and a third subtype that is least developed in their behavior and awareness. In the chapters on the Enneagram styles, I'll discuss the characteristics of each style's subtypes and illustrate them with literary examples.

Levels of Health

In his book *Personality Types*, Don Richard Riso originated the concept of "Levels of Development" for each Enneagram style, a model that describes how individuals can manifest the same Enneagram style very differently, depending on their psychological health. The nine levels Riso describes range from individuals so healthy that they virtually transcend their style, to people afflicted with severe mental illness. Most people, of course, fall somewhere between these two extremes.

For this book I will follow Riso's model but limit myself to three general levels: "healthy," "average" and "unhealthy." In the chapters on the individual styles, I'll offer literary examples of each.

Between the stress and security points, wings, and subtypes, the variations on the nine core styles become considerably more complex. When we factor in levels of health, gender differences and the Enneagram styles associated with different cultures, the mix becomes rich indeed. As we explore literature through the lens of the Enneagram we begin to see not only the extensive variety of human nature but also the underlying patterns of coherence. We also see echoes of our own life stories and more fully understand people whose temperaments differ from our own.

Sources

Jones, James, *From Here to Eternity* (New York: Scribner, 1951)

Shakespeare, William, *Hamlet*

Welty, Eudora, "Death of a Traveling Salesman," in *Selected Stories of Eudora Welty* (New York: The Modern Library, 1936)

Williams, Tennessee, *A Streetcar Named Desire* (New York: New Directions, 1947)

One: The Critic

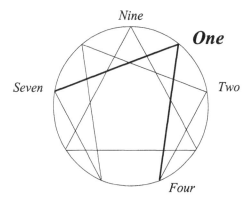

Perfectionistic, self-disciplined, well organized, and unpretentious, the title character of Evan S. Connell's novel *Mr. Bridge* is an exemplary One:

Each morning as soon as he walked into the office he glanced at the photograph of his wife and children which stood on the desk in a silver frame. He had placed the picture exactly where he wanted it, so that it never interfered with his work but at the same time he could see the family as often as he liked. Later pictures had been taken but this one pleased him best: Ruth was five years old, Carolyn three, and Douglas was a baby. The girls were seated on the studio couch, one on either side of their mother, who was holding Douglas in her lap. The photograph was orderly, symmetrical, and serene.

One Monday morning when he entered the office he noticed that the photograph had been moved. Evidently the woman who cleaned the office over the weekend had forgotten where it belonged. He put it back where he wanted it. Then for a few minutes he remained motionless in his swivel chair and stared at the picture; and he wondered again what would have happened to him if he had never met this woman who became his wife. He felt profoundly obligated to her. It seemed to him that the existence of the family was a mysterious accomplishment to which he had contributed very little. She had done this, somehow, almost by herself. He had provided the money and he had made decisions, but these things appeared insignificant when he compared them to what she had done; and he reflected on some lines from a letter by a famous man which he had read not long after meeting her: *Thou only has taught me that I have a heart—thou only has thrown a deep light downward, and upward, into my soul. Thou only has revealed me to myself; for without thy aid, my best knowledge of myself would have been merely to know my own shadow—to watch it flickering on the wall, and mistake its fantasies for my own real actions. Indeed, we are but shadows—we are not endowed with real life, and all that seems most real about us is but the thinnest substance of a dream—till the heart be touched.* These lines had impressed him so that he copied them and kept them a long time; he had often been on the point of reciting them to her because they expressed his own feelings with such lucidity and tenderness.

The idea of life without her caused him to move restlessly.

Then, because it was time to begin work, he cleared his throat, blew his nose, and rang for Julia. (pp. 2-3)

Mr. Bridge's emotional constraint is common in Ones. Although his love for his wife is deep—having even a poetic, transcendent quality—he is uncomfortable expressing it directly. Instead, he turns his energy towards planning his estate so that his family will understand his feelings after his death:

A copy of the will was in the safe-deposit box, and though he knew every word of it he sometimes read it through, searching for possible points of contention. The logic and clarity of the will were pleasing to him; the measured cadence of the sentences he had composed was reassuring, as though the measure of his mind must be respected when it was read aloud at some future date. Often he read to himself particular passages from the will, imagining the delight and surprise with which it would be heard for the first time by his wife and by the children, not merely for the precision of language but because they had no idea of the value of the investments. (pp. 6-7)

Ones have an intense desire to be seen as good and right by people they value; respect is even more important to them than love. Mr. Bridge's pride in his own financial prudence and his fantasy about how much his family will appreciate his foresight reflects values that are central to his Enneagram style.

I call One "The Critic" because people with this style are so preoccupied with perfecting themselves and the world around them that they tend to be unforgiving of mistakes—both their own and others'. When Mr. Bridge takes his car to be lubricated, he instructs the manager of the garage not to change the oil:

That evening when he returned to pick up the car he was met by the manager, who explained apologetically that the oil had been changed.

"I told you not to," said Mr. Bridge.

The manager explained that he had forgotten to tell the mechanic.

"Well," Mr. Bridge said, "I am not going to pay for that oil."

"What we can do is this," the manager said, "we'll let you have it at cost."

Mr. Bridge shook his head. "I intend to pay for the lubrication, nothing more. The mistake is not my fault. I distinctly told you. I will not be charged for something I did not order. I have been parking here for six years and nothing of this sort has happened before. Why does it happen now?"

"It was our fault," the manager said. "We'll take care of it."

And that was how it ended. (p. 15)

Ones have formidable wills and are ready to believe that the errors of others arise from their moral defects. Mr. Bridge is so determined to avoid being cheated—and to be right—that he grows rigidly intolerant.

Ones are part of the triad associated with gut impulses and will. While Eights try to impose their wills by dominating others through explicit or implicit threats, Nines reveal their preoccupation with this issue by avoiding open contests of will and maintaining harmony with others. Ones, by contrast, try to impose their will through moral superiority. A One with little self-awareness like Mr. Bridge may resist a course of action out of principle, even if it means sacrificing what he wants rather than allowing another's will to prevail:

That winter he decided he could afford a Cadillac. For some time he had been thinking about this, but there were two considerations. First, of course, was the expense. The second was more difficult to evaluate because it had to do with taste. Cadillac quite unmistakably symbolized success, and he did not want anybody who observed him in a Cadillac to assume that he was boasting. So, wanting one, he had told himself it would cost too much. But there came a day when he stopped at an agency to get the brochure, and he arranged for a salesman to bring a Cadillac to the house so he could take the family for a ride. . . . He had nearly made up his mind. He was pleased that his wife and son liked the car. The cost troubled him, but he knew he could manage and he felt that the time had come to indulge himself. In the past he had denied himself many things in order to make certain that the family was deprived of nothing. Now, because he had worked hard and was succeeding, and because there were enough securities in the bank so that they would suffer no hardship if he died unexpectedly, he thought he would buy this enormously gratifying piece of machinery. (p. 49)

But the salesman pushes too hard and Mr. Bridge balks at the last moment:

For a few minutes Mr. and Mrs. Bridge remained standing on the driveway to discuss the situation.

"He was so sure of himself," she remarked.

"They're all alike, every last one of them," he answered. "If we decide on a Cadillac I'll go through some other agency. And Lord knows I won't have my initials on it."

He continued to think about the Cadillac, but he could not forget the salesman; and the suggestion that he should advertise himself by putting his initials on the door was so offensive that several weeks after the demonstration he bought a Chrysler. The family liked it, and he himself did not feel quite so conspicuous. He concluded that he had made the proper decision. (p. 51)

Mr. Bridge's desire to maintain an unpretentious facade while enjoying a fine quality car that symbolizes success expresses a conflict that is common in Ones. They often have a running interior dialogue with their inner critic, an inner voice that judges the One even more harshly than he judges others. Mr. Bridge's self-conscious awareness of how he appears to others—another One tendency— is also evident here.

Although Ones can resemble Sixes in their suspiciousness and snap judgments of people, they respond to threatening situations in a decidedly different way. Here is Mr. Bridge on his way home late at night:

He had worked late. Julia had gone home two hours ago. Now the streets were dark. A damp wind was blowing. It was a depressing night to be out and he looked forward to his comfortable home.

At the corner a voice behind him said: "Stick 'em up!"

Mr. Bridge continued walking. He did not believe what he had heard. Either he had not heard what he thought he heard, or if somebody had ordered him to put up his hands it must be a joke.

The command was repeated, and there were footsteps.

Mr. Bridge stopped walking and turned around. Coming toward him was a red-eyed, unshaven man with one hand thrust into the slip pocket of a shabby trench coat.

Mr. Bridge said impatiently: "What is it you want?"

"Give me your money," the man said in a hoarse voice, and he made a threatening gesture.

"Don't be ridiculous," said Mr. Bridge, and walked away.

While driving home he contemplated the incident. Evidently it had been a serious attempt to hold him up. The man might very well have had a gun concealed in his pocket, and it was possible that he was desperate enough to have used it. However, he could not become alarmed as he thought about it any more than he had been alarmed at the time. He felt nothing except a sort of exasperation. The man's presumption was extraordinary. If he had no money he should get a job like everybody else. (pp. 60-61)

Notice Mr. Bridge's rush to judgment, even in a situation where fear and caution would be more sensible. All he sees is that the holdup man is morally wrong, trying to get something without working for it—unlike Mr. Bridge, who would sooner part with his life than give up his hard-earned money.

At other times, despite his rigid standards, Mr. Bridge surprises himself with the intensity of his own feelings:

> Saturday morning he saw Ruth [his daughter] in the back yard getting ready for a sun bath. She had spread a beach towel on the grass near the rose trellis. She was as brown as a Mexican from loitering around the pool at the country club, but evidently she did not think she was brown enough. She untied the straps of her bathing suit, opened a bottle of suntan oil, and began smearing oil on her arms and legs while he watched from the bedroom window. He noticed for the first time that she had become a woman; her body had lengthened and softened. He watched attentively while she poured oil into the palm of her hand and stroked the oil on her skin. Her flesh gleamed in the morning sunlight like varnished cherrywood. Presently she finished oiling herself and lay down on the towel with her arms outstretched as if she had been dancing and fallen exhausted in that position.
>
> Just then Mrs. Bridge entered the bedroom. He turned from the window, caught her by the shoulders and kissed her, forcing his tongue between her teeth. She pulled away. He caught her again and pushed her toward the bed while she murmured doubtfully. (p. 155)

Ones have a built-in Enneagram connection to Seven, a style that can be sensual and licentious. When Ones feel this connection in themselves it can distress them and they may clamp down on their "forbidden" desires, either by denying them or by channeling them into socially acceptable expressions—a defense mechanism psychologists call *reaction formation*. When Mr. Bridge, fighting off his sexual attraction to his daughter, grabs his wife and uses her to discharge his desire, we see reaction formation in action. Helen Palmer has observed that Ones have a "trap door" quality in relation to pleasure; they rigorously control the expression of their feelings, but once the door is opened, their pent-up desires come flooding out.

Later, when Mrs. Bridge asks if her husband finds her attractive, he resists answering her:

> He frowned. "What on earth has gotten into you? All at once for no good reason you behave as if—I don't know what. You were an attractive girl and you are today an attractive woman."
>
> "Am I?"
>
> "You are indeed."
>
> She looked at him playfully. "Would it hurt so much to tell me once

in a while?"

"I'm afraid I'm not good at that sort of business."

"You used to be."

This was both flattering and embarrassing. He pretended to hunt for something. The night seemed unusually still; he glanced at the window and saw trickles of water darting along the glass.

"Tell me, Walter, because I need to know. Do you love me?"

"Love you? Of course," he answered. Just then he heard the boom of thunder overhead, the house almost trembled, and the rain increased.

"Before we met, were in you love with somebody?"

"No."

"Have you been in love since?"

"What?" he asked, incredulous. She rushed over to him and slipped her arms around his waist.

"I'm being silly," she whispered.

"I should say you are." (pp. 158-159)

Note that Mr. Bridge has no inkling of his own heartlessness. Instead he criticizes his wife for her neediness while trying to rationally explain away her sudden need for reassurance. Though Ones may be highly intelligent and observant about details, they are often blind to feelings that most people would empathize with.

Like many Ones, Mr. Bridge is conscientious about attending church, but he finds it difficult to enter into the transcendent feeling of even a joyous religious holiday. In the book's final passage he is in church on Christmas, singing "Joy to the World":

Yet while he was singing he reflected on the word "joy"—the archaic sound of this odd word, and its meaning. He reflected that he had occasionally heard people use this word. Evidently they had experienced joy, or believed they had experienced it. He asked himself if he ever had known it. If so, he could not remember. But he thought he must have known it because he understood the connotation, which would be impossible without having experienced it. However, if he had once known joy it must have been a long time ago. Satisfaction, yes, and pleasure of several sorts, and pride, and possibly a feeling which might be called "rejoicing" after some serious worry or problem had been resolved. There were many such feelings, but none of them should be called "joy." He remembered enthusiasm, hope, and a kind of jubilation or exultation. Cheerfulness, yes, and joviality, and the brief gratification of sex. Gladness, too, fullness of heart, appreciation, and many other emotions. But not joy. No, that belonged to simpler minds. (p. 367)

Characteristically, Mr. Bridge sees his joylessness as a mark of his superiority.

The One's History

As children, Ones often feel emotionally deprived and particularly disconnected from their fathers. The lack of approval they got from the authority figure in their lives is at the root of the irritability and resentment Ones express toward others.

For a One child, parental validation seems elusive, no matter how perfect their behavior, how impressive their achievements. In a sense, when adult Ones criticize others they are using a weapon that was used against them. The voice associated with their internal critic is frequently that of a disapproving father figure like Mr. Bridge.

As parents, Ones can be stingy with praise, partly because they are reluctant to open their own Pandora's box of strong feelings, partly because they want to avoid "spoiling" their own children.

The Silence of the Lambs

In a positive sense, we can see parental high standards at work in Clarice Starling, the heroine of Thomas Harris's police procedural thriller *The Silence of the Lambs*. Starling is an FBI trainee who successfully hunts down a serial killer whom the police have nicknamed Buffalo Bill. Early in her search, she interviews the brilliant and dangerous psychiatrist Hannibal Lecter, imprisoned at an institution for the criminally insane. As Starling questions Lecter, he, in turn, asks her about her childhood. As we learn about Starling's background— especially her mother's courage and her policeman father's dedication—we see how she judges herself by her parents' examples. Here she prepares to offer Lecter better prison conditions in exchange for his psychological profile of the serial killer:

> Starling walked up and down. She gestured to the air. "Hold on, girl," she said aloud. She said it to Catherine Martin [the girl who has been kidnapped by the killer] and she said it to herself. "We're better than this room. We're better than this fucking place," she said aloud. "We're better than wherever he's got you. Help me. Help me. Help me." She thought for an instant of her late parents. She wondered if they would be ashamed of her now—just that question, not its pertinence, no qualifications—the way we always ask it. The answer was no, they would not be ashamed of her.
>
> She washed her face and went out into the hall. (p. 159)

Conscious of her own prejudices and resentments, Starling factors them into her strategies, using her childhood experiences to help her identify with the killer's most recent victim, Catherine:

> Starling could easily have pictured her as a self-absorbed, blunted, boarding-school kid, one of those people who never listen. Starling

knew she had to be careful here because she had her own prejudices and resentments. Starling had done her time in boarding schools, living on scholarships, her grades much better than her clothes. She had seen a lot of kids from rich, troubled families, with too much boarding-school time. She didn't give a damn about some of them, but she had grown to learn that inattention can be a stratagem to avoid pain, and that it is often misread as shallowness and indifference.

Better to think of Catherine as a child sailing with her father, as she was in the film they showed with Senator Martin's plea on television. She wondered if Catherine tried to please her father when she was little. She wondered what Catherine was doing when they came back and told her that her father was dead, of a heart attack at forty-two. Starling was positive Catherine missed him. Missing your father, the common wound, made Starling feel close to this young woman. (p. 208)

Self-awareness is common to healthy individuals of every Enneagram style, but the way Starling consciously uses her own vulnerabilities to psych herself into doing her job more effectively is especially characteristic of healthy Ones. Most Ones, like Mr. Bridge, are unaware of the emotional baggage they carry.

In one interview with Lecter, Starling recalls being ten years old, with both her parents dead, living with foster parents on a ranch. One night she was awakened by the screams of the spring lambs being slaughtered. Knowing that the ranchers bought decrepit horses to fatten up for slaughter, and fearing that they would soon kill an old horse that belonged to her, Starling took the horse and ran away. Lecter asks her:

"You still wake up sometimes, don't you? Wake up in the iron dark with the lambs screaming?"

"Sometimes."

"Do you think if you caught Buffalo Bill yourself and if you made Catherine all right, you could make the lambs stop screaming, do you think they'd be all right too and you wouldn't wake up again in the dark and hear the lambs screaming? Clarice?"

"Yes. I don't know. Maybe." (p. 230)

We understand from this exhange why Starling has such a personal stake in saving the kidnapped young woman. After Starling has rescued Catherine and killed her kidnapper, Starling's boss and mentor says something she has been longing to hear:

He went to his office door. She was going away from him, down the deserted hall. He managed to hail her from his berg of grief: "Starling, your father sees you." (p. 356)

But even this moment of triumph, knowing that she deserves her father's praise—and receiving it symbolically from her boss and mentor—cannot satisfy her for long. In the final passage of the story, Dr. Lecter writes a letter to Starling that shows his understanding of her character:

> Well, Clarice, have the lambs stopped screaming?
> . . . I won't be surprised if the answer is yes and no. The lambs will stop for now. But, Clarice, you judge yourself with all the mercy of the dungeon scales at Threave; you'll have to earn it again and again, the blessed silence. Because it's the plight that drives you, seeing the plight, and the plight will not end, ever. (p. 366)

Even a healthy One can have no lasting respite from the relentless drive to make the world a better place.

Levels of Health

Whatever their level of health, Ones are preoccupied with using their will to perfect themselves. This helps them avoid expressing the powerful feelings that are continually welling up within them—especially anger. The inner critic is a powerful goad to most Ones, who respond by attempting to avoid mistakes and live impeccable lives. To placate this inner voice Ones must seem right and good not only in themselves but in their chosen work, which explains the driven quality common to people of this temperament.

Average Ones tend to have high standards, focus strongly on their work and get lost in details. Quick to criticize others for their moral failings and low standards, they reserve their harshest judgments for themselves. Though anger is the "deadly sin" associated with this Enneagram style, average Ones are rarely conscious of it in themselves.

There is a wide range of average Ones in literature: Evan Connell's Mr. Bridge, Miss Kenton in Kazuo Ishiguro's *The Remains of the Day*, Sergeant Milton Warden in James Jones's *From Here to Eternity*, the title character in P.L. Travers's *Mary Poppins*, Isabella in Shakespeare's *Measure for Measure*, Dr. Stockman in Henrik Ibsen's *An Enemy of the People*, Felix in Neil Simon's *The Odd Couple*, Kyra in David Hare's *Skylight*, Elizabeth Proctor in Arthur Miller's *The Crucible*, Alceste in Molière's *The Misanthrope*, Adolphus Cusins in George Bernard Shaw's *Major Barbara*, and Vivian Bearing in Margaret Edson's play *Wit*.

Healthy Ones like Clarice Starling tend to be more conscious of their underlying resentment and less rigid in their judgments of themselves and others. They forgive mistakes and often have a sense of humor about themselves, albeit a dry one. While a sense of humor about personal characteristics and limitations is a sign of health in all Enneagram styles, it is an especially welcome antidote to the One's perfectionistic self-serious tendencies. In individuals like Nelson Mandela we see the wisdom, tolerance, and generosity of spirit that the healthiest

Ones can embody.

Examples of healthy Ones include: Elinor Dashwood in Jane Austen's *Sense and Sensibility*, Atticus Finch in Harper Lee's *To Kill a Mockingbird*, Katherine in Michael Ondaatje's *The English Patient*, Dorothea Brooke in George Eliot's *Middlemarch*, Constantine Levin in Leo Tolstoy's *Anna Karenina*, Portia in Shakespeare's *The Merchant of Venice*, and Thomas More in Robert Bolt's *A Man for All Seasons*.

Unhealthy Ones can be self-righteous and cruel in their attempts to punish the guilty. Convinced of their own rightness and goodness, they see the world in terms of good and evil, with no moral gray areas. Any deviation from their own rigid code of behavior merits harsh punishment. Puritanical, devoid of compassion for themselves and others, unhealthy Ones are often grim and unhappy. Unhealthy examples in literature include: Javert in Victor Hugo's *Les Miserables*, Stevens in Kazuo Ishiguro's *The Remains of the Day*, Beth in Judith Guest's *Ordinary People*, Angelo in Shakespeare's *Measure for Measure*, Nurse Ratched in Ken Kesey's *One Flew Over the Cuckoo's Nest*, and Allie Fox in Paul Theroux's *The Mosquito Coast*.

Place in Society

Ones are involved in all kinds of work, but they are especially visible in the clergy, in the mental health field, in law enforcement, and in the legal profession—especially as judges and prosecutors. Many Ones can also be found in the military, in education, and in politics. Their patience with detail can make them excellent editors and accountants as well.

Because Ones resist being controlled by others, they are more likely to work as independent contractors, consultants, or free-lancers. In corporate situations, they may be demanding bosses but can also be good trainers and mentors. As employees they are likely to be conscientious, well-organized, and hard-working, especially if they respect their boss. The social value of their work is important to most Ones, and money is rarely the primary factor in their career choice.

Stress and Security Points

The emotional compass of The Critic is wide, ranging from the stress point at Four ("The Aesthete") to the security point at Seven ("The Optimist"). At the Four stress point, Ones tend to be preoccupied with the past, with loss, and with melancholy, while at Seven they embrace future possibilities with optimism. Determined to stay grounded and functional in the face of the opposing lures of Four nostalgia and Seven pie in the sky, Ones tend to focus on the present moment.

Another way of seeing the One emotional arc is in the classic polarities of "soul"—the dark side, the pole of suffering and deprivation, at Four—and "spirit"—the light side, the pole of ecstasy and abundance, at Seven.

Because there is such a strong emotional charge between the poles of Four and Seven, the energy behind a One's ethical preoccupation—"what is right"— is enormous. Moral heroes like Nelson Mandela and moralistic personalities like Hillary Clinton exemplify the force behind Ones' concern for the good, the right, and the true.

Wings

One is located on the Enneagram diagram between the Nine's tendency to have global vision and the Two's desire to help other people. Ones often struggle to balance their Nine-like enjoyment of rumination and pure thought with the more Twoish pleasures of serving others and being appreciated.

In healthy Ones, the combination of the wings brings together the ability to make clear ethical distinctions and the capacity to act in ways that empower others. Thus, Ones can scrupulously examine abstract principles and "big picture" possibilities as well as translate them into ethical action.

Ones with a Nine wing tend to be cooler, stiffer, more philosophical and less in touch with their anger. They are often attached to rules rather than to people. Mr. Bridge's Nine wing is visible in his impatience, his elitism, his protectiveness of his personal privacy, and his discomfort with expressing his feelings even to people close to him.

Ones with a Two wing tend to be more active, emotional, and comfortable working with others, especially if the work makes a visible difference in the world. They also strongly empathize with the suffering of others. Clarice Starling is a good example; she is outgoing, aware of her own and others' feelings, and oriented toward social service.

The Remains of the Day

Kazuo Ishiguro's novel *The Remains of the Day* centers on Stevens, a One with a Nine wing, who narrates the story of his long career as butler of Darlington Hall, one of the great English houses. We come to understand how his obsessiveness about doing his job perfectly and preserving his personal dignity have isolated him from others and left him with the prospect of a lonely old age.

As Stevens describes a butler's duties, we see him preoccupied with rules and disconnected from people. Both are unhealthy expressions of his Nine wing:

> It is, of course, the responsibility of every butler to devote his utmost care in the devising of a staff plan.... I have myself devised many staff plans over the years, and I do not believe I am being unduly boastful if I say that very few ever needed amendment. And if in the present case the staff plan is at fault, blame can be laid at no one's door but my own. At the same time, it is only fair to point out that my task in this instance has been of an unusually difficult order. (p. 5)

Stevens's concern with assigning blame is a One tendency, as is his acknowledgment of his own responsibility. His formal, stiff narrative goes with his Nine wing.

Preserving his own dignity at all costs—in his view the essential quality of "great" butlers—gives rise to his continual failures in personal relationships, most notably with his father and Miss Kenton, a housekeeper at Darlington. In fact, an atmosphere of competition develops between Stevens and Miss Kenton, a One with a Two wing, to see who can perform more perfectly.

When Stevens hires his aging father to work as under-butler, Miss Kenton argues that the duties are too much for a man in his seventies. But Stevens resists lightening the old man's workload until one day, as Miss Kenton predicted, his father drops a heavy tray of tea accessories.

During a large conference that Lord Darlington holds at the estate, Stevens receives word that his father is ill. The following evening he visits the old man, impatient at being taken away from his important duties:

> My father opened his eyes, turned his head a little on the pillow, and looked at me.
>
> 'I hope Father is feeling better now,' I said.
>
> He went on gazing at me for a moment, then asked: 'Everything in hand downstairs?'
>
> 'The situation is rather volatile. It is just after six o'clock, so Father can well imagine the atmosphere in the kitchen at this moment.'
>
> An impatient look crossed my father's face. 'But is everything in hand?' he said again.
>
> 'Yes, I dare say you can rest assured on that. I'm very glad Father is feeling better.'
>
> With some deliberation he withdrew his arms from under the bedclothes and gazed tiredly at the backs of his hands. He continued to do this for some time.
>
> 'I'm glad Father is feeling so much better,' I said again eventually. 'Now really, I'd best be getting back. As I say, the situation is rather volatile.'
>
> He went on looking at his hands for a moment. Then he said slowly: 'I hope I've been a good father to you.'
>
> I laughed a little and said: 'I'm so glad you're feeling better now.'
>
> 'I'm proud of you. A good son. I hope I've been a good father to you. I suppose I haven't.'
>
> 'I'm afraid we're extremely busy now, but we can talk again in the morning.'
>
> My father was still looking at his hands as though he were faintly irritated by them.
>
> 'I'm so glad you're feeling better now,' I said again and took my leave. (p. 97)

Although the his father is clearly dying and longing to connect with his son, Stevens refuses him any comfort. Stevens is a not-very-healthy One, and his insistence on impeccable politeness and formality mask a deeper heartlessness.

His behavior also reflects the common One experience of disconnection from the father figure. Stevens's father, who is also a One, undoubtedly refused his young son nurturance and praise. Now the son is emulating his father, unresponsive to the old man's needs and pain.

Later that evening while Stevens is overseeing the conference, Miss Kenton comes to tell him that his father has died. He accepts her offer to close the old man's eyes and then continues his duties, believing that this is what his father would have wished. At the end of this day, Stevens is proud of the way he handled the situation:

> Of course, it is not for me to suggest that I am worthy of ever being placed alongside the likes of the 'great' butlers of our generation, such as Mr Marshall or Mr Lane—though it should be said there are those who, perhaps out of misguided generosity, tend to do just this. Let me make clear that when I say the conference of 1923, and that night in particular, constituted a turning point in my professional development, I am speaking very much in terms of my own more humble standards. Even so, if you consider the pressures contingent on me that night, you may not think I delude myself unduly if I go so far as to suggest that I did perhaps display, in the face of everything, at least in some modest degree a 'dignity' worthy of someone like Mr Marshall—or come to that, my father. Indeed, why should I deny it? For all its sad associations, whenever I recall that evening today, I find I do so with a large sense of triumph. (p. 110)

Stevens's sense of virtue about his professional behavior as a butler is reaction formation, the One defense. He is actually angry at his father.

In a later scene, Lord Darlington, a German sympathizer who wants to ingratiate himself with German diplomats, instructs Stevens to fire any Jews on the staff. When Stevens tells Miss Kenton that he intends to dismiss the two Jewish maids, their ensuing argument highlights the difference between his Nine wing and her Two wing:

> 'Mr Stevens, I am outraged that you can sit there and utter what you have just done as though you were discussing orders for the larder. I simply cannot believe it. You are saying Ruth and Sarah are to be dismissed on the grounds that they are Jewish?'
>
> 'Miss Kenton, I have just this moment explained the situation to you fully. His lordship has made his decision and there is nothing for you and I to debate over.'
>
> 'Does it not occur to you, Mr Stevens, that to dismiss Ruth and

Sarah on these grounds would be simply—*wrong*? I will not stand for such things. I will not work in a house in which such things can occur.'

'Miss Kenton, I will ask you not to excite yourself and to conduct yourself in a manner befitting your position. This is a very straightforward matter. If his lordship wishes these particular contracts to be discontinued, then there is little more to be said.'

'I am warning you, Mr Stevens, I will not continue to work in such a house. If my girls are dismissed, I will leave also.'

'Miss Kenton, I am surprised to find you reacting in this manner. Surely I don't have to remind you that our professional duty is not to our own foibles and sentiments, but to the wishes of our employer.'

'I am telling you, Mr Stevens, if you dismiss my girls tomorrow, it will be wrong, a sin as any sin ever was one, and I will not continue to work in such a house.'

'Miss Kenton, let me suggest to you that you are hardly well placed to be passing judgments of such a high and mighty nature. The fact is, the world of today is a very complicated and treacherous place. There are many things you and I are simply not in a position to understand concerning, say, the nature of Jewry. Whereas his lordship, I might venture, is somewhat better placed to judge what is for the best.' (pp. 148-149)

After this incident Miss Kenton does not give her notice, although Stevens repeatedly needles her about the subject. When she doesn't respond, he assumes that she is embarrassed, but the reader understands that she is in love with him. Her hopes for a personal relationship with him are doomed, however, since he is determined to protect his dignity and privacy at any cost. Miss Kenton makes a few overtures, flirts with him, and finally tells him that she is considering a marriage proposal from a local man. When Stevens fails to take the hint and simply congratulates her, she gives up and accepts the proposal.

Many years later Stevens arranges a reunion with Miss Kenton when he travels to the West of England. He hopes to persuade her to return as housekeeper at Darlington. As they talk in the tearoom at his hotel Stevens discovers that Miss Kenton's marriage is not as precarious as a letter she had written him had led him to hope. Her daughter is about to have a baby, and she wants to stay nearby. She confesses that she has left her husband three times, and it is evident that she still has strong feelings for Stevens. He asks about her marriage:

'I feel I should answer you, Mr Stevens. As you say, we may not meet again for many years. Yes, I do love my husband. I didn't at first. I didn't at first for a long time. When I left Darlington Hall all those years ago, I never realized I was really, truly leaving. I believe I thought of it as simply another ruse, Mr Stevens, to annoy you. It was a shock to come out here and find myself married. For a long time, I was very unhappy, very unhappy indeed. But then year after year went by, there was the war, Catherine grew up, and one day I realized I loved my husband. You spend so much time with someone, you find you get used to him. He's a kind, steady man, and yes, Mr Stevens, I've grown to love him.'

Miss Kenton fell silent again for a moment. Then she went on:

'But that doesn't mean to say, of course, there aren't occasions now and then—extremely desolate occasions—when you think to yourself: "What a terrible mistake I've made with my life." And you get to thinking about a different life, a *better* life you might have had. For instance, I get to thinking about a life I may have had with you, Mr Stevens. And I suppose that's when I get angry over some trivial little thing and leave. But each time I do so, I realize before long—my rightful place is with my husband. After all, there's no turning back the clock now. One can't be forever dwelling on what might have been. One should realize one has as good as most, perhaps better, and be grateful.'

I do not think I responded immediately, for it took me a moment or two to fully digest these words of Miss Kenton. Moreover, as you might appreciate, their implications were such as to provoke a certain degree of sorrow within me. Indeed—why should I not admit it?—at that moment, my heart was breaking. Before long, however, I turned to her and said with a smile:

'You're very correct, Mrs Benn. As you say, it is too late to turn back the clock. Indeed, I should not be able to rest if I thought such ideas were the cause of unhappiness for you and your husband. We must each of us, as you point out, be grateful for what we *do* have. And from what you tell me, Mrs Benn, you have reason to be contented. In fact, I would venture, what with Mr Benn retiring, and with grandchildren on the way, that you and Mr Benn have some extremely happy years before you. You really mustn't let any more foolish ideas come between yourself and the happiness you deserve.'

'Of course, you're right, Mr Stevens. You're so kind.' (pp. 239-240)

The stifling politeness between them is sustained to the last, despite their mutual love and anguish at parting. The way Stevens maintains his dignity and courtesy in the situation could be a kind of heroism, as he is abandoning any possibility of a close personal relationship in his own life. It is unclear, however, how much he is motivated by a fear of intimacy, characteristic of his Nine wing, and how much his behavior is self-sacrificing, since he knows that Miss Kenton will be happier remaining in her marriage.

A Man for All Seasons

A much healthier One with a Nine wing is Thomas More in Robert Bolt's *A Man for All Seasons*. In Bolt's play we see More, the Chancellor of England and highest-ranking prelate of the Catholic Church, trying and failing to avoid a moral confrontation with Henry VIII over the king's desire to illegally divorce his wife.

Early in the play More, a skilled lawyer and an astute judge of people, refuses to employ Richard Rich, a young man whom he rightly sees as incapable of loyalty. After Rich visits More's house looking for a job and subtly threatens More when he doesn't get it, More's wife, Alice; his daughter, Margaret; and her fiancé, Roper, urge him to arrest Rich:

> ROPER Arrest him.
> ALICE Yes!
> MORE For what?
> ALICE He's dangerous!
> ROPER For libel; he's a spy.
> ALICE He is! Arrest him!
> MARGARET Father, that man's bad.
> MORE There is no law against that.
> ROPER There is! God's law!
> MORE Then God can arrest him.
> ROPER Sophistication upon sophistication!
> MORE No, sheer simplicity. The law, Roper, the law. I know what's legal not what's right. And I'll stick to what's legal.
> ROPER Then you set man's law above God's!
> MORE No, far below; but let me draw your attention to a fact—I'm *not* God. The currents and eddies of right and wrong, which you find such plain sailing, I can't navigate. I'm no voyager. But in the thickets of the law, oh, there I'm a forester. I doubt if there's a man alive who could follow me there, thank God . . .
> *(He says this last to himself)*
> ALICE *(Exasperated, pointing after RICH)* While you talk, he's gone!
> MORE And go he should, if he was the Devil himself, until he broke the law!
> ROPER So now you'd give the Devil benefit of law!
> MORE Yes. What would you do? Cut a great road through the law to get after the Devil?
> ROPER I'd cut down every law in England to do that!
> MORE *(Roused and excited)* Oh? *(Advances on ROPER)* And when the last law was down, and the Devil turned round on you—where would you hide, Roper, the laws all being flat? *(He leaves him)* This country's planted thick with laws from coast to coast—man's laws, not God's—

and if you cut them down—and you're just the man to do it—d'you really think you could stand upright in the winds that would blow then? (*Quietly*) Yes, I'd give the Devil benefit of law, for my own safety's sake. (pp. 64-67)

There are several Ones in action here: More, with a Nine wing; Margaret, who also has a Nine wing; and Roper, a One with a Two wing. Notice how More is concerned with a higher, more abstract form of justice, while Margaret and Roper try to use "rightness" to justify eliminating a potential opponent. More's intellectual bent and trust in his mind as first line of defense are characteristic of a One with a Nine wing. He is a very healthy One, and his daughter is also in the healthy range. Roper, by contrast, is an average One and his volatility is expressive of his Two wing.

Throughout the play we see More cleverly manipulate conversations and events to avoid unnecessary conflict, reflecting his Nine wing's desire to create harmony with others. Resigning his post as Chancellor, he expects to be left in peace, since he has stayed publicly silent about the king's marriage. But an Act of Succession declares the king's second marriage legal and all subjects must swear their allegiance to the Act. When More, in conscience, refuses to do so he is convicted of high treason and imprisoned in the Tower. As he awaits his execution, his wife and daughter visit, hoping to persuade him to change his mind and save his life:

> MORE You want me to swear to the Act of Succession?
>
> MARGARET "God more regards the thoughts of the heart than the words of the mouth." Or so you've always told me.
>
> MORE Yes.
>
> MARGARET Then say the words of the oath and in your heart think otherwise.
>
> MORE What is an oath then but words we say to God?
>
> MARGARET That's very neat.
>
> MORE Do you mean it isn't true?
>
> MARGARET No, it's true.
>
> MORE Then it's a poor argument to call it "neat," Meg. When a man takes an oath, Meg, he's holding his own self in his own hands. Like water. (*He cups his hands*) And if he opens his fingers *then*—he needn't hope to find himself again. Some men aren't capable of this, but I'd be loathe to think your father one of them. . . .
>
> MARGARET (*Emotionally*) But in reason! Haven't you done as much as God can reasonably *want*?
>
> MORE Well . . . finally . . . it isn't a matter of reason; finally it's a matter of love. (pp. 139-140)

Though More has attempted to save himself through clever legalistic ploys, he finally has to choose between his principles and his life. He so intensely loves what he believes is right that he is willing to die for it. His philosophical cast of mind, even in this extreme situation, is especially characteristic of a Nine wing.

Middlemarch

Dorothea Brooke, the protagonist of George Eliot's *Middlemarch*, is a One with a Two wing. The story begins in 1831, a time when the number of social roles for even an upper-class woman were distinctly limited. Unlike her uncle Mr. Brooke, a Nine with whom she lives, Dorothea passionately wants to make the world better. Eliot dryly observes that this may limit her marriage prospects:

> In Mr. Brooke the hereditary strain of Puritan energy was clearly in abeyance; but in his niece Dorothea it glowed alike through faults and virtues, turning sometimes into impatience of her uncle's talk or his way of "letting things be" on his estate, and making her long all the more for the time when she would be of age and have some command of money for generous schemes. She was regarded as an heiress, for not only had the sisters seven hundred a-year each from their parents, but if Dorothea married and had a son, that son would inherit Mr. Brooke's estate, presumably worth about three thousand a year. . . .
>
> And how should Dorothea not marry?—a girl so handsome and with such prospects. Nothing could hinder it but her love of extremes, and her insistence on regulating life according to notions which might cause a wary man to hesitate before he made her an offer, or even might lead her at last to refuse all offers. A young lady of some birth and fortune, who knelt suddenly down on a brick floor by the side of a sick labourer and prayed fervidly as if she thought herself living in the time of the Apostles—who had strange whims of fasting like a Papist, and of sitting up at night to read old theological books! Such a wife might awaken you some fine morning with a new scheme for the application of her income which would interfere with political economy and the keeping of saddle-horses: a man would naturally think twice before he risked himself in such a fellowship. (p. 5)

Ones with either wing are capable of strong religious convictions. Dorothea's conflict between enjoying life's sensuous pleasures and wanting to renounce them, is more common with the Two wing:

> Yet those who approached Dorothea, though prejudiced against her by this alarming hearsay, found that she had a charm unaccountably reconcilable with it. Most men thought her bewitching when she was on horseback. She loved the fresh air and the various aspects of the country, and when her eyes and cheeks glowed with mingled pleasure she looked

very little like a devotee. Riding was an indulgence which she allowed herself in spite of conscientious qualms; she felt that she enjoyed it in a pagan sensuous way, and always looked forward to renouncing it.

She was open, ardent, and not in the least self-admiring; indeed, it was pretty to see how her imagination adorned her sister Celia with attractions altogether superior to her own, and if any gentleman appeared to come to the Grange from some other motive than that of seeing Mr. Brooke, she concluded that he must be in love with Celia. Sir James Chettam, for example, whom she constantly considered from Celia's point of view, inwardly debating whether it would be good for Celia to accept him. That he should be regarded as a suitor to herself would have seemed to her a ridiculous irrelevance. Dorothea, with all her eagerness to know the truths of life, retained very childlike ideas about marriage. ... The really delightful marriage must be where your husband was a sort of father, and could teach you even Hebrew, if you wished it. (p. 6)

Dorothea's unpretentiousness and natural high spirits are characteristic of healthy Ones, especially with a Two wing. But wanting a husband who is a father figure leads her to the worst possible choice: Mr. Casaubon, a clergyman and scholar thirty years her senior and a Five. She is too inexperienced to understand the implications of his cold, self-involved marriage proposal. During their honeymoon in Rome, however, Dorothea's idealism cannot overcome her sense that something is wrong:

Again, the matter-of-course statement and tone of dismissal with which he treated what to her were the most stirring thoughts, was easily accounted for as belonging to the sense of haste and preoccupation in which she herself shared during their engagement. But now, since they had been in Rome, with all the depths of her emotion roused to tumultuous activity, and with life made a new problem by new elements, she had been becoming more and more aware, with a certain terror, that her mind was continually sliding into inward fits of anger and repulsion, or else into forlorn weariness. .... What was fresh to her mind was worn out to his; and such capacity of thought and feeling as had ever been stimulated in him by the general life of mankind had long shrunk to a sort of dried preparation, a lifeless embalmment of knowledge. (p. 187)

Eliot implies that the marriage goes unconsummated and that Dorothea is too naïve to understand what is going on. When Casaubon's young cousin, Will Ladislaw, a Two, visits them in Rome, Casaubon senses an attraction between Will and Dorothea. Later, back at Lowick, her husband's ancestral home, Dorothea's expectations of a husband collide with Casaubon's aversion to intimacy. Now her former optimism gives way to the melancholy of her Four stress point:

In the first minutes when Dorothea looked out she felt nothing but the dreary oppression; then came a keen remembrance, and turning away from the window she walked round the room. The ideas and hopes which were living in her mind when she first saw this room nearly three months before were present now only as memories: she judged them as we judge transient and departed things. All existence seemed to beat with a lower pulse than her own, and her religious faith was a solitary cry, the struggle out of a nightmare in which every object was withering and shrinking away from her. (pp. 261-262)

When Will sends a letter announcing another visit Dorothea and Casaubon clash. Casaubon complains that Dorothea is selfishly urging him to socialize too much. This elicits a Oneish burst of resentment:

There had been no clashing of temper between Dorothea and her husband since that little explosion in Rome, which had left such strong traces in her mind that it had been easier ever since to quell emotion than to incur the consequence of venting it. But this ill-tempered anticipation that she could desire visits which might be disagreeable to her husband, this gratuitous defense of himself against selfish complaint on her part, was too sharp a sting to be meditated on until after it had been resented. Dorothea had thought that she could have been patient with John Milton, but she had never imagined him behaving in this way; and for a moment Mr. Casaubon seemed to be stupidly undiscerning and odiously unjust. Pity, that "newborn babe" which was by-and-by to rule many a storm within her, did not "stride the blast" on this occasion. With her first words, uttered in a tone that shook him, she startled Mr. Casaubon into looking at her, and meeting the flash of her eyes.

"Why do you attribute to me a wish for anything that would annoy you? You speak to me as if I were something you had to contend against. Wait at least till I appear to consult my own pleasure apart from yours."

"Dorothea, you are hasty," answered Mr. Casaubon, nervously.

Decidedly, this woman was too young to be on the formidable level of wifehood—unless she had been pale and featureless and taken everything for granted.

"I think it was you who were first hasty in your false suppositions about my feeling," said Dorothea, in the same tone. The fire was not dissipated yet, and she thought it was ignoble in her husband not to apologise to her.

"We will, if you please, say no more on this subject, Dorothea. I have neither leisure nor energy for this kind of debate." (pp. 269-270)

After this incident, Casaubon has a mental and physical collapse. Lydgate, the family doctor, tells Dorothea that her husband must avoid overwork and "mental agitation." Soon after, Will arrives to stay with Dorothea's uncle. Still oblivious to her husband's unspoken jealousy, Dorothea enjoys an occasional talk with Will. As Casaubon grows increasingly cold, Dorothea finally admits that she is bitter—a difficult moment for this One, who habitually denies her anger:

> She was in the reaction of rebellious anger stronger than any she had felt since her marriage. Instead of tears there came words:—
>
> "What have I done—what am I—that he should treat me so? He never knows what is in my mind—he never cares. What is the use of anything I do? He wishes he had never married me."
>
> She began to hear herself, and was checked into stillness. Like one who has lost his way and is weary, she sat and saw as in one glance all the paths of her young hope which she should never find again. And just as clearly in the miserable light she saw her own and her husband's solitude—how they walked apart so that she was obliged to survey him. If he had drawn her towards him, she would never have surveyed him—never have said, "Is he worth living for?" but would have felt him simply a part of her own life. Now she said bitterly, "It is his fault, not mine." In the jar of her whole being, Pity was overthrown. Was it her fault that she had believed in him—had believed in his worthiness?—And what, exactly, was he?—She was able enough to estimate him—she who waited on his glances with trembling, and shut her best soul in prison, paying it only hidden visits, that she might be petty enough to please him. In such a crisis as this, some women begin to hate. (pp. 406-407)

The now seriously ill Casaubon asks Dorothea to promise that, should he die, she will carry out his wishes—whatever they are. Reluctant to make such an open-ended commitment, she is nevertheless about to dutifully submit. But Casaubon dies before she can agree to the bargain. Already feeling desolate and immersed in her Four stress point, Dorothea is now grief-stricken and remorseful.

Casaubon's will stipulates that Dorothea be disinherited if she marries Will Ladislaw, thus casting aspersions on her honor. Shocked at what the will reveals about her suspicious, vindictive husband, she further learns that Casaubon has cheated his own cousin Will out a share of the family property. Dorothea searches for a way to correct the injustice:

> But now her judgment, instead of being controlled by duteous devotion, was made active by the imbittering discovery that in her past union there had lurked the hidden alienation of secrecy and suspicion. The living, suffering man was no longer before her to awaken her pity: there remained only the retrospect of painful subjection to a husband whose thoughts had been lower than she had believed, whose exorbi-

tant claims for himself had even blinded his scrupulous care for his own character, and made him defeat his own pride by shocking men of ordinary honor. As for the property which was the sign of that broken tie, she would have been glad to be free from it and have nothing more than her original fortune which had been settled on her, if there had not been duties attached to ownership, which she ought not to flinch from. About this property many troublous questions insisted on rising: had she not been right in thinking that the half of it ought to go to Will Ladislaw—but was it not impossible now for her to do that act of justice? Mr. Casaubon had taken a cruelly effective means of hindering her: even with indignation against him in her heart, any act that seemed a triumphant eluding of his purpose revolted her. (p. 470)

Dorothea's concern for the ethics of the situation, even under terrible personal stress, is characteristic of a healthy One. She is determined to put her own unhappiness aside and do good for others—an expression of her Two wing. When a rumor spreads that Dr. Lydgate has taken a bribe from a local banker, Dorothea defends him. When she visits Lydgate's wife, Rosamond, to urge her to have faith in her husband, she finds Will Ladislaw there. Assuming from his embarrassed demeanor that he and Rosalind have been making love, a devastated Dorothea rushes away. The following day, however, she selflessly resolves to revisit Rosamond with her offer of help. Rosamond then tells her that Will had visited her the previous day to explain that he could never love her because he was entirely devoted to Dorothea.

When Will next calls on Dorothea, they finally reveal their deep feelings for each other. But, he reminds her, his poverty and lack of prospects prevent them from marrying. Dorothea wavers for a moment but finally casts aside propriety:

> "Oh, I cannot bear it—my heart will break," said Dorothea, starting from her seat, the flood of her young passion bearing down all the obstructions which had kept her silent—the great tears rising and falling in an instant: "I don't mind about poverty—I hate my wealth."
>
> In an instant Will was close to her and had his arms round her, but she drew her head back and held his away gently that she might go on speaking, her large tear-filled eyes looking at his very simply, while she said in a sobbing childlike way, "We could live quite well on my own fortune—it is too much—seven hundred a-year—I want so little—no new clothes—and I will learn what everything costs." (pp. 773-774)

Here we see the torrent of feeling under a One's controlled demeanor, intensified by her Two wing. Dorothea's standards for herself seem unreasonably high, so we rejoice when she finally surrenders to love and pleasure associated with her Seven security point.

One Flew Over the Cuckoo's Nest

In chilling contrast to George Eliot's heroine, Nurse Ratched in Ken Kesey's *One Flew Over the Cuckoo's Nest* is a very unhealthy One with a Two wing.

The novel, set in a mental hospital, is narrated by a Nine, Chief Bromden, a huge American Indian whom the hospital staff believe is deaf-mute. In the Chief's description of Nurse Ratched we see the self-righteousness of an unhealthy One with a Two wing:

> The Big Nurse tends to get real put out if something keeps her outfit from running like a smooth, accurate, precision-made machine. The slightest thing messy or out of kilter or in the way ties her into a little white knot of tight-smiled fury. She walks around with that same doll smile crimped between her chin and her nose and that same calm whir coming from her eyes, but down inside of her she's tense as steel. I know, I can feel it. And she don't relax a hair till she gets the nuisance attended to—what she calls "adjusted to surroundings."
>
> Under her rule the ward Inside is almost completely adjusted to surroundings. But the thing is she can't be on the ward all the time. She's got to spend some time Outside. So she works with an eye to adjusting the Outside world too. Working alongside others like her who I call the "Combine," which is a huge organization that aims to adjust the Outside as well as she has the Inside, has made her a real veteran at adjusting things. She was already the Big Nurse in the old place when I came in from the Outside so long back, and she'd been dedicating herself to adjustment for God knows how long. (pp. 30-31)

Nurse Ratched's obsession with order and her ability and determination to manipulate others are markers of her Two wing, as is her gift for making others feel the force of her critical judgment, often without saying a word.

Randle McMurphy, the novel's Seven protagonist, gets himself transferred to the mental hospital from a prison work farm, believing that life in the hospital will be easier. But he immediately clashes with Ratched and incites the other patients to rebel against her reign of terror, betting them that he can goad her into losing her cool. One morning he appears wearing only his hat and a towel, and tells her that his clothes were stolen. She assails a nearby black attendant for failing to provide McMurphy with something to cover himself.

> The big black boy . . . ambles off to the linen room to get McMurphy a set of greens—probably ten sizes too small—and ambles back and holds it out to him with a look of the clearest hate I ever saw. McMurphy just looks confused, like he doesn't know how to take the outfit the black boy's handing to him, what with one hand holding the toothbrush and the other hand holding up the towel. He finally winks at

the nurse and shrugs and unwraps the towel, drapes it over her shoulder like she was a wooden rack.

I see he had his shorts on under the towel all along.

I think for a fact that she'd rather he'd of been stark naked under that towel than had on those shorts. She's glaring at those big white whales leaping round on his shorts in pure wordless outrage. That's more'n she can take. It's a full minute before she can pull herself together enough to turn on the least black boy; her voice is shaking out of control, she's so mad.

"Williams . . . I believe . . . you were supposed to have the windows of the Nurses' Station polished by the time I arrived this morning." He scuttles off like a black and white bug. "And you, Washington—and you . . ." Washington shuffles back to his bucket in almost a trot. She looks around again, wondering who else she can light into. She spots me, but by this time some of the other patients are out of the dorm and wondering about the little clutch of us here in the hall. She closes her eyes and concentrates. She can't have them see her face like this, white and warped with fury. She uses all the power of control that's in her. Gradually the lips gather together again under the little white nose, run together, like the red-hot wire had got hot enough to melt, shimmer a second, then click solid as the molten metal sets, growing cold and strangely dull. . . . (pp. 89-90)

Most Ones are terrified of losing control, and Nurse Ratched's formidable grip on her feelings is essential to maintaining her power over others. Ones with a Two wing are more prone to emotional outbursts than Ones with a Nine wing, and McMurphy—a Seven—knows just how to press Ratched's buttons. Unhealthy Ones, however, can be ruthlessly punitive—especially toward Sevens, whom they see as chronically out of control—and the merciless Ratched eventually destroys McMurphy.

Subtypes

Ones are generally focused on improving themselves and the world around them. **Self-Preservation** Ones, whom Oscar Ichazo associates with "anxiety," are preoccupied with physical survival. Self-Preservation Ones are the most "tightly wound" of the One subtypes, the most prone to anxious worry and fear about making mistakes. They often drive themselves to ever-greater productivity, and tend to be extremely task-oriented. They feel guilty about their desires and try to rigorously control what they see as their potentially disastrous self-indulgence. Not surprisingly, Ones who are prone to eating disorders often have this subtype.

Literary examples of Self-Preservation Ones include Mr. Bridge, Thomas More in *A Man for All Seasons*, Constantine Levin in Leo Tolstoy's *Anna Karenina*, Isabella in Shakespeare's *Measure for Measure*, the title character in

Alfred Uhry's play *Driving Miss Daisy*, and Felix Unger in Neil Simon's *The Odd Couple*.

The Odd Couple

In Neil Simon's play, fussy fastidious Felix Unger moves in with his friend Oscar, a sloppy sports writer, while both are getting divorces. Felix immediately takes charge of cleaning up Oscar's apartment, preparing perfect meals and generally driving his new roommate crazy. Early in the play Felix's unhealthy Self-Preservation One issues emerge clearly:

> OSCAR   Felix, why don't you leave yourself alone? Don't tinker.
>
> FELIX   I can't help myself. I drive everyone crazy. A marriage counselor once kicked me out of his office. He wrote on my chart, "Lunatic!" I don't blame her. It's impossible to be married to me.
>
> OSCAR   It takes two to make a rotten marriage.
> (*He lies back down on the couch*)
>
> FELIX   You don't know what I was like at home. I bought her a book and made her write down every penny we spent. Thirty-eight cents for cigarettes; ten cents for a paper. Everything had to go in the book. And then we had a big fight because I said she forgot to write down how much the book was. Who could live with anyone like that?
>
> OSCAR   An accountant! What do I know? We're not perfect. We all have faults.
>
> FELIX   Faults? Heh! Faults. We have a maid who comes in to clean three times a week. And on the other days, Frances does the cleaning. And at night, after they've both cleaned up, I go in and clean the whole place again. I can't help it. I like things clean. Blame it on my mother. I was toilet-trained at five months old.
>
> OSCAR   How do you remember things like that?
>
> FELIX   I loused up the marriage. Nothing was ever right. I used to recook everything. The minute she walked out of the kitchen I would add salt or pepper. It's not that I didn't trust her, it's just that I was a better cook. Well, I cooked myself out of a marriage. (*He bangs his head with the palm of his hand three times*) *God damned idiot!* (p. 246)

Throughout this exchange Felix's anxiety is palpable. Although he sees that his obsession with control and perfection ruined his marriage, he can't help repeating the same pattern with Oscar. All Ones can lacerate themselves about their faults, but the impulse is especially extreme in Self-Preservation Ones. Notice that the areas Felix is most compulsive about—money, cleanliness, cooking—all relate to survival.

Ordinary People

Another vivid Self-Preservation One is Beth in Judith Guest's novel

Ordinary People. Here we see Beth's husband, Cal, remembering a period early in their marriage when her obsession with cleanliness was especially marked:

> On the way back to work he thinks, She never lets herself get trapped. Not strictly true. He can remember a period of their lives when she felt distinctly trapped. When Jordan was two years old, with Connie toddling around after him at ten months, both of them spreading havoc in that tiny northside apartment. *Those first five years just passed in a blur!* he has heard her say gaily at parties. But he remembers them, and remembers the scenes: her figure, tense with fury as she scrubbed the fingermarks from the walls; she bursting suddenly into tears because of a toy left out of place, or a spoonful of food thrown onto the floor from the high chair. And it did not pay him to become exasperated with her. Once he had done so, had shouted at her to forget the damned cleaning schedule for once. She had flown into a rage, railed at him, and flung herself across the bed, in hysterics. Everything had to be perfect, never mind the impossible hardship it worked on her, on them all; never mind the utter lack of meaning in such perfection, weighted as it was against the endless repetition of days, weeks, months. They learned, all of them, that certain things drove her to the point of madness: dirt tracked in on a freshly scrubbed floor; water-spotted shower stalls; articles of clothing left out of place. And, he had to admit, he liked a clean house; he liked the order she brought into his life, perfectionist that she was. (pp. 89-90)

Beth is fairly unhealthy and, unlike Felix Unger, has no perspective on her obsessiveness. We also sense the terror behind her compulsive cleanliness. Self-Preservation Ones assume that without their perfectionistic devotion the world will dissolve into chaos, that their very lives and the lives of their loved ones will be threatened if their vigilance flags. Telling an unhealthy One with this subtype that she is neurotic rarely leads to any insight; more likely it will just enrage her, since she is convinced that survival is at stake.

Social Ones, whom Ichazo calls "nonadaptable," are easier to identify and are the most common One subtype in literature. They are often overtly angry men and women bent on reforming the world around them. They assume that their standards apply to society at large, and don't hesitate to speak out about what they perceive as injustices. Average Social Ones have strong, often moralistic, opinions and can be obsessed with rules and procedures. When less healthy, they see the world in black-and-white and are rigid and punitive.

Literary examples of Social Ones include Clarice Starling in *The Silence of the Lambs*, Atticus Finch in Harper Lee's *To Kill A Mockingbird*, Leah in Barbara Kingsolver's *The Poisonwood Bible*, P. L. Travers's Mary Poppins, Dr. Sloper in Henry James's *Washington Square*, Molly in Alice Adams's *Medicine*

Men, Nurse Ratched in *One Flew Over the Cuckoo's Nest*, Sir Thomas More in *A Man for All Seasons*, Allie Fox in Paul Theroux's *The Mosquito Coast*, Kyra in David Hare's *Skylight*, Dr. Stockman in Ibsen's *An Enemy of the People*, Elizabeth Proctor in Arthur Miller's *The Crucible*, Vivian Bearing in Margaret Edson's *Wit*, and Javert in Victor Hugo's *Les Miserables*.

Les Miserables

Victor Hugo's great novel presents a memorable unhealthy Social One in Javert, the police inspector who relentlessly pursues the hero, Jean Valjean. Right away we see the rigid black-and-white thinking that characterizes this subtype:

> This man was a compound of two sentiments, very simple and very good in themselves, but he almost made them evil by his exaggeration of them; respect for authority and hatred of rebellion; and in his eyes, theft, murder, all crimes, were only forms of rebellion. In his strong and implicit faith he included all who held any function in the state, from the prime minister to the constable. He had nothing but disdain, aversion, and disgust for all who had once overstepped the bounds of the law. He was absolute, and admitted no exceptions. . . . He would have arrested his father if escaping from the galleys, and denounced his mother for violating her ticket of leave. And he would have done it with that sort of interior satisfaction that springs from virtue. His life was a life of privations, isolation, self-denial, and chastity: never any amusement. It was implacable duty, absorbed in the police as the Spartans were absorbed in Sparta, a pitiless detective, a fierce honesty, a marble-hearted informer, Brutus united with Vidocq. (pp. 143-144)

When Javert locates Valjean, his self-righteous delight is that of an unhealthy Social One. Hugo's mixture of horror and compassion for Javert's warped thinking gives this characterization an unusual complexity and dimension:

> Javert was at this moment in heaven. Without clearly defining his own feelings, yet notwithstanding with a confused intuition of his necessity and his success, he, Javert, personified justice, light and truth, in their celestial function as destroyers of evil. He was surrounded and supported by infinite depths of authority, reason, precedent, legal conscience, the vengeance of the law, all the stars in the firmament; he protected order, he hurled forth the thunder of the law, he avenged society, he lent aid to the absolute; he stood erect in a halo of glory; there was in his victory a reminder of defiance and of combat; standing haughty, resplendent, he displayed in full glory the superhuman beastliness of a ferocious archangel. . . .

> Probity, sincerity, candour, conviction, the idea of duty, are things which, mistaken, may become hideous, but which, even though hideous, remain great; their majesty, peculiar to the human conscience, continues in all their horror; they are virtues with a single vice—error. The pitiless, sincere joy of a fanatic in an act of atrocity preserves an indescribably mournful radiance which inspires us with veneration. Without suspecting it, Javert, in his fear-inspiring happiness, was pitiable, like every ignorant man who wins a triumph. Nothing could be more painful and terrible than this face, which revealed what we may call all the evil of good. (pp. 244-245)

Toward the novel's end, Valjean takes Javert as his prisoner and Valjean's comrades expect him to kill the inspector, whom they believe is a political spy. But Valjean takes Javert away from the group, cuts his bonds and releases him. This act of mercy from a man Javert has regarded as wholly evil unnerves the inspector and leads to his eventual suicide. Here the anguished Javert is torn between his duty to bring Valjean to justice and his humanitarian impulses toward a man who spared his life:

> He saw before him two roads, both equally straight; but he saw two; and that terrified him—him who had never in his life known but one straight line. And, bitter anguish, these two roads were contradictory. One of these two straight lines excluded the other. Which of the two was the true one?
>
> His condition was inexpressible. . . .
>
> One thing had astonished him, that Jean Valjean had spared him, and one thing had petrified him, that he, Javert, had spared Jean Valjean.
>
> Where was he? He sought himself and found himself no longer.
>
> What should he do now? Give up Jean Valjean, that was wrong; leave Jean Valjean free, that was wrong. . . . In every course which was open to him, there was a fall. Destiny has certain extremities precipitous upon the impossible, and beyond which life is no more than an abyss. Javert was at one of these extremities. (pp. 1105-1106)

Hugo paints an unforgettable picture of Javert's loathing of his own higher self, which seems to him alien. This unhealthy Social One is so unfamiliar with the idea of a higher perfection—one that goes beyond mere perfectionism—that in the face of it he can only turn on himself:

> He was compelled to recognise the existence of kindness. This convict had been kind. And he himself, wonderful to tell, he had just been kind. Therefore he had become depraved.
>
> He thought himself base. He was a horror to himself.

Javert's ideal was not to be humane, not to be great, not to be sublime; it was to be irreproachable. Now he had just failed.

How had he reached that point? How had all this happened? He could not have told himself. He took his head in his hands, but it was in vain; he could not explain it to himself. (p. 1109)

Ultimately, Javert cannot cope with the awareness that God's law may include a perfection that requires him to violate the mundane standards he has followed all his life, and he commits suicide. A Social One to the end, he first goes to a local police station and prepares a report for his superiors recommending minor changes in police procedures. Even in his personal desperation, his perfectionism and sense of duty compel him to complete his job impeccably.

Although Javert's story illustrates the pathological extreme of a Social One, there is a kind of integrity in his final choice that evokes in the reader both pity and terror.

To Kill A Mockingbird

By contrast, Atticus Finch in Harper Lee's *To Kill A Mockingbird* is a healthy Social One. Set in 1932 in Macon, Georgia, during the Great Depression, the story is told by Atticus's six-year-old daughter Scout. She and her older brother Jem are first seen talking about a neighbor's son named Boo, who only comes out at night and is rumored to be crazy. When Scout later asks her father about Boo, he tells her to stay away from him and "not torment those people."

Atticus, who has a strong Two wing, is a principled lawyer, a widower who loves his kids. He does his best to be a good parent—reading them stories, patiently answering their questions, offering help and guidance in a gentle and loving manner.

When Atticus agrees to defend Tom Robinson, a black man accused of raping a white woman, the atmosphere in town becomes increasingly volatile. Scout begins getting into fights at school with other children. When Atticus asks her why she asks him, "Do you defend niggers?" He replies that he is defending a *Negro*—and that she shouldn't say the other word. When she asks why he's defending the man, Atticus tries to explain, but finally decides that she's too young to understand. He asks her not to get into fights over it, no matter how much the other children provoke her.

Once school is out for the summer, Tom Robinson's trial begins. Brought back from a neighboring town, where he had been taken for his safety, Tom is now in the town jail. One evening the sheriff visits Atticus to warn that there might be trouble that night from a "certain element." Atticus packs a lamp and a chair into his car and drives away.

Jem, who overheard the sheriff's warning, takes Scout and their friend Dil to investigate. In front of the jail they find Atticus in his chair reading. When a mob arrives, intent on lynching the black man, the children make their presence known. Atticus tries to get them to go home, but to no avail. When Scout speaks to one of the men, the father of a boy she knows, the man grows ashamed and suggests the men all leave, which they do. It is clear, however, that Atticus would have been in serious physical danger had the children not appeared. It is not uncommon for Social Ones to put themselves on the line this way, in service of their principles.

Later, at the trial, Atticus proves that it would have been physically impossible for Tom Robinson to cause the injuries sustained by Mae Ella, the white woman he is accused of raping. He further establishes that Bob Ewell, Mae Ella's redneck father, probably beat her and forced her to lie about having been raped. Although Atticus defends Tom superbly, the jury still returns with a guilty verdict.

As the deputies take Tom to another town for safe-keeping, he tries to escape and is killed. Atticus goes to Tom's house to tell his family that Tom is dead. While he is inside, Bob Ewell appears in the yard wanting revenge. Ewell spits in his face, and Atticus, though clearly furious, simply wipes off the spit with his handkerchief, gets into his car and drives away—a powerful example of a healthy Social One's self-control under extreme provocation.

Atticus Finch is a model of the moral hero. The neurotic "inflexibility" that characterizes Social Ones becomes, in him, an unbending and healthy devotion to principle.

Sexual Ones, whom Ichazo associates with "jealousy" or "heat," are focused on finding and maintaining an ideal intimate relationship. This vision of a "perfect mate"—someone who will share the One's high standards and who will be completely faithful—is central to this subtype. Sexual Ones fear that their partners may fall short of their ideals, thus undermining the relationship. Ones with this subtype often exhibit many qualities of Seven: an engaging wit and a magnetic quality that charms potential partners. They are more strongly in touch with their sensual desires, and they may feel deeply conflicted about their sexuality. When less healthy, Sexual Ones tend to be critical and suspicious of their mates, punishing them in an attempt to purge their own sexual feelings.

Some examples of Sexual Ones are: Dorothea in *Middlemarch*, Miss Kenton in *The Remains of the Day*, Portia in *The Merchant of Venice*, Adolphus Cusins in George Bernard Shaw's *Major Barbara*, and Elinor Dashwood in Jane Austen's *Sense and Sensibility*.

Sense and Sensibility

Elinor Dashwood, the oldest of three sisters in Jane Austen's novel, is a healthy Sexual One. The story focuses on the two older sisters and their love lives. Early in the novel, Elinor meets Edward, falls in love with him, and believes that he returns her feelings. One day, however, Edward announces casually that he must leave for an indefinite period. Although distressed at this apparent slight, Elinor is determined—in characteristic One fashion—to keep a tight rein on her feelings:

This desponding turn of [Edward's] mind, though it could not be communicated to Mrs. Dashwood, gave additional pain to them all in the parting, which shortly took place, and left an uncomfortable impression on Elinor's feelings especially, which required some trouble and time to subdue. But as it was her determination to subdue it, and to prevent herself from appearing to suffer more than what all her family suffered on his going away, she did not adopt the method so judiciously employed by Marianne, on a similar occasion, to augment and fix her sorrow, by seeking silence, solitude, and idleness. Their means were as different as their objects, and equally suited to the advancement of each.

Elinor sat down to her drawing-table as soon as he was out of the house, busily employed herself the whole day, neither sought nor avoided the mention of his name, appeared to interest herself almost as much as even in the general concerns of the family, and if, by this conduct, she did not lessen her own grief, it was at least prevented from unnecessary increase, and her mother and sisters were spared much solicitude on her account. . . .

Without shutting herself up from her family, or leaving the house in determined solitude to avoid them, or lying awake the whole night to indulge meditation, Elinor found every day afforded her leisure enough to think of Edward, and of Edward's behaviour, in every possible variety which the different state of her spirits at different times could produce; with tenderness, pity, approbation, censure, and doubt. There were moments in abundance, when, if not by the absence of her mother and sisters, at least by the nature of their employments, conversation was forbidden among them, and every effect of solitude was produced. Her mind was inevitably at liberty; her thoughts could not be chained elsewhere; and the past and the future, on a subject so interesting, must be before her, must force her attention, and engross her memory, her reflection, and her fancy. (pp. 62-63)

Note Elinor's Sexual One tendency to chew over events and consider possible motives for her lover's behavior. Unlike her self-dramatizing sister Marianne, a Sexual Four, Elinor does this in private.

When Elinor learns from Lucy, a conniving Three, that Lucy is engaged to Edward, she is shocked and resentful. While she initially reacts like a victim— her Four stress point—she then takes a more mature view of the situation:

[T]he picture, the letter, the ring, formed altogether such a body of evidence as overcame every fear of condemning him unfairly, and established as a fact which no partiality could set aside, his ill-treatment of herself. Her resentment of such behaviour, her indignation at having been its dupe, for a short time made her feel only for herself; but other ideas, other considerations, soon arose. Had Edward been intentionally deceiving her? Had he feigned a regard for her which he did not feel? Was his engagement to Lucy an engagement of the heart? No; whatever it might once have been, she could not believe it such at present. His affection was all her own. She could not be deceived in that. Her mother, sisters, Fanny, all had been conscious of his regard for her at Norland; it was not an illusion of her own vanity. He certainly loved her. What a softener of the heart was this persuasion! How much could it not tempt her to forgive! He had been blameable, highly blameable in remaining at Norland after he first felt her influence over him to be more than it ought to be. In that, he could not be defended; but if he had injured her, how much more had he injured himself! If her case were pitiable, his was hopeless. His imprudence had made her miserable for a while; but it seemed to have deprived himself of all chance of ever being otherwise. She might in time regain tranquillity; but *he*, what had he to look forward to? Could he ever be tolerably happy with Lucy Steele? Could he, were his affection for herself out of the question, with his integrity, his delicacy, and well-informed mind, be satisfied with a wife like her— illiterate, artful, and selfish? (pp. 81-82)

Not only is Elinor outraged at her lover's lack of standards—a high priority for a Sexual One—but she also feels a healthy compassion for him. In the end, her empathy for his predicament—a reflection of her strong Two wing—eclipses her own sense of injury.

Elinor's One sense of privacy requires that she not impose her sufferings on others, and Sexual Ones can obsess and brood for a long time about unhappy love affairs without those close to them ever suspecting the depth of their unhappiness:

As these considerations occurred to her in painful succession, she wept for him more than for herself. Supported by the conviction of having done nothing to merit her present unhappiness, and consoled by the belief that Edward had done nothing to forfeit her esteem, she thought she could even now, under the first smart of the heavy blow, command herself enough to guard every suspicion of the truth from her mother and sisters. . . .

From their counsel or their conversation she knew she could receive no assistance; their tenderness and sorrow must add to her distress, while her self-command would neither receive encouragement from their example nor from their praise. She was stronger alone, and her own good sense so well supported her, that her firmness was as unshaken, her appearance of cheerfulness as invariable, as, with regrets so poignant and so fresh, it was possible for them to be. (pp. 82-83)

When Marianne learns, four months later, about her sister's misfortune, she assumes, in her Fourish way, that Elinor's continuing cheerfulness has meant that Elinor lacks deep feelings. Elinor sets Marianne straight with a touch of sarcasm:

> "I understand you. You do not suppose that I have ever felt much. For four months, Marianne, I have had all this hanging on my mind, without being at liberty to speak of it to a single creature; knowing that it would make you and my mother most unhappy whenever it were explained to you, yet unable to prepare you for it in the least. . . . And all this has been going on at a time when, as you too well know, it has not been my only unhappiness. If you can think me capable of every feeling—surely you may suppose that I have suffered *now*. The composure of mind with which I have brought myself at present to consider the matter, the consolation that I have been willing to admit, have been the effect of constant and painful exertion; they did not spring up of themselves; they did not occur to relieve my spirits at first; no, Marianne. *Then*, if I had not been bound to silence, perhaps nothing could have kept me entirely—not even what I owed to my dearest friends—from openly showing that I was *very* unhappy." (p. 156)

Later, when Elinor learns from Edward that Lucy has chosen to marry his brother rather than him—and that Edward is therefore free to marry *her*— she can barely contain her feelings:

> Elinor could sit it no longer, She almost ran out of the room, and as soon as the door was closed, burst into tears of joy, which at first she thought would never cease. (p. 215)

Note that, even in her moment of greatest happiness, this One is still reluctant to openly display the depth of her feelings.

> But Elinor, how are *her* feelings to be described? From the moment of learning that Lucy was married to another, that Edward was free, to the moment of his justifying the hopes which had so instantly followed, she was everything by turns but tranquil. But when the second moment had passed—when she found every doubt, every solicitude removed—compared her situation with what so lately it had been—saw him honourably released from his former engagement—saw him instantly profiting by the release, to address herself and declare an affection as tender, as constant as she had ever supposed it to be—she was oppressed, she was overcome by her own felicity; and happily disposed as is the human mind to be easily familiarized with any change for the better, it required several hours to give sedateness to her spirits, or any degree of tranquillity to her heart. (p. 217)

While Ones' habitual behavior can persuade even their family and close friends that they lack passion, the truth is that their feelings are so powerful they fear that expressing them will uncork a volcano. When Sexual Ones find their perfect mate, their capacity for Sevenish joy is boundless.

Measure for Measure

Unhealthy Sexual Ones are often shocked at their own desires. The "trap door" quality is stronger with this subtype and makes them prone to sensual indulgences that later horrify them.

We see this in Angelo, the rigid Sexual One who lusts after the novice nun, Isabella, in Shakespeare's *Measure for Measure*. Early in the play Isabella arrives to plead with Angelo, Deputy of the absent Duke of Vienna, for the life of her brother, Claudio, who has been condemned for fornication. When he first sees her, Angelo is overcome with desire and demands that Isabella come to see him again the following day. After she leaves, he wrestles with his feelings:

> What's this, what's this? Is this her fault or mine?
> The tempter or the tempted, who sins most? Ha!
> Not she: nor doth she tempt: but it is I
> That, lying by the violet in the sun,
> Do as the carrion does, not as the flower,
> Corrupt with virtuous season. Can it be
> That modesty may more betray our sense
> Than woman's lightness? Having waste ground enough,
> Shall we desire to raze the sanctuary
> And pitch our evils there? Oh, fie, fie, fie!
> What dost thou, or what art thou, Angelo?
> Dost thou desire her foully for those things
> That make her good? O, let her brother live!
> Thieves for their robbery have authority
> When judges steal themselves. What, do I love her,
> That I desire to hear her speak again,
> And feast upon her eyes? What is't I dream on?
> O cunning enemy, that to catch a saint,
> With saints dost bait thy hook! Most dangerous
> Is that temptation that doth goad us on
> To sin in loving virtue: never could the strumpet,
> With all her double vigor, art and nature,
> Once stir my temper; but this virtuous maid
> Subdues me quite. Ever till now,
> When men were fond, I smiled and wonder'd how. (II, ii, 161-187)

When Isabella returns the next day, Angelo abandons all pretense of virtue and tries to extort sex from her in exchange for sparing her brother's life. After

Angelo's immorality is unmasked, he admits his fault and asks the Duke to condemn him. This self-punishing quality is especially extreme in unhealthy One characters like Angelo and Javert.

But all Ones suffer to some degree from the critical voice in their heads. Even healthy examples like Clarice Starling, Elinor Dashwood, and Dorothea Brooke are self-accusative. Unlike Fours, Ones conceal their suffering from others, yet their feelings are often deep and intense. At their worst Ones are pitiless and punitive; at their best they are the Enneagram style most likely to be portrayed in literature as moral heroes.

Sources

Austen, Jane, *Sense and Sensibility* (New York: Dodd, Mead, & Co., 1949). First published 1811

Bolt, Robert, *A Man for All Seasons* (New York: Random House, 1962)

Connell, Evan S., *Mr. Bridge* (San Francisco: North Point Press, 1969)

Eliot, George, *Middlemarch* (New York: Barnes & Noble, 1996). First published 1871

Guest, Judith, *Ordinary People* (New York: The Viking Press, 1976)

Harris, Thomas, *The Silence of the Lambs* (New York: St. Martin's Press, 1988)

Hugo, Victor, *Les Miserables*, trans. Charles E. Wilbour (New York: Modern Library, n.d.). First published 1862

Ishiguro, Kazuo, *The Remains of the Day* (New York: Vintage, 1990)

Kesey, Ken, *One Flew Over the Cuckoo's Nest* (New York: Signet, 1963)

Lee, Harper, *To Kill A Mockingbird* (Philadelphia: Lippincott, 1968)

Shakespeare, William, *Measure for Measure*. First produced 1604

Simon, Neil, *The Odd Couple*, in *The Comedy of Neil Simon* (New York: Random House, 1971)

Two: The Lover

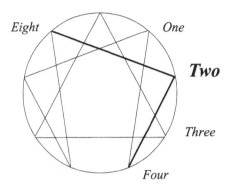

Holden Caulfield, hero of J.D. Salinger's *The Catcher in the Rye*, is a classic example of the Two temperament. As 17-year-old Holden talks with his 10-year-old sister, Phoebe, about the kind of career he might choose, we see the Two's dedication to helping others:

"I couldn't be a scientist. I'm no good in science."

"Well, a lawyer—like Daddy and all."

"Lawyers are all right, I guess—but it doesn't appeal to me," I said. "I mean they're all right if they go around saving innocent guys' lives all the time, and like that, but you don't *do* that kind of stuff if you're a lawyer. All you do is make a lot of dough and play golf and play bridge and buy cars and drink Martinis and look like a hot-shot. And besides. Even if you *did* go around saving guys' lives and all, how would you know if you did it because you really *wanted* to save guys' lives, or because you did it because what you *really* wanted to do was be a terrific lawyer, with everybody slapping you on the back and congratulating you in court when the goddam trial was over, the reporters and everybody, the way it is in the dirty movies? How would you know you weren't being a phony? The trouble is, you *wouldn't.*"

I'm not too sure old Phoebe knew what the hell I was talking about. I mean she's only a little child and all. But she was listening, at least. If somebody at least listens, it's not too bad.

"Daddy's going to kill you. He's going to *kill* you," she said.

I wasn't listening, though. I was thinking about something else—something crazy. "You know what I'd like to be?" I said. "You know what I'd like to be? I mean if I had my goddam choice?"

"What? Stop *swearing*."

"You know that song 'If a body catch a body comin' through the rye?' I'd like—"

"It's 'If a body *meet* a body coming through the rye'!" old Phoebe said. "It's a poem. By Robert *Burns*."

She was right, though. It *is* "If a body meet a body coming through the rye." I didn't know it then, though.

"I thought it was 'If a body catch a body,'" I said. "Anyway, I keep picturing all these little kids playing some game in this big field of rye and all. Thousands of little kids, and nobody's around—nobody big, I mean—except me. And I'm standing on the edge of some crazy cliff. What I have to do, I have to catch everybody if they start to go over the cliff—I mean if they're running and they don't look where they're going I have to come out from somewhere and *catch* them. I'd just be the catcher in the rye and all. I know it's crazy, but that's the only thing I'd really like to be. I know it's crazy." (pp. 172-173)

At their best, Twos are generous, highly emotional, and intense in their relationships. I call Two "The Lover" because people with this temperament generally have a powerful concern for others and empathize with their sufferings. Twos often devote their lives to supporting others and take great pride in this loving service.

Candida

In George Bernard Shaw's play *Candida*, the title character exemplifies the Two's dedication to helping loved ones with their life tasks, as Candida does for her preacher husband, James Morell. The playwright's description of Candida at her first entrance offers a witty portrait of a self-aware Two:

> She is a woman of 33, well built, well nourished, likely, one guesses to become matronly later on, but now quite at her best, with the double charm of youth and motherhood. Her ways are those of a woman who has found that she can always manage people by engaging their affection, and who does so frankly and instinctively without the smallest scruple. So far, she is like any other pretty woman who is just clever enough to make the most of her sexual attractions for trivially selfish ends; but Candida's serene brow, courageous eyes, and well set mouth and chin signify largeness of mind and dignity of character to ennoble her cunning in the affections. (p. 213)

Morell, a Three, introduces his wife to Eugene Marchbanks, a Four, a young poet whom Morell has rescued from personal difficulties. Marchbanks falls in love with Candida, who is 15 years his senior, and persuades Morell that

Candida may return his love.

Candida instinctively understands Marchbanks's hunger for love and beauty. When she confides to her husband that she senses Marchbanks is ready to fall in love with her, it is with Two pride in her potential power over the young poet's life. She explains that Marchbanks's ultimate view of her will depend on how he is introduced to love:

CANDIDA [*explaining*] If he learns it from a good woman, then it will be all right: he will forgive me.
MORELL. Forgive?
CANDIDA. But suppose he learns it from a bad woman, as so many men do, especially poetic men, who imagine all women are angels! Suppose he only discovers the value of love when he has thrown it away and degraded himself in his ignorance! Will he forgive me then, do you think?
MORELL. Forgive you for what?
CANDIDA [*realizing how stupid he is, and a little disappointed, though quite tenderly so*] Don't you understand? [*He shakes his head. She turns to him again, so as to explain with the fondest intimacy*]. I mean, will he forgive me for not teaching him myself? For abandoning him to the bad women for the sake of my goodness, of my purity, as you call it? Ah, James, how little you understand me, to talk of your confidence in my goodness and purity! I would give them both to poor Eugene as willingly as I would give my shawl to a beggar dying of cold, if there were nothing else to restrain me. Put your trust in my love for you, James; for if that went, I should care very little for your sermons: mere phrases that you cheat yourself and others with every day. (p. 242)

Candida's threat to withdraw her love if her husband fails to fully appreciate her may be subtle, but it is real. The iron hand within a velvet glove is characteristic of Twos, whose self-respect is maintained by the love and dependency of others.

In the end, the two men decide that Candida must choose between them. Morell offers her his strength, dignity, protection; Marchbanks his weakness and need. Candida, appalled at their common assumption that she must "belong" to one or the other, deliberately delays choosing until both men are miserable with the suspense:

CANDIDA [*significantly*] I give myself to the weaker of the two.
Eugene divines her meaning at once: his face whitens like steel in a furnace.
MORELL [*bowing his head with the calm of collapse*] I accept your sentence, Candida.
CANDIDA. Do you understand, Eugene?

MARCHBANKS. Oh, I feel I'm lost. He cannot bear the burden.

MORELL [*incredulously, raising his head and voice with comic abruptness*] Do you mean me, Candida?

CANDIDA [*smiles a little*] Let us sit and talk comfortably over it like three friends. [*To Morell*] Sit down, dear. [*Morell, quite lost, takes the chair from the fireside: the children's chair*] Bring me that chair, Eugene. [*She indicates the easy chair. He fetches it silently, even with something like cold strength, and places it next Morell, a little behind him. She sits down. He takes the visitor's chair himself, and sits, inscrutable. When they are all settled she begins, throwing a spell of quietness on them by her calm, sane, tender tone*]. You remember what you told me about yourself, Eugene; how nobody has cared for you since your old nurse died: how those clever fashionable sisters and successful brothers of yours were your mother's and father's pets: how miserable you were at Eton: how your father is trying to starve you into returning to Oxford: how you have had to live without comfort or welcome or refuge: always lonely, and nearly always disliked and misunderstood, poor boy!

MARCHBANKS [*faithful to the nobility of his lot*] I had my books. I had Nature. And at last I met you.

CANDIDA. Never mind that just at present. Now I want you to look at this other boy here: my boy! Spoiled from his cradle. We go once a fortnight to see his parents. You should come with us, Eugene, to see the pictures of the hero of that household. James as a baby! The most wonderful of all babies. James holding his first school prize, won at the ripe age of eight! James as the captain of his eleven! James in his first frock coat! James under all sorts of glorious circumstances! You know how strong he is (I hope he didn't hurt you): how clever he is: how happy. [*With deepening gravity*] Ask James's mother and his three sisters what it cost to save James the trouble of doing anything but be strong and clever and happy. Ask me what it costs to be James's mother and three sisters and wife and mother to his children all in one. Ask Prossy and Maria how troublesome the house is even when we have no visitors to help us to slice the onions. Ask the tradesmen who want to worry James and spoil his beautiful sermons who it is that puts them off. When there is money to give, he gives it: when there is money to refuse, I refuse it. I build a castle of comfort and indulgence and love for him, and stand sentinel always to keep the little vulgar cares out. I make him master here, though he does not know it, and could not tell you a moment ago how it came to be so. [*With sweet irony*] And when he thought I might go away with you, his only anxiety was—what should become of me! And to tempt me to stay he offered me [*leaning forward to stroke his hair caressingly at each phrase*] his strength for my defence! His industry for my livelihood! His dignity for my position!

His—[*relenting*] ah, I am mixing up your beautiful cadences and spoiling them, am I not, darling? [*She lays her cheek fondly against his*].

MORELL [*quite overcome, kneeling beside her chair and embracing her with boyish ingenuousness*] It's all true, every word. What I am you have made me with the labor of your hands and the love of your heart. You are my wife, my mother, my sisters: you are the sum of all loving care to me.

CANDIDA [*in his arms, smiling, to Eugene*] Am I your mother and sisters to you, Eugene?

MARCHBANKS [*rising with a fierce gesture of disgust*] Ah, never. Out, then into the night with me! (pp. 264-267)

This scene provides an amusing composite picture of the Feeling Triad: Candida's Two pride in the control her love and attention gives her over others; Morell's Three blindness to his feelings and his dependence on his wife; and Marchbanks's Four capacity for suffering, which is ultimately a kind of strength.

The Two's History

As children Twos feel ambivalent toward the protective figure in their lives. Usually the father plays this role, but in some cases the mother is the primary provider of structure, guidance, and discipline. Because Twos have mixed feelings about their protector, they develop qualities of the protector's complementary opposite: becoming the motherly, loving, nurturing figure. Their reasoning runs something like this: If I can make others—especially the protective figure—love and depend on me, maybe I will be safe. Winning the protector's affection becomes a template for the Two's later adult relationships.

The World According to Garp

John Irving's novel *The World According to Garp* describes the life and times of Garp, the Two son of Jenny Fields, a feminist leader ahead of her time. Jenny, an Eight, is fiercely independent and unsentimental—her qualities as protective figure much stronger than her qualities as nurturing figure. A nurse in a veterans' hospital, she wants a child but not a husband. Her solution is to become pregnant by a dying, brain-damaged patient whose vocabulary consists of a single word: "Garp." She loses her job when her pregnancy becomes evident, takes a job as nurse in a boys' school, and names her son "T. S. [for Technical Sergeant] Garp."

Garp's story, a sexual comedy of errors, is filled with love, violence, and death. Even as a child, Garp shows a Two's exceptional compassion for others' suffering, When Garp's English teacher is tormented by his students over his foul breath, Garp refuses to participate in this public humiliation:

"G-G-Garp?" stuttered Mr. Tinch, bending close to the boy—who smelled the terrible truth in Senior Honors English Composition. Garp knew he would win the annual creative writing prize. The sole judge was always Tinch. And if he could just pass third-year math, which he was taking for the second time, he would respectably graduate and make his mother very happy.

"Do I have b-b-bad breath, Garp?" Tinch asked.

"'Good' and 'bad' are matters of opinion, sir," Garp said.

"In *your* opinion, G-G-Garp?" Tinch said.

"In *my* opinion," Garp said, without batting an eye, "you've got the best breath of any teacher at this school." And he looked hard across the classroom at Benny Potter from New York—a *born* wise-ass, even Garp would agree—and he stared Benny's grin off Benny's face because Garp's eyes said to Benny that Garp would break Benny's neck if he made a peep.

And Tinch said, "Thank you, Garp," who won the writing prize, despite the note submitted with his last paper.

Mr. Tinch: I lied in class because I didn't want those other assholes to laugh at you. You should know, however, that your breath really is pretty bad. Sorry.   *T.S. Garp*

"You know w-w-what?" Tinch asked Garp when they were alone together, talking about Garp's last story.

"What?" Garp said.

"There's nothing I can d-d-do about my breath," Tinch said. "I think it's because I'm d-d-dying," he said, with a twinkle, "I'm r-r-rotting from the inside out!" But Garp was not amused and he watched for news of Tinch for years after his graduation, relieved that the old gentleman did not appear to have anything terminal. (pp. 66-67)

Garp's instinctive kindness to Tinch is typical of Twos. The style's emotional responsiveness to other people's suffering is also clear in the following scene, in which the adult Garp empathizes with a young girl who has been raped:

Garp had been running in the city park when he found the girl, a naked ten-year-old running ahead of him on the bridle path. When she realized he was gaining on her, she fell down and covered her face, then covered her crotch, then tried to hide her insubstantial breasts. It was a cold day, late fall, and Garp saw the blood on the child's thighs and her frightened, swollen eyes. She screamed and screamed at him.

"What happened to you?" he asked, though he knew very well. He looked all around them, but there was no one there. She hugged her raw knees to her chest and screamed. "I won't hurt you," Garp said. "I want to help you." But the child wailed even louder. My God, of course! Garp thought: the terrible molester had probably said those very words to her, not long ago. "Where did he go?" Garp asked her. Then he changed his tone, trying to convince her he was on her side. "I'll kill him for you," he told her. She stared quietly at him, her head shaking and shaking, her fingers pinching and pinching the tight skin on her arms. "Please," Garp said, "Can you tell me where your clothes are?" He had nothing to give her to wear except his sweaty T-shirt. He was dressed in his running shorts, his running shoes. He pulled his T-shirt off over his head and felt instantly cold; the girl cried out, awfully loud, and hid her face. "No, don't be frightened, it's for you to put on," Garp told her. He let the T-shirt drop on her but she writhed out from under it and kicked at it; then she opened her mouth very wide and bit her own fist. . . .

Garp began to cry. The sky was gray, dead leaves were all around them, and when Garp began to wail aloud, the girl picked up his T-shirt and covered herself with it. They were in this queer position to each other—the child crouched under Garp's T-shirt, cringing at Garp's feet with Garp crying over her—when the mounted park police, a twosome, rode up the bridle path and spotted the apparent child molester with his victim. (p. 141)

Garp becomes a writer and marries Helen, a practical, scholarly, independent woman who resembles his mother. They produce a son, for whom Garp is the primary nurturer.

Like many Twos, Garp has a strong sexual appetite and becomes involved in a number of extra-marital affairs. One night, after having sex with Cindy, his son's baby sitter, he returns home, fearful that the campus police may have seen him throwing away his packet of condoms.

But no one saw him, no one found him out. Even Helen, already asleep, would not have found the smell of sex peculiar; after all, only hours before, he had legitimately acquired the odor. Even so, Garp showered, and slipped cleanly into his own safe bed; he curled against Helen, who murmured some affection; instinctively, she thrust one long thigh over his hip. When he failed to respond, she forced her buttocks back against him. Garp's throat ached at her trust, and at his love for her. He felt fondly the slight swell of Helen's pregnancy. . . . Although he'd agreed with Helen that it would be nice to have a girl, Garp *hoped* for another boy.

Why? he thought. He recalled the girl in the park, his image of the tongueless Ellen James, his own mother's difficult decisions. He felt fortunate to be with Helen; she had her own ambitions and he could not manipulate her. But he remembered the Kärntnerstrasse whores, and Cushie Percy (who would die making a baby). And now—her scent still on him, or at least on his mind, although he had washed—the plundered Little Squab Bones. . . .

Garp didn't want a daughter because of *men*. Because of *bad* men, certainly; but even, he thought, because of men like *me*. (pp. 150-151)

Twos—both male and female—identify with feminine consciousness and vulnerabilities. Garp's concern for his children and his anxiety about their well-being remind us of the "Jewish mother" figure that is a stereotype of Two:

Garp eyed Walt's uneaten pasta as if it were a personal insult. "Why do I bother?" he said. "The child eats nothing."

They finished their meal in silence. Helen knew Garp was thinking up a story to tell Walt after dinner. She knew Garp did this to calm himself whenever he was worried about the children—as if the act of imagining a good story for children was a way to keep children safe forever.

With the children Garp was instinctively generous, loyal as an animal, the most affectionate of fathers; he understood Duncan and Walt deeply and separately. Yet, Helen felt sure, he saw nothing of how his anxiety for the children made the children anxious—tense, even immature. On the one hand he treated them as grownups, but on the other hand he was so protective of them that he was not allowing them to grow up. He did not accept that Duncan was ten, that Walt was five; sometimes the children seemed fixed, as three-year-olds, in his mind.

Helen listened to the story Garp made up for Walt with her usual interest and concern. Like many of the stories Garp told the children, it began as a story for the children and ended up as a story Garp seemed to have made up for Garp. You would think that the children of a writer would have more stories read to them than other children, but Garp preferred that his children listen only to *his* stories. (p. 187)

Helen, a One, obviously understands Garp better than he understands himself. Twos prefer to focus on other people's needs. Searching their own souls generally makes them uncomfortable.

When Garp learns that Helen, a college teacher, is having an affair with one of her students, he responds with histrionics, another Two tendency:

When Helen touched him, he said, "Don't touch me," and went on crying. Helen shut the bedroom door.

"Oh, *don't*," she pleaded. "He isn't worth this; he wasn't *anything*. I just *enjoyed* him," she tried to explain, but Garp shook his head violently and threw his pants at her. He was still only half dressed—an attitude that was perhaps, Helen realized, the most compromising for men: when they were not one thing and also not another. A woman half dressed seemed to have some power, but a man was simply not as handsome as when he was naked, and not as secure as when he was clothed. "Please get dressed," she whispered to him, and handed him back his pants. He took them, he pulled them on; and went on crying.

"I'll do just what you want," she said.

"You won't see him again?" he said to her.

"No, not once," she said. "Not ever again."

"Walt has a cold," Garp said. "He shouldn't even be going out, but it's not too bad for him at a movie. And we won't be late," he added to her. "Go see if he's dressed warmly enough." She did.

He opened her top drawer, where her lingerie was, and pulled the drawer from the dresser; he pushed his face into the wonderful silkiness and scent of her clothes—like a bear holding a great trough of food in his forepaws, and then losing himself in it. When Helen came back into the room and caught him at this, it was almost as if she'd caught him masturbating. Embarrassed, he brought the drawer down across his knee and cracked it; her underwear flew about. He raised the cracked drawer over his head and smacked it down against the edge of the dresser, snapping what felt like the spine of an animal about the size of the drawer. Helen ran from the room and he finished dressing. (pp. 256-257)

Still seething about Helen's affair, Garp takes his sons to a movie, after making her promise that she will break off the affair that evening. Sitting in the movie, Garp frets about his son Walt's fever and his wife's infidelity.

"You should relax, Dad," Duncan suggested, shaking his head. Oh, I *should*, Garp knew; but he couldn't. He thought of Walt, and what a perfect little ass he had, and strong little legs, and how sweet his sweat smelled when he'd been running and his hair was damp behind his ears. A body that perfect should not be sick, he thought. I should have let *Helen* go out on this miserable night; I should have made her call that twerp from her office—and tell him to put it in his ear, Garp thought. Or in a light socket And turn on the juice!

I should have called that candy-ass myself, Garp thought. I should have visited him in the middle of the night. When Garp walked up the aisle to see if they had a phone in the lobby, he heard Walt still coughing.

If she hasn't already gotten in touch with him, Garp thought, I'll tell her *not* to keep trying. I'll tell her it's *my* turn. He was at that point in his feelings toward Helen where he felt betrayed but at the same time honestly loved and important to her; he had not had time enough to ponder *how* betrayed he felt—or how much, truly, she had been trying to keep him in her mind. It was a delicate point, between hating her and loving her terribly—also, he was not without sympathy for whatever she'd wanted; after all, he knew, the shoe on the other foot had also been worn (and was certainly thinner). It even seemed unfair, to Garp, that Helen, who had always meant so well, had been caught like this; she was a good woman and she certainly deserved better luck. But when Helen did not answer the phone, this point of delicacy in Garp's feelings toward her quite suddenly escaped him. He felt only rage, and only betrayal. (pp. 263-264)

Garp's blind fury reflects the Two's connecting point to Eight. He insists on leaving in the middle of the movie, drives home in a blinding sleet storm, and accidentally hits his wife's lover's car in his driveway just as Helen and her lover are in the car making love. The accident kills Walt and seriously injures everyone else.

Levels of Health

Twos at all levels of health seek to win love through serving and helping others. But few have sufficient insight into their own personality dynamics to understand that giving-to-get is sometimes involved in their altruism.

The psychological defense mechanism characteristic of Twos is repression, a banishing of one's own needs from awareness. Because average Twos are out of touch with their personal needs and desires, they unconsciously seek to align themselves with people who can fill those needs. But Twos delude themselves that *they* are the ones filling the needs of others, and their ability to serve others becomes a source of pride. Average Twos are continually in search of reassurance that they are loved and valued.

In literature we see a wide range of average Twos: Holden Caulfield in *The Catcher in the Rye*, Garp in *The World According to Garp*, the title character in Jane Austen's *Emma*, Molly Bloom in James Joyce's *Ulysses*, Dora in Charles Dickens's *David Copperfield*, Amanda in Tennessee Williams's *The Glass Menagerie*, Shakespeare's King Lear and Cleopatra, Will Ladislaw in George Eliot's *Middlemarch*, Emile Zola's Nana, Sophie in William Styron's *Sophie's Choice*, the second Mrs. De Winter in Daphne du Maurier's *Rebecca*, Tereza in Milan Kundera's *The Unbearable Lightness of Being*, Hana in Michael Ondaatje's *The English Patient*, Molina in Manuel Puig's *The Kiss of the Spider Woman*, Norman in Ronald Harwood's *The Dresser*, and the title character in Muriel Spark's *The Prime of Miss Jean Brodie*.

When Twos are healthy, they are altruistic—loving and nurturing others without any expectation of return. They are deeply humble people whose greatest satisfaction is in seeing others' suffering reduced. Unlike average Twos, they are in touch with their own needs and feelings and are able to nurture themselves as well as others.

Healthy Twos in literature include Sidney Carton in Dickens's *A Tale of Two Cities*, Esther in Dickens's *Bleak House*, Flora Poste in Stella Gibbons's

Cold Comfort Farm, Hester Prynne in Nathaniel Hawthorne's *The Scarlet Letter*, the title characters in George Bernard Shaw'*s Major Barbara* and *Candida*, Mr. Darcy in Jane Austen's *Pride and Prejudice*, Mrs. Ramsay in Virginia Woolf's *To the Lighthouse*, Kate Gulden in Anna Quindlen's *One True Thing*, and the black minister in Alan Paton's *Cry, the Beloved Country*.

Unhealthy Twos can become aggressive and manipulative, demanding from others the love that they feel they have earned through their selfless devotion. If this demand is not met, Twos can become bitter at others' "ingratitude" and use their own—often psychosomatic—illnesses as evidence of their self-sacrifice. When Twos deteriorate to this degree, they become so unlovable they actually drive away the love they crave. In extreme pathology, they can become stalkers.

Examples of unhealthy Twos in literature are Gregors Werle in Henrik Ibsen's *The Wild Duck*, the Captain in August Strindberg's *The Father*, Annie in Stephen King's *Misery*, Paula in Roddy Doyle's *The Woman Who Walked into Doors*, Dave in Alice Adams's *Medicine Men*, and Baby Kochamma in Arundhati Roy's *The God of Small Things*.

Place in Society

Twos are found in all lines of work, but they are especially visible in the helping professions. Nurses, massage therapists, physical therapists, dental aides and other professional caregivers are more likely to be Twos, as are nannies, teachers of young children, and school principals. Jobs as restaurant waitstaff, maitre d's, and chefs also appeal to people of this temperament. Twos often choose careers as flight attendants, secretaries, telephone operators, retail salespeople and managers, beauticians, talent agents and personal managers.

Their strong orientation toward people can also lead Twos into careers in show business as actors, singers, dancers, celebrity interviewers, and hosts of children's television shows. Celebrity spouses are sometimes people of this point.

Twos of both sexes commonly devote great energy and attention to nurturing their families, and for many their central "career" is that of homemaker.

Stress and Security Points

The emotional compass of Twos is relatively wide, since they have connections with both sides of the Enneagram diagram, but with only two of the triads. A Two's natural arc is between Eight under stress and Four when secure. It is notable that Twos have qualities of all three of the categories described by Karen Horney: at Eight they are aggressive, at Four they are withdrawn, and in their home style of Two they are compliant and "move towards others" in Horney's terms.

The basic tension for Twos is between wanting to confront and grab power like an Eight versus wanting to experience a self-sufficient depth of feeling at their Four security point. This creates an "I-Thou" issue: where are the appropriate boundaries between the self and the other? If others don't appreciate a Two's helpfulness, the Two may become hysterical, invasive and confrontational. However, if Twos do feel loved and appreciated by others, they gain confidence to explore their own true feelings.

The fact that Twos have no interior line touching the head triad has of course no relation to this type's intelligence; it simply means that thinking is not Twos' first priority.

Wings

The contrast between the One wing and the Three wing is also strong, with a One's sense of duty reinforcing the Two's caretaking, while the Three's need to present a successful image emphasizes the self-serving motivation that is ever-present beneath the Two's stance of helpfulness.

Twos with a One wing tend to be more emotionally controlled and tense than Twos with a Three Wing. Preoccupied with what is right and proper, they are more likely to devote themselves to fostering others' growth and healing, almost on principle.

Garp's One wing is visible in his anxiety about his children, his conscience over his infidelities, and his attention to keeping his household uncluttered. His preoccupation with the social usefulness of his writing is also a mark of the Two with a One wing.

Holden Caulfield, who also has a One wing, is rigid in his judgments of others' cruelty and uncompromising in his desire to find a profession that is compatible with an ethical life. His One-ish black-and-white thinking contributes to his nervous breakdown.

Twos with a Three wing tend to be more seductive, playful, and conscious of the image they present to the world. Both Two and Three are "image" points, defining themselves through the feedback they get from others, so Twos with a Three wing need to be admired and validated more than Twos with a One wing, who are more in touch with their inner compass.

Although Candida is a Two with a Three wing, her high level of health shows in her generosity to others and her lack of expectation of any *quid-pro-quo*. Only when her husband treats her with extreme insensitivity does she remind him of how much he actually depends on her.

To the Lighthouse

Mrs. Ramsay, the protagonist of Virginia Woolf's *To the Lighthouse*, is a healthy Two with a One wing. A 50-year-old mother of eight and wife of a literature professor, she is in Scotland for the summer with her family and assorted house guests. Typically, she is the glue that holds together this disparate group, and she continually focuses on serving them: feeding them, making them feel valued, and using her superb social skills to encourage appropriate romantic matches.

The Two's focus on helping others is visible in Mrs. Ramsay's discussion with her husband about sailing to the nearby Lighthouse the following day. When he argues that the weather looks unpromising, she is distressed about disappointing her six-year-old son, James:

> 'But it may be fine—I expect it will be fine,' said Mrs. Ramsay, making some little twist of the reddish-brown stocking she was knitting, impatiently. If she finished it to-night, if they did go to the Lighthouse after all, it was to be given to the Lighthouse keeper for his little boy, who was threatened with a tuberculous hip; together with a pile of old magazines, and some tobacco, indeed whatever she could find lying about, not really wanted, but only littering the room, to give those poor fellows who must be bored to death sitting all day with nothing to do but polish the lamp and trim the wick and rake about on their scrap of garden, something to amuse them. For how would you like to be shut up for a whole month at a time, and possibly more in stormy weather, upon a rock the size of a tennis lawn? she would ask; and to have no letters or newspapers, and to see nobody; if you were married, not to see your wife, not to know how your children were—if they were ill, if they had fallen down and broken their legs or arms; to see the same dreary waves breaking week after week, and then a dreadful storm coming, and the windows covered with spray, and birds dashed against the lamp, and the whole place rocking, and not be able to put your nose out of doors for fear of being swept into the sea? How would you like that? she asked, addressing herself particularly to her daughters. So she added, rather differently, one must take them whatever comforts one can. (pp. 4-5)

Mrs. Ramsay's Two empathy is evident as she vividly imagines the lives of the lighthouse keepers. As she focuses on helping them she pushes aside her own feelings, especially her impatience with her husband—which, if admitted, might threaten the serenity of their relationship. This is repression, the Two's defense mechanism.

In later passages we see how well Mrs. Ramsay understands what her husband needs from her: in particular, to be reassured about the value of his scholarly work:

> It was sympathy he wanted, to be assured of his genius, first of all, and then to be taken within the circle of life, warmed and soothed, to have his senses restored to him, his barrenness made fertile, and all the rooms of the house made full of life—the drawing-room; behind the drawing-room the kitchen; above the kitchen the bedrooms; and beyond them the nurseries; they must be furnished, they must be filled with life.
>
> Charles Tansley thought him the greatest metaphysician of the time, she said. But he must have more than that. He must have sympathy.

He must be assured that he too lived in the heart of life; was needed; not here only, but all over the world. Flashing her needles, confident, upright, she created drawing-room and kitchen, set them all aglow; bade him take his ease there, go in and out, enjoy himself. She laughed, she knitted. Standing between her knees, very stiff, James felt all her strength flaring up to be drunk and quenched by the beak of brass, the arid scimitar of the male, which smote mercilessly, again and again, demanding sympathy.

He was a failure, he repeated. Well, look then, feel then. Flashing her needles, glancing round about her, out of the window, into the room, at James himself, she assured him, beyond a shadow of a doubt, by her laugh, her poise, her competence (as a nurse carrying a light across a dark room assures a fractious child) that it was real; the house was full; the garden blowing. If he put implicit faith in her, nothing should hurt him; however deep he buried himself or climbed high, not for a second should he find himself without her. So boasting of her capacity to surround and protect, there was scarcely a shell of herself left for her to know herself by; all was so lavished and spent. (p. 42)

She is successful in shoring up her husband's self-respect, but the effort costs her. Being a healthy Two, she is able to acknowledge this:

Filled with her words, like a child who drops off satisfied, he said, at last, looking at her with humble gratitude, restored, renewed, that he would take a turn; he would watch the children playing cricket. He went.

Immediately, Mrs. Ramsay seemed to fold herself together, one petal closed in another, and the whole fabric fell in exhaustion upon itself, so that she had only strength enough to move her finger, in exquisite abandonment to exhaustion, across the page of Grimm's fairy story, while there throbbed through her, like the pulse in a spring which has expanded to its full width and now gently ceases to beat, the rapture of successful creation.

Every throb of this pulse seemed, as he walked away, to enclose her and her husband, and to give to each that solace which two different notes, one high, one low, struck together, seem to give each other as they combine. Yet, as the resonance died, and she turned to the Fairy Tale again, Mrs. Ramsay felt not only exhausted in body (afterwards, not at the time, she always felt this) but also there tinged her physical fatigue some faintly disagreeable sensation with another origin. Not that, as she read aloud the story of the Fisherman's Wife, she knew precisely what it came from; nor did she let herself put into words her dissatisfaction when she realized, at the turn of the page when she stopped and heard dully, ominously, a wave fall, how it came from this: she did not like, even for a second, to feel finer than her husband; and further, could not bear not being entirely sure, when she spoke to him, of the truth of what she said. Universities and people wanting him, lectures and books and their being of the highest importance—all that she did not doubt for a moment; but it was their relation, and his coming to her like that, openly, so that any one could see, that discomposed her; for then people said he depended on her, when they must know that of the two he was infinitely the more important, and what she gave the world, in comparison with what he gave, negligible. But then again, it was the other thing too—not being able to tell him the truth, being afraid, for instance, about the greenhouse room and the expense it would be, fifty pounds perhaps, to mend it; and then about his books, to be afraid that he might guess, what she a little suspected, that his last book was not quite his best book (she gathered that from William Bankes); and then to hide small daily things, and the children seeing it, and the burden it laid on them—all this diminished the entire joy, the pure joy, of the two notes sounding together, and let the sound die on her ear now with a dismal flatness. (pp. 43-45)

At the end of a particularly convivial dinner party, Mrs. Ramsay enjoys the thought that the experience she has created for her guests will ensure her own immortality, in a sense. She sees her party as part of a social fabric that will continue to live through others like the newly engaged Paul and Minta. Although Mrs. Ramsay senses her impending death, she feels no fear about it:

Yes, that was done then, accomplished; and as with all things done, became solemn. Now one thought of it, cleared of chatter and emotion, it seemed always to have been, only was shown now, and so being shown struck everything into stability. They would, she thought, going on again, however long they lived, come back to this night; this moon; this wind; this house: and to her too. It flattered her, where she was most susceptible of flattery, to think how, wound about in their hearts, however long they lived she would be woven; and this, and this, and this, she thought, going upstairs, laughing, but affectionately, at the sofa on the landing (her mother's) at the rocking chair (her father's); at the map of the Hebrides. All that would be revived again in the lives of Paul and Minta; 'the Rayleys'—she tried the new name over; and she felt, with her hand on the nursery door, that community of feeling with other people which emotion gives as if the walls of partition had become so thin that practically (the feeling was one of relief and happiness) it was all one stream, and chairs, tables, maps, were hers, were theirs, it did not matter whose, and Paul and Minta would carry it on when she was dead. (pp. 129-130)

Mrs. Ramsay's joy in the universal connection of all human beings and her consciousness of having a place in the social fabric even beyond her physical life is a mark of the highest level of health in all Enneagram styles, although a Two would still experience it in an especially interpersonal way.

Antony and Cleopatra

Shakespeare's Cleopatra offers a classic example of a Two with a Three wing: seductive, passionate, capricious—one moment vain and shallow, the next loving and generous. *Antony and Cleopatra* tells the story of the ill-fated love affair between the Queen of Egypt and Antony, a rebellious Roman soldier. Antony, an Eight, and Cleopatra are not only lovers but also allies, and at a crucial moment during a sea battle with the Roman fleet the ship carrying Cleopatra retreats. Fearing for her safety, Antony follows her, abandoning the battle and thereby losing it. Later, Antony is ashamed and angry at having fled the battle. Cleopatra, learning of his rage, hopes to rekindle his love by sending word that she has killed herself. But her false report, coupled with Antony's shame, provokes him instead to suicide. After his death Cleopatra takes her own life rather than be led in triumph by the now victorious Caesar.

Early in the play Shakespeare shows us the volatility of this pairing of Two and Eight. The lovers continually jockey for control of the relationship:

CLEOPATRA. If it be love indeed, tell me how much.
ANTONY. There's beggary in the love that can be reckon'd.
CLEOPATRA. I'll set a bourn how far to be beloved.
ANTONY. Then must thou needs find out new heaven, new earth.
[Enter an Attendant.]
ATTENDANT. News, my good lord, from Rome.
ANTONY. Grates me: the sum
CLEOPATRA. Nay, hear them, Antony:
Fulvia [Antony's wife] perchance is angry; or, who knows
If the scarce-bearded Caesaar have not sent
His powerful mandate to you, 'Do this, or this:
Take in that kingdom, and enfranchise that;
Perform't, or else we damn thee.'
ANTONY. How, my love!
CLEOPATRA. Perchance! Nay, and most like'
You must not stay here longer, your dismission
Is come from Caesar; therefore hear it, Antony. . . .
Call in the messengers. As I am Egypt's queen,
Thou blushest, Antony; and that blood of thine
Is Caesar's homager; else so thy cheek pays shame
When shrill-tongued Fulvia scolds. The messengers!
ANTONY. Let Rome in Tiber melt, and the wide arch
Of the ranged empire fall! Here is my space. . . .
CLEOPATRA. Excellent falsehood!

Why did he marry Fulvia, and not love her?
I'll seem the fool I am not; Antony
Will be himself. (I, i, 18-43)

This mixture of sexual and power games that we see in the first half of the play turns deadly when Cleopatra retreats in the heat of battle and Antony concludes that he cannot depend on her support.

Cleopatra's Two manipulativeness, combined with the deceit of her Three wing, is evident in the following passage, which shows the calculation behind her efforts to fascinate her lover:

CLEOPATRA. Where is he?
CHARMIAN. I did not see him since.
CLEOPATRA. See where he is, who's with him, what he does:
I did not send you: if you find him sad,
Say I am dancing; if in mirth, report
That I am sudden sick: quick, and return.
                                        [*Exit Alexas*]
CHARMIAN. Madam, methinks, if you did love him dearly,
You do not hold the method to enforce
The like from him.
CLEOPATRA. What should I do, I do not?
CHARMIAN. In each thing give him way, cross him in nothing.
CLEOPATRA. Thou teachest like a fool; the way to lose him. (I, iii, 1-10)

When a messenger comes to tell her that Antony, for political reasons, has married Octavia, Caesar's sister, Cleopatra flies into a rage and assaults the messenger:

MESSENGER; Madam, he's married to Octavia.
CLEOPATRA. The most infectious pestilence upon thee!
[*Strikes him down*]
MESSENGER. Good madam, patience.
CLEOPATRA. What say you? Hence.
                                [*Strikes him again*]
Horrible villain! Or I'll spurn thine eyes
Like balls before me; I'll unhair thy head:
                                [*She hales him up and down*]
Thou shalt be whipp'd with wire, and stew'd in brine,
Smarting in lingering pickle.
MESSENGER. Gracious madam,
I that do bring the news made not the match.
CLEOPATRA. Say 'tis not so, a province I will give thee,
And make thy fortunes proud: the blow thou hadst

Shall make thy peace for moving me to rage;
And I will boot thee with what gift beside
Thy modesty can beg.
MESSENGER. He's married, madam.
CLEOPATRA. Rogue, thou hast lived too long.
                                        [*Draws a knife*]
MESSENGER. Nay, then I'll run. (II, v, 60-74)

The above passage shows a Two moving to her Eight stress point. An
average-level Two with a Three wing, thwarted in love, is apt to indulge in rages.
    Prevented by Caesar's men from stabbing herself after Antony's death,
Cleopatra ultimately succeeds in taking her life with a poisonous snake brought
to her in a basket of figs. At the play's end, Shakespeare gives this volatile and
sometimes treacherous woman tragic stature in the face of death:

CLEOPATRA. Give me my robe, put on my crown; I have
Immortal longings in me: now no more
The juice of Egypt's grape shall moist this lip:
Yare, yare, good Iras; quick. Methinks I hear
Antony call; I see him rouse himself
To praise my noble act; I hear him mock
The luck of Caesar, which the gods give men
To excuse their after wrath: husband, I come:
Now to that name my courage prove my title! (V, ii, 282-290)

Even in the process of taking her life, Cleopatra imagines her lover praising
her for her nobility, exemplifying the Two's massive need for appreciation. The
arc of Cleopatra's character—from shallow sexual gamesmanship, hysterical
rages, and political power plays to a final dignified embrace of Death as a lover—
shows the emotional range of the Two with a Three wing. In her suicide she
becomes truly queenly, moving to her Four security point and making her end
one of beauty and poetry.

Subtypes

All Twos focus on gaining the love and gratitude of others, though their
strategies for doing this vary with their individual subtype.
    Twos with the **Self-Preservation** subtype, which Oscar Ichazo character-
izes as "me-first," feel entitled to special treatment because of all they have done
for others. There is a childish, tender quality to this subtype, especially in the
average levels. These are the classic caretaker Twos, who project their own needs
onto others and then feel resentful if they do not receive special privileges in
return. The "giving to get" motivation is particularly evident in this variant.
    Examples of this subtype in literature include Aroon in Molly Keane's
Good Behaviour, Little Dora *in David Copperfield*, Baby Kochamma in *The God*

of Small Things and Shakespeare's King Lear.

King Lear

King Lear is a powerfully drawn Self-Preservation Two. When we first meet him he is about to divide his kingdom between his three daughters, but before giving each one her portion he demands to know how much she loves him:

> LEAR: Tell me, my daughters
> (Since now we will divest us both of rule,
> Interest of territory, cares of state),
> Which of you shall we say doth love us most,
> That we our largest bounty may extend
> Where nature doth with merit challenge. Goneril,
> Our eldest-born, speak first. (I, i, 50-57)

The two older daughters, Goneril and Regan, are profuse in their expressions of love, but the youngest, Cordelia, is unable to voice her feelings to her father's satisfaction.

> LEAR. How, how, Cordelia? Mend your speech a little,
> Lest you may mar your fortunes.
> CORDELIA. Good my lord,
> You have begot me, bred me, loved me. I
> Return those duties back as are right fit,
> Obey you, love you, and most honor you.
> Why have my sisters husbands, if they say
> They love you all? Haply, when I shall wed,
> That lord whose hand must take my plight shall carry
> Half my love with him, half my care and duty.
> Sure I shall never marry like my sisters,
> To love my father all.
> LEAR. But goes thy heart with this?
> CORDELIA. Ay, my good lord.
> LEAR. So young, and so untender?
> CORDELIA. So young, my lord and true.
> LEAR. Let it be so, thy truth then be thy dower!
> For, by the sacred radiance of the sun,
> The mysteries of Hecate and the night,
> By all the operation of the orbs
> From whom we do exist and cease to be,
> Here I disclaim all my paternal care,
> Propinquity and property of blood,
> And as a stranger to my heart and me
> Hold thee from this for ever. (I, i, 96-118)

Lear's anger when Cordelia refuses to emulate her sisters' hypocrisy is a typical reaction for a low-to-average level Self-Preservation Two. His motive for giving away his kingdom—to get love and praise from his daughters—is transparent, and his anger may be partly based on Cordelia calling his game. A One, she is just the person to do this. We see Lear's hot temper in his quick move to Eight, the Two's stress point.

After Cordelia has been cast out and Lear's loyal follower Kent is banished for defending her loyalty, the two older daughters band together to deal with their father. One of them, Regan, comments, "'Tis the infirmity of his age, yet he hath ever but slenderly known himself." (I, i, 295-296)

Average to unhealthy Twos typically know themselves "slenderly," repressing their own needs while focusing on having their worth acclaimed by others. Denied the special treatment he feels he deserves, Lear, consistent with his subtype, behaves like a spoiled child.

His tirades increase in intensity as he realizes that his two older daughters, now in control of the kingdom, are unsympathetic with his demands. Wounded by their ingratitude, he vows vengeance:

> LEAR: I will have such revenges on you both
> That all the world shall—I will do such things—
> What they are, yet I know not; but they shall be
> The terrors of the earth. You think I'll weep.
> No, I'll not weep.
> > *Storm and tempest*
> I have full cause of weeping, but this heart
> Shall break into a hundred thousand flaws
> Or ere I'll weep. O Fool, I shall go mad! (II, iv, 270-285)

In the next scene, doing battle with his own colossal pride, Lear does indeed descend into madness: rushing out onto the heath in the midst of the storm, stripping off his clothes and trying to out-shout the tempest in his helpless rage.

Yet even amid his despair and oncoming madness, Lear shows a Two empathy for his nearby jester, concerned about the boy's misery in the midst of the storm:

> LEAR. My wits begin to turn.
> Come on, my boy. How dost, my boy? Art cold?
> I am cold myself. Where is this straw, my fellow?
> The art of our necessities is strange,
> That can make vile things precious. Come, your hovel.
> Poor Fool and knave, I have one part in my heart
> That's sorry yet for thee. (III, iii, 67-73)

In this extremity, Lear is still aware of his common bond with another human being—in contrast to the pride that formerly prevented him from acknowledging his own needs. This is a turning point in the play, and we sense that Lear may ultimately find his way through his madness to a new humility and humanity.

Cordelia, meanwhile, has landed on English shores with an army, having learned of her father's plight. The now ashamed Lear is initially reluctant to confront the daughter he treated so badly. When he finally approaches her, her loving attitude overwhelms him, and he kneels before her:

CORDELIA. O, look upon me, sir,
And hold your hand in benediction o'er me.
You must not kneel.
 LEAR. Pray, do not mock me:
I am a very foolish fond old man,
Fourscore and upward, not an hour more nor less;
And, to deal plainly,
I fear I am not in my perfect mind.
Methinks I should know you and know this man,
Yet I am doubtful; for I am mainly ignorant
What place this is, and all the skill I have
Remembers not these garments, nor I know not
Where I did lodge last night. Do not laugh at me,
For, as I am a man, I think this lady
To be my child Cordelia.
CORDELIA. And so I am, I am.
LEAR. Be your tears wet? Yes, faith. I pray, weep not.
If you have poison for me, I will drink it.
I know you do not love me; for your sisters
Have, as I do remember, done me wrong.
You have some cause, they have not.
CORDELIA. No cause, no cause.
(IV, vii, 57-75)

Cordelia wants her sisters to account for their treatment of Lear, but he wants only to enjoy his new loving relationship with her. Now firmly settled in his Four security point, he is far from his former desire—at his Eight stress point—to take revenge against Goneril and Regan.

CORDELIA. Shall we not see these daughters and these sisters?
LEAR. No, no, no, no! Come, let's away to prison:
We two alone will sing like birds i' th' cage:
When thou dost ask me blessing, I'll kneel down
And ask of thee forgiveness: so we'll live,
And pray, and sing, and tell old tales, and laugh

At gilded butterflies, and hear poor rogues
Talk of court news . . . . (V, ii, 7-14)

A grateful and humble Two now wants only to stay with authentic feeling and relationship, jettisoning all other considerations.

But Lear's moment of joy is not to last. Enemy forces overwhelm Cordelia's camp, and father and daughter are taken away to prison. Although her army eventually wins the day, Cordelia is executed. As Lear re-enters the scene with the dead Cordelia in his arms, his anguish fulfills his own prediction of heartbreak early in the play. But it is a transformed man whose colossal grief we now witness. The suffering is ultimately too much for him, and he is mercifully released in death.

LEAR. And my poor fool is hanged: no, no, no life?
Why should a dog, a horse, a rat, have life,
And thou no breath at all? Thou'lt come no more,
Never, never, never, never, never.
Pray you, undo this button. Thank you, sir.
Do you see this? Look on her. Look, her lips,
Look there, look there.   *He dies.*
(V, iii, 307-313)

It is significant that Lear as a Two, with almost his last breath, asks for and receives help from another person—to release a button on his clothing. His simple "Thank you, sir" implies his respect for his helper and completes the Two character arc from pride to humility. Lear's terrible suffering and madness seem to have burned away his Two limitations of vision. Throughout *King Lear*, which many regard as Shakespeare's greatest play, the theme of seeing and blindness is explored, and culminates in Lear's final lines, when, freed from his pride, he finally sees the world with new eyes.

Good Behaviour

We find another clear Self-Preservation Two in Molly Keane's novel *Good Behaviour*. The story mainly takes place in Ireland, from the eve of the first World War through the 1920s. Aroon, a daughter of country gentry, recalls her childhood and adolescence spent in a venerable country house called Temple Alice. The story is presented as a comedy of manners, and Aroon in some ways resembles Jane Austen's Emma—both Twos and both often mistaken about the motives of others. However, in contrast to the elegant and charming Emma, whom I'll discuss under the Social subtypes, Aroon is unattractive and extremely needy.

In the course of the story, Aroon becomes infatuated with Richard, a close friend of her brother, Hubert, never realizing that Richard and Hubert are lovers. After Hubert is killed in an accident, Aroon continues to fantasize about Richard, ignoring clear implications that he is homosexual.

Twos are adept at repressing not only their hunger for love but also anything that contradicts their self-image as both a loving and a beloved person. Aroon fails to recognize that her adored father has carried on love affairs with many women, including two members of the household staff. Aroon is bitter and cruel towards her unloving critical mother, a fact that the reader comes to understand in the course of the story.

In the book's first scene—which takes place chronologically at the end of the story—we see Aroon serving her elderly, bedridden mother a rabbit mousse she has personally prepared, ignoring her mother's long-established repugnance for rabbit. The mother takes one whiff of the dish and dies. Rose, their servant, accuses Aroon of deliberately bringing on her mother's death:

> ". . . Madam's better off the way she is this red raw minute. She's tired from you—tired to death. Death is right. We're all killed from you and it's a pity it's not yourself lying there and your toes cocked for the grave and not a word more about you, God damn you!"
>
> Yes, she stood there across the bed saying these obscene, unbelievable things. Of course she loved Mummie, all servants did. Of course she was overwrought. I know all that—and she is ignorant to a degree, I allow for that too. Although there was a shocking force in what she said to me, it was beyond all sense or reasons. It was so entirely and dreadfully false that it could not touch me. I felt as tall as a tree standing above all that passionate flood of words. I was determined to be kind to Rose. And understanding. And generous. I am her employer, I thought. I shall raise her wages quite substantially. She will never be able to resist me then, because she is greedy. I can afford to be kind to Rose. She will learn to lean on me. There is nobody in the world who needs me now and I must be kind to somebody. . . .
>
> All my life so far I have done everything for the best reasons and the most unselfish motives. I have lived for the people dearest to me, and I am at a loss to know why their lives have been at times so perplexingly unhappy. I have given them so much, I have given them everything, all I know how to give—Papa, Hubert, Richard, Mummie. At fifty-seven my brain is fairly bright, brighter than ever I sometimes think, and I have a cast-iron memory. (pp. 8-11)

Aroon's Two pride in her own kindness is unshakable, even as she behaves with appalling cruelty and insensitivity. Her assessment of her own acuteness is a joke—she understands nothing, and age has not increased her perceptiveness. This is a Two at her most self-deluded.

The remainder of the novel shows us the events that led to this climactic scene, and by the end of the story we understand why Aroon behaves as she does. Throughout her life, we see that Aroon has been unloved and unlovable, continually misunderstanding the motives of others and assuaging her needs by stuffing herself with food. Always a "big" girl, she becomes in the end gargantuan, and her fixation on food as a self-comforting mechanism is usual for Self-Preservation Twos.

Aroon is deprived of emotional warmth from the beginning of her life, and the only people who seem truly to care for her, her brother and her father, both die. Just before her brother's death in a car accident, his lover, Richard, comes into Aroon's bedroom one night. He kisses her—no more—and makes a good deal of noise in leaving, making sure her father hears him. It's a ruse designed to ward off the father's suspicion that Richard and his son are lovers, but Aroon builds a romantic fantasy around the incident, repressing all subsequent evidence that Richard is homosexual.

Aroon's father suffers a stroke but lives on for many years, cared for by Rose, one of the servants, who clearly is providing him with sexual comforts—though Aroon, being sexually inexperienced, fails to pick up on this. After her father dies—while having sex with Rose—Aroon retreats to her room, leaving Rose to lay out the body:

> Out again in the dark corridor, alone with the thought of my cold bed, I felt a sick shivering go through me. I thought what a crash there would be if I fell, and I almost wished for a disturbance that would bring me some pity. But there was no such thing. Only good behaviour about Death. So I sat down on the floor before I fell down and waited for the weakness to pass over. Sitting there I felt my grief for Papa and my lost love for Richard as joining together. Only Papa had known that we were lovers. Now half my despair was my own secret. No one could take it from me, or lessen it, or tell of it. My great body had been blessed by love. True. It was true. Some merciless shaft had been ready to pierce me with denial. I must run from it, and keep that truth whole for myself. I could hear Rose stirring busily, sure-footed, behind Papa's door, and the idea that soon she might be going to the bathroom for water got me onto my feet. (p. 215)

Here we see Aroon moving to her Four security point, longing for pity while holding on to her fantasies about Richard and her illusory self-image.

As plans are made for Aroon's father's funeral, Richard's father announces that he will attend, and Aroon is sent to meet his train. In the station she asks him for news of Richard and learns that he has gone back to Africa with a man who was one of his schoolmates. Trying hard to keep her repressions from surfacing, Aroon drinks too much at the station, passes out, and misses her father's funeral. Everyone is shocked at her bad behavior. When her father's will is read, however, her social status is redeemed. She learns that her father has left the bulk of his estate to her:

"Yes. Do you understand?—He's left everything to you." [the solicitor says]

I wondered if I could go on breathing naturally, through the delight that lifted me. Twice over now this euphoria of love had elevated my whole body; I was its host. Then the vision changed; it was as though the face of my old world turned away from me—a globe revolving—I was looking into a changed world, where I was a changed person, where my love was recognised and requited. Through the long assuring breaths that followed my sobbing I drew in the truth: that Papa loved me the most. Explicit from the depths of my breathing, like weed anchored far under sea water, I knew a full tide was turning for me. Love and trust were present and whole as they had been once on a summer afternoon. Inexactly present, inexactly lost, the memory fled me as a seal slides into the water with absolute trust in its element. A disturbance on the water closes and there is nothing again. I particularly wanted Rose to hear it again. I was claiming what was mine—his love, his absolute love. I wanted them to understand that he had loved me most. . . . They [her mother and Rose] must be minding dreadfully. Empowered by Papa's love I would be kind to them. Now I had the mild, wonderful power to be kind. Or to reserve kindness. I looked at them with level, considerate eyes. (pp. 244-245)

At last Aroon feels the confirmation of her father's love, but she is so unhealthy that she cannot admit to herself the vengeance she wants to take—and will take—on her disdainful mother and her mother's ally, Rose. This is a downward arc for a Self-Preservation Two—towards increasing self-delusion and pride—in contrast with Lear's upward arc toward self-understanding and humility.

The **Social** Two, which Ichazo associates with "ambition," is familiar in literature. Typical Social Twos seek to enhance their social position through connecting with others, matchmaking, and hosting social events. Popularity is a sign that they are loved, and they bask in being a key figure in their social network. Adept at social climbing, they maneuver to become indispensable to important people. In unhealthy versions, they can become classic co-dependents.

Social Two examples include Mrs. Ramsay in *To the Lighthouse*, Garp, Holden Caulfield, Flora Poste in *Cold Comfort Farm*, Barbara in *Major Barbara*, Esther in *Bleak House*, Nana, Will Ladislaw in *Middlemarch,* Amanda in *The Glass Menagerie* and Emma in Jane Austen's *Emma.*

Emma
The title character in Jane Austen's novel is a Two with a One wing, as well as a clear Social subtype. Emma's attempts to help others to find romance invariably turn out badly. Sensitive to the feelings of others, she has little

awareness of her own needs and desires. Although her manipulative behavior distresses a number of characters, she does no permanent harm, and the book has a "happily ever after" ending common to many Two stories.

Near the beginning of the novel Emma, her father, and their friend and neighbor Mr Knightley, a One, are talking about the recent marriage of Emma's governess. Emma's pride in her matchmaking ability is evident:

> 'Dear Emma bears every thing so well,' said her father. 'But, Mr Knightley, she is really very sorry to lose poor Miss Taylor, and I am sure she *will* miss her more than she thinks for.'
>
> Emma turned away her head, divided between tears and smiles.
>
> 'It is impossible that Emma should not miss such a companion,' said Mr Knightley. 'We should not like her so well as we do, sir, if we could suppose it. But she knows how much the marriage is to Miss Taylor's advantage; she knows how very acceptable it must be at Miss Taylor's time of life to be settled in a home of her own, and how important to her to be secure of a comfortable provision, and therefore cannot allow herself to feel so much pain as pleasure. Every friend of Miss Taylor must be glad to have her so happily married.'
>
> 'And you have forgotten one matter of joy to me,' said Emma, 'and a very considerable one—that I made the match myself. I made the match, you know, four years ago; and to have it take place, and be proved in the right, when so many people said Mr Weston would never marry again, may comfort me for any thing.'
>
> Mr Knightley shook his head at her. Her father fondly replied, 'Ah! My dear, I wish you would not make matches and foretel things, for whatever you say always comes to pass. Pray do not make any more matches.'
>
> 'I promise you to make none for myself, papa; but I must, indeed, for other people. It is the greatest amusement in the world! And after such success, you know! Every body said that Mr Weston would never marry again. Oh dear! no! ... If I had not promoted Mr Weston's visits here, and given many little encouragements, and smoothed many little matters, it might not have come to anything after all. I think you must know Hartfield enough to comprehend that.' (pp. 10-11)

Emma takes Harriet Smith, a Nine, under her wing. Harriet is an illegitimate girl whose simplicity and attractiveness interest Emma—and whose gratitude is especially appealing to a Two. Note that Harriet's social position and limited intelligence offer no threat to Emma, who, as a Social subtype, is keenly competitive for popularity in her circle of friends.

> She was not struck by any thing remarkably clever in Miss Smith's conversation, but she found her altogether very engaging—not inconve-

niently shy, not unwilling to talk—and yet so far from pushing, shewing so proper and becoming a deference, seeming so pleasantly grateful for being admitted to Hartfield, and so artlessly impressed by the appearance of every thing in so superior a style to what she had been used to, that she must have good sense and deserve encouragement. Encouragement should be given. . . . *She* would notice her; she would improve her; she would detach her from her bad acquaintance, and introduce her into good society; she would form her opinions and her manners. It would be an interesting, and certainly a very kind undertaking; highly becoming her own situation in life, her leisure, and powers. (p. 19)

Emma encourages Harriet to turn down a marriage proposal from a young farmer, and to instead believe that Mr Elton, the minister, is an appropriate match for her. When it turns out that Mr Elton is interested in a match with Emma, Harriet is heartbroken and Emma is stricken with remorse for her manipulations:

The hair was curled, and the maid sent away, and Emma sat down to think and be miserable.—It was a wretched business, indeed!—Such an overthrow of every thing she had been wishing for.—Such a development of every thing most unwelcome!—Such a blow for Harriet!— That was the worst of all. Every part of it brought pain and humiliation, of some sort or other; but, compared with the evil to Harriet, all was light; and she would gladly have submitted to feel yet more mistaken—more in error—more disgraced by misjudgment, than she actually was, could the effects of her blunders have been confined to herself.

'If I had not persuaded Harriet into liking the man, I could have borne any thing. He might have doubled his presumption to me—But poor Harriet!'

How she could have been so deceived!—He protested that he had never thought seriously of Harriet—never! She looked back as well as she could; but it was all confusion. She had taken up the idea, she supposed, and made every thing bend to it. His manners, however, must have been unmarked, wavering, dubious, or she could not have been so misled. (p. 103)

Emma's One wing is evident in her self-accusations, but her Two pride reasserts itself.

Her basic competitiveness—and her lack of awareness of it—is visible in her instinctive dislike of the beautiful and accomplished Jane Fairfax. Emma continually compares Jane's musical gifts with her own—to her own detriment—showing us a Two's link to Four envy:

Why she did not like Jane Fairfax might be a difficult question to answer; Mr Knightley had once told her it was because she saw in her the really accomplished young woman, which she wanted to be thought herself; and though the accusation had been eagerly refuted at the time, there were moments of self-examination in which her conscience could not quite acquit her. . . .

It was a dislike so little just—every imputed fault was so magnified by fancy, that she never saw Jane Fairfax the first time after any considerable absence, without feeling that she had injured her; and now, when the due visit was paid, on her arrival, after two years' interval, she was particularly struck with the very appearance and manners, which for those two whole years she had been depreciating. Jane Fairfax was very elegant, remarkably elegant; and she had herself the highest value for elegance. . . . elegance, which whether of person or of mind, she saw so little in Highbury. There, not to be vulgar, was distinction, and merit.

In short, she sat, during the first visit, looking at Jane Fairfax with twofold complacency; the sense of pleasure and the sense of rendering justice, and was determining that she would dislike her no longer. (pp. 125-126)

Emma's neighbor Knightley loves Emma and, as a One, is determined to make her see the truth about herself. He consistently offers her excellent advice, which she consistently ignores, assuming with her Two pride that *she* knows better.

After Emma tries again to make a match for Harriet and again ends up hurting her, she is shocked to realize that Harriet has her sights on Mr Knightley. Suddenly Emma's own feelings for Mr. Knightley become clear:

Why was it so much worse that Harriet should be in love with Mr Knightley, than with Frank Churchill? Why was the evil so dreadfully increased by Harriet's having some hope of a return? It darted through her, with the speed of an arrow, that Mr Knightley must marry no one but herself!

Her own conduct, as well as her own heart, was before her in the same few minutes. She saw it all with a clearness which had never blessed her before. How improperly had she been acting by Harriet! How inconsiderate, how indelicate, how irrational, how unfeeling had been her conduct! What blindness, what madness, had led her on! It struck her with dreadful force, and she was ready to give it every bad name in the world. (p. 308)

As Emma broods on the inappropriate prospective match between Mr. Knightley and Harriet, she finally sees the role her own pride has played in her life. Her One wing comes into play, and she lacerates herself for bringing about the whole situation through her folly:

With insufferable vanity had she believed herself in the secret of everybody's feelings; with unpardonable arrogance proposed to arrange everybody's destiny. She was proved to have been universally mistaken; and she had not quite done nothing—for she had done mischief. (p. 312)

Emma begins to regret having slighted Jane Fairfax, a far more suitable friend, in favor of Harriet, to whom she could merely feel superior.

Mrs. Weston's communications furnished Emma with more food for unpleasant reflection, by increasing her esteem and compassion, and her sense of past injustice towards Miss Fairfax. She bitterly regretted not having sought a closer acquaintance with her, and blushed for the envious feelings which had certainly been, in some measure, the cause. (p. 318)

When Mr Knightley finally declares his feelings to Emma, we see that, even in her happiness, she can still empathize with other people's pain:

While he spoke, Emma's mind was most busy, and, with all the wonderful velocity of thought, had been able—and yet without losing a word—to catch and comprehend the exact truth of the whole; to see that Harriet's hopes had been entirely groundless, a mistake, a delusion, as complete a delusion as any of her own—that Harriet was nothing; that she was every thing herself; that what she had been saying relative to Harriet had been all taken as the language of her own feelings; and that her agitation, her doubts, her reluctance, her discouragement, had been all received as discouragement from herself.—And not only was there time for these convictions, with all their glow of attendant happiness, there was time also to rejoice that Harriet's secret had not escaped her, and to resolve that it need not and should not.—It was all the service she could now render her poor friend. . . . Her way was clear, though not quite smooth.—She spoke then, on being so entreated.—What did she say?— Just what she ought, of course. A lady always does.—She said enough to show there need not be despair—and to invite him to say more himself. . . . (pp. 325-326)

Emma, the essence of a Social Two, understands how to behave well even when her heart is overwhelmed. The reader feels that, through her sufferings, she has grown sufficiently to be worthy of the superb Mr. Knightley.

Medicine Men

A less healthy version of a Social Two is Dave Jacobs, a character in Alice Adams's novel *Medicine Men*. When his lover, Molly, a One, develops a brain tumor, Dave, a physician, insists on overseeing her medical care. More sensitive to the medical hierarchy and his own place in it than he is to Molly, Dave overwhelms her with sexual demands, insisting that sex is good for what ails her:

> Many women complain, with reason, of too little sex in their lives. . . . But Dave overdid it, so that Molly began to feel that he was engaged in some contest with himself. She was sure that he was counting: four times, not bad for a guy almost sixty. Try for five? But that was several too many times for Molly; she could not, was not thirsty anymore. . . .
>
> Invaded is actually what she felt with Dave. Assaulted. He almost never let her peacefully sleep; he kept waking her, prodding her, turning her over. And while he talked a lot about love, how much he loved her, how wonderful to find love twice in his lifetime, to Molly it did not feel like love but rather a form of aggression. She could have been anyone at all, Molly thought, and she often wondered, Why me?
>
> She complained, "You've got to let me sleep. This is crazy. You don't listen. I need more sleep, and I need to be sort of alone to sleep."
>
> "But you're so terribly attractive to me. Aren't you glad?"
>
> Actually she was not glad, but she did not feel that she could tell him that, and so she only repeated, "I've got to get more sleep. I'll never get well with no sleep."
>
> "Love is the greatest cure," he told her, sententiously. (pp. 58-59)

Like most unhealthy Twos, Dave has no idea how overwhelming he can be in an intimate relationship.

Dave takes great pleasure in organizing Molly's medical appointments, using her, in a sense, to enhance his position in the medical establishment. He also takes pride in making himself the hero of the situation, relegating Molly to a minor role:

> "So lucky I could get this appointment." Dave said this many more times than twice when they drove south, down the Peninsula toward Mt. Watson Hospital, and the famous, marvelous Dr. William Donovan. Molly, repeating those words back to herself, became interested in their order, which clearly put the emphasis on "I could get." On "I." Dave was to be the hero of this episode in her life, Molly clearly saw, and in a blurry way she wondered just what her own role was to be; she felt that if Dave was to be heroic she was not. (p. 97)

When Molly finally confronts Dave about his refusal to explain important details like the side effects of her radiation treatments, he makes her feel guilty for not appreciating him:

> "You're getting the best possible, state-of-the-art medical care.

I've seen to that. You don't appreciate—"

Dave never finished that sentence, at that time or later, ever; he never actually said, "You don't appreciate me. But that was a continual subtext, and of course he was right; Molly did not appreciate him, nor what he had done for her. From whatever motives—and whose are ever pure? He had gone and he continued to go to enormous trouble for her. He had taken her to the surgeon who had managed to "get it all," very likely had saved her life. Could another surgeon have done the same? This of course was something Molly would never know. And she tended to focus on the impurity of Dave's motives rather than the results of what he had actually done. She concentrated on his needs to control her, and to *be* with her, as well as his busy joy in a medical setting—and she thought much less of the fact that she was *okay*. She was well, or she would be well, once she got over the effects of radiation—whatever those effects were to be. (pp. 127-128)

Twos' certainty of their own rightness, even when they are most off-base, is possible with all the subtypes. When Molly asks Dave a question about medical ethics, he launches into a diatribe:

[I]n a tired way, as she listened to Dave's rant, Molly recognized that literally nothing she could say would change his view. It was less a question of not believing her than of refusing to hear her. On and on he ranted, his anger fueled by years of righteous, obstinate fury at shrinks (they had no *proof*, they charged high fees, no specific results), plus all his current rage and frustration at the sheer, simple, and inexplicable fact that Molly would not love him. He sometimes suspected that she did not even like him very much. . . . Listening, as she had to do—they were face-to-face, she on her sofa, he on the adjacent leather chair—Molly felt a heating of her blood, and quickening, tightening breath; pure rage is what she felt. The shrieking anger of an overpowered child. Though actually she was neither shrieking nor overpowered.

She stood up. "Dave, now listen to me. Now *listen*. I don't want to hear this crazy stuff. You're just totally, absolutely wrong—" and, as his rant continued—"Dave, just shut up. SHUT UP! Dave, you have to go now. I'm tired. I don't want to see you. Dave, did you hear me? I'm through."

Very ostentatiously, slowly, Dave looked at his watch, and only then he too stood up. "Lord, I'm running late," he said, as though she had not said anything at all.

"Dave, good-bye."

He smiled, with all his big strong bright teeth, and he said, "I'll call you later." (pp. 204-205)

An unhealthy Social Two with a Three wing—aggressive in the pursuit of success and social connections—can literally not hear words that threaten his self-image. To avoid damage to his pride, Dave summons a virtually unassailable combination of defense mechanisms: a Two's repression, a Three's deceit and an Eight's outright denial. Dave's Eightish rage under stress reveals the underlying power game that he is playing, a game he will do anything to win.

The **Sexual** subtype of Two, which Ichazo associates with "seduction/aggression," is characterized by intense focus on emotional and physical intimacy in one-to-one relationships. Seductive Sexual Twos want to be deeply involved in the partner's life, keeping him or her entranced through an impressive repertoire of manipulations and sexual games. If the object of a Sexual Two's affections begins to lose interest, the Two can pursue the lover relentlessly to the point of being overwhelming and even dangerous.

Sexual Twos in literature include Shakespeare's Cleopatra, Jean Brodie in Muriel Spark's *The Prime of Miss Jean Brodie*, Norman in Ronald Harwood's *The Dresser,* Annie in *Misery*, Zola's Nana and Molina in Manuel Puig's *The Kiss of the Spider Woman.*

The Kiss of the Spider Woman

Manuel Puig's novel tells the story of two men sharing a cell in an Argentine prison: Molina, a gay window dresser and a Sexual Two, and Valentin, a dedicated One revolutionary. Molina is obsessed with the fantasy and romance of the movies, and he periodically recounts films stories in an effort to captivate his fellow prisoner. Much of the novel is told in segments of cinematic dialogue between the two men.

In the following passage, Molina describes his ideal man, a married waiter he met while having a meal in a restaurant, and recounts to Valentin his dream of bringing the waiter home to live with him:

> —That he might come to live with me, with my mom and me. And I'd help him, and make him study. And not bother about anything but him, the whole blessed day, getting everything all set for him, his clothes, buying his books, registering him for courses, and little by little I'd convince him that what he had to do was just one thing: never work again. And I'd pass along whatever small amount of money was needed to give the wife for child support, and make him not worry about anything at all, nothing except himself, until he got what he wanted and lost all that sadness of his for good, wouldn't that be marvelous? (p. 69)

Notice Molina's aggressive pursuit of the object of his obsession.

When Molina explains his sexual orientation to the heterosexual Valentin, his Sexual Two identification with the feminine is obvious:

—Well, don't get the idea anything's strange, but if I'm nice to you
... it's because I want to win your friendship, and, why not say it? ...
your affection. Same as I want to be good to my mom because she's a nice
person, who never did anybody any harm, because I love her, because
she's nice, and I want her to love me ... And you too are a very nice
person, very selfless, and you've risked your life for a very noble ideal
... And don't be looking the other way, am I embarrassing you?

—Yes, a little ... But I'm looking at you, see? ...

—And because you're that way ... I respect you, and I'm fond of
you, and I want you to feel the same about me, too ... Because, just look,
my mom's affection for me is, well, it's the only good thing that's
happened to me in my whole life, because she takes me for what I am,
and loves me just that way, plain and simply. And that's like a gift from
heaven, and the only thing that keeps me going, the only thing. (p. 203)

Later it becomes clear that Molina is not only identified with the passive
sexual role but also aroused by its potential dangers. When Valentin suggests that
he should have more self-respect than simply to submit to a male, Molina replies:

—But if a man is ... my husband, he has to give the orders, so he
will feel right. That's the natural thing, because that makes him the ...
man of the house.

—No, the man of the house and the woman of the house have to be
equal with one another. If not, their relation becomes a form of
exploitation.

—But there's no kick to it.

—Why?

—Well, this is very intimate, but since you're asking about it ...
The kick is in the fact that when a man embraces you ... you may feel
a little bit frightened. (pp. 243-244)

Here we see the psychological dynamic behind the Two's preference for a
dominant partner. This paradoxical combination of aggressiveness and a desire
to serve is characteristic of many Twos, quite apart from their sexual orientation.
This may help us understand why Two and Eight is a common combination in
couples.

Ulysses

Molly Bloom in James Joyce's *Ulysses* is a classic Sexual Two. In the last
section of the novel, a stream-of-consciousness monologue, Molly ruminates
about her intimacies with her husband and lovers, and fantasizes about further
sexual adventures. The sexual voraciousness of this subtype is especially evident
in the following section:

of course a woman wants to be embraced 20 times a day almost to make her look young no matter by who so long as to be in love or loved by somebody if the fellow you want isn't there sometimes by the Lord God I was thinking would I go around by the quays there some dark evening where nobodyd know me and pick up a sailor off the sea thatd be hot on for it and not care a pin whose I was only to do it off up in a gate somewhere or one of those wildlooking gipsies in Rathfarnham had their camp pitched near the Bloomfield laundry to try and steal our things if they could (p. 762)

In the book's final passage Molly remembers the sensuality and beauty of the day her husband proposed to her:

the sun shines for you he said the day we were lying among the rhododendrons on Howth head in the grey tweed suit and his straw hat the day I got him to propose to me yes first I gave him the bit of seedcake out of my mouth and it was leapyear like now yes 16 years ago my God after that long kiss I near lost my breath yes he said I was a flower of the mountain yes so we are flowers all a womans body yes that was one true thing he said in his life and the sun shines for you today yes that was why I liked him because I saw he understood or felt what a woman is and I knew I could always get round him and I gave him all the pleasure I could leading him on till he asked me to say yes and I wouldn't answer first only looked out over the sea and the sky I was thinking of so many things he didn't know of . . . O and the sea the sea crimson sometimes like fire and the glorious sunsets and the figtrees in the Alameda gardens yes and all the queer little streets and pink and blue and yellow houses and the rosegardens and the jessamine and the geraniums and cactuses and Gibraltar as a girl where I was a Flower of the mountain yes when I put the rose in my hair like the Andalusian girls used or shall I wear a red yes and how he kissed me under the Moorish wall and I thought well as well him as another and then I asked him with my eyes to ask again yes and then he asked me would I yes to say yes my mountain flower and first I put my arms around him yes and drew him down to me so he could feel my breasts all perfume yes and his heart was going like mad and yes I said yes I will Yes. (pp. 767-768)

Molly's link to her Four security point is clear in her sensuous appreciation of beauty, potently combined here with a Sexual Two's characteristic seductiveness.

The focus on love that we see in Molly Bloom is common to all Twos, and they often fail to understand their own neediness. Their degree of self-delusion ranges from such unhealthy examples as Dave in *Medicine Men* and Aroon in *Good Behaviour* to the extraordinary self-awareness of Mrs. Ramsay in *To the*

Lighthouse. In rare examples there may even be a transcendence of Enneagram type such as we see in King Lear.

Sources
Adams, Alice, *Medicine Men* (New York: Alfred A. Knopf, 1997)
Austen, Jane, *Emma* (London: The Zodiac Press, 1955) First published 1816
Irving, John, *The World According to Garp* (NY: Ballantine, 1978)
Joyce, James, *Ulysses* (New York: The Modern Library, 1934) First published 1914
Keane, Molly, *Good Behaviour* (New York: Alfred A. Knopf, 1981)
Puig, Manuel, *Kiss of the Spider Woman*, trans. Thomas Colchie (New York, Alfred A. Knopf, 1979)
Salinger, J.D., *The Catcher in the Rye* (Boston: Little, Brown, 1951)
Shakespeare, William, *Antony and Cleopatra*. First performed 1606-7
Shakespeare, William, *King Lear*. First performed 1603-1606
Shaw, Bernard, *Candida*, in *Selected Plays with Prefaces* (New York, Dodd, Mead: 1948) First produced 1895
Woolf, Virginia, *To the Lighthouse* (NY: Alfred A. Knopf). First published 1927

Three: The Achiever

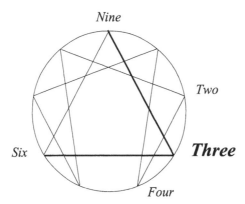

Vain, deceitful, calculating, and charming, Scarlett O'Hara, the heroine of Margaret Mitchell's *Gone with the Wind*, is a quintessential Three:

> By the time Scarlett had undressed and blown out the candle, her plan for tomorrow had worked itself out in every detail. It was a simple plan, for . . . her eyes were centered on the goal and she thought only of the most direct steps by which to reach it.
> . . . From the moment she arrived at Twelve Oaks, she would be her gayest, most spirited self. No one would suspect that she had ever been downhearted because of Ashley and Melanie. And she would flirt with every man there. That would be cruel to Ashley, but it would make him yearn for her all the more. She wouldn't overlook a man of marriageable age, from ginger-whiskered old Frank Kennedy, who was Suellen's beau, on down to shy, quiet, blushing Charles Hamilton, Melanie's brother. They would swarm around her like bees around a hive, and certainly Ashley would be drawn from Melanie to join the circle of her admirers. Then somehow she would maneuver to get a few minutes alone with him, away from the crowd. She hoped everything would work out that way, because it would be more difficult otherwise. But if Ashley didn't make the first move, she would simply have to do it herself. . . .
> Why, by this time tomorrow night, she might be Mrs. Ashley Wilkes! (pp. 71-72)

Scarlett's goal-directedness, strategic planning, and ability to project an image of success are basic Three qualities. She is determined to win Ashley away from his fiancée, Melanie, and the narcissism and self-confidence she shows in the above passage are also common in this Enneagram style. Threes make things happen in this world; their energy, drive, and concern with how others see them often make them successful in business. They can be excellent salespeople, adept at selling themselves first of all, but when they fail to achieve their goals or impress others, underlying feelings of inadequacy often come to the fore. Witness, for instance, Scarlett's humiliation and fury when Ashley refuses to marry her:

> She heard the soft muffled sound of his footsteps dying away down the long hall, and the complete enormity of her actions came over her. She had lost him forever. Now he would hate her and every time he looked at her he would remember how she threw herself at him when he had given her no encouragement at all.
>
> . . .[T]he thought stung her to new rage, rage at herself, at Ashley, at the world. Because she hated herself, she hated them all with the fury of the thwarted and humiliated love of sixteen. Only a little true tenderness had been mixed into her love. Mostly it had been compounded out of vanity and complacent confidence in her own charms. Now she had lost and, greater than her sense of loss, was the fear that she had made a public spectacle of herself. (pp. 118-119)

This hints at the limitations many Threes have in the realm of feelings. People with this style often find it difficult to connect with emotions, both their own and those of others. Although Three is in the heart triad, the group most concerned with feelings, many Threes suppress their emotions and focus instead on presenting a successful and desirable image. Thus when Ashley rejects Scarlett it is an especially painful failure for her.

To save face, Scarlett quickly marries Melanie's brother Charles, who is then killed in an early battle of the Civil War, leaving her a widow with a son. Next she and Melanie travel to Atlanta to stay with Melanie's aunt. After Atlanta falls to the Yankees, Scarlett returns to Tara, her war-torn family homestead. There she finds her mother dead, her father insane, and her sisters seriously ill. Scarlett's rising determination to protect her family and do what is necessary to survive evokes our sympathy:

> Hunger gnawed at her empty stomach again and she said aloud: "As God is my witness, as God is my witness, the Yankees aren't going to lick me. I'm going to live through this, and when it's over, I'm never going to be hungry again. No, nor any of my folks. If I have to steal or kill—as God is my witness, I'm never going to be hungry again." (p. 428)

Scarlett assumes the leadership of the group and becomes a fierce taskmaster for everyone at Tara. When a Yankee soldier appears in the house, she has no scruples about killing him:

No ghost rose from that shallow grave to haunt her in the long nights when she lay awake, too tired to sleep. No feeling of horror or remorse assailed her at the memory. She wondered why, knowing that even a month before she could never have done the deed. Pretty young Mrs. Hamilton, with her dimple and her jingling earbobs and her helpless little ways, blowing a man's face to a pulp and then burying him in a hastily scratched-out hole! Scarlett grinned a little grimly thinking of the consternation such an idea would bring to those who knew her.

"I won't think about it any more," she decided. "It's over and done with and I'd have been a ninny not to kill him. I reckon—I reckon I must have changed a little since coming home or else I couldn't have done it."

She did not think of it consciously but in the back of her mind, whenever she was confronted by an unpleasant and difficult task, the idea lurked giving her strength: "I've done murder and so I can surely do this." (p. 445)

Nine is Three's stress point, and in this passage we see the Three tendency to take on characteristics of Nines when under stress. Throughout the novel, whenever Scarlett is overwhelmed, she defensively postpones thinking about the problem, often vaguely resolving to deal with it tomorrow. As we shall see, Nines frequently procrastinate in just this way.

The end of the war finds Scarlett significantly changed, and her gifts for managing resources and generating cash flow become apparent. When threatened with losing Tara for lack of money to pay the exorbitant Reconstruction taxes, Scarlett decides that marrying Rhett Butler is her best option, although she hates him because he once saw her throw herself at Ashley. When Rhett turns her down, she turns to Frank Kennedy, her sister's beau; she has no compunction about lying to him and betraying her sister in order to secure his proposal:

But she wasn't going to be poor all her life. She wasn't going to sit down and patiently wait for a miracle to help her. She was going to rush into life and wrest from it what she could. Her father had started as a poor immigrant boy and had won the broad acres of Tara. What he had done, his daughter could do. She wasn't like these people who had gambled everything on a Cause that was gone and were content to be proud of having lost that Cause, because it was worth any sacrifice. They drew their courage from the past. She was drawing hers from the future. Frank Kennedy, at present, was her future. At least, he had the store and he had cash money. And if she could only marry him and get her hands on that money, she could make ends meet at Tara for another year. And after that—Frank must buy the sawmill. She could see for herself how quickly the town was rebuilding and anyone who could establish a lumber business now, when there was so little competition, would have a gold mine. (pp. 610-611)

Even before she persuades Frank to marry her, she is planning how to use his money to finance a lucrative business. Less-than-healthy Threes are willing to cut moral corners to insure their economic well being. Scarlett also wastes no time rationalizing her pursuit of Frank. When Threes think of a solution, they often take immediate action without hesitating over feelings or scruples. This capacity can make a Three successful in business but unable to sustain deep personal relationships.

Once Scarlett and Frank are married, she quickly drops her demure and worshipful facade and embraces her calling as a businesswoman:

> A startling thought this, that a woman could handle business matters as well as or better than a man, a revolutionary thought to Scarlett who had been reared in the tradition that men were omniscient and women none too bright. Of course, she had discovered that this was not altogether true but the pleasant fiction still stuck in her mind. Never before had she put this remarkable idea into words. She sat quite still, with the heavy book across her lap, her mouth a little open with surprise, thinking that during the lean months at Tara she had done a man's work and done it well. She had been brought up to believe that a woman alone could accomplish nothing, yet she had managed the plantation without men to help her until Will came. Why, why, her mind stuttered, I believe women could manage everything in the world without men's help—except having babies, and God knows, no woman in her right mind would have babies if she could help it. (p. 620)

Scarlett also borrows money from Rhett to buy a sawmill, demonstrating her gift for deceptive business practices:

> At first the other dealers had laughed at her, laughed with good-natured contempt at the very idea of a woman in business. But now they did not laugh. They swore silently as they saw her ride by. The fact that she was a woman frequently worked in her favor, for she could upon occasion look so helpless and appealing that she melted hearts. With no difficulty whatever she could mutely convey the impression of a brave but timid lady, forced by brutal circumstance into a distasteful position, a helpless little lady who would probably starve if customers didn't buy her lumber. But when ladylike airs failed to get results she was coldly businesslike and willingly undersold her competitors at a loss to herself if it would bring her a new customer. She was not above selling a poor grade of lumber for the price of good lumber if she thought she would not be detected, and she had no scruples about blackguarding the other lumber dealers. With every appearance of reluctance at disclosing the unpleasant truth, she would sigh and tell prospective customers that her competitors' lumber was far too high in price, rotten, full of knot holes and in general of deplorably poor quality.

The first time Scarlett lied in this fashion she felt disconcerted and guilty—disconcerted because the lie sprang so easily and naturally to her lips, guilty because the thought flashed into her mind: What would Mother say?

There was no doubt what Ellen would say to a daughter who told lies and engaged in sharp practices. She would be stunned and incredulous and would speak gentle words that stung despite their gentleness, would talk of honor and honesty and truth and duty to one's neighbor. Momentarily, Scarlett cringed as she pictured the look on her mother's face. And then the picture faded, blotted out by an impulse, hard, unscrupulous and greedy, which had been born in the lean days at Tara and was now strengthened by the present uncertainty of life. So she passed this milestone as she had passed others before it—with a sigh that she was not as Ellen would like her to be, a shrug and a repetition of her unfailing charm: "I'll think of all this later." (pp. 662-663)

Remembering her mother's ethics may give Scarlett momentary pause, but her Nine stress point swings into play, and she puts off thinking about this troubling question.

In fact, Scarlett is prepared to go beyond mere lying to succeed. Although she has evidence that one of her mill managers is abusing the convicts she has leased as workers from the state, she tells the manager to do whatever is necessary to keep the mill profitable.

After Frank dies, Scarlett continues to entertain fantasies of Ashley. But she has grown attracted to Rhett, who has become extremely wealthy through war profiteering. When he proposes to her she is swept away by her feelings—for the first time in her life.

Married to Rhett, an Eight, her disdain for the conventions of social courtesy comes to the surface, and her arrogance costs her many old friends. Now that she has money and success, Scarlett wonders why she isn't happier. She still thinks that if only she had Ashley, a Four, everything would be perfect. However, her perspective on him begins to shift:

"I shouldn't have let him make me look back," she thought despairingly. "I was right when I said I'd never look back. It hurts too much, it drags at your heart till you can't ever do anything else except look back. That's what's wrong with Ashley. He can't look forward any more. He can't see the present, he fears the future, and so he looks back. I never understood it before. I never understood Ashley before. Oh, Ashley, my darling, you shouldn't look back! What good will it do? I shouldn't have let you tempt me into talking of the old days. This is what happens when you look back to happiness, this pain, this heartbreak, this discontent." (p. 925)

Scarlett's Four wing is prominent in this passage. Her fantasy picture of Ashley begins to crack as she realizes that his romantic, regretful Four view of the world could never be her own.

She also begins to experience herself as a feeling person, a healthy step for a Three. Her thoughts about Ashley become more empathetic—she feels for him as a real person, distinct from the fantasy image of him that she has been nursing. In Enneagram terms, this represents a move toward her Six security point, where feelings are real and emotional connections with people bring up doubts and fear.

Scarlett's budding exploration of her feelings is given a massive jolt when a drunken Rhett first confronts her about her fantasies of Ashley. He then carries her up to bed and makes violent love to her. The experience awakens her sexually:

> Two things stood to the fore. She had lived for years with Rhett, slept with him, eaten with him, quarreled with him and borne his child—and yet, she did not know him. The man who had carried her up the dark stairs was a stranger of whose existence she had not dreamed. And now, though she tried to make herself hate him, tried to be indignant, she could not. He had humbled her, hurt her, used her brutally through a wild mad night and she had gloried in it.
>
> Oh, she should be ashamed, should shrink from the very memory of the hot swirling darkness! A lady, a real lady, could never hold up her head after such a night. But, stronger than shame, was the memory of rapture, of the ecstasy of surrender. For the first time in her life she had felt alive, felt passion as sweeping and primitive as the fear she had known the night she fled Atlanta, as dizzy sweet as the cold hate when she had shot the Yankee. . . .
>
> When she thought of meeting him again, face to face in the sober light of day, a nervous tingling embarrassment that carried with it an exciting pleasure enveloped her. (pp. 940-941)

Although Scarlett is aware of her sexuality for the first time, she is unable to attach feelings of love or tenderness to her new-found desire for her husband. He takes his time returning home, and when they next meet they quarrel. The magical moment of sexual connection is never repeated, but Scarlett has become pregnant, and she gives birth to Bonnie, whom Rhett dotes on. When the child is later killed in a riding accident, Scarlett blames Rhett.

In her grief Scarlett realizes the importance of allies and how few she has. We again see her connection to her Six security point, where close relationships with other people are valued:

> Oh, to be with her own kind of people again, those people who had been through the same things and knew how they hurt—and yet how great a part of you they were!
>
> But, somehow, these people had slipped away. She realized that it

was her own fault. She had never cared until now—now that Bonnie was dead and she was lonely and afraid and she saw across her shining dinner table a swarthy sodden stranger disintegrating under her eyes. (pp. 1003-1004)

Scarlett's character arc—from her heartless Three fixation to a genuine emotional connection at her Six security point—is completed as Melanie lies dying:

Why, oh, why, had she not realized before this how much she loved and needed Melanie? But who would have thought of small plain Melanie as a tower of strength? Melanie who was shy to tears before strangers, timid about raising her voice in an opinion of her own, fearful of the disapproval of old ladies, Melanie who lacked the courage to say Boo to a goose? And yet—

Scarlett's mind went back through the years to the still hot noon at Tara when gray smoke curled above a blue-clad body and Melanie stood at the top of the stairs with Charles' saber in her hand. . . .

"Melly is the only woman friend I ever had," she thought forlornly, "the only woman except Mother who really loved me. She's like Mother, too. Everyone who knew her has clung to her skirts."

Suddenly it was as if Ellen were lying behind that closed door, leaving the world for a second time. Suddenly she was standing at Tara again with the world about her ears, desolate with the knowledge that she could not face life without the terrible strength of the weak, the gentle, the tender hearted. (pp. 1012-1013)

Now Scarlett is experiencing her emotions with clarity. This insight also frees her to see through her illusions about Ashley:

"He never really existed at all, except in my imagination," she thought wearily. "I loved something I made up, something that's just as dead as Melly is. I made a pretty suit of clothes and fell in love with it. And when Ashley came riding along, so handsome, so different, I put that suit on him and made him wear it whether it fitted him or not. And I wouldn't see what he really was. I kept on loving the pretty clothes—and not him at all." (p. 1016)

After Melanie's funeral, Scarlett's feelings for Melanie and Ashley deepen even more:

She leaned her head against one of the uprights of the porch and prepared to cry but no tears came. This was a calamity too deep for tears. Her body shook. There still reverberated in her mind the crashes of the two impregnable citadels of her life, thundering to dust about her ears. She stood for a while, trying to summon up her old charm: "I'll think of all this tomorrow when I can stand it better." But the charm had lost its potency. She had to think of two things, now—Melanie and how much she loved and needed her; Ashley and the obstinate blindness that had made her refuse to see him as he really was. And she knew that thoughts of them would hurt just as much tomorrow and all the tomorrows of her life. (pp. 1018-1019)

Scarlett's growth as a person is evident in her acceptance of the emotional pain of life and in the fact that her usual defensive procrastination has lost its potency. She has become capable of truly loving. Realizing that Rhett is the love of her life, Scarlett resolves to renounce her past folly towards him and declare her love, confident that he will understand her as he always has. When they finally meet, he tells her about his grief over Bonnie's death and her response is heartfelt:

Suddenly she was sorry for him, sorry with a completeness that wiped out her own grief and her fear of what his words might mean. It was the first time in her life she had ever been sorry for anyone without feeling contemptuous as well, because it was the first time she had ever approached understanding any other human being. And she could understand his shrewd caginess, so like her own, his obstinate pride that kept him from admitting his love for fear of a rebuff.

"Ah, darling," she said coming forward, hoping he would put out his arms and draw her to his knees. "Darling, I'm so sorry but I'll make it all up to you! We can be so happy, now that we know the truth and—Rhett— look at me, Rhett! There—there can be other babies—not like Bonnie but—"

"Thank you, no," said Rhett, as if he were refusing a piece of bread. "I'll not risk my heart a third time." (pp. 1031-1032)

Scarlett's long journey through average and unhealthy levels of Three to arrive at insight, growth, and the capacity to love now seems all for naught. Her past behavior has destroyed Rhett's love for her. But the final paragraphs of the book show her Three indomitability:

With the spirit of her people who would not know defeat, even when it stared them in the face, she raised her chin. She could get Rhett back. She knew she could. There had never been a man she couldn't get, once she set her mind upon him.

"I'll think of it all tomorrow, at Tara. I can stand it then. Tomorrow, I'll think of some way to get him back. After all, tomorrow is another day." (p. 1037)

The great achievement of Mitchell's novel is that in the end the reader's heart goes out to Scarlett, despite her many flaws. We grieve for her loss of Rhett. We understand that this blow is severe enough to drive her back into unhealthy Three behavior and Nine-like procrastinating.

And we root for her to find some way to get him back.

The Talented Mr. Ripley

Because Threes are able to see themselves as others see them, they are skillful shapers of their public image, able to present themselves in a favorable light and adjust their behavior according to feedback and context.

In Tom Ripley, the ruthless protagonist of Patricia Highsmith's *The Talented Mr. Ripley*, we see a vivid example of this. At the beginning of the story, Tom parlays a slight acquaintance with Dickie Greenleaf, a young man from a wealthy family, into an assignment from Dickie's father to sail to Europe and persuade Dickie to return home to work in the family business.

Aboard the ship, Tom begins rehearsing the role that he will later perfect in Europe. Here he is acquiring props that support his performance:

> He began to play a role on the ship, that of a serious young man with a serious job ahead of him. He was courteous, poised, civilized and preoccupied.
>
> He had a sudden whim for a cap and bought one in the haberdashery, a conservative bluish-grey cap of soft English wool. He could pull its visor down over nearly his whole face when he wanted to nap in his deck-chair, or wanted to look as if he were napping. A cap was the most versatile of headgear, he thought, and he wondered why he had never thought of wearing one before? He could look like a country gentleman, a thug, an Englishman, a Frenchman, or a plain American eccentric, depending on how he wore it. Tom amused himself with it in his room in front of the mirror. He had always thought he had the world's dullest face, a thoroughly forgettable face with a look of docility that he could not understand, and a look also of vague fright that he had never been able to erase. A real conformist's face, he thought. The cap changed all that. It gave him a country air, Greenwich, Connecticut, country. Now he was a young man with a private income, not long out of Princeton, perhaps. He bought a pipe to go with the cap. (p. 34)

Once in Europe, Tom ingratiates himself with Dickie and moves into the latter's villa in a small Italian town. Already a little in love with his host, Tom secretly tries on Dickie's clothes while Dickie is away and fantasizes about what it would be like to be the wealthy young man.

Later, when Dickie, a Seven, makes it clear that he is growing tired of Tom's company, Tom's fantasies mutate into thoughts of killing Dickie and assuming his identity.

He had failed with Dickie, in every way. He hated Dickie, because, however he looked at what had happened, his failing had not been his own fault, not due to anything he had done, but due to Dickie's inhuman stubbornness. And his blatant rudeness! He had offered Dickie friendship, companionship, and respect, everything he had to offer, and Dickie had replied with ingratitude and now hostility. Dickie was just shoving him out in the cold. If he killed him on this trip, Tom thought, he could simply say that some accident had happened. He could— He had just thought of something brilliant: he could become Dickie Greenleaf himself. He could do everything that Dickie did. He could go back to Mongibello first and collect Dickie's things, tell Marge any damned story, set up an apartment in Rome or Paris, receive Dickie's cheque every month and forge Dickie's signature on it. He could step right into Dickie's shoes. He could have Mr. Greenleaf, Sr., eating out of his hand. The danger of it, even the inevitable temporariness of it which he vaguely realized, only made him more enthusiastic. He began to think of *how*. (p. 100)

This is a Three's narcissism descending to a pathological level: if your host is rude to you, it's acceptable to kill him.

Tom proposes a boat trip with Dickie. Out on the water he kills him and dumps his body into the sea. Later, on the train back to Mongibello, Tom feels no horror or remorse: he has simply done what was necessary to acquire the prestige of Dickie's lifestyle, with all the symbolic props that an unhealthy Three craves:

The white, taut sheets of his berth on the train seemed the most wonderful luxury he had ever known. He caressed them with his hands before he turned the light out. And the clean blue-grey blankets, the spanking efficiency of the little black net over his head — Tom had an ecstatic moment when he thought of all the pleasures that lay before him now with Dickie's money, other beds, tables, seas, ships, suitcases, shirts, years of freedom, years of pleasure. Then he turned the light out and put his head down and almost at once fell asleep, happy, content, and utterly, utterly confident, as he had never been before in his life. (pp. 111-112)

After settling into a hotel in Rome, Tom takes on Dickie's identity and begins to feel satisfied with his life for the first time:

He had done so little artificially to change his appearance, but his very expression, Tom thought, was like Dickie's now. He wore a smile that was dangerously welcoming to a stranger, a smile more fit to greet an old friend or a lover. It was Dickie's best and most typical smile when he was in a good humour. Tom was in a good humour. It was Paris. *Wonderful* to sit in a famous café, and to think of tomorrow and tomorrow and tomorrow being Dickie Greenleaf! The cuff links, the white silk shirts, even the old clothes—the worn brown belt with the brass buckle, the old brown grain-leather shoes, the kind advertised in *Punch* as lasting a life-time, the old mustard-coloured coat sweater with the sagging pockets—they were all his and he loved them all. And the black fountain pen with little gold initials. And the wallet, a well-worn alligator wallet from Gucci's. And there was plenty of money to go in it. (p. 126)

Now fully immersed in his longed-for role, Tom plays it to perfection:

He felt alone, yet not at all lonely. It was very much like the feeling on Christmas Eve in Paris, a feeling that everyone was watching him, as if he had an audience made up of the entire world, a feeling that kept him on his mettle, because to make a mistake would be catastrophic. Yet he felt absolutely confident he would not make a mistake. It gave his existence a peculiar, delicious atmosphere of purity, like that, Tom thought, which a fine actor probably feels when he plays an important role on a stage with the conviction that the role he is playing could not be played better by anyone else. He was himself and yet not himself. He felt blameless and free, despite the fact that he consciously controlled every move he made. But he no longer felt tired after several hours of it, as he had at first. He had no need to relax when he was alone. Now, from the moment when he got out of bed and went to brush his teeth, he was Dickie, brushing his teeth with his right elbow jutted out. Dickie rotating the eggshell on his spoon for the last bite. Dickie invariably putting back the first tie he pulled off the rack and selecting a second. He had even produced a painting in Dickie's manner. (pp. 137-138)

When Dickie's friend Freddie Miles arrives in Rome and begins asking about Dickie's whereabouts, Tom murders him. Things begin to unravel when the police investigate Freddie's sudden disappearance and become suspicious about documents Tom has forged with Dickie's signature. Tom realizes he will have to resume his old identity:

He went on packing. This was the end of Dickie Greenleaf, he knew. He hated becoming Thomas Ripley again, hated being nobody, hated putting on his old set of habits again, and feeling that people looked down on him and were bored with him unless he put on an act for them like a clown, feeling incompetent and incapable of doing anything with himself except entertaining people for minutes at a time. He hated going back to himself as he would have hated putting on a shabby suit of clothes, a grease-spotted, unpressed suit of clothes that had not been very good even when it was new. His tears fell on Dickie's blue-and-white-striped shirt that lay uppermost in the suitcase, starched and clean and still as new-looking as when he had first taken it out of Dickie's drawer in Mongibello.

But it had Dickie's initials on the pocket in little red letters. As he packed he began to reckon up defiantly the things of Dickie's that he could still keep because they had no initials, or because no one would remember that they were Dickie's and not his own. Except maybe Marge would remember a few, like the new blue leather address book that Dickie had written only a couple of addresses in, and that Marge had very likely given to him. But he wasn't planning to see Marge again. (p. 192)

Now that Tom's impersonation has succeeded, he has difficulty returning to his true identity, having so thoroughly rejected it.

Next Marge, Dickie's fiancée, appears, along with Dickie's father and a private detective investigating Dickie's disappearance. During a brief visit Marge looks around Tom's apartment for a needle and thread to repair a broken bra strap and finds Dickie's rings in a drawer. Potentially exposed, Tom considers murdering her:

And the fact that he had done it twice before. Those two other times were *facts*, not imagination. He could say he hadn't wanted to do them but he had done them. He didn't want to be a murderer. Sometimes he could absolutely forget that he had murdered, he realized. But sometimes—like now—he couldn't. He had surely forgotten for a while tonight, when he had been thinking about the meaning of possessions, and why he liked to live in Europe.

He twisted on to his side, his feet drawn up on the sofa. He was sweating and shaking. What was happening to him? What had happened? Was he going to blurt out a lot of nonsense tomorrow when he saw Mr. Greenleaf, about Marge falling into the canal, and his screaming for help and jumping in and not finding her? Even with Marge standing there with them, would he go berserk and spill the story out and betray himself as a maniac?

He had to face Mr. Greenleaf with the rings tomorrow. He would have to repeat the story he had told to Marge. He would have to give it details to make it better. He began to invent. His mind steadied. He was imagining a Roman hotel room, Dickie and he standing there talking, and Dickie taking off both his rings and handing them to him. Dickie said: 'It's just as well you don't tell anybody about this. . . . ' (p. 254)

Note how facile and comfortable Tom, as a deteriorated Three, has become with plotting new details and levels of deception.

Faced with the possibility of losing Dickie's money and lifestyle, Tom considers forging a will in which Dickie leaves everything to Tom:

In a way it was asking for trouble, Tom thought. It might start a new investigation of the signatures, on the will and also the remittances, one of the relentless investigations that insurance companies and probably trust companies also launched when it was a matter of money out of their own pockets. But that was the mood he was in. . . . The very chanciness of trying for all of Dickie's money, the peril of it, was irresistible to him. He was so bored after the dreary, eventless weeks in Venice, when each day that went by had seemed to confirm his personal safety and to emphasize the dullness of his existence. . . . Tom had a feeling of emptiness and abeyance that had driven him nearly mad until he made the trip to Munich in his car. When he came back to Venice to pack for Greece and to close his house, the sensation had been worse: he was about to go to Greece, to those ancient heroic islands, as little Tom Ripley, shy and meek, with a dwindling two-thousand-odd in his bank so that he would practically have to think twice before he bought himself even a book on Greek art. It was intolerable. (pp. 276-277)

Tom decides to risk it and succeeds. When he tells Dickie's father that Dickie gave him the rings Marge found in his drawer, Mr. Greenleaf becomes convinced that Dickie took his own life. He also accepts the forged will as legitimate.

Thus in *The Talented Mr. Ripley*, whose "talent" is for deception and ruthlessness, we see a pathological Three's dream-come-true. Out of touch with his feelings and prepared to go to any lengths to maintain his image, he achieves the wealth and lifestyle that he values above all.

The Three's History

The Three's deepest fear is of public disgrace. As we saw in Scarlett and in Tom Ripley, once basic survival needs are met, Threes are concerned primarily with keeping up appearances and being admired for their successes.

Don Richard Riso and Russ Hudson have pointed out that Threes have strong connections with their mothers and depend heavily on maternal approval. If Threes as children fail to win the approval of the nurturing figure, their very survival feels threatened. If the Three child's achievements bring Mother's praise, then he feels safe, and further shapes his behavior to elicit admiration from her and others.

For Three adults, society at large is a mother substitute. How the Three looks, the prestige of his job, the desirability of his mate, the luxury of his lifestyle—all are unconsciously measured by how good they would look to Mom. If she would be dazzled, the Three can feel good about himself; if not, he is desperate and angry. His identity is created by the trappings he collects around him, for without these badges of honor he is not sure who he is.

Levels of Health

Average Threes have a generally positive outlook, with a "can-do" attitude, an appetite for hard work, and an impressive list of accomplishments. They can be stars in the corporate world as well as hard-driving managers of subordinates. Threes at this level can measure their achievements by the size of their income, beating out competitors, and being recognized as good at their job. Because of their image-consciousness, they usually dress well and appropriately, drive a car that advertises their success, choose housing that reflects their status, and select their spouse on the same basis.

The dark side of a Three's image is often expressed through troubled intimate relationships, personal vanity, and an inability to relax. Average Threes are uncomfortable with leisure time; even on vacation they may create demanding schedules and expect others to keep up with them.

Literary examples of average Threes include Scarlett O'Hara, Becky Sharp in William Makepeace Thackeray's *Vanity Fair*, Mark Twain's Tom Sawyer, the title character in F. Scott Fitzgerald's *The Great Gatsby*, Julien Sorel in Stendhal's *The Red and the Black*, the title character in Sinclair Lewis's *Elmer Gantry*, Marc McGranville in John O'Hara's story "How Can I Tell You?", the narrator of John Cheever's story "The Autobiography of a Drummer," Rachel in Barbara Kingsolver's *The Poisonwood Bible*, and R. J. Bowman in Eudora Welty's story "Death of a Traveling Salesman."

Sigmund Freud once defined a healthy individual as someone able to love and work, and when Threes are healthy they find and maintain a balance between work and personal priorities. In touch with their feelings and able to empathize with others, healthy Threes have genuinely intimate relationships. They also bring a quality of "heart" to their work that makes their leadership inspirational. The Horatio Alger novels feature healthy Three protagonists. While Scarlett O'Hara begins *Gone with the Wind* as an average Three, by the story's end she also illustrates this kind of growth.

Unhealthy Threes become entrenched in a heartless, ruthless, competitive stance. They can show great hostility toward anyone who stands in the way of their success. They generally have inflated opinions of their own abilities and are capable of great deceptiveness. If someone threatens to publicly expose the fraudulence of their public image, they are capable of extreme cruelty, violence, and even murder.

Literary examples of unhealthy Threes include Tom Ripley, Shakespeare's Lady Macbeth, Ibsen's Hedda Gabler, Dr. Raleigh Sanderson in Alice Adams's *Medicine Men*, and Richie Arias in Richard North Patterson's novels *Eyes of a Child* and *Degree of Guilt*.

Place in Society

Threes are the chameleons of the Enneagram, able to change their coloration according to what makes them look good in a given situation. As a result, they can be highly successful in jobs and professions that depend on effective self-presentation.

Threes are found in all areas of work, but they show up in disproportionate numbers in sales and advertising. Their focus and dedication make them formidable competitors in sports: they are probably the most common Enneagram style among Olympic athletes. In their quest for astronomical salaries and high status, they often rise to top positions in corporations. They may also be successful as politicians, models, on-camera news reporters and commentators, public relations experts, image consultants, motivational speakers, and success coaches. In the field of medicine, they often play starring roles, for instance as heart surgeons.

Stress and Security Points

Three's security point is Six (The Pessimist). When feeling secure, Threes are able to acknowledge their anxieties. They become more authentic and resist the temptation to create a smokescreen of deceit to bolster their self-image.

The stress point for Three is Nine (The Connector). When Threes are stressed they often become engaged in frantic, ineffectual activity, or they may procrastinate. They also tend to mask their feelings of inadequacy with some form of narcotization—alcohol, drugs, television, or fantasy. Under great stress Threes gone to Nine can also become delusional.

Death of a Salesman

Many American writers have depicted Threes as salesmen, with all the pressures and anxieties that job evokes.

In *Death of a Salesman*, Arthur Miller's famous play, Willy Loman is a poignant portrait of an aging shoe salesman in decline.

Through a flashback to an earlier, happier time, Miller shows Willy impressing his Three philosophy of life on his sons. Bernard, a neighbor boy who has been helping Willy's older son, Biff, with his high school math, has just exited the scene:

WILLY: Bernard is not well liked, is he?
BIFF: He's liked, but he's not well liked.
HAPPY: That's right, Pop.
WILLY: That's just what I mean. Bernard can get the best marks in school, y'understand, but when he gets out in the business world, y'understand, you are going to be five times ahead of him. That's why I thank Almighty God you're both built like Adonises. Because the man who makes an appearance in the business world, the man who creates personal interest, is the man who gets ahead. Be liked and you will never want. You take me, for instance. I never have to wait in line to see a buyer. "Willy Loman is here!" That's all they have to know, and I go right through.
BIFF: Did you knock them dead, Pop?
WILLY: Knocked 'em cold in Providence, slaughtered 'em in Boston. (p. 33)

Now, many years later, Willy senses when he makes his sales calls that his customers are laughing at him—if they notice him at all. He confesses his insecurities to his wife, Linda, but never tells her how he sought solace from this problem with other women.

During Act Two, Willy increasingly retreats from the reality of his failures into fantasy conversations with his brother Ben, who once tried to persuade Willy to join him in a business venture in Africa. In his "talks" with Ben, Willy wants to be validated for his Threeish beliefs: that hard work combined with the right attitude and a likeable image is the key to lasting success.

Later in the play, son Biff confronts Willy with the fact that neither of them is the grand success Willy envisions in his fantasies:

> BIFF: I am not a leader of men, Willy, and neither are you. You were never anything but a hard-working drummer who landed in the ash can like all the rest of them! I'm one dollar an hour, Willy! I tried seven states and couldn't raise it. A buck an hour! Do you gather my meaning? I'm not bringing home any prizes any more, and you're going to stop waiting for me to bring them home.
>
> WILLY, *directly to Biff:* You vengeful, spiteful mut!
>
> *Biff breaks from Happy. Willy, in fright, starts up the stairs. Biff grabs him.*
>
> BIFF, *at the peak of his fury:* Pop, I'm nothing! I'm nothing, Pop. Can't you understand that? There's no spite in it any more. I'm just what I am, that's all.
>
> *Biff's fury has spent itself, and he breaks down, sobbing, holding on to Willy, who dumbly fumbles for Biff's face.*
>
> WILLY, *astonished:* What're you doing? What're you doing? *To Linda:* Why is he crying?
>
> BIFF, *crying, broken:* Will you let me go, for Christ's sake? Will you take that phony dream and burn it before something happens? *Struggling to contain himself, he pulls away and moves to the stairs.* I'll go in the morning. Put him—put him to bed. *Exhausted, Biff moves up the stairs to his room.*
>
> WILLY: *after a long pause, astonished, elevated:* Isn't that—isn't that remarkable? Biff—he likes me!
>
> LINDA: He loves you, Willy!
>
> HAPPY, *deeply moved:* Always did, Pop.
>
> WILLY: Oh, Biff! *Staring wildly:* He cried! Cried to me. *He is choking with his love, and now cries out his promise:* That boy—that boy is going to be magnificent! (pp. 132-133)

After Linda goes upstairs to bed, Willy has a final imaginary conversation with Ben. He speaks of his love for Biff and asks Ben to imagine how magnificent the boy will be with a thousand dollars in his pocket—the amount of Willy's life insurance. Linda wakes up, suddenly afraid, and calls downstairs to Willy. But he is already speeding away in his car toward his suicide.

This scene shows a Three at his Nine stress point, both in Willy's fantasy conversation and in his deluded belief in Biff's great potential. The Six security point is present in the rush of fatherly love that motivates Willy's sacrifice.

The American Dream is basically one of money and success; Willy takes the only way he can see to offer his beloved son an opportunity to pursue this flawed dream. At Willy's funeral, his sons and his friend Charley discuss Willy's reliance on his Three philosophy:

> BIFF: He had the wrong dreams. All, all, wrong.
> HAPPY, *almost ready to fight Biff:* Don't say that!
> BIFF: He never knew who he was.
> CHARLEY, *stopping Happy's movement and reply. To Biff:* Nobody dast blame this man. You don't understand: Willy was a salesman. And for a salesman, there is no rock bottom to the life. He don't put a bolt to a nut, he don't tell you the law or give you medicine. He's a man way out there in the blue, riding on a smile and a shoeshine. And when they start not smiling back—that's an earthquake. And then you get yourself a couple of spots on your hat, and you're finished. Nobody dast blame this man. A salesman is got to dream, boy. It comes with the territory. (p. 138)

In a fitting end to Miller's play, Charley's eulogy expresses compassion for Willy's predicament while implicitly indicting society's Threeish values.

Wings

A Three can have a Two wing, a Four wing, or both wings. Although the worldviews of Two and Four share a focus on feelings, they are in other ways opposed. Twos are drawn toward people, while Fours are more self-absorbed. A Three's neurotic sense of purpose is shaped by the tension between these wings. When they feel unworthy of others' love and insecure about their own intrinsic value, Threes compensate by trying to win love through visible achievements and self-promotion. This is the source of the narcissism that many Enneagram writers have observed in Threes.

Willy Loman's Two wing is not uncommon among Three salespeople. Two qualities like energy, persuasiveness and the ability to focus on others are essential for success in sales. Willy's Two wing is also present in his genuine concern for his sons, although they also represent a narcissistic extension of his own image. Ultimately, Willy accepts that Biff truly loves him, and Willy's final sacrifice is also a gesture of love, albeit in the service of a warped dream of success.

By contrast, Scarlett O'Hara has more of a Four wing, evident in her self-absorption and her romantic longing for Ashley. She is also preoccupied with material security, showing little concern for others until late in the story. Even at the novel's end, her thoughts return to her need for Rhett—not what might be best for *him*. Tom Ripley also has a Four wing, especially visible in his taste for beauty and his sense that he is entitled to the best.

The Great Gatsby

F. Scott Fitzgerald's novel *The Great Gatsby* offers another view of the American Dream that reflects the Three worldview. In this story—surely on most people's short list of candidates for the Great American Novel—Fitzgerald presents his flawed but fascinating central character, Jay Gatsby, through the eyes of another character, Nick Carraway. Gatsby is a Three with a Four wing, and in the course of the story Nick, a Nine with a One wing, discovers a corrupt, possibly criminal side to Gatsby, whom he nevertheless regards as a romantic hero.

Nick, who lives in a small house next door to the mansion Gatsby has recently purchased, is initially dazzled by his new neighbor's charm. His description shows the hope that Threes at their best inspire in others:

> He smiled understandingly—much more than understandingly. It was one of those rare smiles with a quality of eternal reassurance in it, that you may come across four or five times in life. It faced—or seemed to face—the whole eternal world for an instant, and then concentrated on *you* with an irresistible prejudice in your favor. It understood you just so far as you wanted to be understood, believed in you as you would like to believe in yourself, and assured you that it had precisely the impression of you that, at your best, you hoped to convey. Precisely at that point it vanished—and I was looking at an elegant young rough-neck, a year or two over thirty, whose elaborate formality of speech just missed being absurd. (pp. 58-59)

While the guests at Gatsby's elaborate parties whisper about dark secrets in his past, Gatsby offers Nick his own version of his background so Nick won't get "a wrong idea of me from all these stories you hear":

> "I am the son of some wealthy people in the middle west—all dead now. I was brought up in America but educated at Oxford because all my ancestors have been educated there for many years. It is a family tradition."
>
> He looked at me sideways—and I knew why Jordan Baker had believed he was lying. He hurried the phrase "educated at Oxford," or swallowed it or choked on it as though it had bothered him before. And with this doubt his whole statement fell to pieces and I wondered if there wasn't something a little sinister about him after all.
>
> "What part of the middle west?" I inquired casually.
>
> "San Francisco."
>
> "I see."
>
> "My family all died and I came into a good deal of money."
>
> His voice was solemn, as if the memory of that sudden extinction of a clan still haunted him. For a moment I suspected that he was pulling my leg, but a glance at him convinced me otherwise. (p. 78)

Here is a Three safeguarding his image, but he makes an elementary error in geography. Nick, being a conciliatory Nine, declines to call him on it.

Later Nick learns from his friend Jordan Baker of his cousin Daisy's romantic past with Gatsby. Jordan explains that Daisy fell in love with Gatsby, an army lieutenant, four years earlier, but when he went off to war Daisy married Tom Buchanan, a wealthy man from her own social circle. Jordan tells Nick that Gatsby bought his house to be near Daisy. Gatsby wants Nick to invite them both over some afternoon so that he can seize the opportunity to show Daisy his house, which is conveniently next door to Nick's.

Nick issues the invitation, and Gatsby and Daisy reconnect after Nick leaves them alone together. Later Nick and Gatsby wait for Daisy while she goes upstairs to wash her face:

> "My house looks well, doesn't it?" he demanded. "See how the whole front of it catches the light."
>
> I agreed that it was splendid.
>
> "Yes." His eyes went over it, every arched door and square tower. "It took me just three years to earn the money that bought it."
>
> "I thought you inherited your money."
>
> "I did, old sport," he said automatically, "but I lost most of it in the big panic—the panic of the war."
>
> I think he hardly knew what he was saying, for when I asked him what business he was in he answered "That's my affair," before he realized that wasn't an appropriate reply.
>
> "Oh, I've been in several things," he corrected himself. "I was in the drug business and then I was in the oil business. But I'm not in either one now." (p. 109)

Again, the reader senses something fraudulent about Gatsby's shifting stories and carefully prepared replies. His intense focus on Daisy is reminiscent of Scarlett's fixation on Ashley and Tom Ripley's on Dickie: an idealization that has little connection with the actual human being. This psychological process comes easily to Threes with a Four wing. By the end of the afternoon, Nick is struck by the disparity between Gatsby's dream of Daisy and the reality:

> As I went over to say goodbye I saw that the expression of bewilderment had come back into Gatsby's face, as though a faint doubt had occurred to him as to the quality of his present happiness. Almost five years! There must have been moments even that afternoon when Daisy tumbled short of his dreams—not through her own fault but because of the colossal vitality of his illusion. It had gone beyond her, beyond every-thing. He had thrown himself into it with a creative passion, adding to it all the time, decking it out with every bright feather that drifted his way. No amount of fire or freshness can challenge what a man can store up in his ghostly heart. (p. 116)

Nick fills the reader in on Gatsby's true background, which he learned much later. Born James Gatz in North Dakota, he had an encounter at age seventeen that changed his life and fortunes: seeing a large yacht drop anchor in treacherous shallows near a lake shore, he rowed out to warn its owner of the danger. Dan Cody, a fifty-year-old man who had made his fortune in precious metals, took Gatz under his wing. This aspect of the story echoes the Horatio Alger books and other Three rags-to-riches stories:

> To young Gatz, resting on his oars and looking up at the railed deck, that yacht represented all the beauty and glamour in the world. I suppose he smiled at Cody—he had probably discovered that people liked him when he smiled. At any rate Cody asked him a few questions (one of them elicited the brand new name) and found that he was quick and extravagantly ambitious. A few days later he took him to Duluth and bought him a blue coat, six pair of white duck trousers and a yachting cap. And when the *Tuolomee* left for the West Indies and the Barbary Coast Gatsby left too. (p. 120)

Nick tells us that Gatz was employed by his patron for five years as "steward, mate, skipper, secretary, and even jailor" until Cody's sudden death. Although Cody included Gatsby in his will, his other heirs sued and Gatsby was left with only "his singularly appropriate education." Nick tells us that as a result of his experience with Cody "the vague contour of Jay Gatsby had filled out to the substantiality of a man." (p. 121)

In a later scene Daisy comes to one of Gatsby's parties and is offended by his pretentious and excessive style of entertaining. Her husband suspects that Gatsby is a bootlegger and vows to find out who he really is.

A short time later Gatsby fires his servants, explaining to Nick that he needs to avoid gossip, since Daisy now spends many afternoons at his house. Tensions mount when Gatsby and Nick visit Daisy and Tom's house on a hot afternoon:

> "Who wants to go to town?" demanded Daisy insistently. Gatsby's eyes floated toward her. "Ah," she cried, "you look so cool."
> Their eyes met and they stared together at each other, alone in space. With an effort she glanced down at the table.
> "You always look so cool," she repeated.
> She had told him that she loved him, and Tom Buchanan saw. He was astounded. His mouth opened a little and he looked at Gatsby, and then back at Daisy as if he had just recognized her as some one he knew a long time ago. (p. 142)

The situation erupts when Gatsby tells Tom that Daisy is leaving him. Tom reveals that he has been investigating Gatsby's affairs and implies that Gatsby is involved in illegal drug trafficking. Although Gatsby defends himself, Daisy draws away, obviously shocked. Nick observes Gatsby:

> Then I turned back to Gatsby—and was startled at his expression. He
> looked—and this is said in all contempt for the babbled slander of his
> garden—as if he had "killed a man." For a moment the set of his face could
> be described in just that fantastic way.
>
> It passed, and he began to talk excitedly to Daisy, denying every-
> thing, defending his name against accusations that had not been made. But
> with every word she was drawing further and further into herself, so he
> gave that up and only the dead dream fought on as the afternoon slipped
> away, trying to touch what was no longer tangible, struggling unhappily,
> undespairingly, toward that lost voice across the room. (pp. 161-162)

To relieve the tension, Daisy suggests they all go into town. They take two
cars, and on the return trip Daisy drives Gatsby home in Tom's car. Along the way
a woman rushes out in front of the car and is killed. She turns out to be Tom's
mistress, and her angry grieving husband, Wilson, confronts Tom, who he assumes
was driving the car. But Tom tells him the car was Gatsby's and gives him
directions to Gatsby's house. When Wilson finds Gatsby in his swimming pool,
he shoots him, and then kills himself.

When Nick tries to assemble a group to attend Gatsby's funeral, no one can
be found. Tom and Daisy have left town, leaving no address and no return date. In
Gatsby's house, Nick answers the phone and learns, by chance, the full extent of
Gatsby's criminal business dealings. Gatsby's father arrives for the funeral and
shows Nick a copy of a book Gatsby had as a child. Handwritten in the back is a
self-development "schedule" that could have come from a Horatio Alger story.

In the end, Gatsby embodies both the best and the worst of his Enneagram
style—the Three's natural charm, energy, and ambition, but also the deceit, vanity,
and willingness to cut moral and ethical corners.

Subtypes

Self-Preservation Threes, whom Oscar Ichazo associates with "security,"
are the most dedicated to work as a means of survival. More than other subtypes,
they can be distinctly workaholic, driven by the need for money and possessions
as the only source of security. Willy Loman has this subtype, as does Bowman in
Eudora Welty's story "Death of a Traveling Salesman" (discussed in Part One and
below). Other literary examples include Marc McGranville in John O'Hara's story
"How Can I Tell You?", the narrator of John Cheever's story "The Autobiography
of a Drummer," and Levene in David Mamet's play *Glengarry Glen Ross*.

Struggling Upward

Self-Preservation Threes are the heroes in all of Horatio Alger's books. They
are energetic, ambitious individuals who achieve financial security through hard
work, honesty, and timely help from wealthy and successful patrons. Typical

Alger titles—which themselves have the flavor of this subtype—include *Slow and Sure*, *Try and Trust*, and *Strong and Steady*.

One of Alger's most popular books was *Struggling Upward*, the story of Luke Larkin:

> ... the son of a carpenter's widow, living on narrow means, and so compelled to exercise the strictest economy. Luke worked where he could, helping the farmers in hay-time, and ready to do odd jobs for any one in the village who desired his services. He filled the position of janitor at the school which he attended, sweeping out twice a week and making the fires. He had a pleasant expression, and a bright, resolute look, a warm heart, and a clear intellect, and was probably, in spite of his poverty, the most popular boy in Groveton. (pp. 3-4)

Over the course of the story Luke, who has a Two wing, overcomes poverty, fraud, snobbery and assorted evildoers to make a new life for himself. The plot involves stolen government bonds, blackmail and other nefarious doings, but Luke triumphs in the end, his victory sweetened by generous financial rewards from grateful patrons.

"Death of a Traveling Salesman"

R. J. Bowman, the central character in Eudora Welty's story "Death of a Traveling Salesman," is also a Self-Preservation Three with a Two wing. As the story begins, Bowman, who has traveled for fourteen years through Mississippi selling shoes, is feeling ill and suddenly finds himself lost:

> There was not a house in sight. ... There was no use wishing he were back in bed, though.
> By paying the hotel doctor his bill he had proved his recovery. He had not even been sorry when the pretty trained nurse said good-bye. He did not like illness, he distrusted it, as he distrusted the road without signposts. It angered him. He had given the nurse a really expensive bracelet, just because she was packing up her bag and leaving.
> But now—what if in fourteen years on the road he had never been ill before and never had an accident? His record was broken, and he had even begun almost to question it. ... He had gradually put up at better hotels, in the bigger towns, but weren't they all, eternally, stuffy in summer and drafty in winter? Women? He could only remember little rooms within little rooms, like a nest of Chinese paper boxes, and if he thought of one woman he saw the worn loneliness that the furniture of that room seemed built of. And he himself—he was a man who always wore rather wide-brimmed black hats, and in the wavy hotel mirrors had looked something like a bullfighter, as he paused for that inevitable instant on the landing, walking downstairs to supper. ... (pp. 232-233)

We see here not only the absence of intimate relationships in this Self-Preservation Three's life but also Bowman's denial of his illness. He has paid the bill, he reasons, therefore he must be recovered. Breaking his perfect work record is obviously a blow to this workaholic Three.

Next he has car trouble and seeks help at a farmhouse:

> ... it was so still. The silence of the fields seemed to enter and move familiarly through the house. The wind used the open hall. He felt that he was in a mysterious, quiet, cool danger. It was necessary to do what? . . . To talk.
>
> "I have a nice line of women's low-priced shoes . . ." he said.
>
> But the woman answered, "Sonny'll be here. He's strong. Sonny'll move your car." (p. 239)

As a Self-Preservation Three, Bowman believes work is a means to security so any hint of anxiety sends him automatically into his sales pitch, however inappropriate. Sonny, the woman's husband, comes home and then leaves to pull Bowman's car out of the ditch. Alone with the woman, Bowman wrestles with his feelings:

> [Bowman] felt a curious and strong emotion, not fear, rise up in him.
>
> This time, when his heart leapt, something—his soul—seemed to leap too, like a little colt invited out of a pen. He stared at the woman while the frantic nimbleness of his feeling made his head sway. He could not move; there was nothing he could do, unless perhaps he might embrace this woman who sat there growing old and shapeless before him.
>
> But he wanted to leap up, to say to her, I have been sick and I found out then, only then, how lonely I am. Is it too late? My heart puts up a struggle inside me, and you may have heard it, protesting against emptiness. . . . It should be full, he would rush on to tell her, thinking of his heart now as a deep lake, it should be holding love like other hearts. It should be flooded with love. There would be a warm spring day. . . . Come and stand in my heart, whoever you are, and a whole river would cover your feet and rise higher and take your knees in whirlpools, and draw you down to itself, your whole body, your heart too.
>
> But he moved a trembling hand across his eyes, and looked at the placid crouching woman across the room. She was still as a statue. He felt ashamed and exhausted by the thought that he might, in one more moment, have tried by simple words and embraces to communicate some strange thing—something which seemed always to have just escaped him. . . . (pp. 243-244)

Welty clearly means for us to see Bowman's illness as a symbol of his life-long emotional incapacity. Sonny, the woman's husband, returns, having successfully pulled the salesman's car out of the ditch it was stuck in. Bowman offers to pay the couple for their help, but they refuse. He tells them that he's still sick and asks if he can stay the night, and they agree. Later, as they eat supper, Bowman realizes that his initial impression of his hosts was mistaken. Preoccupied with his own troubles, he had failed to observe the woman closely. She is not old, as he had originally thought, but young and pregnant:

> Bowman could not speak. He was shocked with knowing what was really in this house. A marriage, a fruitful marriage. That simple thing. Anyone could have had that.
> Somehow he felt unable to be indignant or protest, although some sort of joke had certainly been played upon him. There was nothing remote or mysterious here—only something private. The only secret was the ancient communication between two people. (p. 251)

The woman's pregnancy and the couple's close relationship shock Bowman because his heart has been closed to such possibilities. Later he lies sleepless by the fire, suddenly aware of how his preoccupation with work has limited his life. Money is the only thing he has to give this couple, and he leaves all he has under a lamp on the table. Feeling "ashamed" of his emotional poverty, he starts running toward his car:

> Just as he reached the road, where his car seemed to sit in the moonlight like a boat, his heart began to give off tremendous explosions like a rifle, bang bang bang.
> He sank in fright onto the road, his bags falling about him. He felt as if all this had happened before. He covered his heart with both hands to keep anyone from hearing the noise it made.
> But nobody heard it. (p. 253)

These are the last lines of the story. Though Eudora Welty was almost certainly unfamiliar with the Enneagram, her story vividly and touchingly portrays the predicament of a Self-Preservation Three. While trying to protect his heart, Bowman dies without ever having truly shared it with another person.

Social Threes, whom Ichazo associates with "prestige," seek social status and the trappings of success. Charming and at ease with others, Threes with this subtype look for external acknowledgment that they are moving up in the world and are accepted in the social circles they aspire to join.

Literary exemplars of this subtype include Tom Ripley, Jay Gatsby, Lavinia in T. S. Eliot's *The Cocktail Party*, Shakespeare's Lady Macbeth, and Julian Sorel in Stendhal's *The Red and the Black*.

The Red and the Black

Julien Sorel is an especially clear Social Three. He is an ambitious carpenter's son who makes his way in the world through hypocrisy and seduction and is eventually guillotined for shooting his mistress. Before he dies, however, he rejects his life-long pattern of deception and achieves a kind of emotional authenticity.

Early in the story Julien is determined to succeed, working hard to impress his benign elderly teacher and dreaming of having the success of his idol, Napoleon. But if a career as a priest will bring him more money, he is quite willing to adjust:

> Julien expressed only devout sentiments in Monsieur Chélan's presence. Who could have guessed that those girlish features, so pale and so gentle, concealed an implacable determination to expose himself to a thousand deaths rather than fail to make a fortune.
>
> For Julien, to make a fortune was first to leave Verrières; he loathed his native countryside. All that he saw there chilled his imagination.
>
> Since childhood he had been given to moments of exaltation. At such times he dreamed exultantly of how, one day, he would be presented to the beautiful women of Paris, and how he would contrive to attract their attention by some brilliant exploit. Why should he not be loved by them as Napoleon, while yet a poor man, had been loved by the radiant Madame de Beauharnais? For many years Julien had probably not let one hour of his life go by without reminding himself that Bonaparte, an obscure lieutenant with no fortune, had made himself master of the world with his sword. That idea consoled him for his misfortunes, which seemed great to him, and redoubled his joys when he had any. . . .
>
> "When Bonaparte made his name for himself, France was afraid of being invaded; military ability was vital and timely. Today one sees forty-year-old priests receiving a hundred thousand francs a year, three times the pay of Napoleon's famous generals. A priest is the thing to be." (p. 18)

Julien's father arranges for him to be a tutor in the house of Monsieur de Renal, and Julien soon becomes Madame de Renal's lover. Even while making love to her, however, he is playing a role, unable to honestly feel and express his emotions:

> Several hours later, when Julien left Madame de Renal's bedroom he had, to put it in the style of a novel, nothing further to desire. . . .
>
> But, even at the most gratifying moments, the victim of an eccentric pride, he still pretended to play the part of a man accustomed to subjugating women: he made incredible conscious efforts to destroy everything that was most likable in himself. Instead of being attentive to the passion he aroused and to the remorse that heightened its violence, he never ceased to see the word *duty* before his eyes. He dreaded a fearful regret and eternal

ridicule if he deviated from the ideal model he set up for himself to follow. In a word, it was precisely what made Julien a superior being that prevented him from enjoying the happiness that offered itself so freely to him. He was like the young girl of sixteen who has exquisite color and who, to go to a ball, is foolish enough to put on rouge. . . .

My God! to be happy, to be loved, is that all it is? was Julien's first thought upon returning to his own room. He was in that state of amazement and uneasy disquiet into which the soul falls when it has just obtained what it has long desired. It is accustomed to desiring, finds nothing further to desire, and has as yet no memories. Like the soldier who returns from parade, Julien was exclusively absorbed in going over all the details of his conduct. "Did I miss anything I owe to myself? Did I play my part well?"

And what part? That of a man accustomed to shining with women. (pp. 76-77)

After Julien's illicit relationship with Madame de Renal is exposed, he is forced to leave the household. He becomes secretary to the Marquis de la Mole and quickly becomes engaged to the wealthy Marquis's daughter. When Madame de Renal writes to the Marquis that Julien is a fortune hunter, however, the engagement is broken. Julien, despondent over the destruction of his ambitions, finds Madame de Renal praying in church and shoots her. Although he only wounds her slightly, he is put on trial and sentenced to death. Later, in prison, he realizes the depth of his love for Madame de Renal:

Upon being returned to the prison, Julien was placed in the cell reserved for those condemned to death. He, who ordinarily noticed even the most insignificant details, was not aware that he was not being taken back to his dungeon. He was thinking of what he would say to Madame de Renal if, before the last moment, it might be granted him to see her. He was thinking that she would interrupt him, and wanted to be able to express all his remorse in his first word. After such an action, how can I convince her that I love her alone? For after all it was either ambition or love of Mathilde that made me want to kill her.

Lying down on the bed, he noticed the coarse muslin sheets. His eyes came open. Ah, yes, I'm in the condemned cell, he thought. That's right. . . .

Julien went on. By the Lord, if I meet the Christians' God, I'm lost; He is a despot, and as such He is full of ideas of vengeance; His Bible speaks only of frightful punishments. I have never loved Him; I have never even been willing to believe that anyone could love Him sincerely. He is pitiless (and he recalled several passages from the Bible). He will punish me in an abominable manner. . . .

But if I meet Fénelon's God! He will say to me, perhaps: "Much will be forgiven you, because you have greatly loved. . . ."

Have I greatly loved? Oh, I loved Madame de Renal, but I've behaved atrociously. In that, as in other things, simple and modest worth was forsaken for what glittered. . . .

But then, what prospects! Colonel of Hussars, if we had a war; legation secretary during peace time; later on, ambassador—for I should soon have mastered the art—and even if I had never been anything but a fool, has the Marquis de la Mole's son-in-law any rivalry to fear? All my blunders would have been excused, or rather counted as merits. A man of merit, reveling in the most splendid existence in Vienna or in London. . . .

"Not precisely, Monsieur. Guillotined in three days." (pp. 313-314)

Despite his genuine spiritual unfolding, Julien ultimately falls back into his fantasy of realizing his ambitions. We see him quickly alternate between the unhealthy Three fantasy of the prestige he might have achieved and the honest acknowledgement of what is actually in store for him (his Six security point). His Threeish struggle for authenticity continues right to the end.

Macbeth

Shakespeare's Lady Macbeth is another vivid Social Three. Here we see her ruthlessly plotting to murder Duncan, the King of Scotland, in order to advance her and her husband's social standing:

The raven himself is hoarse
That croaks the fatal entrance of Duncan
Under my battlements. Come, you spirits
That tend on mortal thoughts, unsex me here,
And fill me from the crown to the toe top-full
Of direst cruelty! Make thick my blood;
Stop up the access and passage to remorse,
That no compunctious visitings of nature
Shake my fell purpose, nor keep peace between
The effect and it! Come to my woman's breasts,
And take my milk for gall, you murdering ministers,
Wherever in your sightless substances
You wait on nature's mischief! Come, thick night,
And pall thee in the dunnest smoke of hell,
That my keen knife see not the wound it makes,
Nor heaven peep through the blanket of the dark,
To cry 'Hold, hold!' (I, v, 39-55)

Lady Macbeth persuades her husband to murder Duncan. But when Macbeth, a Nine, loses his nerve she goads him on with taunts about his lack of manliness. Her ambition and determination are characteristic of the Social subtype, and in the following speech we see her playing the role of a pathological success coach:

> LADY MACBETH: Was the hope drunk
> Wherein you dress'd yourself? Hath it slept since?
> And wakes it now, to look so green and pale
> At what it did so freely? From this time
> Such I account thy love. Art thou afeard
> To be the same in thine own act and valor
> As thou art in desire? Wouldst thou have that
> Which thou esteem'st the ornament of life,
> And live a coward in thine own esteem
> Letting 'I dare not' wait upon 'I would,'
> Like the poor cat i' the adage?
> MACBETH: Prithee, peace:
> I dare do all that may become a man;
> Who dares do more is none.
> LADY MACBETH: What beast was't, then,
> That made you break this enterprise to me?
> When you durst do it, then you were a man. . . .
> I have given suck, and know
> How tender 'tis to love the babe that milks me:
> I would, while it was smiling in my face,
> Have pluck'd my nipple from his boneless gums,
> And dash'd the brains out, had I so sworn as you
> Have done to this.
> MACBETH: If we should fail?
> LADY MACBETH: We fail!
> But screw your courage to the sticking-place
> And we'll not fail. (I, vii, 36-62)

After the murder, when Macbeth returns to their chamber still holding the murder weapons, two bloody daggers, Lady Macbeth sends him back to plant the knives near the King's attendants, so they will be suspected of the murder:

> MACBETH: I'll go no more:
> I am afraid to think what I have done;
> Look on't again I dare not.
> LADY MACBETH: Infirm of purpose!
> Give me the daggers: the sleeping and the dead
> Are but as pictures: 'tis the eye of childhood
> That fears a painted devil. If he do bleed,

I'll gild the faces of the grooms withal;
For it must seem their guilt. (II, iii, 50-57)

Toward the end of the play, after Macbeth has become King, Lady Macbeth becomes mysteriously ill. At one point she is walking in her sleep, trying to rub away blood she sees on her hands, reliving the night when she urged her husband to murder:

LADY MACBETH: Out, damned spot! Out I say!—One: two: why, then, 'tis time to do't.—Hell is murky!—Fie, my lord, fie! A soldier, and afeard? What need we fear who knows it, when none can call our power to account?—Yet who would have thought the old man to have had so much blood in him. . . . Here's the smell of the blood still: all the perfumes of Arabia will not sweeten this little hand. Oh, oh, oh! (V, i, 39-59)

In Enneagram terms, this is a Three moving into the fragmentation of her Nine stress point. For all her earlier self-appraisal as confident and ruthless in pursuit of social prestige, remnants of Lady Macbeth's feelings have survived. Shakespeare makes it clear that her guilt and horror are the essential causes of her illness and death.

Sexual Threes, whom Ichazo associates with "virility/femininity," want above all to be desired by others. Their self-images hinge on being sexually attractive and they work at maintaining their physical appearance. Sexual Threes are generally not interested in real intimacy, and may be promiscuous as they try to reassure themselves of their desirability. They think of themselves as sexual "stars" and, even in intimate encounters, may stand outside themselves, watching and admiring their own prowess.

Literary examples include: Scarlett O'Hara, Sukie Rougement in John Updike's *The Witches of Eastwick*, Rosamond Yancy in George Eliot's *Middlemarch*, Rachel in Barbara Kingsolver's *The Poisonwood Bible*, Myra in Jim Thompson's *The Grifters*, and Dr. Raleigh Sanderson in Alice Adams's *Medicine Men*.

Medicine Men

Dr. Raleigh "Sandy" Sanderson is a Sexual Three with a Two wing. In the following passage we see a comic juxtaposition between his preoccupation with his sexual prowess and his sense that using coarse language to describe sexual activity detracts from his self-image:

Since he had always laid nurses, Dr. Raleigh Sanderson felt that laying nurses did not count; it did not constitute infidelity to Felicia, his official (and unofficial) lady. And "lay" is the word that he would have used for his encounters with nurses. "Fuck" in his mind was a dirty word;

making love was what he and Felicia did—although sometimes they fucked, dirtily, on a sweaty afternoon. What Raleigh used to do with Connie, his wife, he thought of as simply that, as "doing it." But he laid nurses; Sandy did not think of himself as "getting laid," even though more often than not these days it was he who lay down, allowing the bouncy nurse to bring him to climax with her hands or her mouth, or both. He much disliked the vulgar, graphic expressions for these activities. Even "oral sex" was too explicit for Sandy.

Like so many people, Sandy was convinced that his sexual drives were exceptionally strong. As proof of such strength, he cited (to himself; he was not given to even semi-public boasting) the extreme and compelling arousal that he often experienced at the end of a successful operation, and almost all his operations were successful; his record was world-renowned. His skill was indeed quite fantastic; sometimes Sandy himself was amazed at what went on beneath his hands, the incredible speed and precision with which his fingers moved, all racing toward the instant at which he knew: This heart is all right now, I've repaired (or replaced) the valve, I've saved it. Of course he could not know absolutely for days or weeks, even months, that the heart was really functioning on its own. Still, there was always the moment when, within his own heart, he *knew*, and he lived for that moment, that peak. Further recovery on the part of the patient was anticlimactic, and basically uninteresting to Sandy. It was boring to have to keep seeing those patients again and again, listening to their parade of minor symptoms, their major gratitude. But the operations themselves—they thrilled him still. No other word for it, he was thrilled. It was thrilling work that he did.

Small wonder, then, that after such an exciting, deeply felt triumph he should feel himself excited in a sexual way, as well as in his own heart.

Not surprisingly, Sandy thought considerably about that organ, that marvelous muscle: his personal heart. He admired its strength, and its clear superiority to those lesser hearts that he operated on, and fixed: hearts enlarged or those with leaking valves, those damaged by early rheumatic fever, or simply born bad, defective. As his heart was born strong and good. A superior heart.

And he had kept in shape. Played racquetball and tennis at his club, swam at Tahoe in the summer and worked out on an exercise bike almost every day. Made love to lively Felicia a lot, in recent years, and sometimes laid nurses.

No wonder that even his hair was still so enviably thick and lively. He wondered about those guys, like Dave Jacobs, who went bald. (pp. 16-17)

Author Adams devises an appropriate comeuppance for this monster of sexual vanity: he develops prostate problems. Running scared, he tries to bully

Felicia, but she responds by ending the relationship. His sexual self-image now further threatened, he considers murdering her:

> Going down in the elevator, for some reason he found himself thinking intensively about O.J. Simpson. He got off, is what Sandy was thinking. And Nicole did not get by with sleeping around—blonde spoiled bitch. But then he had to remind himself of several obvious facts: One was that O.J. had much more money than he did, although luckily he himself was not exactly poor. Not without resources. But O.J. was black, with a wild black lawyer, lots of lawyers, and a bunch of blacks on his jury. Suppose he, Sandy, had a jury full of doctors—straight, non-Jewish doctors? They'd hang him, they'd love to. He knew that. (p. 217)

Sandy does try to kill Felicia, but she and her new lover thwart him by setting a trap in her garden, where he breaks his ankle. In the end, his prostate problems threaten to end not only his sexual adventures but his life—an ironic punishment for his vanity, deceit, and heartlessness.

Middlemarch

Rosamond Yancy in George Eliot's *Middlemarch* is another Sexual Three. An important subplot in this classic novel set in the 1830s involves the courtship and marriage between Rosamond, the beautiful but spoiled daughter of a local merchant, and Lydgate, an aristocratic and idealistic but impoverished young doctor.

When Lydgate, a Seven, first meets Rosamond, he admires not only her beauty but her musical gifts, and she is canny enough to parlay his interest into a formal courtship. She is aware of her image and her effect on men in a way that brings to mind Scarlett O'Hara:

> Poor Lydgate! Or shall I say, Poor Rosamond! Each lived in a world of which the other knew nothing. It had not occurred to Lydgate that he had been a subject of eager meditation to Rosamond, who had neither any reason for throwing her marriage into distant perspective, nor any pathological studies to divert her mind from that ruminating habit, that inward repetition of looks, words, and phrases, which makes a large part of the lives of most girls. He had not meant to look at her or speak to her with more than the inevitable amount of admiration and compliment which a man must give to a beautiful girl; indeed, it seemed to him that his enjoyment of her music had remained almost silent, for he feared falling into the rudeness of telling her his great surprise at her possession of such accomplishment. But Rosamond had registered every look and word, and estimated them as the opening incidents of a preconceived romance—incidents which gather value from the foreseen development and climax. In Rosamond's romance it was not necessary to imagine much about the

inward life of the hero, or of his serious business in the world: of course, he had a profession and was clever, as well as sufficiently handsome; but the piquant fact about Lydgate was his good birth, which distinguished him from all Middlemarch admirers, and presented marriage as a prospect of rising in rank and getting a little nearer to that celestial condition on earth in which she would have nothing to do with vulgar people. . . . It was part of Rosamond's cleverness to discern very subtly the faintest aroma of rank, and once when she had seen the Miss Brookes accompanying their uncle at the county assizes, and seated among the aristocracy, she had envied them, notwithstanding their plain dress. (pp. 156-157)

Preoccupied with making men fall in love with her, Rosamond focuses on creating the perfect image to ensnare Lydgate. Notice how hard she works to bait this sexual trap:

Rosamond, in fact, was entirely occupied not exactly with Tertius Lydgate as he was in himself, but with his relation to her; and it was excusable in a girl who was accustomed to hear that all young men might, could, would be, or actually were in love with her, to believe at once that Lydgate could be no exception. His looks and words meant more to her than other men's, because she cared more for them: she thought of them diligently, and diligently attended to that perfection of appearance, behaviour, sentiments, and all other elegancies, which would find in Lydgate a more adequate admirer than she had yet been conscious of.

For Rosamond, though she would never do anything that was disagreeable to her, was industrious; and now more than ever she was active in sketching her landscapes and market-carts and portraits of friends, in practising her music, and in being from morning till night her own standard of a perfect lady, having always an audience in her own consciousness, with sometimes the not unwelcome addition of a more variable external audience in the numerous visitors of the house. (pp. 157-158)

Once Lydgate and Rosamond are married, he discovers that she has no intention of deferring to his wishes or decisions, but goes her own way. Sexual Threes, for all their allure, often have little capacity for real intimacy:

There was gathering within him an amazed sense of his powerlessness over Rosamond. His superior knowledge and mental force, instead of being, as he had imagined, a shrine to consult on all occasions, was simply set aside on every practical question. He had regarded Rosamond's cleverness as precisely of the receptive kind which became a woman. He was now beginning to find out what that cleverness was—what was the shape into which it had run as into a close network aloof and independent.

No one quicker than Rosamond to see causes and effects which lay within the track of her own tastes and interests: she had seen clearly Lydgate's pre-eminence in Middlemarch society, and could go on imaginatively tracing still more agreeable social effects when his talent should have advanced him; but for her, his professional and scientific ambition had no other relation to these desirable effects than if they had been the fortunate discovery of an ill-smelling oil. (p. 557)

When Lydgate discovers that Rosamond has secretly written to his uncle asking for money on Lydgate's behalf, he is furious with her:

"... You have always been counteracting me secretly. You delude me with a false assent, and then I am at the mercy of your devices. If you mean to resist every wish I express, say so and defy me. I shall at least know what I am doing then."

It is a terrible moment in young lives when the closeness of love's bond has turned to this power of galling. In spite of Rosamond's self-control a tear fell silently and rolled over her lips. She still said nothing; but under that quietude was hidden an intense effect: she was in such entire disgust with her husband that she wished that she had never seen him. Sir Godwin's rudeness towards her and utter want of feeling ranged him with Dover and all other creditors—disagreeable people who only thought of themselves, and did not mind how annoying they were to her. Even her father was unkind, and might have done more for them. In fact there was but one person in Rosamond's world whom she did not regard as blameworthy, and that was the graceful creature with blond plaits and with little hands crossed before her, who had never expressed herself unbecomingly, and had always acted for the best—the best naturally being what she best liked. (p. 633)

All Rosamond can think of is her own self-justification and comfort. This is the same willful quality we saw in Scarlett O'Hara.

As she continues her tactics and Lydgate fulminates against them, the bad feelings between them escalate. Now Rosamond begins to think of other men who might treat her better and the sexual competitiveness and hunger for flattery of her subtype emerge more clearly:

The hard and contemptuous words which had fallen from her husband in his anger had deeply offended that vanity which he had at first called into active enjoyment; and what she regarded as his perverse way of looking at things, kept up a secret repulsion, which made her receive all his tenderness as a poor substitute for the happiness he had failed to give her. They were at a disadvantage with their neighbours, and there was no longer any outlook towards Quallingham—there was no outlook anywhere except in an occasional letter from Will Ladislaw. She had felt stung and disappointed by Will's resolution to quit Middlemarch, for in spite of what she knew and guessed about his admiration for Dorothea, she secretly cherished the belief that he had, or would necessarily come to have, much more admiration for herself; Rosamond being one of those women who live much in the idea that each man they meet would have preferred them if the preference had not been hopeless. Mrs. Causabon was all very well; but Will's interest in her dated before he knew Mrs. Lydgate. Rosamond took his way of talking to herself, which was a mixture of playful fault-finding and hyperbolical gallantry, as the disguise of a deeper feeling; and in his presence she felt that agreeable titillation of vanity and sense of romantic drama which Lydgate's presence had no longer the magic to create. She even fancied—what will not men and women fancy in these matters?—that Will exaggerated his admiration for Mrs. Casaubon in order to pique herself. In this way poor Rosamond's brain had been busy before Will's departure. He would have made, she thought, a much more suitable husband for her than she had found in Lydgate. No notion could have been falser than this, for Rosamond's discontent in her marriage was due to the conditions of marriage itself, to its demand for self-suppression and tolerance, and not to the nature of her husband; but the easy conception of an unreal Better had a sentimental charm which diverted her ennui. She constructed a little romance which was to vary the flatness of her life: Will Ladislaw was always to be a bachelor and live near her, always to be at her command, and have an understood though never fully expressed passion for her, which would be sending out lambent flames every now and then in interesting scenes. (pp. 716-717)

Throughout *Middlemarch*, Rosamond remains an average Sexual Three: preoccupied with presenting herself in an alluring light while failing to understand the give and take required for a workable marriage. For all her narcissism and posturing, however, Rosamond turns out in the end to have more generosity of spirit than the reader expects of her.

In great literary works characters of all Enneagram styles have the capacity to surprise us with unexpected virtues as well as unexpected vices. Perhaps because America is so devoted to Three values, American writers tend to be especially critical of this temperament. But multi-dimensional Three characters like Scarlett O'Hara, Gatsby, Willy Loman, Bowman, and Julien Sorel help us sympathize with this style's struggle for authenticity—and the way all of us, whatever our Enneagram style, share the need to become our best selves.

Sources

Adams, Alice, *Medicine Men* (New York: Alfred A. Knopf, 1997)
Alger, Horatio, *Struggling Upward* (Philadelphia: Porter & Coates, 1890)
Eliot, George, *Middlemarch* (New York: Barnes & Noble, Inc., 1996). First published 1871
Fitzgerald, F. Scott, *The Great Gatsby* (New York: Charles Scribner's Sons, 1925)
Highsmith, Patricia, *The Talented Mr. Ripley* (New York: Vintage, 1992). First published 1955
Miller, Arthur, *Death of a Salesman* (New York: Viking Press, 1949)
Mitchell, Margaret, *Gone with the Wind* (New York: Macmillan, 1936)
Shakespeare, William, *Macbeth*. First produced 1606
Stendhal, *The Red and the Black*, trans. Joan Charles (New York: Literary Guild of America, 1949). First published 1831
Welty, Eudora, "Death of a Traveling Salesman," in *Selected Stories of Eudora Welty* (New York: The Modern Library, 1936)

Four: The Aesthete

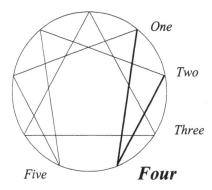

One

Two

Three

Five   **Four**

Many qualities of Enneagram Fours are evident in the narrator of Marcel Proust's six-volume novel *Remembrance of Things Past*. In *Swann's Way*, the first volume, the narrator describes his childhood in a melancholy tone, with a sense of nostalgia for what he has lost. Like many Fours, he finds his identity through his memories:

> I lost all sense of the place in which I had gone to sleep, and when I awoke at midnight, not knowing where I was, I could not be sure at first who I was; I had only the most rudimentary sense of existence, such as may lurk and flicker in the depths of an animal's consciousness; I was more destitute of human qualities than the cave-dweller; but then the memory, not yet of the place in which I was, but of various other places where I had lived, and might now very possibly be, would come like a rope let down from heaven to draw me up out of the abyss of non-being, from which I could never have escaped by myself: in a flash I would traverse and surmount centuries of civilisation, and out of a half-visualized succession of oil-lamps, followed by shirts with turned-down collars, would put together by degrees the component parts of my ego. (pp. 7-8)

The narrator's ego is fluid and he relies on memory to continually shore up his self-image and anchor himself to the world. The loss or insufficiency of love is also a preoccupation with Fours, as we see in the narrator's recollections of his childhood bed-time rituals:

My sole consolation when I went upstairs for the night was that Mamma would come in and kiss me after I was in bed. But this good night lasted for so short a time: she went down again so soon that the moment in which I heard her climb the stairs, and then caught the sound of her garden dress of blue muslin, from which hung little tassels of plaited straw, rustling along the double-doored corridor, was for me a moment of the keenest sorrow. So much did I love that good night that I reached the stage of hoping that it would come as late as possible, so as to prolong the time of respite during which Mamma would not yet have appeared. Sometimes when, after kissing me, she opened the door to go, I longed to call her back, to say to her "Kiss me just once again," but I knew that then she would at once look displeased, for the concession which she made to my wretchedness and agitation in coming up to me with this kiss of peace always annoyed my father, who thought such ceremonies absurd, and she would have liked to try to induce me to outgrow the need, the custom of having her there at all, which was a very different thing from letting the custom grow up of my asking her for an additional kiss when she was already crossing the threshold. And to see her look displeased destroyed all the sense of tranquility she had brought me a moment before. (p. 17)

Four is part of the triad associated with the heart and feelings. While Twos focus on the needs of others and try to earn love through helpful service, Threes avoid their feelings in order to better focus on their work, so that others will admire their achievements. Fours, by contrast, examine their feelings in detail, hoping that they will establish the Four's authenticity, which will then make the Four lovable. One element of their authenticity or "specialness," as Fours see it, is a capacity for deep feeling and an intense longing for love. Yet this very intensity often causes others to recoil from the Four's neediness.

Proust's narrator remembers being sent to bed early during his parents' dinner party and sending a letter to his mother via a servant, hoping that it would bring her upstairs to play out their usual bedtime ritual. Remembering the pain he felt when the ploy failed, the narrator compares his childhood agony over his mother's rejection with the pain of Swann, his parents' dinner guest, over his love for a woman named Odette:

As for the agony through which I had just passed, I imagined that Swann would have laughed heartily at it if he had read my letter and had guessed its purpose; whereas, on the contrary, as I was to learn in due course, a similar anguish had been the bane of his life for many years, and no one perhaps could have understood my feelings at that moment so well as himself; to him, that anguish which lies in knowing that the creature one adores is in some place of enjoyment where oneself is not and cannot follow—to him that anguish came through Love, to which it is in a sense predestined, by which it must be equipped and adapted; but when, as had befallen me, such an anguish possesses one's soul before Love has yet entered into one's life, then it must drift, awaiting Love's coming, vague and free, without precise attachment, at the disposal of one sentiment today, of another tomorrow, of filial piety or affection for a comrade. (pp. 41-42)

The Four's readiness to suffer from love is striking. Even as a boy, the narrator seems to be rehearsing for a future adult drama of love, loss, and suffering. Catching sight of Swann's daughter, Gilberte, he immediately begins constructing fantasies around her, imagining himself in love with her:

I realised both the rare worth of a creature such as Mlle. Swann, and, at the same time, how coarse and ignorant I should appear to her; and I felt so keenly how pleasant and yet how impossible it would be for me to become her friend that I was filled at once with longing and with despair. And usually, from this time forth, when I thought of her, I would see her standing before the porch of a cathedral, explaining to me what each of the statues meant, and, with a smile which was my highest commendation, presenting me, as her friend, to Bergotte. And invariably the charm of all the fancies which the thought of cathedrals used to inspire in me, the charm of the hills and valleys of the Ile-de-France and of the plains of Normandy, would radiate brightness and beauty over the picture I had formed in my mind of Mlle. Swann; nothing more remained but to know and to love her. (pp. 140-141)

Here is a Four creating his own sense of inadequacy by anticipating that his love for an idealized person will be unrequited.

As the story continues, it also becomes clear that the narrator doubts his gifts as a writer:

Perhaps this want of talent, this black cavity which gaped in my mind when I ransacked it for the theme of my future writings, was itself no more, either, than an unsubstantial illusion, and would be brought to an end by the intervention of my father, who would arrange with the Government and with Providence that I should be the first writer of my day. But at other times, while my parents were growing impatient at seeing me loiter behind instead of following them, my actual life, instead of seeming an artificial creation by my father, and one which he could modify as he chose, appeared, on the contrary, to be comprised in a larger reality which had not been created for my benefit, from whose judgments there was no appeal, in the heart of which I was bound, helpless, without friend or ally, and beyond which no further possibilities lay concealed. It was evident to me then that I existed in the same manner as all other men, that I must grow old, that I must die like them, and that among them I was to be distinguished merely as one of those who have no aptitude for writing. And so, utterly despondent, I renounced literature for ever, despite the encouragements that had been given me by Bloch. This intimate, spontaneous feeling, this sense of the nullity of my intellect, prevailed against all the flattering speeches that might be lavished upon me, as a wicked man, when everyone is loud in the praise of his good deeds, is gnawed by the secret remorse of conscience. (pp. 248-249)

A familiar theme of Fours is their continual hope of rescue—in this case by the narrator's father. Fours also have trouble facing their own ordinariness. The narrator is ready to give up his aspirations to write, without really trying, suggesting a self-defeating quality that is also characteristic of many less-than-healthy Fours.

While the narrator feels continually insecure, he compensates with an abiding sense of his own specialness and fantasizes that others will recognize it. Here he sees the aristocratic Mme. De Guermantes in church and imagines that she has looked on him with understanding and appreciation. Note how he sets himself up to be disappointed—another pattern of Fours. While this increases his suffering, he also enjoys it:

And I, remembering the glance which she had let fall upon me during the service, blue as a ray of sunlight that had penetrated the window of Gilbert the Bad, said to myself "Of course, she is thinking about me." I fancied that I had found favour in her sight, that she would continue to think of me after she had left the church, and would, perhaps, grow pensive again, that evening, at Guermantes, on my account. And at once I fell in love with her, for if it is sometimes enough to make us love a woman that she looks on us with contempt, as I supposed Mlle. Swann to have done, while we imagine that she cannot ever be ours, it is enough, also, sometimes that she looks on us kindly, as Mme. De Guermantes did then, while we think of her as almost ours already. Her eyes waxed blue as a periwinkle flower, wholly beyond my reach, yet dedicated by her to me; and the sun, bursting out again from behind a threatening cloud and darting full force of its rays on to the Square and into the sacristy, shed a geranium glow over the red carpet laid down for the wedding, along which Mme. De Guermantes smilingly advanced, and covered its woolen texture with a nap of rosy velvet, a bloom of light, giving it that sort of tenderness, of solemn sweetness in the pomp of a joyful celebration, which characterise certain pages of Lohengrin, certain paintings by Carpaccio, and make us understand how Baudelaire was able to apply to the sound of the trumpet the epithet 'delicious.' (p. 255)

For all their readiness to suffer—especially for Love—Fours can take passionate delight in the beauty of the world.

The Four's History

As children, Fours often feel disconnected from both of their parents. As they compensate for the resulting sense of emotional deprivation, they struggle to find an appropriate balance for their feelings. Fours are especially prone to envy—the feeling that they lack what others possess.

Fours often lack parental role models for equanimity—the Four virtue—and have difficulty controlling their passions. Aware from their earliest years of wanting what they could not have—their parents' unconditional love—Fours eventually find comfort in a familiar feeling of longing. They continually hark back to moments when they were happy to reassure themselves that they can survive in the present. But the very expectation that pain and loss are love's inevitable outcome creates a self-fulfilling prophecy that colors—and sometimes dooms—relationships throughout their lives.

The Four defense mechanism is *introjection*, the tendency to create an idealized internal picture of another person and turn him or her into an object of love. Since real people rarely live up to ideal images, an introjecting Four may have trouble relating to whomever they see this way, even if that person loves the Four in reality. In fact, the Four may create a physical or psychological distance, so that the real person will go away and the Four can return to the safety of loving his ideal. When Proust's narrator is finally invited to play with Gilberte, the object of his adoration, he is confounded by the prospect of seeing his fantasies fulfilled:

> She was in fact summoning me to cross the snowy lawn to her camp, to 'take the field,' which the sun, by casting over it a rosy gleam, the metallic lustre of old and worn brocades, had turned into a Field of the Cloth of Gold.
>
> This day, which I had begun with so many misgivings, was, as it happened, one of the few on which I was not unduly wretched.
>
> For, although I no longer thought, now, of anything save not to let a single day pass without seeing Gilberte . . . yet those moments which I spent in her company, for which I had waited with so much impatience all night and morning, for which I had quivered with excitement, to which I would have sacrificed everything else in the world, were by no means happy moments; well did I know it, for they were only moments in my life on which I concentrated a scrupulous, undistracted attention, and yet I could not discover in them one atom of pleasure. All the time I was away from Gilberte, I wanted to see her, because, having incessantly sought to form a mental picture of her, I was unable, in the end, to do so, and did not know exactly to what my love corresponded. (pp. 572-573)

Note the difficulty this Four has when forced to align his introjected picture with what is actually happening. A situation that promises to fulfill his dreams instead makes him acutely unhappy, a more familiar feeling. Many Fours are uncomfortable with happiness, especially the mundane ordinary kind.

Anna Karenina

The tragic heroine of Leo Tolstoy's *Anna Karenina* is another classic Four. Vivacious, beautiful, concerned for others, Anna seems healthy when we first meet her. In the following passage we see her through the appreciative eyes of Kitty, a Two:

> Anna was not at all like a society woman, or like the mother of an eight-year-old son, but would rather have resembled a twenty-year-old girl in the suppleness of her movements, her freshness, and the vivacity that played about her face and kept breaking through in a smile or a look, if it had not been for the grave and occasionally sad expression in her eyes, which struck Kitty and attracted her. Kitty felt that Anna was completely simple and hid nothing, but that she had within her another, higher world of interests, complex and poetical, that were beyond Kitty's reach. (p. 75)

Early in the story we learn that Anna has come to Moscow to mediate a quarrel between her brother and his wife, Dolly, and that her mission has been successful. At a ball, Count Vronsky—whom Dolly's sister, Kitty, expects to marry—becomes fascinated with Anna. Aware of Kitty's disappointment and insecure about her own attraction to the dashing Count, Anna decides to take an early train home and end the awkward situation. But Vronsky, a Seven, takes the same train, and when they meet he tells Anna he is there because of her. Although she begs him to forget their meeting, she is secretly thrilled:

> Without remembering either her own words or his, she understood instinctively that this momentary conversation had brought them terribly close together; she was frightened by this and gladdened. She stood still for a few seconds, went into the carriage and sat down. The state of tension that had tormented her at first was not only renewed but heightened to a point where she was afraid that something in her that was stretched too far would break any minute. She did not sleep all night. But there was nothing gloomy or disagreeable in this tension, or in the visions which filled her imagination; on the contrary, they had something joyful, glowing, and exciting. (p. 109)

Anna's intense response to Vronsky is characteristic of her Enneagram style. Immediately she imagines exciting romantic scenarios. But once the two become lovers, Anna is ashamed of betraying her husband. Her hysterical reaction shocks Vronsky:

> "Anna, Anna!" he said in a trembling voice. "Anna—for God's sake!"
>
> But the louder he spoke the lower drooped her once proud and gay, but now shame-stricken head; writhing she slipped off the sofa and was sitting on the floor, at his feet; she would have fallen on the carpet if he had not held her.
>
> "My God! Forgive me!" she said sobbing, pressing his hand to her breast.
>
> She felt so sinful, so guilty, that the only thing left for her to do was to humble herself and beg to be forgiven; now she had no one in her life but him, so she addressed her plea for forgiveness to him too. As she looked at him she felt her own humiliation physically, and could say nothing further. . . . The shame she felt at her own spiritual nakedness crushed her, and communicated itself to him. . . .
>
> "Everything is finished," she said. "I have nothing but you now. Remember that." (pp. 156-157)

Anna is capable of destroying her newfound happiness with her own excessive emotion, a pattern that arises out of an average Four's extreme neediness.

Her Fourish gift for suffering is even more evident when she becomes pregnant by Vronsky. He tries to persuade her to leave her husband, but she fears losing her son. In prerevolutionary Russia only the innocent party could obtain a divorce, and then with difficulty. The guilty party could not remarry, and lost custody of any children. Anna begs Vronsky not to speak to her of this possibility again:

> "I know"—she interrupted him—"how painful it is for your truthful nature to lie, and I pity you. I often think of how you've ruined your life for my sake."
>
> "I was thinking the same thing just now," he said, "how you could sacrifice because of me. I can't forgive myself for your being unhappy."
>
> "Unhappy—I?" she said, coming close and looking at him with a rapturous smile of love, "I—am like someone starving who's been given something to eat. It may be that he's still cold, and his clothes are torn, and he's ashamed of himself, but he's not unhappy. I unhappy? No—this is my happiness—" (p. 201)

Anna is now in her neurotic element: a situation where every possible choice brings suffering can be a comfortable resting place for the Four. In a sense, many Fours are unable to accept love except in a context of suffering, since the pain serves to intensify and authenticate their passion.

After Anna nearly dies giving birth to Vronsky's daughter, her husband tries to reconcile with her. Although she admires Karenin's goodness and is still ashamed of her own behavior, she is too mired in her suffering to accept his overture:

> My making him unhappy was inevitable, she thought, but I don't want to profit by this unhappiness; I'm suffering too and shall go on suffering: I've deprived myself of what I treasured most—my good name and my son. What I did was wrong and because of that I don't wish for happiness, I don't want a divorce and I shall go on suffering from shame and from the loss of my son. (p. 495)

She begins to see no alternative to the divorce, even though she knows it means permanent separation from her son. Meanwhile, her relationship with Vronsky goes from bad to worse, mostly because of her obsessive and unfounded jealousy. Having disintegrated to an unhealthy level, her self-destructiveness becomes increasingly prominent:

> The irritation that divided them had no external cause, and every attempt to clear things up not only failed to eliminate it, but increased it. It was an inner irritation, which for her was due to the diminishing of his love, and for him to a regret that for her sake he had put himself in a distressing situation that she, instead of alleviating, was making even more distressing. Neither one ever mentioned the cause of their irritation but each thought the other in the wrong and attempted to prove it to the other at every opportunity.
> For her he—all of him, with all his habits, thoughts, and desires, his whole spiritual and physical temperament—was just one thing: love for women, and this love, which she felt ought to be concentrated altogether on her alone, was diminishing. Consequently, to her mind, he must have transferred a part of this love to other women, or some other woman. She grew jealous: she was not jealous of any particular woman, but of the diminution of his love. Since she had no object for her jealousy she looked for one. At the slightest hint she would transfer her jealousy from one object to another. . . .
> And since she was jealous Anna kept losing her temper with him; she seized on everything to justify her indignation. She blamed him for all the hardships of her situation. The painful state of anticipation she had to undergo in Moscow, suspended in midair; Karenin's dilatory indecisiveness; her own solitude—she attributed everything to him: if he loved her he would understand the full hardship of her situation and get her out of it. It was he who was to blame for her living in Moscow and not in the country. (pp. 785-786)

Anna becomes obsessed with relocating to the country, convinced the move will restore the loving relationship she and Vronsky originally had. Vronsky agrees to go with her but says he must postpone the trip a few days because of business. Anna gives him an ultimatum: they must leave by Monday or not at all. Although she is aware of her self-destructiveness, she is unable to keep herself from continually needling him. Exasperated, he finally demands to know what she wants of him and she replies:

"What can I want? I can only want you not to leave me, as you are thinking of doing," she said, understanding everything he had left unsaid. "But I don't want that—that's secondary. What I want is love, and there is none. Therefore everything is finished!"

She started toward the door.

"Wait! W-a-i-t!" said Vronsky, not changing the morose set of his brows, but holding her back by the hand. "What is the matter? I said we had to put off leaving for three days, and on that you said to me I was lying, that I'm dishonorable."

"Yes, I repeat, that a man who reproaches me by saying he has sacrificed everything for my sake," she said, remembering the words used in a still earlier quarrel, "is worse than dishonorable—he is heartless!"

"No—there are limits to endurance!" he cried, and abruptly let go her hand.

He hates me, that's clear, she thought, and without looking round, in silence, her steps uncertain, she left the room.

He loves some other woman, that's even clearer, she said to herself, as she went into her own room. I want love, and there is none. Therefore everything is finished, she said, repeating her own words, and it must be finished.

But how? she asked herself, and sat down in the armchair before the mirror.

. . . She had some obscure thought in her mind; it was the only thing that interested her but she could not quite get hold of it. When she recalled Karenin again, she also recalled the time she had been ill after the birth of the child, and the feeling that at that time would not leave her: Why didn't I die? She recalled her words at the time, and the feeling she had had. Suddenly she realized what was in her heart. Yes—that was the thought that was the only thing that could solve everything.

Yes—die! she thought. Both Karenin's shame and his disgrace, and Seryozha's, and my own dreadful shame—everything will be saved by my death. Die—then he'll feel sorry, he'll love me, and suffer for me.

With a fixed smile of self-pity she sat down in the arm-chair, taking off and putting on the rings on her left hand, and vividly imagining to herself from all angles his feelings after her death. (pp. 790-791)

Anna's sense that her death is the answer is a solution that unhealthy Fours leap to easily. Death is a kind of ultimate bargaining chip to gain her lover's devotion.

Arriving at the train station, Anna sends her coachman to buy her a ticket. Vronsky's coachman appears with a note from him reassuring her that he loves her and will join her as soon as he can. But it is too late to reverse course. Bent on taking revenge against her lover, Anna throws herself under a train.

At their unhealthy extreme Fours are more likely than most Enneagram styles to attempt suicide, usually to punish others for not loving the Four sufficiently.

Levels of Health

Even when they are not professional artists, average Fours see themselves as artistic and romantic, people passionately absorbed with creating beauty in their lives. They use their imaginations to heighten their already intense feelings, and sometimes feel overwhelmed by their own emotionality. Although their inner life is intense, they can seem withdrawn and self-absorbed. In relationships they are hypersensitive, emotionally vulnerable, and quick to feel victimized. Average Fours see themselves as "special" and can be disdainful of lesser mortals, yet their willfulness and lack of practicality often make them ineffective.

Literature offers us many examples of average Fours. Among them are: Anna Karenina, Swann in Proust's *Swann's Way*, Heathcliff in Emily Brontë's *Wuthering Heights*, the title character in Gustave Flaubert's *Madame Bovary*, Marianne in Jane Austen's *Sense and Sensibility*, Werther in Goethe's *The Sorrows of Young Werther*, Quentin in William Faulkner's *The Sound and the Fury*, Orsino and Olivia in Shakespeare's *Twelfth Night*, Shakespeare's Richard II, Laura in Tennessee Williams's *The Glass Menagerie*, Mrs. Penniman in Henry James's *Washington Square*, Pushkin's Eugene Onegin, the title character in John Fowles's *The French Lieutenant's Woman*, Gustave Aschenbach in Thomas Mann's *Death in Venice*, and the title character in Anton Chekov's *Ivanov*.

Healthy Fours, like Proust's narrator in *Swann's Way*, use their sensitivity and imagination to express themselves in art. They often transmute their personal suffering into gifts that they offer the world. Other healthy Fours apply their acute self-awareness to exploring their inner workings and expressing their individuality; they live authentic, emotionally honest lives and have a distinctive personal style. Although their primary focus is internal and they enjoy solitude, healthy Fours are generally compassionate and respectful toward others.

Healthy Fours include Thea Kronborg in Willa Cather's *The Song of the Lark*, Alexandre Dumas's Camille, David Hare's Esme in *Amy's View*, Antonio in Shakespeare's *The Merchant of Venice*, Adam Dalgleish in P.D. James's *Devices and Desires,* and the title character in Edmund Rostand's *Cyrano de Bergerac.*

Unhealthy Fours can be deeply depressed, overwhelmed with personal shame, and bitterly angry with themselves and others. Unable to function, they are alienated from society, wracked with despair, and preoccupied with death. They may turn to drugs or alcohol to mask their self-hatred and are prone to suicide.

Unhealthy Fours in literature include: O in Pauline Réage's *The Story of O*, Blanche DuBois in Tennessee Williams's *A Streetcar Named Desire*, Shakespeare's Richard III, Esther Greenwood in Sylvia Plath's *The Bell Jar*, Lestat in Anne Rice's *Interview with the Vampire*, Edwin Arlington Robinson's "Miniver Cheevy," and Robert Browning's vengeful monk in "Soliloquy of the Spanish Cloister."

Place in Society

Although Fours are found in a variety of jobs and professions, they are especially visible in the arts, as poets, novelists, actors, musicians, composers, painters, sculptors, and architects. Fours are also drawn to work in fashion, all realms of design, museums, journalism, advertising, and education. Their affinities for beautiful environments and "elite" people lead them to succeed in work that demands taste and expertise.

Fours may also be attracted to professions like medicine—as plastic surgeons, for example—and psychotherapy, where their ability to understand and compassionately handle emotional extremes is a major asset. Fours can also do well in business, especially in companies involved with such aesthetic-related products as cosmetics, clothing, and works of art. Many Fours are most effective when working independently. They are not well-suited to regimented situations where their creative input is unwelcome or irrelevant.

In America's predominantly Three culture well-paid, visible success is a central value, and the "pursuit of happiness" is a high priority. Both these goals are at odds with the Four world view, which encompasses deep feeling, a capacity for suffering and an ability to contemplate death without flinching. Though Fours are often viewed as "outsiders," they may bring balance to a culture that refuses to acknowledge the "dark" side of life. In this sense, American Fours are unsung heroes.

Stress and Security Points

Under stress, Fours take on characteristics of Twos: fearful of being outcast because of their innate defectiveness, they become avid people-pleasers whose personal neediness is uncomfortably obvious. When feeling secure, Fours take on the qualities of Ones. They become cool and somewhat critical, able to make accurate assessments of individuals and ethical situations. This connection also lessens the Fours' characteristic emotional turmoil.

Healthy Fours have great emotional depth, but unhealthy Fours can swing between hysterical people-pleasing at Two and compulsive perfectionism at

One. A basic issue in Fours' emotional compass is their ambivalence about people: Are others to be courted indiscriminately to stave off the Four's fear of isolation—the perspective of the Two stress point—or are people to be evaluated with an intelligent, discerning eye that accurately pegs their character as well as their beauty—the perspective of the One security point?

Wings

In Fours, the contrast between the Three wing and the Five wing is particularly marked, since Three is an aggressive style and Five, like Four, is withdrawn.

Average Fours with a Three wing tend to be more active, dramatic, and emotionally expressive than Fours with a Five wing. They are also more concerned with projecting a vivid, distinctive image. Fours with this wing can also be competitive, elitist, preoccupied with questions of taste and elegance.

Anna Karenina's Three wing is visible in her vivacity and charm as well as her strong drive to be part of the social elite. Her aggressiveness toward her lover when his interest in her seems to be diminishing is also characteristic of the Three wing.

Fours with a Five wing tend to be more self-contained, rational, and analytical. Gentle but passionate, they are less concerned with projecting a dramatic image and more observant of their environment and other people. Though often extremely intense, Fours with this wing can be more insecure both socially and personally.

Proust's narrator is an example: a shy, sensitive loner who is brilliantly insightful about the world around him but also insecure about his gifts as a writer. His labyrinthine writing style seems designed more to please himself than to appeal to a general audience. Like most Fours he is preoccupied with suffering, but his creative achievements reflect the healthy levels of his Enneagram style.

The Glass Menagerie

Laura, the reclusive, sensitive sister in Tennessee Williams's *The Glass Menagerie*, is a less healthy Four with a Five wing. So shy she cannot hold a job and without creative outlets for her sensibilities, she focuses her longing and imagination on her collection of miniature glass animals, which seem to symbolize her own beauty and fragility. Her mother Amanda's desperate effort to find her a suitor prompts her brother to bring a work mate home for dinner.

He turns out to be the one boy Laura ever liked in high school, and when she first learns the identity of this "gentleman caller," she is overcome with emotion:

LAURA [with an altered look]: What did you say his name was?
AMANDA: O'Connor.
LAURA: What is his first name?
AMANDA: I don't remember. Oh, yes, I do. It was—Jim!

[Laura sways slightly and catches hold of a chair.]

LAURA [faintly]: Not—Jim!

AMANDA: Yes, that was it, it was Jim! I've never known a Jim that wasn't nice!

LAURA: Are you sure his name is Jim O'Connor?

AMANDA: Yes. Why?

LAURA: Is he the one that Tom used to know in high school?

AMANDA: He didn't say so. I think he just got to know him at the warehouse.

LAURA: There was a Jim O'Connor we both knew in high school— [then, with effort] If that is the one that Tom is bringing to dinner— you'll have to excuse me, I won't come to the table.

AMANDA: What sort of nonsense is this?

LAURA: You asked me once if I'd ever liked a boy. Don't you remember I showed you this boy's picture?

AMANDA: You mean the boy you showed me in the yearbook?

LAURA: Yes, that boy.

AMANDA: Laura, Laura, were you in love with that boy?

LAURA: I don't know, Mother. All I know is I couldn't sit at the table if it was him! (pp. 72-73)

Here we see the Four defense mechanism of introjection at work. Having formed an idealized picture of Jim in her mind, Laura panics at the prospect of having to relate to him in person.

After dinner, Amanda contrives to leave Jim alone with Laura in the living room, and Laura reminds him that they knew each other in high school. He asks about her life since, and she tells him she took a business course but had to abandon it because it gave her indigestion. All she can manage now, she says, is to care for her collection of glass animals. Jim, a Three, gives Laura a pep talk on how to get over her "inferiority complex." Charmed by her sweetness, he insists on dancing with her, despite the fact that she wears a leg brace. They accidentally knock her glass unicorn off the table, and its horn breaks off. Her light-hearted reaction to this delights Jim, and he kisses her. Suddenly aware that he is in dangerous waters, he confesses to Laura that he is engaged and won't be able to pursue his interest in her:

JIM: . . . I can't call up next week and—ask for a date. I thought I had better explain the situation in case you—misunderstood it and—I hurt your feelings. . . .

[There is a pause. Slowly, very slowly, Laura's look changes, her eyes returning slowly from his to the glass figure in her palm. Amanda utters another gay laugh in the kitchenette.]

LAURA [faintly]: You—won't—call again?

JIM: No, Laura, I can't. [He rises from the sofa.] As I was just explaining, I've—got strings on me, Laura, I've—been going steady! I go out all the time with a girl named Betty. She's a home-girl like you, and Catholic, and Irish, and in a great many ways we—get along fine. I met her last summer on a moonlight boat trip up the river to Alton, on the Majestic. Well—right away from the start it was—love! . . . Being in love has made a new man of me!
[Leaning stiffly forward, clutching the arm of the sofa, Laura struggles visibly with her storm. But Jim is oblivious; she is a long way off.]
The power of love is really pretty tremendous! Love is something that—changes the whole world, Laura!
[The storm abates a little and Laura leans back. He notices her again.]
It happened that Betty's aunt took sick, she got a wire and had to go to Centralia. So Tom—when he asked me to dinner—I naturally just accepted the invitation, not knowing that you—that he—that I— [He stops awkwardly.] Huh—I'm a stumblejohn!
[He flops back on the sofa. The holy candles on the altar of Laura's face have been snuffed out. There is a look of almost infinite desolation. Jim glances at her uneasily.]
I wish that you would—say something.

[She bites her lip which was trembling and then bravely smiles. She opens her hand again on the broken glass figure. Then she gently takes his hand and raises it level with her own. She carefully places the unicorn in the palm of his hand, then pushes his fingers closed upon it.]
What are you—doing that for? You want me to have him? Laura?
[She nods.]
What for?
LAURA: A—souvenir . . . .
[She rises unsteadily and crouches beside the Victrola to wind it up.]
(pp. 107-109)

The play makes clear that, with Laura's dream of an actual relationship now destroyed, she will never develop a relationship with a man. It also implies that this incident pushes her over the edge into madness, a not uncommon outcome for a very unhealthy Four with a Five wing.

The Sorrows of Young Werther

In the title character of Johann Wolfgang von Goethe's *The Sorrows of Young Werther* we find an unhealthy Four with a Three wing. As we saw with Anna Karenina, Fours with this wing are capable of extravagant emotionality, and unhealthy fictional examples often commit suicide, usually over unrequited love. Fours with either wing can create romantic fantasies and form attachments to inappropriate people. Young Werther does this with Charlotte, who is engaged to another man.

Werther's story is told mostly through letters to his friend Wilhelm. In the first one, dated May 4, 1771, Werther introduces the theme of unhappiness over love. He has left his home town, he writes, partly to escape an unpleasant situation with a woman. Note his Fourish tone of lamentation:

> ... My dear friend, I promise you, I will change; I will no longer, as has always been my habit, continue to ruminate on every petty annoyance which fate may have in store for me; I will enjoy the present, and the past shall be for me the past. No doubt you are right, my best of friends, there would be far less suffering among mankind, if men—and God knows why they are so constituted—did not use their imaginations so assiduously in recalling the memory of past sorrow, instead of bearing an indifferent present. (p. 5)

No sooner has Werther settled into his new environment than he is seized by a Fourish longing for what is not present. Although he was initially delighted with the beauty of the setting, it now leaves him dissatisfied:

> It is so strange how, when I came here first and looked out upon that lovely valley from the hills, I felt charmed with everything around me—the little wood opposite—how delightful to sit in its shade! How fine the view from that summit!—that delightful chain of hills, and the exquisite valleys at their feet!—could I but lose myself amongst them! ... but alas! when we rush towards our goal, when the distant there becomes the present here, all is the same; we are as poor and limited as ever, and our soul still languishes for unattainable happiness. (p. 20)

After meeting Charlotte and falling in love with her, Werther is predictably crushed when Albert, her fiancé, arrives on the scene. Once again we see a Four, whose unconscious agenda includes the need to suffer, contrive to place himself in an untenable romantic position.

Werther asks to borrow Albert's pistols for a journey, and Albert, a One, agrees. When Werther impulsively points one of the pistols at his own head, the ensuing conversation details the Four fascination with death and sense of exemption from ordinary social standards:

> With a sudden motion I pointed the mouth of the pistol to my forehead, over the right eye. "What are you doing?" cried Albert, turning the pistol away. "It's not loaded," I said. "Even so," he asked with impatience, "what is the meaning of this? I can't imagine how a man can be so mad as to shoot himself; the very idea of it shocks me."
>
> "Oh, you people!" I said, "why do you always have to label an action and call it mad or wise, good or bad? What does all that mean?

That you have fathomed the motives of these actions? That you can explain with certainty why they happened, why they had to happen? If you could, you would be less hasty with your 'labels.'"

"But you will admit," said Albert, "that some actions are wrong, let them spring from whatever motives they may." I granted it, and shrugged my shoulders.

"Still," I continued, "there are some exceptions here too. Theft is a crime, but the man who commits it from extreme poverty to save his family from starvation, does he deserve pity or punishment? Who shall throw the first stone at a husband who in just rage sacrifices his faithless wife and her perfidious seducer. Or at the young girl who in an hour of rapture forgets herself in the overwhelming joys of love? Even our laws, cold and pedantic as they are, relent in such cases, and withhold their punishment."

"That is quite another thing," said Albert, "because a man under the influence of violent passion loses all reasoning power and is regarded as drunk or insane."

"Oh, you rationalists," I replied, smiling. "Passion! Drunkenness! Madness! You moral creatures, so calm and so righteous! You abhor the drunken man and detest the eccentric; you pass by, like the Levite, and thank God, like the Pharisee, that you are not one of them. I have been drunk more than once, my passions have always bordered on madness, and I'm not ashamed to confess it. I've learned in my own way that all extraordinary men who have done great and improbable things have ever been decried by the world as drunk or insane. And in ordinary life too, is it not intolerable that no one can undertake anything noble or generous without having everybody say, 'That fellow is drunk, he is mad'? Shame on you, ye sages!" (pp. 32-33)

Werther takes a job as an ambassador's aide and accompanies him to his post in a foreign country. Seeing the "inferior" quality of the people around him, Werther feels better about himself. The chronic insecurity of Fours is based on their habit of continually comparing themselves to others:

All will yet be well; you were quite right, my friend: since I have had to associate with other people and see what they do and how they live, I have become better satisfied with myself. For this is our nature, that we are ever anxious to compare ourselves with others; and our happiness or misery depends on the things and people with whom we compare ourselves. And nothing is more dangerous than solitude; our imagination, always disposed to rise high, nourished by the fantastic images of the poets, seems to project for us a chain of beings of whom we ourselves seem the most inferior. All things appear more perfect than they really are, and all seem superior to us. This is quite natural. We feel so often our own imperfections, and imagine that we perceive in others the qualities we do not possess, attributing to them also all that we have ourselves. And thus we form the idea of a perfect, happy man—a creature entirely of our own imagination.

But when, in spite of weakness and disappointments, we do our daily work in earnest, we shall find that with all false starts and compromises, we make better headway than others who have wind and tide with them; and it gives one a real feeling of self to keep pace with others or outstrip them in the race. (p. 43)

Here we see the beginning of Werther's connection to One, the Four's security point. When Fours shift their focus away from their own feelings to specific tasks and goals, they become more comfortable and effective in the world.

But Werther's preoccupation with the sorrows of his past is too deep not to reassert itself. No one, he feels, has suffered more than he. Charlotte tells Werther he is deceiving himself, seeking his own destruction, that he must not be so excessive in his feelings for her, since she cannot reciprocate. Werther responds by writing her a letter that is found, sealed, in his desk after his suicide. It is reminiscent of Anna Karenina's impulse to punish her lover with her own death:

My mind is made up, Charlotte: I am resolved to die! I am writing you this without any romantic sentimentality, on this morning of the day when I am to see you for the last time. When you read this, my dearest, the cool grave will cover the stiff remains of that restless and unhappy man who, in the last moments of his life, knows no greater bliss than to converse with you! I have passed a dreadful night—or rather, a propitious one; for it has given me resolution, it has fixed my purpose. I am resolved to die. . . . It is not despair, but the certainty that I have reached the end, and must sacrifice myself for you. Yes, Charlotte, why should I not say it? One of us three must go: it shall be Werther. O Beloved! this heart, excited by rage and fury, has often had the monstrous impulse to murder your husband—you—myself! Now, it is decided. And in the bright, quiet evenings of summer, when you wander toward the mountains, let your thoughts turn to me: recollect how often you watched me coming to meet you from the valley; then, look toward the churchyard to my grave, and, by the light of the setting sun, mark how the evening breeze waves the tall grass which grows above my tomb. I was calm when I began this, but now, when I see it all so vividly, I am weeping like a child. (pp. 73-74)

Subtypes

Fours generally focus on what is missing in their lives, which produces a sense of dissatisfaction with themselves and their situation. **Self-Preservation**

Fours, whom Oscar Ichazo describes as "dauntless, reckless," are often less conscious than other subtypes of the envy that underlies their character. Many have a strong drive to acquire material possessions and create an elegant lifestyle. To this end they can be financially profligate or even reckless. Needing, like all Fours, to feel strong emotion, Self-Preservation Fours generate it by putting themselves at risk. They are good at handling emotional extremes and find dangerous situations stimulating.

Literary examples of this subtype include Chekov's Ivanov, Esme in David Hare's play *Amy's View*, the narrator of Isak Dineson's memoir *Out of Africa*, and Emma Bovary in Flaubert's *Madame Bovary*.

Madame Bovary

Emma Bovary, the protagonist of Gustave Flaubert's famous nineteenth-century novel, is a Self-Preservation Four with a Three wing.

Self-Preservation Fours often have a quality of sensuality about them, and this is apparent even in Emma's childhood. When her father sends her to be schooled in a convent at age thirteen, her reaction to her religious surroundings is more aesthetic than spiritual:

> Far from being bored at first at the convent, she took pleasure in the society of the good sisters, who, to amuse her, took her to the chapel, which one entered from the refectory by a long corridor. She played very little during recreation hours, knew her catechism well, and it was she who always answered Monsieur le Vicaire's difficult questions. Living thus, without ever leaving the warm atmosphere of the class-rooms, and amid these pale-faced women wearing rosaries with brass crosses, she was softly lulled by the mystic langour exhaled in the perfumes of the altar, the freshness of the holy water, and the lights of the tapers. Instead of attending to mass, she looked at the pious vignettes with their azure borders in her book, and she loved the sick lamb, the sacred heart pierced with sharp arrows, or the poor Jesus sinking beneath the cross he carries. She tried, by way of mortification, to eat nothing a whole day. She puzzled her head to find some vow to fulfil.
>
> When she went to confession, she invented little sins in order that she might stay there longer, kneeling in the shadow, her hands joined, her face against the grating beneath the whispering of the priest. The comparisons of betrothed, husband, celestial lover, and eternal marriage, that recur in sermons, stirred within her soul depths of unexpected sweetness. (pp. 40-41)

After several years Emma grows impatient with the spiritual discipline of convent life. Searching for a rescuer, she marries Charles, a provincial doctor who is a Nine. But her idealized picture of marriage soon crumbles before her actual experience. To compensate, she begins to long for settings, environments, and possessions that are missing from her life with her stolid husband.

In one scene Emma and Charles are invited to a ball, where she dances with a Viscount. The memory of this preoccupies her for some time:

> The memory of this ball, then, became an occupation for Emma. Whenever the Wednesday came round she said to herself as she awoke, "Ah! I was there a week—a fort night—three weeks ago." And little by little the faces grew confused in her remembrance. She forgot the tune of the quadrilles; she no longer saw the liveries and appointments so distinctly; some details escaped her, but the regret remained with her. (pp. 63-64)

Notice here the implicit focus on luxury. Preoccupied with her own unhappiness, Emma also envies others:

> Would this misery last for ever? Would she never issue from it? Yet she was as good as all the women who were living happily. She had seen duchesses at Vaubyessard with clumsier waists and commoner ways, and she execrated the injustice of God. She leant her head against the walls to weep; she envied lives of stir; longed for masked balls, for violent pleasures, with all the wildness, that she did not know, but that these must surely yield. (p. 75)

When Emma becomes pregnant, she dreams of having a son, hoping that producing a male heir will give her a solid social status and thereby eliminate her feelings of insecurity and victimization. When she learns that her baby is a girl, she turns her head away and faints. From this moment on, she basically ignores her daughter.

Next she develops an infatuation with Léon, a local clerk:

> But she was eaten up with desires, with rage, with hate. That dress with the narrow folds hid a distracted heart, of whose torment those chaste lips said nothing. She was in love with Léon, and sought solitude that she might with the more ease delight in his image. The sight of his form troubled the voluptuousness of this meditation. Emma thrilled at the sound of his step; then in his presence the emotion subsided, and afterwards there remained to her only an immense astonishment that ended in sorrow. (p. 125)

This is more introjection. Anna cherishes her interior picture of Léon, only to be disappointed by his actual presence.

Offered work in Paris, Léon leaves town. Soon after Emma meets Rodolphe, a Seven, who woos her in a way calculated to appeal to her romantic fantasies. They quickly become lovers.

After six months of regular meetings, Rodolphe's interest begins to flag. Anxious about losing his love, Emma moves to her Two stress point and passionately declares her devotion:

> "Oh," she went on, "I love you! I love you so that I could not live without you, do you see? There are times when I long to see you again, when I am torn by all the anger of love. I ask myself, Where is he? Perhaps he is talking to other women. They smile upon him; he approaches. Oh, no; no one else pleases you. There are some more beautiful, but I love you best. I know how to love best. I am your servant, your concubine! You are my king, my idol! You are good, you are beautiful, you are clever, you are strong!" (p. 218)

Desperate to rekindle Rodolphe's passion, Emma begs him to take her away. When he instead decides to break off the relationship, she contemplates suicide.

She takes to her bed, desperately ill, and her husband nurses her until she recovers. By now Charles has serious money worries, partly due to Emma's extravagance. But the situation is worse than he knows: Emma has spent huge sums on fashionable clothing and sunk the couple so far in debt that they risk having their household furniture seized.

Oblivious to the consequences of her actions, Emma travels frequently to a nearby city, supposedly to take music lessons, but really to meet with Léon. Consistent with her subtype, she becomes increasingly unstable and reckless as the relationship continues:

> And what an outburst the next Thursday at the hotel in their room with Léon. She laughed, cried, sang, sent for sherbets, wanted to smoke cigarettes, seemed to him wild and extravagant, but adorable, superb.
>
> He did not know what recreation of her whole being drove her more and more to plunge into the pleasures of life. She was becoming irritable, greedy, voluptuous; and she walked about the streets with him carrying her head high, without fear, so she said, of compromising herself. (p. 316)

Despite her wild behavior, Emma is unhappy with Léon, too. No amount of extravagance can fill her longing for what she doesn't have—though she has no idea what that might be. The sense of something missing in her relationship with Léon leads her to more financial recklessness and she lays out her own money for luxurious hotel suites in which to hold their trysts.

Faced with the imminent loss of her furniture because of her extravagance, she begs Rodolphe, her former lover, for money to pay her debts. After he refuses, she rushes to the shop of the local pharmacist, a friend of her husband's, finds a jar of arsenic and consumes some of it. Despite Charles's efforts to save her, she dies after suffering horribly.

Emma's belief that she can shore up her negative self-image by surrounding herself with luxury is common to her subtype. But no amount of material comfort can fill the emptiness that an unhealthy Self-Preservation Four can feel at the core of her being.

Social Fours, whom Ichazo associates with "shame," are driven by a strong sense of inner defect and the expectation that others will see their flaws and reject them. They are powerfully aware of what is missing in their lives, intensely envious of those who have it, and may even be ashamed of their own envy. Unhealthy Social Fours fear that their many defects make them unable to function in society, and they may have trouble holding down jobs.

Examples in literature include Anna Karenina, Proust's narrator and Swann in *Swann's Way*, Blanche DuBois in *A Streetcar Named Desire*, Laura in *The Glass Menagerie*, Chekov's Ivanov, Ophelia in *Hamlet*, O in Pauline Réage's *The Story of O*, the title character in John Fowles's *The French Lieutenant's Woman* and Adam Dalgleish in *Devices and Desires*.

Devices and Desires

Adam Dalgleish, the hero of P.D. James's detective series, is a healthy Social Four with a Five wing. Socially reticent, he nevertheless makes practical contributions to the world through his work as a brilliant police detective while also producing critically acclaimed volumes of poetry.

At the beginning of *Devices and Desires*, Dalgliesh takes a two-week leave from his job as "Scotland Yard's most intelligent inspector" to put the affairs of his aunt in order. She recently died, leaving him a large fortune and a converted windmill at Larksoken on the north-east coast of Norfolk:

> And then there were family papers and his aunt's books, particularly her comprehensive library of ornithology, to be looked at and sorted and their disposal decided upon. These were pleasurable tasks. Even in boyhood he had disliked taking a holiday totally without purpose. He didn't know from what roots of childhood guilt or imagined responsibility had grown this curious masochism, which in his middle years had returned with added authority. But he was glad that there was a job to be done in Norfolk, not least because he knew that the journey had an element of flight. After four years of silence his new book of poetry, *A Case to Answer and Other Poems*, had been published to considerable critical acclaim, which was surprisingly gratifying, and to even wider public interest which, less surprisingly, he was finding more difficult to take. (pp. 9-10)

Dalgleish's built-in link to One (the Four security point) is evident in his reluctance to take a vacation without some purpose. When a colleague asks him to investigate a serial murderer in Norfolk who may also be killing women in London, Dalgleish is relieved. Ones are oriented toward work and feel most comfortable when there is a task to be accomplished. Healthy Fours, not content to focus primarily on their feelings, have a similar bent.

Dalgleish's ambivalence about the success of his books and his reluctance to do the usual promotion for his poetry reflects an anxiety about making personal appearances that is not uncommon for shy Fours with a Five wing. Here he is talking with his publisher's Publicity Director:

> "Anyone would think you didn't want to be read." [says Bill Costello, the Publicity Director]
> And did he want to be read? Certainly he wanted some people to read him, one person in particular, and having read the poems he wanted her to approve. Humiliating but true. As for the others: well, he supposed that the truth was that he wanted people to read the poems but not be coerced into buying them, an overfastidiousness which he could hardly expect Herne & Illingworth [his publishers] to share. He was aware of Bill's anxious, supplicating eyes, like those of a small boy who sees the bowl of sweets rapidly disappearing from his reach. His reluctance to co-operate seemed to him typical of much in himself that he disliked. There was a certain illogicality, surely, in wanting to be published but not caring particularly whether he was bought. The fact that he found the more public manifestations of fame distasteful didn't mean that he was free of vanity, only that he was better at controlling it and that in him it took a more reticent form. After all, he had a job, an assured pension and now his aunt's considerable fortune. He didn't have to care. He saw himself as unreasonably privileged compared with Colin McKay, who probably saw him—and who could blame Colin?—as a snobbish, oversensitive dilettante. (pp. 15-16)

Notice how Dalgleish compares himself with others and the undertone of envy in his thoughts. Idealistic Social Fours tend to resist doing anything that is not ethically impeccable—especially self-promotion. Dalgleish is also self-critical, another expression of his security point.

His Four penchant for privacy, even for isolation, is also tempered by the realism and objectivity of his link to One. We see the combination as Dalgleish chats with his neighbor Alice Mair:

> Dalgliesh was interested that Alice Mair apparently knew so much about local affairs. He had thought of her as essentially a private woman who would be very little concerned with her neighbours or their problems. And what about himself? In his deliberations whether to sell or keep on the Mill as a holiday home he had seen it as a refuge from London, eccentric and remote, providing a temporary escape from the

demands of his job and the pressures of success. But how far, even as an occasional visitor, could he isolate himself from the community, from their private tragedies no less than their dinner parties? It would be simple enough to avoid their hospitality, given sufficient ruthlessness, and he had never lacked that when it came to safeguarding his privacy. But the less tangible demands of neighbourliness might be less easily shrugged away. It was in London that you could live anonymously, could create your own ambience, could deliberately fabricate the persona which you chose to present to the world. In the country you lived as a social being and at the valuation of others. (pp. 31-32)

Dalgleish's ruminations also reveal the "image" consciousness that is present in the whole heart/feeling triad.

Later Dalgleish is talking with Rickards, the Inspector in charge of investigating the Norfolk serial murders. When Rickards mentions in passing that his wife has decided, near the end of her first pregnancy, to go to stay with her mother, Dalgleish's complex reaction reveals his personal history:

[Rickards] added: "I suppose it's natural for an only daughter to want to be with her mother at a time like this, particularly with a first baby."

Dalgliesh's wife hadn't wanted to be with her mother, she had wanted to be with him, had wanted it with such intensity that he had wondered afterwards whether she might have felt a premonition. He could remember that, although he could no longer recall her face. His memory for her, which for years, a traitor to grief and to their love, he had resolutely tried to suppress because the pain had seemed unbearable, had gradually been replaced by a boyish, romantic dream of gentleness and beauty now fixed for ever beyond the depredation of time. His newborn son's face he could still recall vividly and sometimes did in his dreams, that white unsullied look of sweet knowledgeable contentment, as if, in a brief moment of life, he had seen and known all there was to know, seen it and rejected it. . . .

Whatever mysterious spirit had unlocked the verse, it had freed him for other human satisfactions, for love; or was it the other way around? Had love unlocked the verse? It seemed even to have affected his job. Grinding the coffee beans, he pondered life's smaller ambiguities. When the poetry hadn't come, the job had seemed not only irksome but occasionally repellent. Now he was happy enough to let Rickards impose on his solitude to use him as a sounding board. The new benignity and tolerance a little disconcerted him. Success in moderation was no doubt better for the character than failure, but too much of it and he would lose his cutting edge. (pp. 69-70)

The Four theme of loss is clearly here, but we see Dalgleish's healthy response to it—using it to offer a creative gift to the world in the form of his poetry. The "irksome" aspect of his police job again reflects the Four's connection to One—and a One's resentment.

Even a healthy Four like Dalgleish is preoccupied with his own feelings. He is, however, a keen observer of others as we see from his descriptions of three women at a dinner party:

> On the other side of their host sat Meg Dennison, delicately but unfussily peeling her grapes with pink-tipped fingers. Hilary Robarts's sultry handsomeness emphasized her own very different look, an old-fashioned, carefully tended but unselfconscious prettiness which reminded him of photographs of the late 1930s. Their clothes pointed up the contrast. Hilary wore a shirt-waister dress in multicoloured Indian cotton, three buttons at the neck undone. Meg Dennison was in a long black skirt and a blue-patterned silk blouse with a bow at the neck. But it was their hostess who was the most elegant. The long shift in fine dark-brown wool worn with a heavy necklace of silver and amber hid her angularity and emphasized the strength and regularity of the strong features. Beside her Meg Dennison's prettiness was diminished almost to insipidity and Hilary Robarts's strong-coloured cotton looked tawdry. (p. 83)

Not only does he assess the aesthetic qualities of the women's clothes, he also finds keys to their characters in the way they dress. This observant analytical capacity is usual in Fours with a Five wing.

Several days later, while walking on a beach, Dalgliesh discovers the body of Hilary Robarts. After he reports the murder, he stands watch near the body and ruminates in this Fourish way:

> No murderer had ever left his imprint more clearly on a victim than had the Whistler. Why, then, did he feel this unease, the sense that it was less straightforward than it seemed?
>
> He wriggled his heels and buttocks more comfortably into the shingle and prepared to wait. The cold moonlight, the constant falling of the waves and the sense of that stiffening body behind him induced a gentle melancholy, a contemplation of mortality including his own. *Timor mortis conturbat me.* He thought: In youth we take egregious risks because death has no reality for us. Youth goes caparisoned in immortality. It is only in middle age that we are shadowed by the awareness of the transitoriness of life. And the fear of death, however, irrational, was surely natural, whether one thought of it as annihilation or as a rite of passage. Every cell in the body was programmed for life; all healthy creatures clung to life until their last breath. How hard to

accept, and yet how comforting, was the gradual realization that the universal enemy might come at last as a friend. Perhaps this was part of the attraction of his job, that the process of detection dignified the individual death, even the death of the least attractive, the most unworthy, mirroring in its excessive interest in clues and motives man's perennial fascination with the mystery of his mortality, providing, too, a comforting illusion of a moral universe in which innocence could be avenged, right vindicated, order restored. But nothing was restored, certainly not life, and the only justice vindicated was the uncertain justice of men. The job certainly had a fascination for him which went beyond its intellectual challenge, or the excuse it gave for his rigorously enforced privacy. But now he had inherited enough money to make it redundant. (pp. 173-174)

After two other women die mysteriously in a boating accident that might be related to Hilary Robarts's murder, Dalgliesh interviews Pascoe, who lived with one of them. Dalgliesh's thoughts reveal his Two stress point:

Pascoe looked at Dalgliesh with the frustration and anger of an uncomprehending child. ". . . I didn't think you could be angry and grieving at the same time. I ought to be mourning her, but all I can feel is this terrible anger."

"Oh yes," said Dalgliesh. "You can feel anger and grief together. That's the commonest reaction to bereavement."

Suddenly Pascoe began crying. The empty beer can rattled against the table, and he bent his head low over it, his shoulders shaking. Women, thought Dalgliesh, are better at coping with grief than we are. He had seen them so many times, the women police officers moving unconsciously to take the grieving mother, the lost child in their arms. Some men were good at it too, of course. Rickards had been in the old days. He himself was good with the words, but, then, words were his trade. What he found difficult was what came so spontaneously to the truly generous at heart, the willingness to touch and be touched. He thought: I'm here on false pretences. If I were not, perhaps I too could feel adequate.(p. 410)

Note again the sense of social inadequacy.

When Rickards believes he has found the murderer of Hilary Robarts, Dalgliesh disagrees. He explains his reasoning to the skeptical Rickards, a Six, before leaving for London and emotionally withdrawing from the case:

[I]t wasn't his case. Within two days he would be back in London. Any more dirty work which MI5 wanted done they would have to do themselves. He had already interfered more than was strictly justified and certainly more than he had found agreeable. He told himself that it would be dishonest to blame either Rickards or the murderer for the fact that most of the decisions he had come to the headland to make were still undecided.

That unexpected spurt of envy had induced a mild self-disgust which wasn't helped by the discovery that he had left the book he was currently reading, A.N. Wilson's biography of Tolstoy, in the room at the top of the tower. It was providing satisfaction and consolation of which at the present he felt particularly in need. (p. 456)

Dalgleish's "mild self-disgust" is common in shame-based Social Fours. A healthy Four, with a strong link to his One security point, might well find a biography of Tolstoy, who was a One, especially satisfying.

Since so many Four literary characters come to tragic ends, it is inspiring to find a complex, engaging, and positive Four hero in Adam Dalgleish.

A Streetcar Named Desire

Blanche DuBois in Tennessee Williams's classic *A Streetcar Named Desire* is an unhealthy Social Four with a Three wing. In Part One I discussed the way Blanche continually shifts between her Two stress point and her One security point. Her rampant social insecurity is also characteristic of her subtype.

When Blanche tells her sister that their childhood home, Belle Reve, has been lost, Stella is shocked. Defensively believing Stella blames her, Blanche counterattacks so aggressively that she drives Stella to tears:

STELLA: But how did it go? What happened?
BLANCHE: You're a fine one to ask me how it went!
STELLA: Blanche!
BLANCHE: You're a fine one to sit there accusing me of it!
STELLA: Blanche!
BLANCHE: I, I, I took the blows in my face and my body! All of those deaths! The long parade to the graveyard! Father, mother! Margaret, that dreadful way! So big with it, it couldn't be put in a coffin! But had to be burned like rubbish! You just came home in time for the funerals, Stella. And funerals are pretty compared to deaths. Funerals are quiet, but deaths—not always. Sometimes their breathing is hoarse, and sometimes it rattles, and sometimes they even cry out to you, "Don't let me go!" Even the old, sometimes, say, "Don't let me go." As if you were able to stop them! But funerals are quiet, with pretty flowers. And, oh, what gorgeous boxes they pack them away in! Unless you were there at the bed when they cried out, "Hold me!" you'd never suspect there was the struggle for breath and bleeding. You didn't dream, but I saw! Saw! Saw! And now you sit there telling me with your eyes that I let the place go! How in hell do you think all that sickness and dying

was paid for? Death is expensive, Miss Stella! And old Cousin Jessie's right after Margaret's, hers! Why, the Grim Reaper had put up his tent on our doorstep! . . . Stella, Belle Reve was his headquarters! Honey— that's how it slipped through my fingers! Which of them left us a fortune? Which of them left a cent of insurance even? Only poor Jessie—one hundred to pay for her coffin. That was all, Stella! And I with my pitiful salary at the school. Yes, accuse me! Sit there and stare at me, thinking I let the place go! I let the place go? Where were you! In bed with your—Polack! (pp. 21-22)

Here again, the hysterical quality of the Two stress point is evident in Blanche's melodramatic speech. Unhealthy Social Fours, plagued by insecurity and expecting to be rejected, often make accusative pre-emptive strikes at others. Not infrequently, the other person responds with hurt, anger, and the rejection the Four was expecting in the first place. In the Four's view, she is proved right— and the downward spiral continues. We saw the same pattern in Anna Karenina, another Social subtype, when she unfairly accused Vronsky of rejecting her.

Blanche's search for a rescuer is an especially strong tendency in average to unhealthy Fours, and for a time it looks as though she has found one in Stanley's friend Mitch. But when the truth about her situation comes out—her promiscuity, her sexual involvement with one of her high school students, her expulsion from her home town—her dream of rescue is shattered and she descends into madness.

Sexual Fours, whom Ichazo associates with "competition," are more aggressive than the other Four subtypes. They can develop intense attractions to people, and their relationships can be stormy. Jealous and possessive, they often have ambivalent feelings toward their lovers: hatred mixed with love and admiration. Sexual Fours tend to become competitive with their lovers, envying the lovers' good qualities, then rejecting them for even tiny imperfections. Some female Sexual Fours can have a castrating quality. Very unhealthy Fours with this subtype are capable of crimes of passion.

Literary examples of Sexual Fours include Salieri in Peter Shaffer's play *Amadeus*, Shakespeare's Richard III, Gilbert Osmond in Henry James's *The Portrait of a Lady*, Thea Kronborg in Willa Cather's *The Song of the Lark*, and Marianne Dashwood in Jane Austen's *Sense and Sensibility*.

Sense and Sensibility

In *Sense and Sensibility* the character of Marianne offers an excellent portrait of an average Sexual Four. This novel of manners, love, and marriage emphasizes the relationship between marriage prospects and financial resources in early nineteenth century England, and the way this limited choices for women. The story especially contrasts the temperaments of two sisters, Elinor, a One, and Marianne, a Four with a Three wing.

When Marianne falls in love with the dashing Willoughby, a Seven, Elinor watches her sister's headlong intensity and lack of judgment with concern:

> Elinor could not be surprised at their attachment. She only wished that it were less openly shown, and once or twice did venture to suggest the propriety of some self-command to Marianne. But Marianne abhorred all concealment where no real disgrace could attend unreserve; and to aim at the restraint of sentiments which were not in themselves illaudable, appeared to her not merely an unnecessary effort, but a disgraceful subjection of reason to commonplace and mistaken notions. Willoughby thought the same; and their behaviour, at all times, was an illustration of their opinions.
> ... Such conduct made them of course most exceedingly laughed at; but ridicule could not shame, and seemed hardly to provoke them. (pp. 31-32)

When Willoughby announces that he is leaving for an indefinite period of time, Marianne is inconsolable. Sexual Fours are the most dramatic of all the Four subtypes, and they often stoke their own grief:

> The evening passed off in the equal indulgence of feeling. She [Marianne] played over every favourite song that she had been used to play to Willoughby, every air in which their voices had been oftenest joined, and sat at the instrument gazing on every line of music that he had written out for her, till her heart was so heavy that no further sadness could be gained; and this nourishment of grief was every day applied. She spent whole hours at the pianoforte alternately singing and crying, her voice often totally suspended by her tears. In books, too, as well as in music, she courted the misery which a contrast between the past and present was certain of giving. She read nothing but what they had been used to read together.
> Such violence of affliction indeed could not be supported for ever; it sunk within a few days into a calmer melancholy; but these employments, to which she daily recurred, her solitary walks and silent meditations, still produced occasional effusions of sorrow as lively as ever. (p. 50)

When Willoughby later transfers his affections to another woman, it is revealed that Marianne impetuously wrote him letters that expressed her feelings for him so strongly that she has "compromised" her virtue. Although distressed, Marianne passionately defends her own wrongheadedness:

> "Elinor, I have been cruelly used, but not by Willoughby."
> "Dearest Marianne, who but himself? By whom can he have been

instigated?"

"By all the world, rather than by his own heart. I could rather believe every creature of my acquaintance leagued together to ruin me in his opinion, than believe his nature capable of such cruelty. This woman of whom he writes—whoever she be—or any one, in short, but your own dear self, mamma, and Edward, may have been so barbarous to belie me. Beyond you three, is there a creature in the world whom I would not rather suspect of evil than Willoughby, whose heart I know so well?" (p. 112)

Later, Marianne learns that Elinor has been quietly agonizing over the surprise revelation that the man she loves is engaged to another woman. Stunned by the contrast between Elinor's conduct and her own, Marianne suddenly sees how excessive her own responses have been. The shock of this insight moves her to her One security point, where she is helped by her sister's example:

". . . Do not, my dearest Elinor, let your kindness defend what I know your judgment must censure. My illness has made me think—it has given me leisure and calmness for serious recollection. . . . I saw that my own feelings had prepared my sufferings, and that my want of fortitude under them had almost led me to the grave. My illness, I well knew, had been entirely brought on by myself, by such negligence of my own health as I felt even at the time to be wrong. Had I died, it would have been self-destruction. I did not know my danger till the danger was removed; but with such feelings as these reflections gave me, I wonder at my recovery—wonder that the very eagerness of my desire to live, to have time for atonement to my God, and to you all, did not kill me at once. . . . Your example was before me; but to what avail? Was I more considerate of you and your comfort? Did I imitate your forbearance, or lessen your restraints, by taking any part in those offices of general complaisance or particular gratitude which you had hitherto been left to discharge alone? No; not less when I knew you to be unhappy, than when I had believed you at ease, did I turn away from every exertion of duty or friendship; scarcely allowed sorrow to exist but with me, regretting only that heart which desired and wronged me, and leaving you, for whom I professed an unbounded affection, to be miserable for my sake. . . . The future must be my proof. I have laid down my plan, and if I am capable of adhering to it, my feelings shall be governed and my temper improved. They shall no longer worry others, nor torture myself. I shall now live solely for my family. . . . As for Willoughby, to say that I shall soon or that I shall ever forget him, would be idle. His remembrance can be overcome by no change of circumstances or opinions. But it shall be regulated, it shall be checked by religion, by reason, by constant employment." (pp. 206-208)

Marianne's shift to One gives her the emotional balance to accept the proposal of another suitor, Colonel Brandon. Here she contemplates her happiness in more realistic terms:

> Instead of falling a sacrifice to an irresistible passion, as once she had fondly flattered herself with expecting, instead of remaining even for ever with her mother, and finding her only pleasures in retirement and study, as afterwards in her more calm and sober judgment she had determined on, she found herself, at nineteen, submitting to new attachments, entering on new duties, placed in a new home, a wife, the mistress of a family, and the patroness of a village. . . . Marianne could never love by halves; and her whole heart became in time, as much devoted to her husband, as it had once been to Willoughby. (p. 227)

A loving One—who represents the Four's security point—can help a Four achieve more emotional balance. Elinor's generosity and steadfast sisterly love brings Marianne to a change in attitude that opens her to a happy marriage.

In the contrast between two sisters we see the power of true love to correct the imbalances of strongly contrasting personalities. Love allows Elinor to express her One passion (sensibility), lessening her excessive self-discipline, while it encourages Marianne's practicality (sense), reining in her excessive Four passion and self-absorption.

The Portrait of a Lady

In Henry James's novel *The Portrait of a Lady* we see the power of an unhealthy Sexual Four to poison an intimate relationship. Gilbert Osmond, a Four with a Five wing, is one of the great evil characters in literature. At the root of his malevolence is an envy of his wife Isabel's goodness, and the story details his systematic attempt to destroy her.

When Isabel, a Seven, first meets Osmond, she finds him difficult to categorize:

> Isabel had never met a person of so fine a grain. . . . He was certainly fastidious and critical; he was probably irritable. His sensibility had governed him—possibly governed him too much; it had made him impatient of vulgar troubles and had led him to live by himself, in a serene, impersonal way, thinking about art and beauty and history. He had consulted his taste in everything—his taste alone, perhaps; that was what made him so different from every one else. . . . [S]uch shyness as his—the shyness of ticklish nerves and fine perceptions—was perfectly consistent with the best breeding. Indeed, it was almost a proof of superior qualities. (pp. 241-243)

Osmond, in turn, feels extremely satisfied with the impression he has made on Isabel:

> In general Osmond took his pleasure singly; he was usually
> disgusted with something that seemed to him ugly or offensive; his mind
> was rarely visited with moods of comprehensive satisfaction. But at
> present he was happy—happier than he had perhaps ever been in his life;
> and the feeling had a large foundation. This was simply the sense of
> success—the most agreeable emotion of the human heart. Osmond had
> never had too much of it; in this respect he had never been spoiled; as
> he knew perfectly well and often reminded himself. "Ah no, I have not
> been spoiled; certainly I have not been spoiled," he used to repeat to
> himself. "If I do succeed before I die, I shall have earned it well.". . . We
> have seen that she thought him "fine"; and Gilbert Osmond returned the
> compliment. We have also seen (or heard) that he had a great dread of
> vulgarity, and on this score his mind was at rest with regard to our young
> lady. He was not afraid that she would disgust him or irritate him; he had
> no fear that she would even, in the more special sense of the word,
> displease him. If she was too eager, she could be taught to be less so; that
> was a fault which diminished with growing knowledge. She might defy
> him, she might anger him; this was another matter from displeasing him,
> and on the whole a less serious one. If a woman were ungraceful and
> common, her whole quality was vitiated, and one could take no precau-
> tions against that; one's own delicacy would avail little. If, however, she
> were only willful and high-tempered, the defect might be managed with
> comparative ease; for had one not a will of one's own that one had been
> keeping for years in the best condition—as pure and keen as a sword
> protected by its sheath? (pp. 280-282)

Along with the unhealthy Four qualities of self-absorption and selfishness,
we see the Sexual Four's interest in dissecting the personality of a potential
partner.

Soon after they marry, Osmond begins to pressure Isabel to persuade her
friend Lord Warburton to marry Osmond's daughter, Pansy. At first Isabel
agrees to the plan, but then, out of affection for Pansy, lets Warburton know that
the girl actually loves another man. When Warburton backs away from Pansy,
Osmond blames Isabel and she suddenly realizes that Osmond hates her:

> She remembered perfectly the first sign he had given of it—it had
> been like the bell that was to ring up the curtain upon the real drama of
> their life. He said to her one day that she had too many ideas, and that
> she must get rid of them. He had told her that already, before their
> marriage; but then she had not noticed it; it came back to her only
> afterwards. This time she might well notice it, because he had really
> meant it. . . . He had expected his wife to feel with him and for him, to

enter into his opinions, his ambitions, his preferences. . . . It was her scorn of his assumptions—it was that that made him draw himself up. . . . When one had a wife who gave one that sensation there was nothing left but to hate her!

She was morally certain now that this feeling of hatred, which at first had been a refuge and a refreshment, had become the occupation and comfort of Osmond's life. The feeling was deep, because it was sincere; he had a revelation that, after all, she could dispense with him. (pp. 396-401)

Osmond's malignant hatred and envy of Isabel's originality and independence are characteristic of the unhealthy Sexual Four. He wants to destroy her out of competitive spite, since he knows that he can never have her natural gifts himself.

By the novel's end, Isabel learns the truth about the depth of Osmond's deception, and realizes she must escape him. Meanwhile, however, he has succeeded in making her married life a hell on earth—driven by an unhealthy Sexual Four's hate-filled envy.

"Soliloquy of the Spanish Cloister"

Robert Browning's dramatic monologue, "Soliloquy of the Spanish Cloister," offers a stunning portrait of a vicious Sexual Four. The narrator's hatred of a fellow monk is all the more horrifying for taking place in a cloister, where one would expect gentleness and piety.

I

Gr-r-r—there go, my heart's abhorrence!
Water your damned flower-pots, do!
If hate killed men, Brother Lawrence,
God's blood, would not mine kill you!
What? Your myrtle-bush wants trimming?
Oh, that rose has prior claims—
Needs its leaden vase filled brimming?
Hell dry you up with its flames!

The friar's envy of Brother Lawrence's simplicity and saintliness leads him to scheme about ways to trick a genuinely good man into damnation:

VII

There's a great text in Galatians,
Once you trip on it, entails
Twenty-nine distinct damnations,
One sure, if another fails:
If I trip him just a-dying,

Sure of heaven as sure can be,
Spin him round and send him flying
Off to hell, a Manichee?

VIII
Or, my scrofulous French novel
On grey paper with blunt type!
Simply glance at it, you grovel
Hand and foot in Belial's gripe:
If I double down its pages
At the woeful sixteenth print,
When he gathers his greengages,
Ope a sieve and slip it in't?

As the narrator plans Brother Lawrence's downfall, by trapping the monk into committing various mortal sins, his own familiarity with sins of the flesh suggests the depth of his hypocrisy. The more he plots against his fellow friar, the blacker his own soul appears.

Eventually, he considers a bargain with Satan, pledging his own soul—while leaving a loophole in the deal—if Satan will destroy a rose-acacia plant that Brother Lawrence loves:

IX
Or, there's Satan!—one might venture
Pledge one's soul to him, yet leave
Such a flaw in the indenture
As he'd miss till, past retrieve,
Blasted lay that rose-acacia
We're so proud of! Hy Zy, Hine . . .
'St, there's Vespers! Plena gratia
Ave, Virgo! Gr-r-r—you swine!

What the narrator fails to see, of course, is that his own soul is already damned by his deadly sin of envy.

Browning's friar is a deeply unhealthy Four. The range of this style otherwise extends from the dazzling creativity and eloquence of Proust's narrator in *Swann's Way* to the disorientation and pathos of Blanche DuBois in *A Streetcar Named Desire*; from the clarity, creative gifts and practical skills of Adam Dalgleish in *Devices and Desires* to the mean-spirited destructiveness of Gilbert Osmond in *The Portrait of a Lady*. Whether Fours are extraordinary artists, productive citizens, lost souls, or vindictive destroyers, their presence in society continually reminds us of the suffering inherent in the human condition.

Sources

Austen, Jane, *Sense and Sensibility* (NY: Dodd, Mead, 1949). First published 1811

Browning, Robert, "Soliloquy of the Spanish Cloister," in *An Oxford Anthology of English Poetry* (NY: Oxford University Press, 1956), pp. 949-950

Flaubert, Gustave, *Madame Bovary*, trans. Eleanor Marx Aveling (NY: The Modern Library, 1950). First published 1857

Goethe, Johann Wolfgang von, *The Sorrows of Young Werther*, trans. Victor Lange (NY: Suhrkamp, 1988). First published 1774

James, Henry, *The Portrait of a Lady* (NY: Barnes & Noble). First published 1881

James, P. D., *Devices and Desires* (NY: Warner Books, 1989)

Proust, Marcel, *Swann's Way*, trans. C.K. Scott Moncrieff (NY: Modern Library, 1928). First published 1913

Tolstoy, Leo, *Anna Karenina*, trans. Joel Carmichael (NY: Bantam, 1960). First published 1877

Williams, Tennessee, *A Streetcar Named Desire* (New York: New Directions, 1947)

The Glass Menagerie (NY: New Directions, 1945)

Five: The Analyst

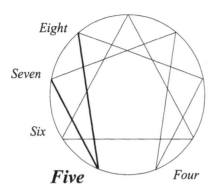

Meet detective Sherlock Holmes, the quintessential Five created by Arthur Conan Doyle. In the following scene from the early novella *A Study in Scarlet* we find Holmes talking with Dr. Watson, a Nine, whom he has recently met:

> [Holmes says:] "Observation with me is second nature. You appeared to be surprised when I told you, on our first meeting, that you had come from Afghanistan."
>
> "You were told, no doubt."
>
> "Nothing of the sort. I *knew* you came from Afghanistan. From long habit the train of thoughts ran so swiftly though my mind that I arrived at the conclusion without being conscious of the intermediate steps. There were such steps, however. The train of reasons ran, 'Here is a gentleman of a medical type, but with the air of a military man. Clearly an army doctor, then. He has just come from the tropics, for his face is dark, and that is not the natural tint of his skin, for his wrists are fair. He has undergone hardship and sickness, as his haggard face says clearly. His left arm has been injured. He holds it in a stiff and unnatural manner. Where in the tropics could an English army doctor have seen much hardship and got his arm wounded? Clearly in Afghanistan.' The whole train of thought did not occupy a second. I then remarked that you came from Afghanistan, and you were astonished." (p. 24)

Fives are especially noted for their ability to observe minute details and use their extraordinary deductive powers to draw conclusions from what they see. Earlier in the story, the man who will introduce Watson to Holmes describes the detective:

> "Holmes is a little too scientific for my tastes—it approaches to cold-bloodedness. I could imagine his giving a friend a little pinch of the latest vegetable alkaloid, not out of malevolence, you understand, but simply out of a spirit of inquiry in order to have an accurate idea of the effects. To do him justice, I think that he would take it himself with the same readiness. He appears to have a passion for definite and exact knowledge." (p. 17)

Emotional coolness, detachment, and a strong cognitive orientation are characteristic of Fives, who use knowledge as a defense in a dangerous world. Where Fours hide in their feelings to cope with life's disappointments, Fives use their minds as a bulwark against the world's intrusions. For Fives, a large storehouse of precise knowledge gives them a feeling of mastery over their environment. Although the Five's "deadly sin" is avarice—the tendency to greedily hoard—people with this style hoard knowledge more often than they do money.

The Stranger

In the opening passage of Albert Camus's classic novel *The Stranger*, Mersault, the Five protagonist, is oddly unmoved by his mother's death:

> Mother died today. Or, maybe, yesterday; I can't be sure. The telegram from the Home says: YOUR MOTHER PASSED AWAY. FUNERAL TOMORROW. DEEP SYMPATHY. Which leaves the matter doubtful; it could have been yesterday.
> The Home for Aged Persons is at Marengo, some fifty miles from Algiers. With the two-o'clock bus I should get there well before nightfall. Then I can spend the night there, keeping the usual vigil beside the body, and be back here by tomorrow evening. I have fixed up with my employer for two days' leave; obviously, under the circumstances, he couldn't refuse. Still, I had an idea he looked annoyed, and I said, without thinking: "Sorry, sir, but it's not my fault, you know."
> Afterwards it struck me I needn't have said that. I had no reason to excuse myself; it was up to him to express his sympathy and so forth. Probably he will do so the day after tomorrow, when he sees me in black. For the present, it's almost as if Mother weren't really dead. The funeral will bring it home to me, put an official seal on it, so to speak. . . . (pp. 1-2)

The day after his mother's funeral Mersault meets a young woman at a public swimming pool and ends up spending the night with her. Shortly after this interlude he goes to the seashore with a male friend. There he intercedes in a fight between his friend and an Arab and takes away his friend's gun, to prevent violence. Later, when Mersault returns to the beach alone, he sees the Arab, feels threatened by him, and shoots him.

Awaiting trial, Mersault finds himself explicitly accused of murder and implicitly indicted for his heartless reaction to his mother's death. Even his court-appointed lawyer seems disturbed by Mersault's lack of feeling:

> Sitting on the bed, he said that they'd been making investigations into my private life. They had learned that my mother died recently in a home. Inquiries had been conducted at Marengo and the police informed that I'd shown "great callousness" at my mother's funeral.
>
> "You must understand," the lawyer said, "that I don't relish having to question you about such a matter. But it has much importance, and, unless I find some way of answering the charge of 'callousness,' I shall be handicapped in conducting your defense. And that is where you, and only you, can help me."
>
> He went on to ask if I had felt grief on that "sad occasion." The question struck me as an odd one; I'd have been much embarrassed if I'd had to ask anyone a thing like that.
>
> I answered that, of recent years, I'd rather lost the habit of noting my feelings, and hardly knew what to answer. I could truthfully say I'd been quite fond of Mother—but really that didn't mean much. All normal people, I added as an afterthought, had more or less desired the death of those they loved, at some time or another.
>
> Here the lawyer interrupted me, looking greatly perturbed.
>
> "You must promise me not to say anything of that sort at the trial, or to the examining magistrate."
>
> I promised, to satisfy him, but I explained that my physical condition at any given moment often influenced my feelings. For instance, on the day I attended Mother's funeral, I was fagged out and only half awake. So, really, I hardly took stock of what was happening. Anyhow, I could assure him of one thing: that I'd rather Mother hadn't died.
>
> The lawyer, however, looked displeased. "That's not enough," he said curtly.
>
> After considering for a bit he asked me if he could say that on that day I had kept my feelings under control.
>
> "No," I said. "That wouldn't be true."
>
> He gave me a queer look, as if I slightly revolted him; then informed me, in an almost hostile tone, that in any case the head of the Home and some of the staff would be cited as witnesses.
>
> "And that might do you a very nasty turn," he concluded.
>
> When I suggested that Mother's death had no connection with the charge against me, he merely replied that this remark showed I'd never had any dealings with the law. (pp. 79-81)

Mersault's disassociated response to his lawyer's revulsion shows a Five's rigorous focus on logic. He also fails to comprehend what his lack of emotion might cost him. Many unhealthy Fives have trouble feeling empathy, so they don't understand how much it matters to others.

In jail awaiting trial, Mersault is mildly distressed at being forbidden to smoke. He adapts by fixing his thoughts elsewhere:

> Except for these privations I wasn't too unhappy. Yet again, the whole problem was: how to kill time. After a while, however, once I'd learned the trick of remembering things, I never had a moment's boredom. Sometimes I would exercise my memory on my bedroom and, starting from a corner, make the round, noting every object I saw on the way. At first it was over in a minute or two. But each time I repeated the experience, it took a little longer. I made a point of visualizing every piece of furniture, and each article upon or in it, and then every detail of each article, and finally the details of the details, so to speak: a tiny dent or incrustation, or a chipped edge, and the exact grain and color of the woodwork. At the same time I forced myself to keep my inventory in mind from start to finish, in the right order and omitting no item. With the result that, after a few weeks, I could spend hours merely in listing the objects in my bedroom. I found that the more I thought, the more details, half-forgotten or malobserved, floated up from my memory. There seemed no end to them. (p. 98)

Mersault's meaningless mental exercises are designed to block his fears about his potential fate. This response is consistent with the Seven stress point, where Fives become like Sevens and distract themselves from danger.

After Mersault is found guilty and condemned to death, he occupies himself with thinking about possible ways to avoid his fate:

> This problem of a loophole obsesses me; I am always wondering if there have been cases of condemned prisoners' escaping from the implacable machinery of justice at the last moment, breaking through the police cordon, vanishing in the nick of time before the guillotine falls. Often and often I blame myself for not having given more attention to accounts of public executions. One should always take an interest in such matters. There's never any knowing what one may come to. Like everyone else I'd read descriptions of executions in the papers. But technical books dealing with this subject must certainly exist; only I'd never felt sufficiently interested to look them up. And in these books I might have found escape stories. Surely they'd have told me that in one case, anyhow, the wheels had stopped; that once, if only once, in that inexorable march of events, chance or luck had played a happy part. Just once! In a way I think that single instance would have satisfied me. My

emotion would have done the rest. (pp. 136-137)

It's not unusual for a Five to believe that the solution to a problem—even his own death sentence—can be found through acquiring more information. Fives also guard themselves against surprises, as we see in the following passage:

> They always came for one at dawn; that much I knew. So, really, all my nights were spent in waiting for that dawn. I have never liked being taken by surprise. When something happens to me I want to be ready for it. That's why I got into the habit of sleeping off and on in the daytime and watching through the night for the first hint of daybreak in the dark dome above. The worst period of the night was that vague hour when, I knew, they usually come; once it was after midnight I waited, listening intently. Never before had my ears perceived so many noises, such tiny sounds. Still, I must say I was lucky in one respect; never during any of those periods did I hear footsteps. Mother used to say that however miserable one is, there's always something to be thankful for. And each morning, when the sky brightened and light began to flood my cell, I agreed with her. (pp. 141-142)

Mersault makes a kind of peace with his impending death by becoming acutely aware of how alive he is in the present moment. His final thoughts are of his mother and her death:

> With death so near, Mother must have felt like someone on the brink of freedom, ready to start life all over again. No one, no one in the world had any right to weep for her. And I, too, felt ready to start life all over again. It was as if that great rush of anger had washed me clean, emptied me of hope, and, gazing up at the dark sky spangled with its signs and stars, for the first time, the first, I laid my heart open to the benign indifference of the universe. To feel it so like myself, indeed, so brotherly, made me realize that I'd been happy, and that I was happy still. For all to be accomplished, for me to feel less lonely, all that remained to hope was that on the day of my execution there should be a huge crowd of spectators and that they should greet me with howls of execration. (p. 154)

In this, the final paragraph of Camus's novel, we see Mersault's Fiveish lack of feeling give way to the direct anger and ability to confront others that are characteristic of Fives at their Eight security point. Facing his execution, Mersault for the first time experiences the life force coursing through his body. He is even comforted by the horror others have for him, since it at least proves that he has been alive.

Smilla's Sense of Snow

Peter Hoeg's suspense novel *Smilla's Sense of Snow* offers a multi-dimensional portrait of a female Five. Smilla Qaavigaaq Jasperson, who is part Inuit and part Danish, lives in Copenhagen. At 37, she is single, childless, and moody. Although her peerless scientific expertise about the properties of snow and ice could earn her a prominent place in Danish society, she disdains most social and professional connections and lives a solitary life. When her neighbor, seven-year-old Isaiah, falls to his death off the top of their apartment building, Smilla studies the boy's footprints in the rooftop snow and concludes that the fall was no accident.

Here she discusses the circumstances of the boy's death with the investigating detective:

> "Time to go downstairs." [says the detective]
> At that moment I am clear about nothing, only confused. But I have so much confusion to spare that I could give some of it away. So I don't budge.
> "Strange way to play, don't you think?" I ask him.
> Some people might say that I'm vain. And I wouldn't exactly contradict them. I may have my reasons for it. At any rate, my clothes are what makes him listen to me now. The cashmere sweater, the fur hat, the gloves. He certainly would like to send me downstairs. But he can see that I look like an elegant lady. And he doesn't meet very many elegant ladies on the rooftops of Copenhagen. So he hesitates for a moment.
> "What do you mean?"
> "When you were that age," I say, "and your father and mother hadn't come home from the salt mines yet, and you were playing alone up on the roof of the barracks for the homeless, did you run in a straight line along the edge?"
> He chews on that.
> "I grew up in Jutland," he says. But he doesn't take his eyes off me as he speaks. (p. 10)

Like a good researcher, Smilla is able to tolerate uncertainty, without demanding closure, in her quest for understanding. She observes the detective closely, noting that he responds to her elegant clothes and pegs her as upper class. She then uses this to advantage in her own investigation of Isaiah's death, getting the detective to give her more latitude and share his information. Her awareness of the image she presents suggests a Four wing, but as a Five she is indifferent to how others see her except when it helps her acquire useful information.

In a later scene, Smilla displays other common Five attitudes:

> I feel the same way about solitude as some people feel about the

blessing of the church. It's the light of grace for me. I never close my
door behind me without the awareness that I am carrying out an act of
mercy toward myself. Cantor illustrated the concept of infinity for his
students by telling them that there was once a man who had a hotel with
an infinite number of rooms, and the hotel was fully occupied. Then one
more guest arrived. So the owner moved the guest in room number 1 into
room number 2; the guest in room number 2 into number 3; the guest in
3 into room 4, and so on. In that way room number 1 became vacant for
the new guest.

What delights me about this story is that everyone involved, the
guests and the owner, accept it as perfectly natural to carry out an infinite
number of operations so that one guest can have peace and quiet in a
room of his own. That is a great tribute to solitude.

I realize, as well, that I have furnished my apartment like a hotel
room—without overcoming the impression that the person living here
is in transit. Whenever I feel a need to explain it to myself, I think about
the fact that my mother's family, and she herself, were more or less
nomads. In terms of an excuse it's a weak explanation. (p. 11)

Smilla's use of complex intellectual concepts to support her penchant for
solitude and her enjoyment of having few possessions are both marks of her
Enneagram style.

Some average Fives resist not only paying the cost of physical luxuries but
also the emotional cost of grief:

I thought that I would grieve. I spoke to the police officers and
offered Juliane [Isaiah's mother] a shoulder to lean on and took her over
to a friend's place and came back, and the whole time I held my grief at
bay with my left hand. Now it should be my turn to give in to sorrow.

But it's not yet time. Grief is a gift, something you have to earn. I
make myself a cup of peppermint tea and go over to stand by the
window. But nothing happens. Maybe because there's still one little
thing I have to do, a single thing unfinished, the kind that can block a
flood of emotions. (pp. 11-12)

Smilla cared deeply for Isaiah by the time of his death, but remembers how
she initially resisted the connection:

For a moment I think it's a dog lying on the stairs. Then I see that
it's a child, and on this particular day that is not much better.
"Beat it, you little shit," I say.
Isaiah looks up.
"*Peerit*," he says. Beat it yourself.
There aren't many Danes who can tell by looking at me. They think

there's a trace of something Asian, especially when I put a shadow under my cheekbones. But the boy on the stairs looks right at me with a gaze that cuts straight through to what he and I have in common. It's the kind of look you see in newborns. Later it vanishes, sometimes reappearing in extremely old people. This could be one reason I've never burdened my life with children—I've thought too much about why people lose the courage to look each other in the eye.

"Will you read me a story?"

I have a book in my hand. That's what prompted his question.

You might say that he looks like a forest elf. But since he is filthy, dressed only in underpants, and glistening with sweat, you might also say he looks like a seal pup.

"Piss off," I say.

"Don't you like kids?"

"I eat kids."

He steps aside.

"*Salluvutit*, you're lying," he says as I go past.

At that moment I see two things in him that somehow link us together. I see that he is alone. The way someone in exile will always be. And I see that he is not afraid of solitude.

"What's the book?" he shouts after me.

"Euclid's *Elements*," I say, slamming the door. (pp. 13-14)

In Smilla's initial rudeness to Isaiah, she reacts readily with the aggression of her Eight security point. Her respect for the way the child stands up to her is similar to the way Eights appreciate people who stand their ground.

Smilla's Eight connection is also evident in her lack of social niceties and the way she is willing to make others uncomfortable if it helps her get information. Her investigation of Isaiah's death leads her to a tough-talking pathologist. Their conversation strengthens her suspicion that the fall from the roof was not accidental:

"We all have our phobias," I say. "Something that we're truly terrified of. I have mine. You probably have yours, when you take off that bulletproof white coat. Do you know what Isaiah's was? It was heights. He would race up to the second floor. But from there he crawled, with his eyes closed and both hands on the banister. Picture that—every day, on the stairway, inside the building, with sweat on his forehead and his knees buckling, five minutes to get from the second to the fourth floor. . . ."

There's a good long pause before he replies. "Nevertheless, he *was* up there."

"Yes," I say, "he was. But you could have tried a hydraulic lift. You could have tried a Hercules crane and you still wouldn't have budged him even a foot up that scaffolding. What puzzles me, what keeps me awake at night, is wondering what made him go up there at all." (pp. 22-23)

In Smilla's attitude toward phobias, we see a reflection of the Five's distinctive position in the so-called "fear" triad. Fives often use isolation and stockpiles of knowledge as tools to ward off their own phobic tendencies, unlike Sixes, who seek safety through trustworthy allies, and Sevens, who continually distract themselves to escape their underlying anxieties.

Smilla also displays the natural ability of many Fives to think in symbols, especially those related to mathematics or maps:

> I only have to look at a map once and the landscape rises up from the paper. It's not something that I learned. Although, of course, I had to acquire a nomenclature, a system of symbols. The ridged elevation peaks on the topographical maps of the Geodesic Institute. The red and green parabolas on the military maps of the ice pack. The discus-shaped, grayish-white photographs of the X-band radar. The multi-spectrum scans of LANDSAT 3. The candy-colored sediment maps of the geologists. The red-and-blue thermal photographs. But in the truest sense it has been like learning a new alphabet. Which you then forget about as soon as you start reading. (p. 80)

Although petite, Smilla is battle-ready and physically capable of doing great damage in a fight. Even as a child, she was able to take forceful Eightish action when the situation required it:

> The misconception that violence always favors the physically strong has spread to a large segment of the population. It's not correct. The results of a fight are a matter of speed in the first few yards. When I moved out to Skovgards School after six months at Rugmarkens School, I encountered for the first time the classic Danish persecution of those who are different. In the school we came from, we were all foreigners and in the same boat. In my new class I was the only one with black hair and broken Danish. There was one boy in particular, from one of the older classes, who was really quite brutal. I found out where he lived. Then I got up early and waited for him where he crossed Skovshoved Road. He was thirty pounds heavier than I was. He didn't have a chance. He never got the couple of minutes that he needed to work himself into a trance. I hit him right in the face and broke his nose. I kicked him on one kneecap and then on the other, to bring him down to a more acceptable height. It took twelve stitches to put his nasal septum back in place. No one ever really believed that it could have been me. (pp. 86-87)

Smilla's physical daring is supported by her lightning-fast mind. As a Five she leads with her head, first calculating mentally and then acting boldly. An Eight, by contrast, would be more likely to use physical force as a first line of defense.

When Smilla and a mechanic who was also a friend of Isaiah's become lovers, she is torn between her Five need for privacy and autonomy, and her desire for connection.

There in bed, happiness comes over me. Not like something that belongs to me, but like a wheel of fire rolling through the room and the world.

For a moment I think I'll manage to let it pass and be able to lie there, aware of what I have, and not wish for anything more.

The next moment I want to hang on. I want it to continue. He has to lie beside me tomorrow, too. This is my chance. My only, my last chance.

I swing my legs onto the floor. Now I'm panic-stricken.

This is what I've been working to avoid for thirty-seven years. I've systematically practiced the only thing in the world that is worth learning. How to renounce. I've stopped hoping for anything. When experienced humility becomes an Olympic discipline, I'll be on the national team.

I've never had any patience for other people's unhappy love affairs. I hate their weakness. . . .

There's one thing that is forbidden on journeys by sled, and that is whimpering. Whining is a virus, a lethal, infectious, epidemic disease. I refuse to listen to it. I refuse to be saddled with these orgies of emotional pettiness.

That's why I'm scared now. Standing there on his floor, next to his bed, I can hear something. It's coming from inside me, and it's a whimper. It's the fear that what has been given to me won't last. It's the sound of all the unhappy love stories I've never wanted to listen to. Now it sounds as if they're all contained within me. (pp. 181-182)

Her Fiveish terror of falling in love leads Smilla to deny that it is happening to her:

Falling in love has been greatly overrated. Falling in love consists of 45 percent fear of not being accepted and 45 percent manic hope that *this time* the fear will be put to shame, and a modest 10 percent frail awareness of the possibility of love.

I don't fall in love anymore. Just like I don't get the mumps.

But of course anyone can be overpowered by love. The last few weeks I've allowed myself to think about him for a few minutes each night. I give my mind permission and then watch how my body yearns and how I still remember him from the time before I really noticed him. I see his solicitude, remember his stutter, his embraces, and the awareness of the enormous core of his personality. When these images start to radiate too much longing, I cut them off. At least I try to.

I haven't fallen in love. I see things too clearly for that. Falling in love is a form of madness. Closely related to hatred, coldness, resentment, intoxication, and suicide.

Occasionally—not often, but occasionally—I'm reminded of the times in my life when I've fallen in love. That's what's happening now. (p. 321)

Smilla's anxiety about the risks of intimacy is shared by many Fives. She Fourishly yearns for love, but when she feels it she uses her reason to cut it off.

Near the story's end, Smilla is still trying to resolve Isaiah's death. She gets a job as a stewardess on a ship owned by the novel's villain and bound for a remote island off Greenland. Caught snooping in an unauthorized area of the ship, she faces her possible doom:

Nothing was more reassuring to me than the knowledge that I would die. In these moments of clarity—and you see yourself clearly only when you see yourself as a stranger—all despair, all gaiety, all depression vanish and are replaced by calm. For me death was not something scary or a state of being or an event that would happen to me. It was a focusing on the now, an aid, an ally in the effort to be mentally present. (p. 395)

Although in a life-threatening situation, Smilla's control of her emotions allows her to maintain her mental acuity.

During the story's finale, Smilla endures great physical pain while remaining focused on her goal. In fact, she finally solves the puzzle of Isaiah's death through sheer mental alertness.

Author Hoeg's depiction of Smilla as a Five hero is all the more powerful for its depiction of the psychological price—in emotional constriction and isolation—that Fives pay for their mental mastery of the world.

The Five's History

As children Fives typically feel vulnerable to engulfment by one or both of their parents. Anxious about being overwhelmed, Five children withdraw into their own minds, relying on their powers of observation and analysis to keep them safe.

In contrast to Fours, who long for intimate relationships, Fives avoid such connections for fear of losing control over their lives. Better, the Five thinks, to detach from feelings as much as possible and rely on my certain strengths of intellect than to face the emotional helplessness that comes with giving and receiving love.

Levels of Health

Fives at all levels of health seek to maintain their safety by relying on their mental faculties and minimizing contact with others. The psychological defense mechanism used by Fives is *isolation of affect*—a deliberate tamping down of emotions that protects the Five's fragile core from violation. Focused on issues of safety and security, Fives often see others as more dangerous than helpful.

Average Fives are preoccupied with their own mental processes. They enjoy accumulating information and achieving mastery in their fields. Emotionally detached, they resist having intimate relationships. Often tense and intense, they tend toward cynicism and iconoclasm.

Average Fives lack an emotional language. They are not devoid of feeling, but they prefer to process their feelings in private, and generally avoid revealing their emotions to others—even life partners. The tendency to detach and withdraw in the face of others' emotion is in direct proportion to Fives' fear of violation.

In literature we see a range of average Fives: Mersault in *The Stranger*, Smilla in *Smilla's Sense of Snow*, Neara in Russsell Hoban's *Turtle Diary*, Thersites in Shakespeare's *Troilus and Cressida*, Feste in Shakespeare's *Twelfth Night*, the Fool in Shakespeare's *King Lear*, Stephen Dedalus in James Joyce's *Portrait of the Artist as a Young Man* and *Ulysses*, Joseph K. in Franz Kafka's *The Trial*, Adah in Barabara Kingsolver's *The Poisonwood Bible*, Anna Wulf in Doris Lessing's *The Golden Notebook*, Thomas Mann's Doctor Faustus, Peggy in Elizabeth McCracken's *The Giant's House: A Romance*, Almásy in Michael Ondaatje's *The English Patient*, David Lurie in J.M. Coetzee's *Disgrace*, Christopher Banks in Kazuo Ishiguro's *When We Were Orphans*, and George in Edward Albee's *Who's Afraid of Virginia Woolf?*

Healthy Fives are extraordinarily alert and inventive, capable of original insights into the patterns of nature and human life. In love with knowledge, they master whatever subjects interest them and can become world-class experts in their chosen field. Healthy Fives are independent and often display a wry humor.

Literary examples include Beth in Louisa Mae Alcott's *Little Women*, Arthur Conan Doyle's Sherlock Holmes, C. S. Lewis in William Nicholson's play *Shadowlands*, Joseph Knecht in Hermann Hesse's *The Glass Bead Game (Magister Ludi)*, and Catherine in David Auburn's play *Proof*.

Unhealthy Fives can become physically and mentally out of touch with reality and people, obsessed with negative thoughts and bizarre ideas, subject to phobias and distortions of reality. When extremely unhealthy, their quest for respite from the torments of their own mind may lead them to suicide or psychosis.

Examples of unhealthy Fives in literature include Samuel Beckett's Molloy, Scrooge in Charles Dickens's *A Christmas Carol*, Casaubon in George Eliot's

Middlemarch, Frederick Clegg in John Fowles's *The Collector*, Janet Frame in her autobiography *An Angel at My Table*, Hannibal Lecter in Thomas Harris's *The Silence of the Lambs*, William in Russell Hoban's *Turtle Diary*, Gustave Aschenbach in Thomas Mann's *Death in Venice*, and Herman Melville's Bartleby.

Place in Society

Although Fives are found in all professions, they are especially prominent in scientific and technical fields where mastering difficult concepts and original thinking are highly prized. Work with computers attracts many Fives because it permits the autonomy they crave. Fives are also drawn to work as researchers and scholars, historians, teachers, and social scientists. Their skill as observers and analysts often leads them to jobs as reporters, psychologists, philosophers, and scientists. Their preference for working alone fits them for work as mathematicians, accountants, engineers, auto mechanics and machinists.

Five artists—including fiction writers, poets, painters, sculptors, composers, and musicians—can produce work that is notable for both its distinctive vision and technical brilliance. Fives are also attracted to careers as magicians, perhaps because they enjoy mastering the difficult technical skills involved in creating illusions. Professional chess players and designers of computer games are often Fives, as well.

Stress and Security Points

Five's connecting points are Seven and Eight, both aggressive styles. Although Five is a withdrawn style, Fives tend to react strongly when their detached stance meets significant challenges from the outer world. Under stress, Fives may take on the hyperactive characteristics of the average Seven. Seeking activities that will distract them from their growing anxieties, they can suffer from mental overload and be unable to focus in depth on subjects or situations that require their attention.

When Fives feel secure, they realize that the knowledge and mastery they have acquired are sufficient to support their active participation in society. At their Eight security point, they tend to move into the strong leadership stance, becoming confident of their power and able to stand their ground.

Wings

There is a marked contrast between Fives with a Four wing and those with a Six wing. While Four is a withdrawn style, reinforcing the Five's instinct to detach from others, Six is both compliant and dependent—giving Fives with a Six wing more desire to move toward others.

Average Fives with a Four wing tend to be detached from their personal feelings but passionate about aesthetic and ethical issues. Absorbed in analyzing how the world works, they are self-conscious about sharing their ideas with others. They can be enormously creative and original; Five artists often have this wing.

In *Smilla's Sense of Snow*, Smilla's Four wing is especially evident in the way she resists personal relationships. When the boy Isaiah attempts to befriend her, her rudeness to him signals her extreme fear of being intruded upon. Although she accepts the mechanic as her lover, she remains uncomfortable about their intimacy as well. Unlike a Four, she is clear about her core identity and mistrusts her feelings. Far from longing to be rescued, as a Four might, Smilla is able and determined to rescue herself.

Average Fives with a Six wing want to be liked by others, and they generally have better social skills than Fives with a Four wing. Although they mistrust most people, their awareness of the value of allies motivates them to engage with a few trusted friends.

In Camus's *The Stranger*, Mersault's Six wing shows in his ability to connect with the young woman at a public swimming pool and the man he accompanies to the seashore. Mersault's lack of interest in aesthetic, ethical, and emotional matters clashes with the Four French culture that condemns him—as much for his lack of feeling towards his mother as for murdering the Arab.

Turtle Diary

The two central characters in Russell Hoban's *Turtle Diary* offer contrasting examples of the wings of Five. A quixotic quest to free the sea turtles at the London Zoo unites this unlikely pair: Neara H., a writer of children's books, a Five with a Four wing, and William G., a bookstore employee, who has a Six wing. After conspiring with the turtles' keeper, they arrange to release the animals into the open sea, finding freedom for themselves in the process. Although there is no romance between them, both Neara and William are better able to connect with other people as a result of their joint mission.

The beginning of the story finds William at a crisis point. He has long ago lost touch with his ex-wife and daughters and is almost completely without personal connections:

> I had a sort of bursting feeling as if my self were a wall round me that I couldn't knock down or climb over. I have no talent, no Zen like that of the gibbons. Once, twice, long ago. Out of it, away and in the clear. What's the use of remembering. Out of it was at the same time into it. There's a wall inside the self as well. Can't get through any more. Can't live is what it amounts to. No place to live. Get through the days, the seasons, oh yes. But no place to be. No way to hold the sun in the eye, be held by it swimming, swimming.
>
> The wax people downstairs at Madame Tussaud's contemplating in wax their crimes get through the days, the nights, the seasons. The thought escapes me, there was more to it. Prisons are all we know how to make, even in wax. No wax sea turtles, thank God for that.

There they were in the golden-green murk of their little box of sea, their little bedsitter of ocean. . . . Thousands of miles in their speechless eyes, submarine skies in their flipper-wings. (p. 23)

William's fragmented thinking shows a Five's strong link to his Seven stress point. Although he is walled off from his true feelings, he senses the turtles are real and identifies with their imprisonment.

Neara, too, feels a strong connection with the turtles' plight, but for different reasons:

At three o'clock in the morning I sat in the dark looking out of the window down at the square where the fountain is not and I thought about the turtles. The essence of it is that they can find something and they are not being allowed to do it. What more can you do to a creature, short of killing it, than prevent it from finding what it can find? How must they feel? Is there a sense in them of green ocean, white surf and hot sand? Probably not. But there *is* a drive in them to find it as they swoop in their golden-green light with their flippers clicking against the glass as they turn. Is there anything to be done about it? My mind is not an organizational one. (p. 48)

Neara projects her Four-like yearning and desperation onto the turtles: they are trapped and so is she. Her wing also shows in her concern for what they must be feeling.

When Neara talks with the turtles' keeper about returning them to the sea, he tells her of William's independent interest in doing the same thing. She struggles to work up the social courage to introduce herself to William:

I went to the bookshop. The man and I said hello to each other and I went to the Natural History section where I turned the pages of books without looking at them. My heart was pounding somewhat and I found myself mentally rehearsing what I would say. I always do that, I can't help it. Even when I go to the Post Office I say in my mind before I reach the window, 'Twenty stamps at 3p, please.' Then I say it aloud at the window. 'I wonder if you too are thinking about the turtles?' I would say. Or 'Perhaps we had better discuss the turtles?' I cursed him for not being man enough to speak up and broach the subject when it loomed so large and visible between us. (p. 70)

Rehearsing social interactions, even mundane ones, is a Five tendency.

Throughout *Turtle Diary* Neara and William are instinctively aware of each other's feelings, although Neara is healthier than William. Here, conscious that William is despairing and possibly suicidal, Neara visits his apartment after prying his address out of his co-worker. William is spooked by Neara's intuitive understanding of his mental state:

> It was absolutely uncanny, gave me the creeps. That woman actually thought I'd been thinking of suicide.
>
> I *had* been thinking of it right enough, I often do, always have the idea of it huddled like a sick ape in a corner of my mind. But I'd never do it. At least I don't think I'd do it, can't imagine a state of mind in which I'd do it. Well, that's not true either. I *can* imagine the state of mind, I've been in it often enough. No place for the self to sit down and catch its breath. Just being hurried, hurried out of existence. . . . As the mind moves forward the self is pushed back, everything multiplies itself like mirrors receding laboriously to infinity, repeating endlessly even the earwax in the ears, the silence in the eyes. (p. 95)

William's Six wing is evident in the way his fear afflicts his ability to think clearly.

Later in the story William and Neara carry out their plan and release the turtles into the ocean near the English resort town of Polperro. Drinking champagne to celebrate their achievement, Neara experiences a peak moment of love and forgiveness:

> 'Here's wishing them luck,' we said, and drank to the turtles. The waves were silver under the moon, the spray flew up from the rocks on either side of the harbour entrance, there was a beacon on the headland. The champagne tasted like clear and bubbling bright new mornings without end. We gulped it greedily and threw the empty bottle into the ocean. The ocean was rough and real, always real, only real. It wasn't Polperro's fault that the place had to go begging with souvenirs and money-boxes and a model village. I forgave Polperro, loved it for what it had been and what it now was, for its happiness and sorrow by the sea. I forgave myself for not loving it before, loved myself for loving it now. I forgave everybody everything, felt the Caister two-stone in the pocket of my mac, flung it out into the moonlit ocean. (pp. 158-159)

Fours have strong issues about aesthetics and ethics, and find ugliness and money-grubbing offensive, especially in a beautiful natural setting. In this transcendent moment Neara's Four wing is able not only to feel love—a breakthrough for a Five—but to do so without longing for its object to be more worthy.

William has his own epiphany after releasing the turtles, glorying in his new-found ability to live in the present and without his usual Sixish fears:

> When I felt the wind on my face and saw that the tide was in it seemed all at once that I didn't need any answers to anything. The tide

and the moon, the beacon on the headland and the wind were so *here*, so *this*, so *now* that nothing else was required. I felt free of myself, unlumbered. (p. 160)

When William returns to London, he suddenly finds the courage to confront Sandor, his house-mate, about the latter's habit of leaving the bathtub and kitchen filthy. This leads to a physical fight, and William suddenly finds more of his personal power:

> Go ahead and squeeze, I thought.... I was getting angry. There was a redness silently exploding in my mind. Violence. Lovely. Bumpitty bump.
>
> I was on the landing feeling quite wrenched and pulled about. Mr Sandor was one flight down, rubbing himself in various places and looking up at me with great concentration. Now he's *really* going to be angry, I thought. I didn't mind. I didn't care if we killed each other.
>
> Mrs Inchcliff came racing up the stairs. She'd never smoked, stairs were nothing to her even at sixty. 'What's happening?' she said. 'Why is everyone lying on the floor? Are you both all right?'
>
> 'We have collision,' said Sandor. 'Down we tumble.' He was still staring at me and I saw in his face that he saw in my face that I wasn't afraid of him any more. (p. 174)

For Neara, freeing the turtles has released new creative energies in her: she now begins to experiment with a new way of writing. For her, as for William, this represents a Five's move to the Eight security point.

When Neara returns to tell the turtles' keeper that they have been released, she ends up in his arms weeping, and the two become lovers. Happy in her relationship with this simple, loving man, a Nine, Neara suddenly realizes how lonely she has been:

> I didn't know how lonely I'd been until the loneliness stopped. . . . George had given me so much that even if there came a time without George I could bear it now and not step carefully or build my broken eggshell with mad patience. He hadn't done anything special, it was simply his way of being. Like him I found that I no longer minded being alive. And the turtles were swimming, there was always that to fall back on. (p. 203)

Now that Neara has confidence in her own creative center, we sense that she is going to write something remarkable.

William, too, continues to feel the reverberations of releasing the turtles. When a woman in his boarding house commits suicide he experiences empathy, possibly for the first time—a significant step toward psychological health for a Five. He also connects with his fellow-boarders in a new way:

> The morning had nothing special to recommend it. . . . But I felt good.
>
> At lunch-time I bought a bottle of Moët-Chandon and went up to the Zoo. In the tube I thought about Miss Neap and Mr Sandor and Mrs Inchcliff. With no funeral to go to we'd found ourselves drawn together somehow and remembering her but not altogether mournfully. In fact we all got drunk and Sandor sang gypsy songs. Rather well too. Odd but not really. If Flora Angelica Neap was going to be an undeparted presence she'd have to share the good times as well as the bad. And I could imagine good times, why I don't know. Nothing was different or better and I didn't think I was either but I didn't mind being alive at the moment. After all who knew what might happen. (p. 210)

William's depression has lifted, and the positive aspects of the Five's Six wing are visible in his ability to take pleasure in being part of a social group. Like Neara, he has been freed by freeing the turtles.

Subtypes

All Fives focus on finding ways of preserving their safety and autonomy in the world, but their strategies for doing this vary according to their subtype.

Self-Preservation Fives, whom Oscar Ichazo characterizes as "castle," tend to be the most fragile, shy and withdrawn. Their basic strategy is to minimize personal needs and social contacts. Intent on creating a safe place to which they can retreat from a dangerous world, they are easily exhausted by others and need solitary time in familiar surroundings to recoup their energies. Self-Preservation Fives may also stockpile supplies as a way of feeling prepared for any contingency.

Examples of this subtype in literature include Mersault in *The Stranger*, both William and Neara in *Turtle Diary*, Joseph K. in Franz Kafka's *The Trial*, Adah Price in Barbara Kingsolver's *The Poisonwood Bible*, Janet Frame in her autobiography *An Angel at My Table*, Catherine in David Auburn's play *Proof*, and Scrooge in Charles Dickens's *A Christmas Carol*.

A Christmas Carol

In Dickens's classic story we first see Ebenezer Scrooge, an unhealthy Self-Preservation Five, sitting in his office on Christmas Eve:

> Oh! But he was a tight-fisted hand at the grindstone, Scrooge! A squeezing, wrenching, grasping, scraping, clutching, covetous old sinner! Hard and sharp as flint, from which no steel had ever struck out generous fire; secret, and self-contained, and solitary as an oyster. (p. 4)

When Scrooge's nephew comes to invite him to Christmas dinner, Scrooge makes it clear that he sees the holiday entirely in economic terms:

"Bah!" said Scrooge, "Humbug!" . . .

"Don't be cross, uncle," said the nephew.

"What else can I be," returned the uncle, "when I live in such a world of fools as this? Merry Christmas! Out upon Merry Christmas! What's Christmas time to you but a time for paying bills without money; a time for finding yourself a year older, but not an hour richer; a time for balancing your books and having every item in 'em through a round dozen of months presented dead against you? If I could work my will," said Scrooge, indignantly, "every idiot who goes about with 'Merry Christmas' on his lips, should be boiled with his own pudding, and buried with a stake of holly through his heart. He should!" (pp. 5-6)

As a Self-Preservation Five Scrooge hoards his resources, but being confrontational also helps him emotionally distance others, including his nephew.

Later, when the ghost of Scrooge's former business partner, Jacob Marley, appears to Scrooge, he doubts the apparition's reality:

"You don't believe in me," observed the Ghost.

"I don't," said Scrooge.

"What evidence would you have of my reality beyond that of your senses?"

"I don't know," said Scrooge.

"Why do you doubt your senses?"

"Because," said Scrooge, "a little thing affects them. A slight disorder of the stomach makes them cheats. You may be an undigested bit of beef, a blot of mustard, a crumb of cheese, a fragment of an underdone potato. There's more of gravy than of grave about you, whatever you are!" (p. 14)

Self-Preservation subtypes of all Enneagram styles have a strong awareness of food, a basic necessity for survival. Here it's Scrooge's criterion for what is real.

Marley's ghost warns Scrooge that he will be haunted by Three Spirits, who will help Scrooge avoid the disastrous path that Marley himself took. The first spirit, the Ghost of Christmas Past, is a childlike yet aged figure. It shows Scrooge a scene from his youth when his fiancée broke off their engagement because he loved money more than he loved her.

"Our contract is an old one [she says]. It was made when we were both poor and content to be so, until, in good season, we could improve our worldly fortune by our patient industry. You *are* changed. When it was made, you were another man. . . . But if you were free to-day, to-morrow, yesterday, can even I believe that you would choose a dower-less girl—you who, in your very confidence with her, weigh everything by Gain: or, choosing her, if for a moment you were false enough to your one guiding principle to do so, do I not know that your repentance and regret would surely follow? I do; and I release you. With a full heart, for the love of him you once were."

He was about to speak; but with her head turned from him, she resumed.

"You may—the memory of what is past half makes me hope you will—have pain in this. A very, very brief time, and you will dismiss the recollection of it, gladly, as an unprofitable dream, from which it happened well that you awoke. May you be happy in the life you have chosen!"

She left him, and they parted. (pp. 30-31)

The idea that a loving relationship might offer something valuable in itself is hard for a Self-Preservation Five to conceive; all the young Scrooge sees is that it is a potential drain on his limited resources.

Next, the Ghost of Christmas Present appears, as a hearty, jovial middle-aged man. He shows Scrooge the household of his clerk, Bob Crachit. Seeing the family happy despite their poverty and the chronic illness of the youngest child, Tiny Tim, Scrooge is amazed. Touched by the boy's spirit and sweetness, Scrooge feels concern for another human being for the first time.

The last spirit, the Ghost of Christmas Yet To Come, gives Scrooge a frightening preview of his own lonely death. Among other things, Scrooge watches strangers steal his treasured belongings, even his bed linen and the shirt off his corpse. When he awakens from this nightmare, secure in his own bedroom, he is suddenly filled with joy and resolves to mend his ways. He acts immediately on his change of heart:

Scrooge was better than his word. He did it all, and infinitely more; and to Tiny Tim, who did NOT die, he was a second father. He became as good a friend, as good a master, and as good a man, as the good old city knew, or any other good old city, town, or borough, in the good old world. Some people laughed to see the alteration in him, but he let them laugh, and little heeded them; for he was wise enough to know that nothing ever happened on this globe, for good, at which some people did not have their fill of laughter in the outset; and knowing that such as these would be blind anyway, he thought it quite as well that they should wrinkle up their eyes in grins, as have the malady in less attractive forms. His own heart laughed: and that was quite enough for him. (pp. 72-73)

By the end of Dickens's story Scrooge is taking positive action through the force of his Eight security point. He has escaped the fearful isolation of his Self-Preservation subtype to become part of the human race.

The Poisonwood Bible

Adah Price in Barbara Kingsolver's *The Poisonwood Bible* offers a multi-dimensional portrait of a Self-Preservation Five with a Four wing. The story is told by the wife and four daughters of Nathan Price, a fierce evangelical Baptist who takes his family and mission to the Belgian Congo in 1959. It is an epic of the family's tragic undoing and remarkable reconstruction over the course of three decades.

Adah, one of the daughters and a twin crippled from birth, is a keen observer of everything around her, but she rarely speaks and is considered mute by most people. Here she describes her disability:

> My right side drags. I was born with half my brain dried up like a prune, deprived of blood by an unfortunate fetal mishap. My twin sister, Leah, and I are identical in theory, just as in theory we are all made in God's image. Leah and Adah began our life as images mirror perfect. We have the same eyes dark and chestnut hair. But I am a lame gallimaufry and she remains perfect.
>
> Oh, I can easily imagine the fetal mishap: we were inside the womb together dum-de-dum when Leah suddenly turned and declared, Adah you are just too slow. I am taking all the nourishment here and going on ahead. She grew strong as I grew weak. (Yes! Jesus loves me!) And so it came to pass, in the Eden of our mother's womb, I was cannibalized by my sister.
>
> Officially my condition is called hemiplegia. *Hemi* is half, hemisphere, hemmed-in, hemlock, hem and haw, *Plegia* is the cessation of motion. After our complicated birth, physicians in Atlanta pronounced many diagnoses on my asymmetrical brain, including Wernicke's and Broca's aphasia, and sent my parents home over the icy roads on Christmas Eve with one-half a set of perfect twins and the prediction that I might possibly someday learn to read but would never speak a word.
>
> . . .
>
> I am prone to let the doctors' prophecy rest and keep my thoughts to myself. Silence has many advantages. When you do not speak, other people presume you to be deaf or feeble-minded and promptly make a show of their own limitations. Only occasionally do I find I have to break my peace: shout or be lost in the shuffle. But mostly am lost in the shuffle. I write and draw in my notebook and read anything I please.
>
> It is true I do not speak as well as I can think. But that is true of most people, as nearly as I can tell. (pp. 33-34)

As a Self-Preservation Five, Adah used the doctor's prophecy as an excuse to avoid social contact—thus securing the isolation that becomes her safe haven.

When Adah was in elementary school it became clear that she had special gifts with numbers, an ability seen in some Fives:

> In third grade I began to sum up our grocery bill in my head, silently write it down and hand it over, faster than Delma Royce could total it on her cash register. This became a famous event and never failed to draw a crowd. I had no idea why. I merely felt drawn in by those rattling, loose numbers needing their call to order. No one seemed to realize calculating sums requires only the most basic machinery and good concentration. Poetry is far more difficult. And palindromes, with their perfect, satisfying taste: Draw a level award! Yet it is always the thin gray grocery sums that make an impression.
>
> My hobby is to ignore the awards and excel when I choose. . . .(p.57)

Adah also has a knack for creating palindromes—formations of words that are identical when read forward or backward. Her sardonic sense of humor is revealed in her private pot-shots at her self-important father and his mission:

> The Reverend towered over the rickety altar, his fiery crew cut bristling like a woodpecker's cockade. When the Spirit passed through him he groaned, throwing body and soul into this weekly purge. The "Amen enema," as I call it. My palindrome for the Reverend. (p. 69)

Adah has a penchant for seeing unexpected connections. She connects the birth and death of her sister, Ruth May, in a way that resonates with the writings of her poet-hero, Emily Dickinson. Note her clarity and detachment as she describes the process of dying, even though the victim is her sister:

> *Because I could not stop for Death—He kindly stopped for me.*
> I was not present at Ruth May's birth but I have seen it now, because I saw each step of it played out in reverse at the end of her life. The closing parenthesis, at the end of the palindrome that was Ruth May. Her final gulp of air as hungry as a baby's first breath. That last howling scream, exactly like the first, and then at the end a fixed, steadfast moving backward out of this world. After the howl, wide-eyed silence without breath. Her bluish face creased with a pressure closing in, the near proximity of the other-than-life that crowds down around the edges of living. Her eyes closed up tightly, and her swollen lips clamped shut. Her spine curved, and her limbs drew in more and more tightly until she seemed impossibly small. While we watched without comprehension, she moved away to where none of us wanted to follow. Ruth May shrank back through the narrow passage between this brief fabric of light and all the rest of what there is for us: the long waiting. Now she will wait the rest of the time. It will be exactly as long as the time that passed before she was born. (p. 365)

Years later, when Adah attends medical school, she has an opportunity to undergo a program of neurological re-education that will remove her disability:

> I am losing my slant.
> In medical school I have been befriended by an upstart neurologist, who believes I am acting out a great lifelong falsehood. Adah's False Hood. In his opinion, an injury to the brain occurring as early as mine should have no lasting effects on physical mobility. He insists there should have been complete compensation in the undamaged part of my cerebral cortex, and that my dragging right side is merely holding on to a habit it learned in infancy. I scoffed at him, of course. I was unprepared to accept that my whole sense of *Adah* was founded on a misunderstanding between my body and my brain. (p. 438)

As a Self–Preservation Five she has to decide whether to surrender the "castle" of her disability.

Many years later, in 1985, she considers her new identity:

> Personally I have stolen an arm and a leg. I am still Adah but you would hardly know me now, without my slant. I walk without any noticeable limp. Oddly enough, it has taken me years to accept my new position. I find I no longer have *Ada*, the mystery of coming and going. Along with my split-body drag I lost my ability to read in the old way. When I open a book, the words sort themselves into narrow-minded single file on the page; the mirror-image poems erase themselves half-formed in my mind. I miss those poems. Sometimes at night, in secret, I still limp purposefully around my apartment, like Mr. Hyde, trying to recover my old ways of seeing and thinking. Like Jekyll I crave that particular darkness curled up within me. Sometimes it almost comes. The books on the shelf rise up in solid lines of singing color, the world drops out, and its hidden shapes snap forward to meet my eyes. But it never lasts. By morning light, the books are all hunched together again with their spines turned out, fossilized, inanimate. (p. 492)

Losing her disability feels like losing a part of her core self, the refuge that allowed Adah her distinct and valuable perspective and kept her safe.

Her self-image is still that of a limited person, and her uncertainty about her core identity is another mark of her Four wing:

> Tall and straight I may appear, but I will always be Ada inside. A crooked little person trying to tell the truth. The power is in the balance: we are our injuries, as much as we are our successes. (p. 496)

Like a number of Self-Preservation Fives, Adah has well-thought-out reasons for never marrying:

I have not married either, for different reasons. The famous upstart neurologist wanted to be my lover, it turned out, and actually won me to his bed for a time. But slowly it dawned upon my love-drunk skull: he had only welcomed me there after devising his program to make me whole! He was the first of several men to suffer the ice storms of Adah, I'm afraid.

This is my test: I imagine them back there in the moonlight with the ground all around us boiling with ants. Now, which one, the crooked walker, or the darling perfection? I know how they would choose. Any man who admires my body now is a traitor to the previous Adah. So there you are. (pp. 531-532)

Like most average Self-Preservation Fives, Adah finds it easy to cut off intimate relationships and is ultimately most comfortable in solitude.

Fives with a **Social** subtype, whom Ichazo associates with "totems," seek to become part of society's intellectual elite through mastery of special knowledge. Social Fives are often scientists and academics who enjoy analyzing social trends and exchanging complex ideas with their peers. They find safety and satisfaction in the social status that accompanies their affiliations.

Social Fives in literature include Sherlock Holmes, Thomas Mann's Doctor Faustus, Stephen Dedalus in James Joyce's *Portrait of the Artist as a Young Man* and *Ulysses*, George in Edward Albee's *Who's Afraid of Virginia Woolf?*, Anna Wulf in Doris Lessing's *The Golden Notebook*, C.S. Lewis in William Nicholson's *Shadowlands*, Casaubon in George Eliot's *Middlemarch*, Christopher Banks in Kazuo Ishiguro's *When We Were Orphans*, and Joseph Knecht in Hermann Hesse's *The Glass Bead Game (Magister Ludi)*.

The Glass Bead Game (Magister Ludi)
Joseph Knecht in Hermann Hesse's dense and difficult but poetic novel is a healthy Social Five. As a boy Knecht is sent to Castalia, the school for the secular order of intellectuals who have dedicated their lives to the Glass Bead Game.

In a letter to his friend Tegularius, Knecht recalls the intellectual excitement of life at the school:

"Let me remind you of the time the two of us, assigned to the same group, were so eagerly working on our first sketches for Glass Bead Games. Do you recall a certain day and a certain game? Our group leader had given us various suggestions and proposed all sorts of themes for us to choose from. We had just arrived at the delicate transition from astronomy, mathematics, and physics to the sciences of language and history, and the leader was a virtuoso in the art of setting traps for eager beginners like us and luring us on to the thin ice of impermissible abstractions and analogies. He would slip into our hands tempting baubles taken from etymology and comparative linguistics, and enjoyed seeing us grab them and come to grief. We counted Greek quantities until we were worn out, only to feel the rug pulled out from under us when he suddenly confronted us with the possibility, in fact the necessity, of accentual instead of a quantitative scansion, and so on. In formal terms he did his job brilliantly, and quite properly, although I did not like the spirit of it. . . . I suddenly realized that in the language, or at any rate in the spirit of the Glass Bead Game, everything actually was all-meaningful, that every symbol and combination of symbols led not hither and yon, not to single examples, experiments, and proofs, but into the center, the mystery and innermost heart of the world, into primal knowledge. Every transition from major to minor in a sonata, every transformation of a myth or a religious cult, every classical or artistic formulation was, I realized in that flashing moment, if seen with a truly meditative mind, nothing but a direct route into the interior of the cosmic mystery, where in the alternation between inhaling and exhaling, between heaven and earth, between Yin and Yang, holiness is forever being created." (pp. 118-119)

In the rarified atmosphere of this exclusive society, the Glass Bead Game represents the primary "totem"—the system of secret knowledge that the students strive to master. Knecht's excitement at glimpsing the mystery of the universe is consistent with his subtype. Later, he begins to realize that mastering the game is not necessarily the same as grasping the game's larger meaning:

"I imagine," Knecht wrote to his patron, "that one can be an excellent Glass Bead Game player, even a virtuoso, and perhaps even a thoroughly competent Magister Ludi, without having any inkling of the real mystery of the Game and its ultimate meaning. It might even be that one who does guess or know the truth might prove a greater danger to the Game, were he to become a specialist in the Game, or a Game leader. . . . Because I think I have come close to the meaning of the Glass Bead Game, it will be better for me and for others if I do not make the Game my profession, but instead shift to music." (pp. 121-122)

Despite his reservations, Knecht is named Magister Ludi—Master of the Glass Bead Game. He accepts the honor and its responsibilities with grace but feels ambivalent about becoming part of the Castalian hierarchy.

As the years pass, Knecht's chosen way of life continues to trouble him. Eventually, he decides to send a "circular letter" to the leaders of the Order, asking to be released from his post as Magister Ludi and allowed to leave the Order. His chief reasons have to do with the insularity of the Order and its abdication of its responsibility for taking action in the larger world:

"... Ruling does not require qualities of stupidity and coarseness, as conceited intellectuals sometimes think. But it does require whole-hearted delight in extraverted activity, a bent for identifying oneself with outward goals, and of course also a certain swiftness and lack of scruple about the choice of ways to attain success. And these are traits that a scholar—for we do not wish to call ourselves sages—may not have and does not have, because for us contemplation is more important than action, and in the choice of ways to attain our goals we have learned to be as scrupulous and wary as is humanly possible.

Therefore it is not our business to rule and not our business to engage in politics. . . ." (p. 358)

Knecht continues to struggle with his need for taking active Eightish action—the Five's security point. But this is contrary to the Order's philosophy:

And what about the virtues of serenity, firm tempo and courage? They dwindled in size perhaps, but remained intact. Even if he might not be advancing on his own, but was only being led, even if what he was undergoing was not independent transcending, but merely a revolving of the space outside him around himself as its center, the virtues persisted and retained their value and their potency. They consisted in affirmation instead of negation, in acceptance instead of evasion. And perhaps there might even be some small virtue in his conducting himself as if he were the master and an active focus, in accepting life and self-deception—with its corollary self-determination and responsibility—without examining these things too closely. Perhaps it was inherently virtuous that for unknown reasons he was by nature more inclined to acting than acquiring knowledge, that he was more instinctual than intellectual. (pp. 379-380)

After Knecht leaves the Order, he feels a great sense of freedom and innocence. His action represents a Five's mature choice to integrate thought with action:

Everything was new again, mysterious, promising; all that had been could recur, and many new things as well. It was long, long since he had looked out upon the day and the world and seen them as so unburdened, so beautiful and innocent. The happiness of freedom, of commanding his own destiny, flooded through him like a strong drink. How long it was since he had last had this feeling, last entertained this lovely and rapturous illusion. (p. 406)

For a Social Five, leaving the safety of affiliation with a prestigious group is a heroic act, and Knecht's exuberance at his freedom is a mark of a Five at his healthiest.

The Golden Notebook

Novelist Anna Wulf, an average Social Five with a Six wing, is the protagonist of Doris Lessing's *The Golden Notebook*. At the beginning of the story Anna keeps four notebooks related to different facets of her life. In a notebook with a black cover, she reviews the African experience of her earlier years. In a red one she records her political life and growing disillusionment with the Communist Party. In a yellow notebook she writes a novel in which the heroine's thoughts and experiences echo Anna's own. And in a blue one she keeps a personal diary. The way Anna physically separates life reflects the Five inner defense of mental and emotional compartmentalization.

Anna despairs of ever focusing her abilities sufficiently to write a novel that will have a significant impact on society:

> I am incapable of writing the only kind of novel which interests me: a book powered with an intellectual or moral passion strong enough to create order, to create a new way of looking at life. It is because I am too diffused. I have decided never to write another novel. I have fifty "subjects" I could write about; and they would be competent enough. If there is one thing we can be sure of, it is that competent and informative novels will continue to pour from the publishing houses. I have only one, and the least important of the qualities necessary to write at all, and that is curiosity. . . . I am interested only in stretching myself, on living as fully as I can. When I said that to Mother Sugar [her psychoanalyst] she replied with the small nod of satisfaction people use for these resounding truths, that the artist writes out of an incapacity to live. I remember the nausea I felt when she said it. . . . But extraordinary how this old stuff issued so fresh and magisterial from the lips of psychoanalysis. (pp. 59-60)

Here we see the Five's stress point, Seven. The fragmented Anna is beset by so many possibilities for her second novel that she is unable to choose any of them. Her ambivalence about authority, personified by her psychoanalyst, reflects her Six wing.

The Social Five need to affiliate with a like-minded group is implicit in Anna's membership in the Communist Party, and her doubts about the Party also point to issues with authority. She is also keenly aware of group dynamics:

> All the time I am thinking: Not once does one of us say: something is fundamentally wrong; yet the implication of what we say amounts to that. I can't stop thinking about this phenomenon—that when two of us meet, our discussions are on a totally different level than when there are three people present. Two people, and it is two persons, from a critical tradition, discussing politics as people not communists would discuss them. (By people not communists I mean that they wouldn't be recognised

as communists, except for the jargon, by an outsider listening in.) But more than two, and a different spirit altogether is present. This is particularly true of what is said about Stalin. Although I am quite prepared to believe that he is mad and a murderer (though remembering always what Michael says—that this is a time when it is impossible to know the truth about anything), I like to hear people use that tone of simple, friendly respect for him. Because if that tone were to be thrown aside, something very important would go with it, paradoxically enough, a faith in the possibilities of democracy, of decency. A dream would be dead—for our time, at least. (p. 288)

While Anna's psychotherapy has put her in touch with her feelings, she still dissociates from the painful ones:

I put myself back into the state of mind I was in when I went to Mother Sugar. I can't feel, I said. I don't care about anyone in the world except Janet [her daughter]. Seven years ago now?—something like that. When I left her I said: You've taught me to cry, thank you for nothing, you've given me back feeling, and it's too painful.

How old-fashioned of me to seek a witch-doctor to be taught to feel. Because now I think of it, I see that people everywhere are trying not to feel. Cool, cool, cool, that's the word. That's the banner. From America first, but now us. I think of the groups of young people, political and social around London. Tommy's friends, the new socialists—that's what they have in common, a quality of measured emotion, coolness.

In a world as terrible as this, limit emotion. How odd I didn't see it before. (pp. 520-521)

Anna's troubled love affair with Saul, an American writer, leads her to abandon her fragmented practice of writing in four different notebooks. She buys a notebook with a golden cover and writes in that alone, seeming to move toward more integration of her personality. But she also experiences the rapid mood swings of her Seven stress point:

As his feet went down the stairs, my mood of self-disgust went with him. I sat and luxuriated in my body. Even a small dry wrinkling of skin on the inside of my thigh, the beginning of being old, gave me pleasure. I was thinking: Yes, that's as it should be, I've been so happy in my life, I shan't care about being old. But even as I said it, the security leaked away again. I was back in disgust. I stood in the centre of the big room, naked, letting the heat strike me from the three points of heat, and I knew, and it was an illumination—one of those things one has always known, but never really understood before—that all sanity depends on this: that it should be a delight to feel heat strike the skin, a delight to stand upright, knowing the bones are moving easily under the flesh. If this goes, then the conviction of life goes too. But I could feel none of this. The texture of the carpet was abhorrent to me, a dead processed thing; my body was a thin, meagre, spiky sort of vegetable, like an unsunned plant; and when I touched the hair on my head it was dead. I felt the floor bulge up under me. The walls were losing their density. I knew I was moving down into a new dimension, further away from sanity than I had ever been. (p. 585)

Anna's personality is growing more fragile and she senses herself on the verge of disintegrating. After Saul leaves her, she has a brief affair with another man, then starts clipping newspapers and pasting the clippings on her walls, a further sign of fragmentation:

It was as if she, Anna, were a central point of awareness, being attacked by a million unco-ordinated facts, and the central point would disappear if she proved unable to weigh and balance the facts, take them all into account. . . .
It occurred to her that she was going mad. This was "the break-down" she had foreseen; the "cracking-up." Yet it did not seem to her that she was even slightly mad; but rather that people who were not as obsessed as she was with the inchoate world mirrored in the newspapers were all out of touch with an awful necessity. Yet she knew she was mad. (pp. 619-621)

At the end of *The Golden Notebook*, Anna tells a friend that she plans to get a job and abandon writing altogether, but the reader knows that she will continue and eventually thrive. Doris Lessing, the most autobiographical of novelists, ultimately *did* emerge from her own psychological crisis to create what critics have described as a breakthrough work of fiction.

Fives with a **Sexual** subtype, whom Ichazo associates with "confidence," like to share confidences with the few people they trust. Sexual Fives are generally more willing to risk emotional contact than Self-Preservation or Social Fives. But the ambivalence they feel about being close to others often gives a love-hate cast to their relationships.

Literary examples of this subtype include Frederick Clegg in John Fowles's *The Collector*, Hannibal Lecter in Thomas Harris's *The Silence of the Lambs* and *Hannibal*, Peggy Cort in Elizabeth McCracken's *The Giant's House: A Romance*, Maurice Bendrix in Graham Greene's *The End of the Affair*, and Almásy in Michael Ondaatje's *The English Patient*.

The English Patient

Ladislas de Almásy, a Sexual Five with a Four wing, is Ondaatje's "English patient." Nameless and hideously burned in a plane crash, he lies in an Italian villa at the end of 1944, tended by a nurse. He tells her and others bits and pieces of his life story, but his identity—and even his nationality—is unclear. By the book's end, the reader understands that he took part in an international geographical expedition exploring the desert, had a tragic love affair with the wife of a colleague, and gave helpful information about the desert's topography to the German side during World War II.

Early in Almásy's relationship with Katharine, a One, we see his ambivalence about intimacy:

> She picks up a cushion and places it onto her lap as a shield against him. "If you make love to me I won't lie about it. If I make love to you I won't lie about it."
> She moves the cushion against her heart, as if she would suffocate that part of herself which has broken free.
> "What do you hate most?" he asks.
> "A lie. And you?"
> "Ownership," he says. "When you leave me, forget me." (p. 152)

Almásy's hatred of "ownership" reflects his fear of engulfment and his vulnerability to losing himself in the relationship, while Katharine's hatred of lying is characteristic of a One.

Almásy's affinity with the desert illustrates a Five's comfort with minimalism:

> He sweeps his arm across plates and glasses on a restaurant table so she might look up somewhere else in the city hearing this cause of noise. When he is without her. He, who has never felt alone in the miles of longitude between desert towns. A man in a desert can hold absence in his cupped hands knowing it is something that feeds him more than water. There is a plant he knows of near El Taj, whose heart, if one cuts it out, is replaced with a fluid containing herbal goodness. Every morning one can drink the liquid the amount of a missing heart. The plant continues to flourish for a year before it dies from some lack or other.
> He lies in his room surrounded by the pale maps. He is without Katharine. His hunger wishes to burn down all social rules, all courtesy.
> Her life with others no longer interests him. He wants only her stalking beauty, her theatre of expressions. He wants the minute and secret reflection between them, the depth of field minimal, their foreignness intimate like two pages of a closed book. (pp. 154-155)

Note Almásy's strong desire to share secrets, his intensity toward his beloved, and his vision of the two of them against the world. All are characteristic of the Sexual Five.

No longer able to betray her husband, Katharine ends the affair, but Almásy remains obsessed with her. Her husband, who has learned about the affair, takes Katharine flying and deliberately crashes his plane into Almásy, who is on the ground, in an attempt to kill the lovers and himself. The husband dies, but Almásy survives and takes the injured Katharine into a desert cave. There she reveals her bitterness over the way he treated her after their breakup:

How did you hate me? She whispers in the Cave of Swimmers, talking through her pain of injuries. A broken wrist. Shattered ribs. You were terrible to me. That's when my husband suspected you. I still hate that about you—disappearing into deserts or bars.

You left me in Groppi Park.

Because you didn't want me as anything else.

Because you said your husband was going mad. Well, he went mad.

Not for a long time. I went mad before he did, you killed everything in me. Kiss me, will you. Stop defending yourself. Kiss me and call me by my name.

Their bodies had met in perfumes, in sweat, frantic to get under that thin film with a tongue or a tooth, as if they each could grip character there and during love pull it right off the body of the other.

Now there is no talcum on her arm, no rose water on her thigh.

You think you are an iconoclast, but you're not. You just move, or replace what you cannot have. If you fail at something you retreat into something else. Nothing changes you. How many women did you have? I left you because I knew I could never change you. You would stand in the room so still sometimes, so wordless sometimes, as if the greatest betrayal of yourself would be to reveal one more inch of your character. (pp. 173-174)

Katharine is astute enough to see the depth of Almásy's stinginess. While a Sexual Five might think he is sharing secrets, to a One it looks as though he's holding back.

A Sexual Five's conflict about being in an intimate relationship can lead him to continually undermine it. Almásy's push-pull attitude towards intimacy also reflects his Four wing, which intensifies his fear of being engulfed:

Women want everything of a lover. And too often I would sink below the surface. So armies disappear under sand. And there was her fear of her husband, her belief in her honour, my old desire for self-sufficiency, my disappearances, her suspicions of me, my disbelief that she loved me. The paranoia and claustrophobia of hidden love.

"I think you have become inhuman," she said to me.

"I'm not the only betrayer."

"I don't think you care—that this has happened among us. You slide past everything with your fear and hate of ownership, of owning, of being owned, of being named. You think this is a virtue. I think you are inhuman. If I leave you, who will you go to? Would you find another lover?"

I said nothing.

"Deny it, damn you." (p. 238)

An average Sexual Five like Almásy can have trouble seeing beyond his own fears and empathizing with the feelings of his beloved.

The Giant's House: A Romance

Peggy Cort, the narrator of Elizabeth McCracken's novel *The Giant's House: A Romance*, offers another vivid example of a Sexual Five, again with a Four wing. Peggy, a young librarian in a small Massachusetts town, comes to know and love James Sweatt, a Nine, an "over-tall" eleven-year-old boy who grows into an eight-foot giant.

As a librarian and a Five, Peggy longs to communicate to others the importance of books as a source of knowledge. For a Sexual Five, sharing information is a form of intimacy:

Even at age eleven, James asked me how to find things in the catalog. He told me of books he liked, wanting something similar. He recognized me as an expert. Despite popular theories, I believe people fall in love based not on good looks or fate but on knowledge. . . .

Nowadays, trendy librarians, wanting to be important, say Knowledge is power. I know better. *Knowledge is love.* (pp. 7-8)

When James's mother commits suicide, his aunt remarks that the mother seemed outwardly happy. Peggy mulls this:

Not sad? To me she seemed the saddest person in the world, a woman completely perplexed by her life and its trappings. Being myself a sad person, I recognized that much. My own sadness isn't something I admit to people. If someone asked, yes, I think I might. If someone noticed and inquired, I would explain—I think I would explain—that I am a fundamentally sad person, a fundamentally unlovable person, a person who spends her life longing for a number of things she cannot bring herself to name or define. (pp. 64-65)

Peggy's Four wing is visible here. But Fives, unlike Fours, are often uncomfortable talking about their feelings.

When the now adolescent James breaks his leg and is hospitalized in

Boston, Peggy visits him and makes awkward attempts to comfort him. Suddenly she realizes that her feelings for him have progressed beyond friendship to a kind of obsession. True to her Sexual subtype, she quickly decides to make this relationship the focus of her life:

> The rest of the world fell in love, and the physics baffled me. I could see it happen—God knows, all around I saw falling couples—but I did not understand the emotional gravity that allowed their descent.
>
> And then, like Newton, I felt it smack me over the head.
>
> Those people had made a decision, and then they fell; they did not find themselves hip deep in love and wonder how they got there. For years I'd waited for someone to love me: that was the permission I needed to fall in love myself, as though I were a pin sunk deep in a purse, waiting for a magnet to prove me metal. When that did not happen, I'd thought of myself as *unlovable*.
>
> But now, with James lonely in his hospital room, I realized that waiting like that was hopeless. I could wait forever and he might never know to love me back and I would live and then die with a tiny awful feeling that could have been love, had it ever seen light or oxygen.
>
> Well, I'd change that. I would love him. It would be as easy as keeping his gaze, easy as saying, This is what to do. I would perfect my love for him, never care what others thought of me, or even what he was thinking of me. It was *this* I'd waited for all my life: a love that would make me useful, a love that would occupy all my time. (pp. 76-77)

Resolving to dedicate herself to James, Peggy feels a sense of comfort about narrowing her world and giving up other options.

Again, sharing confidences with a loved one is equivalent to intimacy for this subtype:

> Now I understood. I was saving myself for James. *Myself* meant only my secrets. Any other commodities (my youth, my virginity, any brand of innocence or hope) I'd years ago lost, a gambler who didn't understand the game. My secrets were all I'd saved, all these years the only thing I hadn't and wouldn't cash in on just anyone. If you poured out yourself to anyone who might for a moment listen, on just a usual day—it struck me as cheap, the way some girls' mothers used the word. I was saving what was left of myself for James. (p. 101)

As a Sexual Five, Peggy is not necessarily adept at sexual intimacy or even comfortable with the prospect:

> Nowadays sex is the guest you should always expect, because it's supposed to knock down your door without an invitation: you might as

well be prepared. If you haven't set a place at the table, you are called naive or repressed.

But sometimes, honestly, the mind makes calibrations, but not for sex, because sex is not coming to you, sex is down the street wrecking your neighbor's house, sex has—for any number of reasons—washed its hands of you, even if you are not done with it, even if the breakup is not mutual. In which case, if you are lucky and you work very hard, you learn not only to be satisfied by other things, you start to long for them. And you don't feel starved; you find your hungers are simply different, as if you've dropped your Western upbringing for a childhood in a country where ice cream is unheard of, available only in books.

And so I stared at the hand [James's] on the tabletop, wanting it to come toward me even if I wasn't sure for what. (p. 107)

When James proposes to Peggy, they are both filled with complex emotions, knowing that sex is impossible because of his condition:

I thought about sitting up, taking his hand. I didn't know if he wanted me to, and I couldn't think about what I wanted. . . . Every part of me was waiting.

"Do you want to get married, Peggy," he said. "We could, you know. I mean, I wouldn't be a good *husband*—"

Then I was sitting up, I did take his hand. "Yes—" I said.

"No, I wouldn't," he answered. "I mean, not like a real husband. But we still could. If you wanted."

What I wanted was to drag him into bed with me—not for the sex he was delicately reminding me he was incapable of, not even for kissing. Just so we could be closer. Just so I could explain how little I needed. It's hard, I thought, to have a conversation like this without lying down. (p. 201)

After James dies, Peggy understands more about why she chose to love him:

Did I love him because I knew this moment would come, when James who I'd poured my love into, would be gone, because I knew my love, my pourable love, was limited, and if I'd decanted it into someone whose prognosis was better I would have run out by our fifteenth anniversary (is that tin? paper? steel?) and would have then become the bitter empty person everyone knew I was destined to be, only with the company of my unfortunate husband?

Maybe I'd loved him because I knew he'd leave me. Maybe, once. It wasn't worth it. (pp. 227-228)

A Sexual Five's need for connection can be continually at odds with her sense that her inner resources are too limited to sustain a long-term relationship. The fact that James would leave her was an emotionally safer option than having to sustain a long-term relationship.

Peggy has more insight into her pattern than most Fives. Although the possibility of intellectual self-knowledge always exists for Fives, their challenge is to move into full connection with their emotions and the physical world.

In this chapter we have seen a range of examples, extending from such fixated personalities as Mersault in *The Stranger* to fully transformed individuals such as Knecht in *The Glass Bead Game*. Five artists, such as Neara in *Turtle Diary* and Anna in *The Golden Notebook* often find the possibility of significant evolution through their work. Relatively healthy Fives like Sherlock Holmes and Smilla frequently make important contributions to society.

Sources

Camus, Albert, *The Stranger*, trans. Stuart Gilbert (New York: Alfred A. Knopf, 1974). First published 1942

Dickens, Charles, *A Christmas Carol*, in *Christmas Books by Charles Dickens* (London: Macmillan, 1956). First published 1843

Doyle, Arthur Conan, *A Study in Scarlet*, in *The Complete Sherlock Holmes* (New York: Doubleday). First published 1887

Hesse, Hermann, *The Glass Bead Game (Magister Ludi)*, trans. Richard and Clara Winston (New York: Holt, Rinehart and Winston, 1969). First published 1943

Hoban, Russell, *Turtle Diary* (New York: Random House, 1975)

Hoeg, Peter, S*milla's Sense of Snow* (New York: Farrar Straus and Giroux, 1993)

Kingsolver, Barbara, *The Poisonwood Bible* (New York: HarperCollins, 1998)

Lessing, Doris, *The Golden Notebook* (New York: Perennial, 1999). First published 1962

McCracken, Elizabeth, *The Giant's House: A Romance* (New York: Dial Press, 1996)

Ondaatje, Michael, *The English Patient* (New York: Vintage, 1993)

Six: The Pessimist

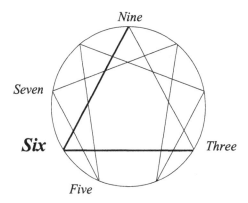

In Shakespeare's Hamlet we see the pessimism, fearfulness, and vacillation of the Enneagram Six:

To be, or not to be: that is the question:
Whether 'tis nobler in the mind to suffer
The slings and arrows of outrageous fortune,
Or to take arms against a sea of troubles,
And by opposing end them. To die, to sleep—
No more—and by a sleep to say we end
The heartache, and the thousand natural shocks
That flesh is heir to! 'Tis a consummation
Devoutly to be wished. To die, to sleep—
To sleep—perchance to dream: ay, there's the rub,
For in that sleep of death what dreams may come
When we have shuffled off this mortal coil,
Must give us pause. There's the respect
That makes calamity of so long life:
For who would bear the whips and scorns of time,
Th' oppressor's wrong, the proud man's contumely,
The pangs of despised love, the law's delay,
The insolence of office, and the spurns
That patient merit of th' unworthy takes,
When he himself might his quietus make
With a bare bodkin? Who would fardels bear,
To grunt and sweat under a weary life,

But that the dread of something after death,
The undiscovered country, from whose bourn
No traveler returns, puzzles the will,
And makes us rather bear those ills we have,
Than fly to others that we know not of?
Thus conscience does make cowards of us all,
And thus the native hue of resolution
Is sicklied o'er with the pale cast of thought,
And enterprises of great pitch and moment,
With this regard their currents turn awry,
And lose the name of action. (III, i, 56-88)

Hamlet, the Prince of Denmark, is the most famous of literary Sixes, and this soliloquy illustrates many aspects of The Pessimist's character. Hamlet's mental agility, high anxiety, and negative outlook are all evident in what are certainly Shakespeare's most familiar lines.

The Six is the central point in the triad at the left side of the Enneagram diagram, associated with the head, thinking and fear. In each of the triads, the middle Ennegram style exemplifies the most disordered version of that triad's main preoccupation. In the "To be or not to be" soliloquy we see how fear distorts Hamlet's thinking process. He is literally so scared he can't think straight.

Sixes can be a difficult Enneagram style to identify, primarily because of their contradictory qualities. Hamlet is at one moment funny, the next tragic; one moment compassionate, the next insulting; one moment poetic, the next crude; one moment tender, the next violent; one moment self-confident, the next insecure; one moment brilliant, the next deranged; one moment resolute, the next procrastinating.

I have heard many Sixes describe an experience that Don Richard Riso and Russ Hudson have called "the inner committee"—continually shuttling back and forth between contrasting points of view. This process, evident in Hamlet's soliloquy, is one aspect of the confused thinking that is characteristic of this style.

Hamlet's speech takes place in the middle of Shakespeare's tragedy, but it is only tenuously related to what has gone before. In a previous scene Hamlet was preoccupied with arranging to have the visiting troupe of actors present a performance he hoped would shock his uncle, Claudius, into revealing his guilt in the murder of Hamlet's father. Then, suddenly, the Prince is preoccupied with suicide. This sort of leap in logic—from resolving to kill his uncle and avenge his father's murder to ruminating about killing himself—is typical of distorted Six thinking. Hamlet's further leap within the speech—from the idea of death as surcease from life's trials to the idea of death as possible prelude to an even worse afterlife—reflects his Six preoccupation with worst-case scenarios.

Yet even in the midst of his mental turmoil, Hamlet correctly identifies his basic (Six) issues: cowardice and the tendency to let thinking prevent action. One of Hamlet's qualities that has fascinated actors, audiences, and scholars over four centuries is his self-awareness. In the "To be or not to be" soliloquy he performs a feat of self-analysis that would dazzle a modern psychotherapist. But Hamlet's brilliance cannot avert the play's final tragedy, which arises out of his character as much as out of events.

Hamlet moves from Sixish vacillation and doubt to the Six stress point of Three (The Achiever), which is associated with action. Now he is finally able to take action, but it is reckless and counterproductive: psychologically brutalizing Ophelia, killing Polonius, terrorizing his mother, leaping into Ophelia's grave. Ultimately he moves to his Nine security point (The Connector), associated with a philosophical outlook. He accepts his fate and manifests a calmer frame of mind based on a wider perspective. Skillful dramatist that Shakespeare was, it is possible he decided to insert the "To be or not to be" soliloquy to emphasize the breadth of Hamlet's character arc and contrast this speech with his final Nineish acceptance of the human condition:

> If it be now, 'tis not to come; if it be not to come, it will be now; if it be not now, yet it will come. The readiness is all. . . . Let be. (V, ii, 220-225)

Sixes are generally immobilized by fear, and Hamlet's transcendence of his fear is the arc of a Six tragic hero.

Crime and Punishment

Where in *Hamlet* the final outcome is tragic, we see a distinctly different arc in Fyodor Dostoevsky's classic novel *Crime and Punishment*. Raskolnikov, a young student, murders an old woman for her money, then acts in ways that eventually lead to his capture and conviction. Although sentenced to prison, he is redeemed by the love of the selfless Sonia, a Nine. At the story's end, we see Raskolnikov ecstatic at the prospect of his ultimate release. Dostoevsky's great achievement is not only in showing the deranged thought process that leads this unhealthy Six to murder but also in gaining the reader's sympathies for Raskolnikov despite the horror of his crime.

The distorted mentality of this unlikely hero begins with his assumptions about reality. Like many Sixes, Raskolnikov fails to consider the "big picture." He fails to understand that murder is not an alternative in a civilized society. In a way, he is like a hamster on an exercise wheel, going round and round in the cage of his own mind, oblivious to the wider world. His thinking process becomes self-referential, and he never pulls back to examine his basic assumptions.

For instance, when Raskolnikov contemplates the murder, he is preoccupied with justifying the act on absurd grounds: that the old woman—a pawnbroker—is a blight on society, or that he himself is a "special" person whose recourse to violence is justified by his having gotten away with the murder.

Even though Raskolnikov fails to consciously recognize his own guilt, his actions continually betray him: he faints at the police station when the murder is mentioned, although he is not a suspect. He hints at his guilt to a police inspector; he confesses the crime to the woman he loves as well as to his sister. Although his original motive for murder was money, he stashes his loot in an inaccessible place and never touches it. Raskolnikov's interior monologue as he contemplates committing the murder has some themes in common with Hamlet's "To be or not to be" soliloquy:

> He felt utterly broken: darkness and confusion were in his soul. He rested his elbows on his knees and leaned his head on his hands.
> "Good God!" he cried, "can it be, can it be, that I shall really take an axe, that I shall strike her on the head, split her skull open . . . that I shall tread in the sticky warm blood, break the lock, steal and tremble; hide, all spattered in the blood . . . with the axe. . . . Good God, can it be?"
> He was shaking like a leaf as he said this.
> "But why am I going on like this?" he continued, sitting up again, as it were profound amazement. "I knew that I could never bring myself to it, so what have I been torturing myself for till now? . . . Why am I going over it again, then? Why am I still hesitating? As I came down the stairs yesterday, I said to myself that it was base, loathsome, vile, vile . . . the very thought of it made me feel sick and filled me with horror.
> "No, I couldn't do it, I couldn't do it! Granted, granted that there is no flaw in all that reasoning, that all that I have concluded this last month is clear as day, true as arithmetic. . . . My God! Anyway I couldn't bring myself to it! I couldn't do it, I couldn't do it! Why, why then am I still . . . ?" (pp. 53-54)

Raskolnikov's obsession with the subject, in spite of his terror, is characteristic of a Six. Like Hamlet, he is highly intelligent but a muddled thinker.

Raskolnikov is the author of a well-regarded treatise on the psychology of the criminal mind in which he notes the tendency of the criminal to expose himself. He ponders this possibility as he contemplates the murder of the old woman:

> [I]n his opinion the chief reason lay not so much in the material impossibility of concealing the crime as in the criminal himself. Almost every criminal is subject to a failure of will and reasoning power by a childish and phenomenal heedlessness, at the very instant when prudence and caution are most essential. . . .
> When he reached these conclusions, he decided that in his own case there could not be such a morbid reaction, that his reason and will would remain unimpaired at the time of carrying out his design, for the single reason that his design was "not a crime . . . ." (pp. 63-64)

Skillful novelists sometimes reveal their characters by having one describe another. In *Crime and Punishment*, Razumihin, a Two, gives his impressions of his friend Raskolnikov to the latter's mother:

> [H]e is morose, gloomy, proud and haughty, and of late—and perhaps for a long time before—he has been suspicious and fanciful. He has a noble nature and a kind heart. He does not like showing his feelings and would rather do a cruel thing than open his heart freely. Sometimes, though, he is not at all morbid, but simply cold and inhumanly callous; it's as though he were alternating between two characters. Sometimes he is fearfully reserved! He says he is so busy that everything is a hindrance, and yet he lies in bed doing nothing. He doesn't jeer at things, not because he hasn't the wit, but as though he hadn't time to waste on such trifles. He never listens to what is said to him. He is never interested in what interests other people at any given moment. He thinks very highly of himself and perhaps he is right." (p. 187)

In view of Razumihin's comments, it is interesting to note that in Russian the name Raskolnikov means "split."

The contradictory nature of Sixes is another similarity between Hamlet and Raskolnikov, especially visible in the two contrasting ways they manifest fear: through aggressiveness or through open anxiety. Psychologists commonly call this the "fight or flight" syndrome. Aggressive or "counterphobic" Sixes like Hamlet are often unaware of their fear and seem eager to pick fights, to avoid being attacked first by others. "Phobic" Sixes like Raskolnikov are more aware of their fear, and tend to flee from the dangers they perceive. Some writers on the Enneagram consider "phobic" and "counterphobic" Sixes distinct categories, but it seems to me that all Six individuals are mixtures of these two aspects. The so-called "counterphobic" Six is like an abused dog who has become a "fear biter," as opposed to a nervous animal who cringes at every sound.

In his treatise on the criminal mind Raskolnikov offers a brilliant analysis of "phobic" and "counterphobic" individuals:

> The first category, generally speaking, are men conservative in temperament and law-abiding; they live under control and love to be controlled. To my thinking it is their duty to be controlled, because that's their vocation, and there is nothing humiliating in it for them. The second category all transgress the law; they are destroyers or disposed to destruction according to their capacities. The crimes of these men are of course relative and varied; for the most part they seek in very varied ways the destruction of the present for the sake of the better. (p. 227)

Raskolnikov's unexamined assumption here is that *all* people are like him. One quality that he ascribes to the first category of men is a subservience to

202 The Literary Enneagram

authority. This is a major issue with Sixes, who either cleave to authority through affiliation with groups—organized religions, labor unions, professions like the military or the police—or are highly resistant to it. This second group of Sixes probably makes up a significant portion of the prison population.

Another strong issue with all Sixes—and what they consider their chief virtue—is loyalty, and Raskolnikov's crime is an expression of loyalty to his mother and his sister. Toward the end of the book, he confesses the murder to his beloved Sonia and describes his rationale:

> "[T]o turn one's back upon everything, to forget one's mother and decorously accept the insults inflicted on one's sister. Why should one? When one has buried them, to burden oneself with others—wife and children—and to leave them again without a farthing? So I resolved to gain possession of the old woman's money and to use it for my first years without worrying my mother, to keep myself at the university and for a little while after leaving it—and to do this all on a broad, thorough scale, so as to build up a completely new career and enter upon a new life of independence. . . . Well . . . that's all. . . . Well, of course in killing the old woman I did wrong. . . . Well, that's enough."
>
> He struggled to the end of his speech in exhaustion and let his head sink.
>
> "Oh, that's not it, that's not it," Sonia cried in distress. "How could one . . . no, that's not right, not right."
>
> "You see yourself that it's not right. But I've spoken truly, it's the truth."
>
> "As though that could be the truth! Good God!"
>
> "I've only killed a louse, Sonia, a useless, loathsome, harmful creature."
>
> "A human being—a louse!"
>
> "I too know it wasn't a louse," he answered, looking strangely at her. "But I am talking nonsense, Sonia," he added. "I've been talking nonsense a long time . . . ." (p. 358)

He continues rambling about the need to take power, to prove his courage, a Six under stress moving to Three, rationalizing his need to take action, any action, however appalling:

> "I divined then, Sonia," he went on eagerly, "that power is only vouchsafed to the man who dares to stoop and pick it up. There is only one thing, one thing needful: one has only to dare! Then for the first time in my life an idea took shape in my mind which no one had ever thought of before me, no one! I saw clear as daylight how strange it is that not a single person living in this mad world has had the daring to go straight for it all and send it flying to the devil! I . . . I wanted *to have the daring*

... and I killed her. I only wanted to have the daring, Sonia! That was the whole cause of it!" (pp. 359-360)

After some further rambling, he gets closer to the point:

"I wanted to find out then and quickly whether I was a louse like everybody else or a man. Whether I can step over barriers or not, whether I dare stoop to pick up or not, whether I am a trembling creature or whether I have the *right* . . . "
"To kill? Have the right to kill?" Sonia clasped her hands.
(pp. 360-361)

After he is sentenced and imprisoned, Sonia follows him to Siberia. In despair, he suffers for a year in the labor camp unable to repent, reproaching himself for not having the courage to commit suicide. Finally, through Sonia's steadfast love, Raskolnikov begins to understand his crime and punishment, and we see him move, as Hamlet did, to the more optimistic and philosophical viewpoint characteristic of a Nine, the Six's security point. We see him develop both insight and faith:

How it happened he did not know. But all at once something seemed to seize him and fling him at her feet. He wept and threw his arms round her knees. For the first instant she was terribly frightened and she turned pale. She jumped up and looked at him trembling. But at the same moment she understood, and a light of infinite happiness came into her eyes. She knew and had no doubt that he loved her beyond everything and that at last the moment had come. . . .
They wanted to speak, but could not; tears stood in their eyes. They were both pale and thin; but those sick pale faces were bright with the dawn of a new future, of a full resurrection into a new life. They were renewed by love; the heart of each held infinite sources of life for the heart of the other.
They resolved to wait and be patient. They had another seven years to wait, and what terrible suffering and what infinite happiness before them! But he had risen again and he knew it and felt it in all his being, while she—she only lived in his life. (p. 471)

I have discussed in some detail the character arcs of Hamlet and Raskolnikov in order to show the flawed thinking, suspiciousness, loyalty, authority issues, pessimism and contradictory qualities common to Sixes. In both Hamlet and Raskolnikov the *distortion of the thinking process* is marked. As they move beyond the anxiety that drives their skewed mental process, both characters evolve and transform. The upward arc for Six characters generally shows them transcending fear and manifesting true courage, whether the ultimate outcome is life—as for Raskolnikov—or death—as for Hamlet.

The Six's History

For many Sixes, the deepest anxiety is that they will be unable to survive without help and guidance. Like Hamlet, they tend to have strong connections with their father and seek safety through a relationship with him or some other authority figure. Because they distrust their ability to make important decisions and take care of themselves, they constantly search for beliefs and life strategies that will lend them security.

Final Payments

Isabel Moore, the Six protagonist of Mary Gordon's novel *Final Payments*, is typical in her attachment to her father, a Catholic theologian and professor. Isabel's mother died in an accident when she was two, and her father hired a housekeeper, Margaret, who stayed with them over the next eleven years. Aware that the woman had ambitions to marry her father, Isabel succeeded in thwarting them. At nineteen Isabel had her first sexual experience, with a young man who was a student of her father's; her father caught them in bed together and vented his rage on the boy. Three weeks later her father had a stroke that incapacitated him, and Isabel took care of him until his death, eleven years later.

The Six's sense of insecurity, of needing a program for her life, of being actually grateful for limitations that offer a sense of order and clear boundaries is evident from the beginning of the novel, right after the death of Isabel's father:

> You may wonder, as many have wondered, why I did it, why I stayed with my father all those years. Does it suggest both the monstrosity and the confusion of the issue if I say that the day Dr. MacCauley told me about my father's stroke was of my whole life the day I felt most purely alive? Certainty was mine, and purity; I was encased in meaning like crystal. It was less than three weeks after my father found me with David Lowe. Perhaps after the dull, drowning misery of those weeks, the news that brought me the possibility of a visible martyrdom was sheer relief: a grapefruit ice that cleanses the palate between courses of a heavy meal. During those weeks we barely spoke; neither of us could invent the mechanism of forgiveness. Then my father had his stroke. In its way, it suited us to perfection.
>   . . . and if I smelt his sick breath and wished for him only to be dead—still, I knew this was mine. This was my life, inevitable to me as my own body. I could not share that life any more than I could give my own body over. It is too simple to say, but I must say it: I loved him very much; I loved him more than anyone else. (pp. 4-5)

Isabel declines over the course of the book, becoming involved in a self-destructive relationship with a friend's husband and eventually devoting herself to care for the now ailing Margaret. This is a classic Six downward spiral, moving from general insecurity to an unhealthy masochism, here made possible by the spiteful and demanding Margaret.

Isabel's redemption comes from two sources: the persistent devotion of her friends in the face of her self-destructiveness, and her Catholic faith, through which she ultimately resolves her desire for a life that includes personal pleasure:

> It is one of the marvels of a Catholic education that the impulse of a few words can bring whole narratives to light with an immediacy and a clarity that are utterly absorbing. "The poor you have always with you." I knew where Christ had said that: at the house of Martha and Mary. Mary had opened a jar of ointment over Christ's feet. Spikenard, I remembered. And she wiped his feet with her hair. Judas had rebuked her; he had said that the ointment ought to be sold for the poor. . . . And Christ had said to Judas, Mary at his feet, her hair spread out around him, "The poor you have always with you; but me you have not always."
>
> And until that moment, climbing the dark stairs in a rage to my ugly room, it was a passage I had not understood. It seemed to justify to me the excesses of centuries of fat, tyrannical bankers. But now I understood. What Christ was saying, what he meant, was that the pleasures of that hair, that ointment, must be taken. Because the accidents of death would deprive us soon enough. We must not deprive ourselves, our loved ones, of the luxury of our extravagant affections. We must not try to second-guess death by refusing to love the ones we loved in favor of the anonymous poor. . . .
>
> I knew now I must open the jar of ointment. I must open my life. I knew now that I must leave [Margaret's house]. (pp. 298-299)

Isabel's character arc is a common one for Sixes. With the support of trusted allies and the power of her religious faith, she is able to break through her distorted thinking and release herself from her masochistic downward spiral. It's an unexpected twist in Gordon's novel that Catholic dogma, far from encouraging Isabel to ever-escalating self-denial, actually helps her justify moving toward light and life.

Levels of Health

As with other Enneagram temperaments, healthy Sixes are more difficult to identify than average or unhealthy exemplars. More than other styles, however, the variations within the Six group are enormous.

Average Sixes tend to be wary, insecure, conscious of safety and security, loyal to those they trust, pessimistic, complex and contradictory. Many long for an authority they can rely on or ally themselves with people and institutions that seem confident and trustworthy. Other average Sixes can be rebellious and resist alliances with any kind of authority.

Literary examples include Katharina in Shakespeare's *The Taming of the Shrew*, Shylock in Shakespeare's *The Merchant of Venice*, Wormold in Graham

Greene's *Our Man in Havana*, Leamas in John le Carré's *The Spy Who Came in from the Cold*, Isabel Moore in Mary Gordon's *Final Payments*, Maeve in Alice McDermott's *Charming Billy*, Mitchell Stephens, Esq. in Russell Banks's *The Sweet Hereafter*, Bernard Sampson in Len Deighton's *Hope*, and Rudy Baylor in John Grisham's *The Rainmaker*.

Healthy Sixes are courageous, make strong reciprocal bonds with others, are affectionate and reliable in their relationships and responsible in their service to the larger community. Notable for their persistence and hard work, they have a gift for cooperative problem solving and even leadership. Celia Coplestone in T. S. Eliot's *The Cocktail Party* and Viola in Shakespeare's *Twelfth Night* are good examples.

Unhealthy Sixes may be masochistic or violent, but are fundamentally irrational in their actions. Fictional stories about them often end in psychosis, suicide, or violence. Examples of unhealthy Sixes on a downward spiral include Ahab in Herman Melville's *Moby-Dick*, Satan in John Milton's *Paradise Lost*, Captain Queeg in Herman Wouk's *The Caine Mutiny*, Lilly Dillon in Jim Thompson's *The Grifters*, and Will in Alice Adams's *Medicine Men*.

Place in Society

Sixes contribute an essential ingredient to the working of the world. They are often followers who are reliable, careful, and cooperative with others. They keep households, businesses, and institutions running smoothly. People with this style are rarely top-level leaders, but they play a crucial role in every leader's support system. The Six's innate gifts for assessing whom to trust and for steadfast loyalty are easy to take for granted, but without them there would be little in this world we could rely on.

Sixes are found in all occupations, but they show up in disproportionate numbers in the legal profession, the military, and police work, as well as in the prison inmate population. They are also visible in labor unions, civil service jobs, nonprofit organizations, and religious institutions. Sixes' analytical abilities and capacity to probe for the truth make them natural psychotherapists and spies. Their comfort level with worst-case scenarios may lead them into professions like oncology and social work. Their ability to connect with people can lead them to become politicians, actors and stand-up comedians. Their drive to prove their courage in the face of danger can make jobs as test pilots, stunt men or women, and race car drivers attractive to them.

Stress and Security Points

Under stress Sixes move to Three (The Achiever) and generally take on the negative qualities of Threes. Some become workaholics; others—like Hamlet, Raskolnikov and Isabel Moore—act impulsively and irresponsibly, making their situations worse. Taking blind action is a kind of safety valve for the pressure created by Sixes' anxiety; as their tension builds they find release in doing something. A Six at Three may also become devious and deceitful.

When Sixes feel secure, they often adopt the positive qualities of Nine (The Connector). Their fear dissolves, and they become philosophical, trusting, and optimistic. As their perspective broadens, they grow mellow and relaxed and may admit a spiritual dimension to their lives—something we see in Hamlet, Raskolnikov and Isabel. Secure within themselves, they can then act with true courage.

Wings

The world views of Five and Seven, the wings of Six, are in many ways opposed. While Fives are primarily concerned with social self-protectiveness, preventing others from encroaching on their world and maintaining their boundaries with vast stores of knowledge, Sevens are preoccupied with pleasure, new ideas, and expanding their options.

A Six with a strong Five wing is likely to be more intellectual, more intense, more careful about making connections with people. Five is a withdrawn style, and a Six's desire for approval from and connection with others is diminished by a strong Five wing. They may, in fact, be wary of affiliations. Both Hamlet and Raskolnikov are Sixes with a Five wing, as are Ahab in *Moby-Dick* and Milton's Satan in *Paradise Lost*.

Sixes with a Seven wing are more open to connection with people, more inclined to deflect their anxiety with humor, casual sexual encounters, and alcohol or drug use. They may also be more energetic—even a bit manic—as well as voluble. Not surprisingly, this group includes many well-known stand-up comedians. Sevens aggressively pursue fun and adventure as a way of denying their core terror. Sixes with a Seven wing do the same thing.

The Spy Who Came in from the Cold

Another Six with a Five wing is Alec Leamas, the title character of John le Carré's classic thriller *The Spy Who Came in From the Cold*. Spy stories are generally a Six genre, in their preoccupation with "us versus them" themes and their undercurrent of anxiety about who is to be trusted. In this story, Leamas leads a hermetic existence, detached from the ordinary world of human affection and relationship:

> A man who lives a part, not to others but alone, is exposed to obvious psychological dangers. In itself, the practice of deception is not particularly exacting; it is a matter of experience, of professional *expertise*, it is a facility most of us can acquire. But while a confidence trickster, a play-actor or a gambler can return from his performance to the ranks of his admirers, the secret agent enjoys no such relief. For him deception is first a matter of self-defense. He must protect himself not only from without but from within, and against the most natural of impulses: though he earn a fortune, his role may forbid him the purchase of a razor; though he be erudite, it can befall him to mumble nothing but

208 The Literary Enneagram

banalities; though he be an affectionate husband and father, he must under all circumstances withhold himself from those in whom he should naturally confide.

Aware of the overwhelming temptations which assail a man permanently isolated in his deceit, Leamas resorted to the course which armed him best; even when he was alone, he compelled himself to live with the personality he had assumed. . . . The qualities he exhibited to Fiedler, the restless uncertainty, the protective arrogance concealing shame, were not approximations but extensions of qualities he actually possessed; hence also the slight dragging of the feet, the aspect of personal neglect, the indifference to food, and an increasing reliance on alcohol and tobacco. When alone, he remained faithful to these habits. He would even exaggerate them a little, mumbling to himself about the iniquities of his Service.

Only very rarely, as now, going to bed that evening, did he allow himself the dangerous luxury of admitting the great lie he lived. (pp. 142-143)

Leamas's living a lie, even to himself, is related to his stress point. Threeish deceit has become so familiar to him that even his self-loathing is blunted. Unlike the average Three, however, Leamas recognizes the implications lying can have for his personal life. He longs for relationship, and this is his area of vulnerability as well as what is most noble in his character. At the novel's end, he learns that the people he most trusted have been planning the death of the woman he loves. Rather than live in a world of such treachery, Leamas deliberately chooses to die. This triumph of principle over the safety of affiliation is a supremely heroic gesture for a Six.

The Witches of Eastwick

Jane Smart, one of the witches in John Updike's *The Witches of Eastwick*, is another Six with a Five wing. Updike's novel tells the story of three divorced women friends, all of whom have occult powers and all of whom lust after Darryl, a newcomer to their New England town who may or may not be the Devil. Each of the witches dabbles in one of the arts: Jane—whom Updike describes as "hot, short, concentrated like a pencil point" (p. 5)—is a cellist, while Alexandra, a Nine, is a sculptor and Sukie, a Three, is a writer.

Jane's prickly persona nicely illustrates a Six with a Five wing:

One credited to Jane Smart's angry dark brow, as she slammed herself into her old moss-green Plymouth Valiant, with its worn door latch, a certain distinction, an inner boiling such as had in other cloistral towns produced Emily Dickinson's verses and Emily Brontë's inspired novel. (pp. 209-210)

After Darryl marries Jenny, a young woman whom the witches had befriended, they jealously decide to hex the new bride. Jane, the Six with a Five wing, has the most intense response:

"Don't you just *hate* her?" Sukie asked Alexandra. "I mean, we all understood he was to be yours if he was to be anybody's, among the three of us, once the novelty and everything wore off. Isn't that so, Jane?"

"It is not so" was the definite response. "Darryl and I are both musical. And we're dirty."

"Who says Lexa and I aren't dirty?" Sukie protested.

"You work at it," Jane said. "But you have other tendencies too. You both have goody-goody sides. You haven't committed yourselves the way I have. For me, there is nobody except Darryl. . . . What can we *do*?" Jane asked rhetorically. Her black hair, brushed from a central part in two severe wings, fell forward, eclipsing her face, and was swiftly brushed back. "It's obvious. We can *hex* her."

The word, like a shooting star suddenly making its scratch on the sky, commanded silence.

"You can hex her yourself if you feel that vehement," Alexandra said. "You don't need us."

"I do. It needs the three of us. This mustn't be a little hex, so she'll just get hives and a headache for a week."

Sukie asked after a pause, "What *will* she get?"

Jane's thin lips clamped shut upon a bad-luck word, the Latin for "crab." "I think it's obvious, from the other night, where her anxieties lie. When a person has a fear like that it takes just the teeniest-weeniest psychokinetic push to make it come true." (pp. 235-237)

After Jenny dies of cancer, Jane sits in her house alone late at night playing Bach and brooding about life and death:

Moving on after this savoring to the first minuet, Jane most distinctly heard—it was not a question of hearing, she *embodied*—the war between chords and the single line that was always trying to escape them but could not. Her bow was carving out shapes within a substance, within a blankness, within a silence. The outside of things was sunshine and scatter; the inside of everything was death. Maria, the princess, Jenny: a procession. . . .

On she spun. Usually she had trouble with these gappy sharped and flatted runs but tonight she flew along them, deeper, higher, deeper, *spiccato*, *legato*. The two voices struck against each other, the last revival of that fluttering, that receding, returning theme, still to be quelled. So this was what men had been murmuring about, monopolizing, all these centuries, death; no wonder they had kept it to themselves, no wonder they had kept it from women, let the women do their nursing and hatching, keeping a bad thing going while they, *they*, men, distributed among themselves the true treasure, onyx and ebony and unalloyed gold, the substance of glory and release. Until now Jenny's death has been simply an erasure in Jane's mind, a nothing; now it had its tactile structure, a branched and sumptuous complexity, a sensuous downpulling fathoms more flirtatious than that tug upon our ankles the retreating waves on the beach gave amid the tumbling pebbles, that wonderful weary weighty sigh the sea gives with each wave. It was as if Jenny's poor poisoned body had become intertwined, vein and vein and sinew and sinew, with Jane's own, like the body of a drowned woman with seaweed, and both were rising, the one eventually to be shed by the other but for now interlaced, one with the other, in those revolving luminescent depths. The gigue bristled and prickled under her fingers; the eighth-note thirds underlying the running sixteenth grew ominous; there was a hopeless churning, a pulling down, a grisly *fortissimo* flurry, and a last run down and then skippingly up the scale to the cry capping the crescendo, the thin curt cry of that terminal *d*. . . .

Jane rose from her chair. She had a killing pain between her shoulder blades and her face streamed with tears. It was twenty after four. (pp. 276-278)

Jane's contradictory feelings of harshness and sensitivity reflect the emotional intensity common to many Sixes with a Five wing. We see the same pattern in Hamlet and Raskolnikov.

A Passage to India

In E.M. Forster's novel *A Passage to India*, Dr. Aziz is the Six with a Seven wing. In this early scene Aziz has just met Mrs. Moore, an elderly English Nine, in the garden of a mosque. As they discuss Major Callender, Dr. Aziz's boss, Mrs. Moore admits that she does not much like Mrs. Callender. Aziz takes this as a license to vent his complaints:

He burst out with: "She has just taken my tonga without my permission—do you call that being charming?—and Major Callender interrupts me night after night from where I am dining with my friends and I go at once, breaking up a most pleasant entertainment, and he is not there and not even a message. Is this charming, pray? But what does it matter? I can do nothing and he knows it. I am just a subordinate, my time is of no value, the verandah is good enough for an Indian, yes, yes, let him stand, and Mrs. Callender takes my carriage and cuts me dead . . . ."

She listened.

He was excited partly by his wrongs, but much more by the

knowledge that someone sympathized with them. It was this that led him to repeat, exaggerate, contradict. She had proved her sympathy by criticizing her fellow-countrywoman to him, but even earlier he had known. The flame that not even beauty can nourish was springing up, and though his words were querulous his heart began to glow secretly. Presently it burst into speech.

"You understand me, you know what others feel. Oh, if others resembled you!" (p. 21)

Visible in this brief exchange are a Six's concern with hierarchies as well as the need to be liked. Dr. Aziz also demonstrates a tendency to complain that is especially characteristic of the Six with a Seven wing.

A few pages later we see the quicksilver emotional changes that can go with this wing—and which many Six comedians use as the basis of their humor. In this scene, Aziz is preparing to commune with his dead wife:

And unlocking a drawer, he took out his wife's photograph. He gazed at it, and tears spouted from his eyes. He thought, "How unhappy I am!" But because he really was unhappy, another emotion soon mingled with his self-pity: he desired to remember his wife and could not. Why could he remember people whom he did not love? They were always so vivid to him, whereas the more he looked at this photograph, the less he saw. She had eluded him thus, ever since they had carried her to her tomb. He had known that she would pass from his hands and eyes, but had thought she could live in his mind, not realizing that the very fact that we have loved the dead increases their unreality, and that the more passionately we invoke them the further they recede. A piece of brown cardboard and three children—that was all that was left of his wife. It was unbearable, and he thought again, "How unhappy I am!" and became happier. He had breathed for an instant the mortal air that surrounds Orientals and all men, and he drew back from it with a gasp, for he was young. "Never, never shall I get over this," he told himself. "Most certainly my career is a failure, and my sons will be badly brought up." Since it was certain, he strove to avert it, and looked at some notes he had made on a case at the hospital. Perhaps some day a rich person might require this particular operation, and he gain a large sum. The notes interesting him on their own account, he locked the photograph up again. Its moment was over, and he did not think about his wife any more. (pp. 58-59)

Aziz's distractibility is also a marker of a Six with a Seven wing. People with this temperament can emotionally turn on a dime, full of anguish one moment and absorbed in something completely different in the next.

Mrs. Dalloway

We also see this changeability in Mrs. Dalloway, the title character of Virginia Woolf's novel. At one point during the story Clarissa and Richard Dalloway give a party in their elegant London home. One of their guests, Sir William Bradshaw, a distinguished psychiatrist, explains that he has arrived late because one of his patients committed suicide. Clarissa thinks to herself:

> What business had the Bradshaws to talk of death at her party? A young man had killed himself. And they talked of it at her party—the Bradshaws, talked of death. He had killed himself—but how? Always her body went through it first, when she was told, suddenly, of an accident; her dress flamed, her body burnt. He had thrown himself from a window. Up had flashed the ground; through him, blundering, bruising, went the rusty spikes. There he lay with a thud, thud, thud in his brain, and then a suffocation of blackness. So she saw it. But why had he done it? And the Bradshaws talked of it at her party! (p. 200)

Clarissa then ruminates about what might have been going through the young man's mind just before he flung himself from the window:

> Or there were the poets and thinkers. Suppose he had had that passion, and had gone to Sir William Bradshaw, a great doctor yet to her obscurely evil, without sex or lust, extremely polite to women, but capable of some indescribable outrage—forcing your soul, that was it— if this young man had gone to him, and Sir William had impressed him, like that, with his power, might he not then have said (indeed she felt it now), Life is made intolerable; they make life intolerable, men like that?
>
> Then (she had felt it only this morning) there was the terror; the overwhelming incapacity, one's parents giving it into one's hands, this life, to be lived to the end, to be walked with serenely; there was in the depths of her heart an awful fear. Even now, quite often if Richard had not been there reading the *Times*, so that she could crouch like a bird and gradually revive, send roaring up that immeasurable delight, rubbing stick to stick, one thing with another, she must have perished. But that young man had killed himself.
>
> Somehow it was her disaster—her disgrace. It was her punishment to see sink and disappear here a man, there a woman, in this profound darkness, and she forced to stand here in her evening dress. She had schemed; she had pilfered. She was never wholly admirable. She had wanted success. Lady Bexborough and the rest of it. And once she had walked on the terrace at Bourton.
>
> It was due to Richard; she had never been so happy. Nothing could be slow enough; nothing last too long. No pleasure could equal, she thought, straightening the chairs, pushing in one book on the shelf, this

having done with the triumphs of youth, lost herself in the process of living, to find it, with a shock of delight, as the sun rose, as the day sank. (pp. 201-202)

In Clarissa Dalloway we see how an average Six's disordered thinking can lead her to choose not what she wants but what she *fears least*. The young Clarissa, faced with two men who wanted to marry her, rejected Peter, a Four—the love of her life, whom she still continually thinks about thirty years later—and chose Richard, a Nine—a safe and comfortable choice. Woolf implies that Clarissa's marital choice was inevitable, even wise, given the depth of her existential terror.

Clarissa's Seven wing is evident in her continual see-sawing between terror and ecstasy. The terror for her is always present, just beneath the surface, and it drives her to seek diversions through giving parties. She is also reassured by the affectionate but not too passionate relationship with her husband. If need be, she can even distract herself with keeping the chairs straightened. But the urge to stay in continual motion is more usual with the Seven wing.

Subtypes

In Sixes, the subtypes are especially distinct. The **Self-Preservation** variant, which Oscar Ichazo associates with "warmth," is more phobic. People with this subtype seek security through winning the support of stronger people or groups. The most obviously dependent of the Six subtypes, they fear taking risks and resist moving beyond familiar patterns. Clarissa in *Mrs. Dalloway*, Wormold in Graham Greene's *Our Man in Havana*, The Cowardly Lion in *The Wizard of Oz*, and Maeve in Alice McDermott's *Charming Billy* are examples.

Charming Billy

Maeve, the widow of the title character in Alice McDermott's *Charming Billy*, is the daughter of an alcoholic father. She is plain looking, loyal, and doggedly devoted to her alcoholic husband, Billy, who has spent most of his life mourning a fiancée he mistakenly believes is dead.

Maeve first meets Billy when she accompanies her father to buy shoes at a store where Billy works. Right away we see a timidity that is common in many Self-Preservation Sixes:

Looking on, Maeve saw her father's future with this kind and attentive young man before she had the courage to imagine her own. Or rather, being nun-taught, lives-of-the-saints-saturated (the quiet, handmaiden saints who, if they had not chosen the better part, were freed by their bustling about with food and drink and dishes from ever having to form a sentence, or even a clear thought, about how they loved Him and why), she saw that only through her father's life, which was all the life she had planned to know, would he gain any part in hers. (pp. 152-153)

In Maeve's history we see her early awareness of the precariousness of life, something Self-Preservation Sixes are especially attuned to:

> Maeve was only eight when her mother died—my father getting the story in her tiny kitchen, over all those cups of tea and slivers of cake she had served him after they'd gotten Billy into bed, over all those nights she had summoned him. There had been another child, an older sister, who died of lead poisoning when Maeve was very small. A policeman's daughter, Maeve had gotten some sense early on of the precariousness of life, the risk taken by simply walking out the apartment door. Her mother, all false courage, touched her father's back, the hem of his coat, as he went out, saving the intake of breath, the sign of the cross, for the moment she saw him gain the street. Anything might happen, and did, and Maeve felt the heavy weight of her grieving father's hand on her shoulder. He might have shipped her off to female relatives, but he managed instead to trade in his beat for a desk job so he could stay alive for her. The nuns at her school were more than happy to take the child in for as many hours as he needed them to, and Maeve spoke often—or as often as she spoke of anything—of the pleasant afternoons she had spent in the tiny courtyard of the convent beside her school . . . or in its seldom-visited front room, where the silence was palpable, luxurious, punctuated as it was by the soft steps of the sisters going through the hall or up the stairs or stopping in to bring her a glass of ginger ale and some digestive biscuits on a saucer. . . . (p. 154)

Self-Preservation Sixes find the routines of daily life a haven of security. Sixes' natural anxieties about the future become more manageable when they repeat behavior that has proven safe in the past; there is a sense of permanence, of unchanging stability.

We also see how Maeve's experience with her father's drinking laid the groundwork for a future life with an alcoholic husband:

> There was no question, when she finished school, of having to find a job—which made her the envy of most of her girl friends, who were struggling with stenography and switchboards, and getting to the subway by eight. There was no question, either, that she would join the nuns for good. She did the shopping and cleaned the house and cooked his meals. Lipstick was for weekends, a movie with the girls, a Saturday afternoon at the stores along Jamaica Avenue. Her father drank most evenings, but it was a man's right and, with a wife in her grave, his only solace. And when things got out of hand—when, in his cups, he growled at her or cursed her or waved his arms about as if her love and attention were cobwebs she'd draped around him—there were the nuns to go to, who would listen quietly and advise prayer, but also make sure that the

pastor crooked his finger at the old man next time he and Maeve were at Mass. So she had the attention of men, too; her father when he was feeling fond of her and the priests when he was giving her trouble, and the butcher and the fellow at the newsstand, and even on occasion some boys she had known from school, not the best-looking ones, of course, the homely mostly, the bad-skinned and wet-palmed, the untalkative (which meant a long night of short questions and short answers for them both) who saw in her plainness, her lack of prospects, their own advantage. (p. 155)

Maeve's soliciting attention is related to the way Self-Preservation Sixes will create a network of allies who offer various kinds of protection. But her attraction to Billy, who is mourning his dead fiancée and already an alcoholic, suggests her simultaneous desire to keep her life within familiar limits:

Bringing her father to the store was her way of showing Billy her life in one sweeping glance. Bringing her girl friend was a flirtation with despair—if he fell in love with her talkative friend, Maeve would, at least, in her lifetime, know him. Walking in alone was a dream, but as it turned out, it was another girl's dream. She was the plain one with the father, the one who without him would have become a nun. She was the one who, having chosen this part, must stand steadily by as his future was formed for her (p. 156)

Like many Self-Preservation Sixes, Maeve feels inadequate to the task of shaping her own life, yet she feels a fierce desire to connect with Billy, whose situation reminds her of her father's, who also grieved for a lost love. Continuity is especially comforting to this subtype.

Billy and Maeve marry, and after a long life together Billy dies. His funeral is followed by a gathering of relatives and friends back at their house. As Maeve listens to the platitudes of the local Monsignor, who tries to comfort her with the Catholic idea of resurrection, she is preoccupied:

Maeve lifted her head, but did not raise her eyes. You could see in the stubborn set of her jaw that it was not a figurative life that she wanted for Billy at this moment but a literal one, his literal presence, coming in with the dog as she dozed, opening the cookie jar where they kept the dog biscuits, hanging the chain on the hook by the back door. Their life together, even as it was, simply going on. It was the same literal presence the Legion lady had spoken of earlier, the literal presence, even in a dream, that contained the actual sound of his voice in her ear . . . and the actual weight of him beside her, admiring the flowers, putting her mind at ease. She wanted the real pressure of his hand against hers. (p. 178)

The Self-Preservation issues predominate: Billy's physical presence and reassurance are what Maeve needs, not abstract ideas about spiritual truths.

When Maeve tells the gathering about a time when Billy was drunk, we again see how she found security in a situation that, for all its horrors, was at least familiar. Later, Dan Lynch, the best man at Maeve and Billy's wedding, offers his opinion about why this troubled marriage suited her:

> "Were they happy?" Dan said finally. "Billy and Maeve. Do you think? Were they ever close?" He would not look either of us in the eye, as if the question had embarrassed him.
>
> "She put up with him," my father said, knowing it wasn't an answer.
>
> "She chose to," Dan Lynch said. Now he raised his head. "She chose him, and as far as I can see he fit her to a T. Her old man all over again. Someone to maneuver, to shore up. An alcoholic with a shadow across his heart. An alcoholic because he had a shadow across his heart, the way I see it." He shook his head, squinting into the dim room. "I don't begrudge her her tears, of course, but I wonder, too. Would she have known what to do with a sober man, with the full force of the affection of a sober man who'd never loved another?" (p. 222)

This is the kind of bargain an unevolved Self-Preservation Six feels comfortable making. Maeve avoided the emotional challenge of marrying a non-alcoholic, loving partner and found a kind of security that, to a fearful Self-Preservation Six, was ample compensation for its limitations.

In the **Social** Six subtype, which Ichazo associates with "duty," we find people who are anxious about the social order and who may even be social activists. Social Sixes are sensitive to group norms, conscious of authority issues, and fearful of making mistakes. Sixes with this subtype generally display a mixture of phobic and counterphobic behavior, and we see that combination in such contrasting characters as Hamlet, Miguel de Cervantes's Don Quixote, Shylock in Shakespeare's *The Merchant of Venice*, Celia Coplestone in T. S. Eliot's *The Cocktail Party*, and Mitchell Stephens in Russell Banks's *The Sweet Hereafter*.

The Sweet Hereafter

Some Social Sixes can act like angry, judgmental Ones. This is certainly true of Mitchell Stephens, Esq., in *The Sweet Hereafter*. Mitchell, a personal-injury lawyer, comes to a small upstate New York town after a school bus accident kills most of the town's children. He visits the children's parents, trying to get their cooperation for a class-action lawsuit against the town, the bus company, or some corporate "deep pockets" who may be responsible for flaws in the bus's design.

Mitchell's own family life is in shambles: he is divorced and fiercely loyal to a daughter who is a manipulative drug addict. He displaces his anger about his troubled relationships onto more abstract issues of social irresponsibility, fulminating against the rich and powerful and the injuries they have caused his potential clients:

[W]e're permanently pissed off . . . and practicing law is a way to be socially useful at the same time, that's all. It's like a discipline; it organizes and controls us; probably keeps us from being homicidal. A kind of Zen is what. Some people equally pissed off are able to focus their rage by becoming cops or soldiers or martial arts instructors; those who become lawyers, however, especially litigators like me, are a little too intelligent, or maybe too intellectual is all, to become cops. (I've known some pretty smart cops, but not many intellectual ones.) So instead of learning how to break bricks and two-by-fours with our hands or bust chain-snatchers in subways, we sneak off to law school and put on three-piece suits and come roaring out like banshees, all teeth and claws and fire and smoke.

Certainly we get paid well for it, which is a satisfaction, yes, but not a motivation, because the real satisfaction, the true motivation, is the carnage and the smoldering aftermath and the trophy heads that get hung up on the den wall. I love it.

That's why I spent most of six months up there in Sam Dent, practically becoming a citizen. Not my idea of a winter vacation, believe me. But anytime I hear about a case like that school bus disaster up there, I turn into a heat-seeking missile, homing in on a target that I know in my bones is going to turn out to be some bungling corrupt state agency or some multinational corporation that's cost-accounted the difference between a ten-cent bolt and a million-dollar out-of-court settlement and has decided to sacrifice a few lives for the difference. They do that, work the bottom line; I've seen it play out over and over again, until you start to wonder about the human species. They're like clever monkeys, that's all. They calculate ahead of time what it will cost them to assure safety versus what they're likely to be forced to settle for damages when the missing bolt sends the bus over a cliff, and they simply choose the cheaper option. And it's up to people like me to make it cheaper to build the bus with that extra bolt, or add the extra yard of guardrail, or drain the quarry. That's the only check you've got against them. That's the only way you can ensure moral responsibility in this society. Make it cheaper.

So that winter morning when I picked up the paper and read about this terrible event in a small town upstate, with all those kids lost, I knew instantly what the story was; I knew at once that it wasn't an "accident" at all. There are no accidents. I don't even know what the word means, and I never trust anyone who says he does. I knew that somebody somewhere had made a decision to cut a corner in order to save a few pennies, and now the state or the manufacturer of the bus or the town, somebody, was busy lining up a troop of smoothies to negotiate with a bunch of grief-stricken bumpkins a settlement that wouldn't displease the accountants. I packed a bag and headed north, like I said, pissed off. (pp. 90-92)

Mitchell's ruminations nicely capture the way a counterphobic Social Six thinks and also what would motivate him to choose a profession like the law.

The Cocktail Party

Celia Coplestone in T. S. Eliot's play *The Cocktail Party* offers a contrasting example of a Social Six. Celia, whom Eliot clearly intends us to see as saintly, is uncertain about the right course for her life. Disillusioned about relationships after the breakup of a love affair, she seeks advice from a psychiatrist, Sir Henry Harcourt-Reilly:

CELIA: Well, there are two things I can't understand,
Which you might consider symptoms. But first I must tell you
That I should really *like* to think there's something wrong with me—
Because, if there isn't, then there's something wrong,
Or at least, very different from what it seemed to be,
With the world itself—and that's much more frightening!
That would be terrible. So I'd rather believe
There is something wrong with me, that could be put right.
I'd do anything you told me, to get back to normality. (p. 359)

Like most Sixes, Celia relies strongly on authority. But she has a dawning sense that something is wrong with the world—a more frightening prospect than something being wrong with *her*, since as a Social Six she gives "the world" her power in some form.

REILLY: We must find out about you, before we decide
What *is* normality. You say there are two things:
What is the first?
CELIA: An awareness of solitude. . . .
REILLY: So you want to see no one?
CELIA: No . . . It isn't that I *want* to be alone,
But that everyone's alone—or so it seems to me.
They make noises, and think they are talking to each other;
They make faces, and think they understand each other.
And I'm sure that they don't. Is that a delusion?
REILLY: A delusion is something we must return from.

There are other states of mind, which we take to be delusion,
But which we have to accept and go on from.
And the second symptom?
CELIA: That's stranger still
It sounds ridiculous—but the only word for it
That I can find, is a sense of sin. (pp. 359-360)

When Reilly asks Celia what she means by a sense of sin, it's clear that she is not talking about sin in the usual sense of immorality. She has a Six's tolerance for doubt and ambiguity as she searches for understanding:

CELIA: It's not the feeling of anything I've ever done,
Which I might get away from, or of anything in me
I couldn't get rid of—but of emptiness, of failure
Towards someone, or something, outside of myself;
And I feel I must . . . atone—is that the word?
Can you treat a patient for such a state of mind? (p. 362)

Celia presumes that there is a higher order, and relates to this imagined authority with feelings of duty and even guilt—a common pattern for Social Sixes.

In the midst of her own disillusionment and hunger for meaning, she still feels compassion for her former lover:

REILLY: And this man. What does he now seem like, to you?
CELIA: Like a child who has wandered into a forest
Playing with an imaginary playmate
And suddenly discovers he is only a child
Lost in a forest, wanting to go home.
REILLY: Compassion may be already a clue
Towards finding your own way out of the forest.
CELIA: But even if I find my way out of the forest
I shall be left with the inconsolable memory
Of the treasure I went into the forest to find
And never found, and which was not there
And perhaps is not anywhere? But if not anywhere,
Why do I feel guilty at not having found it?
REILLY: Disillusion can become itself an illusion
If we rest in it.
CEILA: I cannot argue.
It's not that I'm afraid of being hurt again:
Nothing again can either hurt or heal
I have thought at moments that the ecstasy is real
Although those who experience it may have no reality. . . .

And if that is all meaningless, I want to be cured
Of a craving for something I cannot find
And of the shame of never finding it.
Can you cure me? (pp. 362-363)

The idealism and sense of personal shame Celia expresses are also a pattern in Social Sixes.

Reilly says that her condition is curable, but she must choose the form of her own treatment. He can, for instance, help her become reconciled to the human condition, if that is her choice. Like other Social Sixes, Celia is willing to suffer to be certain she is on the right path:

CELIA: I know I ought to be able to accept that
If I might still have it. Yet it leaves me cold.
Perhaps that's just a part of my illness,
But I feel it would be a kind of surrender—
No, not a surrender—more like a betrayal.
You see, I think I really had a vision of something
Though I don't know what it is. I don't want to forget it.
I want to live with it. I could do without everything,
Put up with anything, if I might cherish it.
In fact, I think it would really be dishonest
For me, now, to try to make a life with *any*body!
I couldn't give anyone the kind of love—
I wish I could—which belongs to that life.
Oh, I'm afraid this sounds like raving!
Or just cantankerousness . . . still,
If there's no other way . . . then I feel just hopeless. (p. 364)

Here we see Celia wrestling with the basic Six issue of "betrayal" and again demonstrating the quality of doubt. Her idealistic vision of a higher purpose is common to Social Sixes.

REILLY: There *is* another way, if you have the courage.
The first I could describe in familiar terms
Because you have seen it, as we all have seen it,
Illustrated, more or less, in lives of those about us.
The second is unknown, and so requires faith—
The kind of faith that issues from despair.
The destination cannot be described;
You will know very little until you get there;
You will journey blind. But the way leads towards possession
Of what you have sought for in the wrong place.
CELIA: That sounds like what I want. But what is my duty?

REILLY: Whichever way you choose will prescribe its own duty.
CELIA: Which way is better?
REILLY: Neither way is better.
Both ways are necessary. It is also necessary
To make a choice between them.
CELIA: Then I choose the second.
REILLY: It is a terrifying journey.
CELIA: I am not frightened
But glad. I suppose it is a lonely way?
REILLY: No lonelier than the other. But those who take the other
Can forget their loneliness. You will not forget yours.
Each way means loneliness—and communion.
Both ways avoid the final desolation
Of solitude in the phantasmal world
Of imagination, shuffling memories and desires
CELIA: That is the hell I have been in. (pp. 364-365)

Reilly explains that she must be ready to be leave immediately for the "sanatorium," and the blessing he gives her has religious overtones.

After Celia departs, Reilly discusses her case with his friend and colleague Julia:

JULIA: . . . It's the thought of Celia that weighs upon my mind.
REILLY: Of Celia?
JULIA: Of Celia.
REILLY: But when I said just now
That she would go far, you agreed with me.
JULIA: Oh yes, she will go far. And we know where she is going.
But what do we know of the terrors of the journey?
You and I don't know the process by which the human is
Transhumanised: what do we know
Of the kind of suffering they must under go
On the way of illumination? (p. 367)

In the last act of the play, we learn that Celia joined a nursing order, was sent to Africa, and died horribly during a native uprising when she refused to leave her patients. She was crucified near an ant hill, and Eliot makes it clear that she was unconsciously seeking martyrdom.

The **Sexual** subtype of Six, which Ichazo associates with "strength" and "beauty," shows more bravado than the other two, attempting to compensate for fears by looking powerful and/or seductive. In their belligerence, contrariness, and counterphobic "strength," Sexual Sixes often resemble Eights. Those preoccupied with "beauty" are somewhat more phobic and use their sexual allure to attract support. Literary examples of this subtype include Raskolnikov in *Crime and Punishment*, Ahab in Melville's *Moby-Dick*, Satan in Milton's *Paradise Lost*, Lilly Dillon in Jim Thompson's *The Grifters*, Will in Alice Adams's *Medicine Men*, and Katharina in Shakespeare's *The Taming of the Shrew*.

The Taming of the Shrew

Shakespeare's Katharina is the elder of two daughters and under pressure to marry so that her sister may also find a husband. Petruchio, a Sexual Eight searching for a rich wife, woos and wins Katharina, despite her reputation as a "shrew": bad-tempered, quarrelsome, defiant of authority, "curst." After they marry, he contrives to keep her hungry, sleepless and sexually frustrated—all ostensibly for her benefit:

> KATHARINA: The more my wrong, the more his spite appears:
> What, did he marry me to famish me?
> Beggars, that come unto my father's door,
> Upon entreaty have a present alms;
> If not, elsewhere they meet with charity:
> But I, who never knew how to entreat,
> Nor never needed that I should entreat,
> Am starved for meat, giddy for lack of sleep,
> With oaths kept waking and with brawling fed:
> And that which spites me more than all these wants,
> He does it under name of perfect love;
> As who should say, if I should sleep or eat,
> Twere deadly sickness or else present death. (IV, iii, 2-14)

In the "name of perfect love" Petruchio refuses to argue with Katharina or even speak crossly to her. This stops her counterphobic aggressiveness in its tracks. When she has no negative response from Petruchio against which to argue, her underlying fear comes to the surface.

Petruchio continues his campaign to "tame" her by announcing a plan to take her to visit her father, then abruptly cancels the journey when she corrects him after he has deliberately misstated the time of day.

Petruchio obviously wants Katharina's complete subjection to his authority. While on the surface this is a feminist's nightmare, for a Six there is a kind of comforting certainty in it: Katharina knows exactly where she stands and how the marital game is to be played. Shortly thereafter she capitulates to her husband's authority, and her "taming" is complete.

Eventually, she and Petruchio do travel to her father's house, where they join the celebration of her sister Bianca's wedding. Talking to his friends, Petruchio wagers that, of three wives summoned by their husbands, Katharina will come the quickest. After he wins the bet, Katharina offers her philosophy of marriage to her sister and the other bride:

> KATHARINA: Fie, fie! Unknit that threatening unkind brow,
> And dart not scornful glances from those eyes,
> To wound thy lord, thy king, thy governor. . . .
> Thy husband is thy lord, thy life, thy keeper,
> Thy head, thy sovereign; one that cares for thee,
> And for thy maintenance commits his body
> To painful labor both by sea and land,
> To watch the night in storms, the day in cold,
> Whilst thou liest warm at home, secure and safe;
> And craves no other tribute at thy hands
> But love, fair looks and true obedience;
> Too little payment for so great a debt. . . .
> I am ashamed that women are so simple
> To offer war where they should kneel for peace. . . .
> Come, come, you froward and unable worms!
> My mind hath been as big as one of yours,
> My heart as great, my reason haply more,
> To bandy word for word and frown for frown;
> But now I see our lances are but straws,
> Our strength as weak, our weakness past compare. . . .
> And place your hands below your husband's foot:
> In token of which duty, if he please,
> My hand is ready; may it do him ease.
> PETRUCHIO: Why, there's a wench! Come on, and kiss me, Kate.
> (V, ii, 136-180)

Thus we see a Sexual Six "tamed" by a Sexual Eight. Shakespeare's subtext suggests that Katharina is aware of the erotic advantages of having a husband whose strength is greater than her own. Petruchio's reply implies that a lively session in the bedchamber may be in the offing as the "strength" of a Sexual Six meets the staying power of a Sexual Eight.

Moby-Dick

Ahab, in Herman Melville's great novel *Moby-Dick*, is another Sexual Six. Captain of the whaling ship Pequod, he sets sail from Nantucket in search of Moby Dick, the great white whale who, in a previous encounter, cost Ahab a leg. Defying all reason—and in the face of stories about the whale's destructive power—Ahab heedlessly risks his ship and crew while he obsessively seeks vengeance. In the end, Ahab, the ship and crew are lost; all except Ishmael, the novel's narrator, who survives the disaster by floating on a wooden coffin until he is rescued.

Early in the story Ishmael, looking for a berth on the Pequod, asks another sea captain about Ahab, and we get our first description of this complex Six character:

"He's a queer man, Captain Ahab—so some think—but a good one. Oh, thou'lt like him well enough; no fear, no fear. He's a grand, ungodly, god-like man, Captain Ahab; doesn't speak much; but when he does speak, then you may well listen. Mark ye, be forewarned; Ahab's above the common; Ahab's been in colleges, as well as 'mong the cannibals; been used to deeper wonders than the waves; fixed his fiery lance in mightier, stranger foes than whales. . . . I know Captain Ahab well; I've sailed with him as mate years ago; I know what he is—a good man—something like me—only there's a good deal more of him. Aye, aye, I know that he was never very jolly; and I know that on the passage home he was a little out of his mind for a spell; but it was the sharp shooting pains in his bleeding stump that brought that about, as any one might see. I know, too, that ever since he lost his leg last voyage by that accursed whale, he's been a kind of moody—desperate moody, and savage sometimes; but that will all pass off. . . . Besides, my boy, he has a wife—not three voyages wedded—a sweet, resigned girl. Think of that; by that sweet girl that old man has a child; hold ye then there can be any utter, hopeless harm in Ahab? No, no, my lad; stricken, blasted, if he be, Ahab has his humanities!" (pp. 82-83)

The captain sees Ahab as an essentially decent, if troubled, man. The Six ability to engage others on a human level is noticable even in an unhealthy specimen like Ahab.

Once the voyage is underway, Ishmael watches as Ahab nails a gold piece to the mast and promises it to the first crew member who sights Moby Dick. Starbuck, a One and the ship's first mate, asks if this is the whale who took off Ahab's leg:

"Who told thee that?" cried Ahab; then pausing, "Aye, Starbuck; aye, my hearties all round; it was Moby Dick that dismasted me; Moby Dick that brought me to this dead stump I stand on now. Aye, aye," he shouted with a terrific, loud, animal sob, like that of a heart-stricken moose; "Aye, aye! It was that accursed white whale that razeed me; made a poor pegging lubber of me for ever and a day!" Then tossing both arms, with measureless imprecations he shouted out: "Aye, aye! and I'll chase him round Good Hope, and round the Horn, and round the Norway Maelstrom, and round perdition's flames before I give him up. . . . (pp. 155-156)

The Sexual subtype of any Enneagram style is often the most intense. Here the intensity of Ahab's thoughts engenders a kind of paranoia that gets projected onto Moby Dick. This is shocking to Starbuck, who represents the voice of reason throughout the story:

> "Vengeance on a dumb brute!" cried Starbuck, "that simply smote thee from blindest instinct! Madness! To be enraged with a dumb thing, Captain Ahab, seems blasphemous."
>
> "Hark ye yet again,—the little lower layer. All visible objects, man, are but as pasteboard masks. But in each event—in the living act, the undoubted deed—there, some unknown but still reasoning thing puts forth the mouldings of its feature from behind the unreasoning mask. If man will strike, strike through the mask! How can the prisoner reach outside except by thrusting through the wall? To me, the white whale is that wall, shoved near to me. Sometimes I think there's naught beyond. But 'tis enough. He tasks me; he heaps me; I see in him outrageous strength, with an inscrutable malice sinewing it. That inscrutable thing is chiefly what I hate; and be the white whale agent, or be the white whale principal, I will wreak that hate upon him. Talk not to me of blasphemy, man; I'd strike the sun if it insulted me. For could the sun do that, then could I do the other; since there is ever a sort of fair play herein, jealousy presiding over all creations. But not my master, man, is even that fair play. Who's over me? Truth hath no confines. Take off thine eye! more intolerable than fiends' glarings is a doltish stare! So, so; thou reddenest and palest; my heat has melted thee to anger-glow. But look ye, Starbuck, what is said in heat, that thing unsays itself. There are men from whom warm words are small indignity. I mean not to incense thee. Let it go. . . ." (pp. 156-157)

Despite his passionate determination to pursue the whale, Ahab is aware, as all Sixes are, of the importance of alliances. He knows he needs Starbuck's help if his quest is to succeed, and we see him come close to apologizing for his intemperateness.

Later, sitting in his cabin alone, Ahab is pleased with how well he has imbued his principal crew members with his own passion for destroying the white whale:

> 'Twas not so hard a task. I thought to find one stubborn, at the least; but my one cogged circle fits into all their various wheels, and they revolve. Or, if you will, like so many ant-hills of powder, they all stand before me; and I their match. Oh, hard! that to fire others, the match itself must needs be wasting! What I've dared, I've willed; and what I've willed, I'll do! They think me mad—Starbuck does; but I'm demoniac, I am madness maddened! The wild madness that's only calm to comprehend itself! The prophecy was that I should be dismembered;

and—Aye! I lost this leg. I now prophesy that I will dismember my dismemberer. Now, then, be the prophet and the fulfiller one. That's more than ye, ye great gods, ever were. I laugh and hoot at ye, ye cricket-players, ye pugilists, ye deaf Burkes and blind Bendigoes! I will not say as schoolboys do to bullies,—Take some one of your own size; don't pommel *me!* No, ye've knocked me down, and I am up again; but *ye* have run and hidden. Come forth from behind your cotton bags! I have no long gun to reach ye. Come, Ahab's compliments to ye; come and see if ye can swerve me. Swerve me? ye cannot swerve me, else ye swerve yourselves! man has ye there. Swerve me? the path to my fixed purpose is laid with iron rails, whereon my soul is grooved to run. Over unsounded gorges, through the rifled hearts of mountains, under torrents' beds, unerringly I rush! Naught's an obstacle, naught's an angle to the iron way! (pp. 160-161)

Ahab seems to be defying nature and God, pitting his own will against the cosmic order. These are authority issues on a colossal scale.

Some Sexual Sixes seek battles that test their strength and their ability to endure mental anguish:

Often, when forced from his hammock by exhausting and intoler-ably vivid dreams of the night . . . Ahab would burst from his state room, as though escaping from a bed that was on fire. . . . For, at such times, crazy Ahab, the scheming, unappeasedly steadfast hunter of the white whale; this Ahab that had gone to his hammock, was not the agent that so caused him to burst from it in horror again. The latter was the eternal, living principle or soul in him; and in sleep, being for the time dissociated from the characterizing mind, which at other times em-ployed it for its outer vehicle or agent, it spontaneously sought escape from the scorching contiguity of the frantic thing, of which, for the time it was no longer an integral. But as the mind does not exist unless leagued with the soul, therefore it must have been that, in Ahab's case, yielding up all his thoughts and fancies to his one supreme purpose; that purpose, by its own sheer inveteracy of will, forced itself against gods and devils into a kind of self-assumed, independent being of its own. . . . God help thee, old man, thy thoughts have created a creature in thee; and he whose intense thinking thus makes him a Prometheus; a vulture feeds upon that heart for ever; that vulture the very creature he creates. (pp. 191-192)

We see that Ahab's suffering, typical of all Sixes, is thought-induced. As we saw with Hamlet and Raskolnikov, distorted thinking can inflame a Six to the point where his only hope for release seems to lie in violent action.

Ahab's crazed thinking leads him to further conclude that pleasure is frivolous and that the gods themselves are melancholy. This kind of pessimism is particularly evident in Sixes with a Five wing:

> For, thought Ahab, while even the highest earthly felicities ever have a certain unsignifying pettiness lurking in them, but, at bottom, all heart-woes, a mystic significance and in some men, an archangelic grandeur; so do their diligent tracings-out not belie the obvious deduction. To train the genealogies of these high mortal miseries carries us at last among the sourceless primogenitures of the gods; so that, in the face of all the glad, hay-making suns, and soft-cymballing, round harvest-moons, we must needs give in to this; that the gods themselves are not for ever glad. The ineffaceable, sad birthmark in the brow of man is but the stamp of sorrow in the signers. (p. 426)

Ishmael has already noted that Ahab has a birthmark resembling a fork of lightning that begins on his forehead, continues down his face and neck—and perhaps further down his body. To Ishmael, Ahab looks as though he has been struck by lightning.

Indeed, Ahab seems to have a particular affinity with lightning. Later, during a storm, he refuses to let the lightning rods attached to the ship's masts be grounded in the sea, and the masts catch fire. The entire crew watches the amazing sight. As the flames leap higher, Ahab makes a lengthy invocation to the powers that burn within him and consume him, concluding with the lines:

> Oh, thou foundling fire, thou hermit immemorial, thou too hast thy incommunicable riddle, thy unparticipated grief. Here again with haughty agony, I ready my sire. Leap! leap up, and lick the sky! I leap with thee; I burn with thee; would fain be welded with thee; defyingly I worship thee!" (p. 462)

This is a Sexual Six at once defying and identifying with the forces of nature—both divine and diabolic—that the flames represent to him.

As Ahab girds himself for his final battle with Moby Dick, he seems aware of the colossal folly of it—and of his whole life. His humanity shows itself again in his concern for Starbuck's safety, his desire to save the mate from the inevitable destruction he has set in motion:

> "Oh, Starbuck! it is a mild, mild wind, and a mild looking sky. On such a day—very much such a sweetness as this—I struck my first whale—a boy-harpooneer of eighteen! Forty—forty—forty years ago!—ago! Forty years of continual whaling! forty years of privation, and peril, and storm-time! forty years on the pitiless sea! for forty years has Ahab forsaken the peaceful land, for forty years to make war on the horrors of the deep! Aye and yes, Starbuck, out of those forty years I have not spent three ashore. When I think of this life I have led; the desolation of

solitude it has been; the masoned, walled-town of a Captain's exclusive-ness, which admits but small entrance to any sympathy from the green country without—oh, weariness! heaviness! . . . away, whole oceans away, from that young girl-wife I wedded past fifty, and sailed for Cape Horn the next day, leaving but one dent in my marriage pillow—wife? wife?—rather a widow with her husband alive! Aye, I widowed that poor girl when I married her, Starbuck; and then, the madness, the frenzy, the boiling blood and the smoking brow, with which, for a thousand lowerings old Ahab has furiously, foamingly chased his prey—more a demon than a man!—aye, aye! what a forty years' fool—fool—old fool, has old Ahab been! . . . Close! stand close to me, Starbuck; let me look into a human eye; it is better than to gaze into sea or sky; better than to gaze upon God. By the green land; by the bright hearth-stone! this is the magic glass, man; I see my wife and my child in thine eye. No, no; stay on board, on board!—lower not when I do; when branded Ahab gives chase to Moby Dick. That hazard shall not be thine. No, no! not with the far away home I see in that eye! (pp. 491-492)

Starbuck pleads with Ahab to turn away from the confrontation with Moby Dick and head for home. But Ahab's course is set, and he feels that this encounter is his destiny:

But Ahab's glance was averted; like a blighted fruit tree he shook, and cast his last, cindered apple to the soil.

"What is it, what nameless inscrutable, unearthly thing is it; what cozzening, hidden lord and master, and cruel, remorseless emperor commands me; that against all natural lovings and longings, I so keep pushing, and crowding, and jamming myself on all the time; recklessly making me ready to do what in my own proper, natural heart, I durst not so much as dare? Is Ahab, Ahab? Is it I, God, or who, that lifts this arm? But if the great sun move not of himself; but is as an errand-boy in heaven; nor one single star can revolve, but by some invisible power; how then can this one small heart beat; this one small brain think thoughts; unless God does that beating, does that thinking, does that living and not I. By heaven, man, we are turned round and round in this world, like yonder windlass, and Fate is the handspike. (p. 493)

Once the whale is located and the chase begins, Starbuck continues to beg Ahab to stop it. But the irrational captain is impervious. On the final day, Ahab muses about the limitations of the human faculty of thought:

"What a lovely day again! were it a new-made world, and made for a summerhouse to the angels, and this morning the first of its throwing open to them, a fairer day could not dawn upon that world. Here's food for thought, had Ahab time to think; but Ahab never thinks; he only feels, feels, feels; *that's* tingling enough for mortal man! to think's audacity. God only has that right and privilege." (p. 510)

All Sixes tend towards flawed thinking, but Sexual Sixes are more capable of acting out their misdirected thoughts through extremes of feeling and action.

The white whale is sighted and the battle ensues. Moby Dick strikes the ship with his tail, dealing it a fatal blow. Now in his whaleboat, Ahab prepares to hurl his harpoon, believing that his grandeur as a human being depends on the intensity of his feeling, not on his ability to think:

Ho, ho! from all your furthest bounds, pour ye now in, ye bold billows of my whole foregone life, and top this one piled comber of my death! Towards thee I roll, thou all-destroying but unconquering whale; to the last I grapple with thee; from hell's heart I stab at thee; for hate's sake I spit my last breath at thee. Sink all coffins and all hearses to one common pool! and since neither can be mine, let me then tow to pieces, while still chasing thee, though tied to thee, thou damned whale! *Thus,* I give up the spear!"

The harpoon was darted; the stricken whale flew forward; with igniting velocity the line ran through the groove;—ran foul. Ahab stooped to clear it; he did clear it; but the flying turn caught him round the neck, and voicelessly as Turkish mutes bowstring their victim, he was shot out of the boat, ere the crew knew he was gone. Next instant, the heavy eye-splice in the rope's final end flew out of the dark-empty tub, knocked down an oarsman, and smiting the sea, disappeared in its depths. (pp. 519-520)

Thus a Sexual Six, defiant to the end, goes to his death in a stunning final display of willfulness, anguish, and folly.

Among Six literary examples, we see a great range: from the mad but titanic Ahab to the timid Maeve in *Charming Billy*. I also know of no other Enneagram point whose literary characters so often transcend their style: Celia Coplestone in *The Cocktail Party*, Raskolnikov in *Crime and Punishment*, and Hamlet.

Sources
Banks, Russell, *The Sweet Hereafter* (New York: HarperCollins, 1991)

Dostoevsky, Fyodor, *Crime and Punishment*, trans. Constance Garnett (New York: Bantam, 1981). First published 1866

Eliot, T. S. *The Cocktail Party* in *The Complete Poems and Plays 1909-1950* (New York: Harcourt Brace Jovanovich, 1971). First published 1950

Forster, E.M., *A Passage to India* (New York: Harcourt Brace Jovanovich, 1924)

Gordon, Mary, *Final Payments* (New York: Ballantine, 1978)

Le Carré, John, *The Spy Who Came in from the Cold* (New York: Ballantine, 1963)

McDermott, Alice, *Charming Billy* (New York: Farrar, Straus and Giroux, 1998)

Melville, Herman, *Moby-Dick* (New York: Bantam, 1981). First published 1851

Shakespeare, William, *Hamlet*. First produced 1601-2

_____ *The Taming of the Shrew*. First produced 1593-4

Updike, John, *The Witches of Eastwick* (New York: Alfred A. Knopf, 1984)

Woolf, Virginia, *Mrs. Dalloway* (New York: Harcourt Brace, 1925)

Seven: The Optimist

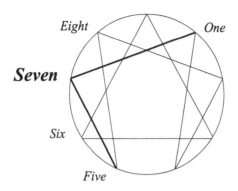

Eight *One*

Seven

Six

Five

J.M. Barrie's play *Peter Pan* is a classic Seven story, featuring adventure and fun, personified by Peter, the eternal boy. In Act One, Peter flies through the window of the bedroom shared by the Darling children, Wendy and her two younger brothers. When Wendy asks him about his background he offers only whimsical answers:

WENDY. Where do you live?
PETER. Second to the right and then straight on till morning.
WENDY. What a funny address!
PETER. No, it isn't.
WENDY. I mean, is that what they put on the letters?
PETER. Don't get any letters.
WENDY. But your mother gets letters?
PETER. Don't have a mother.
WENDY. Peter!
(*She leaps out of bed to put her arms round him, but he draws back; he does not know why, but he knows he must draw back.*)
PETER. You mustn't touch me.
WENDY. Why?
PETER. No one must ever touch me.
WENDY. Why?
PETER. I don't know.
(*He is never touched by any one in the play.*)
WENDY. No wonder you were crying.
PETER. I wasn't crying. But I can't get my shadow to stick on.
WENDY. It has come off! How awful. (pp. 62-63)

We see in Peter qualities common in Sevens: charm, energy, a disengagement from the mother, resistance to being touched by others and an inability to connect with the darker side of his own nature.

On the island where Peter takes Wendy and her brothers is a troop of lost boys, who are delighted to pretend that Wendy is their mother. Wendy, a Two, enjoys her maternal role and persuades the lost boys to go home with her, assuring them that her mother and father will adopt them:

> WENDY (*insinuatingly*). Get your clothes, Peter.
> PETER (*Skipping and playing fairy music on his pipes, the only music he knows*). I am not going with you, Wendy.
> WENDY. Yes, Peter!
> PETER. No.
> (*The lost ones run back gaily, each carrying a stick with a bundle on the end of it.*)
> WENDY. Peter isn't coming!
> (*All the faces go blank.*)
> JOHN (*even JOHN*). Peter not coming!
> TOOTLES (*overthrown*). Why, Peter?
> PETER (*his pipes more riotous than ever*). I just want always to be a little boy and to have fun. (pp. 142-143)

Peter's riotous pipe playing betrays his anxiety over Wendy's demands for commitment. After he returns Wendy and her brothers home safely, their mother offers to adopt Peter.

> MRS. DARLING (*from the window*). Peter, where are you? Let me adopt you too.
> (*She is the loveliest age for a woman, but too old to see PETER clearly.*)
> PETER. Would you send me to school?
> MRS. DARLING (*obligingly*). Yes.
> PETER. And then to an office?
> MRS. DARLING. I suppose so.
> PETER. Soon I should be a man?
> MRS. DARLING. Very soon.
> PETER (*passionately*). I don't want to go to school and learn solemn things. No one is going to catch me, lady, and make me a man. I want always to be a little boy and to have fun.
> (*So perhaps he thinks, but it is only his greatest pretend.*) (pp. 185-186)

Barrie's comment acknowledges the inherent limitations of the Seven style. For all Peter's charm, energy and audacity, he refuses to accept the implications of the human condition—including the inevitability of aging and death—which sentences him to a life without dimension.

Breakfast at Tiffany's

Holly Golightly, the central character of Truman Capote's novella *Breakfast at Tiffany's*, offers another vivid example of a Seven. Beautiful and chic, Holly is part of the fashionable set in New York City in the 1950s. Coming from a rural background and with limited education, she makes ends meet by contributions from men she dates. Her primary ambition is to land a rich husband.

Holly's story is told by an equally impoverished young neighbor, an aspiring writer whose name we never learn. He first sees her coming up the stairs of their building, followed by a man who is upset that she won't allow him into her apartment:

> [H]e plunged down the stairs, slamming a fist against the wall. Just as he reached the bottom, the door of the girl's apartment opened and she poked out her head.
>
> "Oh, Mr. Arbuck . . ."
>
> He turned back, a smile of relief oiling his face: she'd only been teasing.
>
> "The next time a girl wants a little powder-room change," she called, not teasing at all, "take my advice, darling: *don't* give her twenty cents!" (pp. 233-234)

Sevens like Holly often fear having their options limited by inadequate resources, and when people are ungenerous with them, they can turn off very quickly.

Holly later meets the writer when she climbs up the fire escape to his apartment to avoid another unpleasant man who is inside her flat. Right away she tells the writer she will help him get published because he looks like her brother Fred. In fact, she decides to call him Fred, and her lack of interest in him apart from his relevance to herself reflects the narcissism that is prevalent in Sevens.

Like many Sevens, Holly also has trouble with commitment:

> She was still hugging the cat. "Poor slob," she said, tickling his head, "poor slob without a name. It's a little inconvenient, his not having a name. But I haven't any right to give him one: he'll have to wait until he *belongs* to somebody. We just sort of took up by the river one day, we don't belong to each other: he's an independent, and so am I. I don't want to own anything until I know I've found the place where me and things belong together. I'm not quite sure where that is just yet. But I know what it's like." She smiled, and let the cat drop to the floor. "It's like Tiffany's," she said. . . . "Listen. You know those days when you've got the mean reds?"
>
> "Same as the blues?"
>
> "No," she said slowly. "No, the blues are because you're getting fat or maybe it's been raining too long. You're sad, that's all. But the

mean reds are horrible. You're afraid and you sweat like hell, but you don't know what you're afraid of. Except something bad is going to happen, only you don't know what it is. You've had that feeling?"

"Quite often. Some people call it *angst*."

"All right. *Angst*. But what do you do about it?"

"Well, a drink helps."

"I've tried that. I've tried aspirin, too. Rusty thinks I should smoke marijuana, and I did for a while, but it only makes me giggle. What I've found does the most good is just to get into a taxi and go to Tiffany's. It calms me down right away, the quietness and the proud look of it; nothing very bad could happen to you there, not with those kind men in their nice suits, and that lovely smell of silver and alligator wallets. If I could find a real-life place that made me feel like Tiffany's, then I'd buy some furniture and give the cat a name." (pp. 246-247)

The "mean reds" is Holly's Sevenish euphemism for fear. Holly's time-tested way of dealing with this negative emotion is to take a taxi to Tiffany's—the source of all the quality things that money can buy—the equivalent of Peter Pan's Never land.

Sevens often display an appetite for the forbidden and the madcap, and Holly enjoys the adrenaline rush she gets from flouting the law:

Passing a Woolworth's, she gripped my arm: "Let's steal something," she said, pulling me into the store, where at once there seemed a pressure of eyes, as though we were already under suspicion. "Come on. Don't be chicken." She scouted a counter piled with paper pumpkins and Halloween masks. The saleslady was occupied with a group of nuns who were trying on masks. Holly picked up a mask and slipped it over her face; she chose another and put it on mine; then she took my hand and we walked away. It was as simple as that. Outside, we ran a few blocks, I think to make it more dramatic; but also because, as I'd discovered, successful theft exhilarates. I wondered if she'd often stolen. "I used to," she said. "I mean I had to. If I wanted anything. But I still do it every now and then, sort of to keep my hand in." (p. 254)

Sevens are often idealistic, and we see Holly's idealism in bizarre conjunctions with her self-interest and pragmatism. When she finds herself pregnant by her Brazilian lover, José, she expects to marry him, although he has not yet proposed:

"I wish, please don't laugh—but I wish I'd been a virgin for him, for José. Not that I've warmed the multitudes some people say: I don't blame the bastards for *saying* it, I've always thrown out such a jazzy line. Really, though, I toted up the other night, and I've only had eleven lovers—not counting anything that happened before I was thirteen because, after all, that just *doesn't* count. Eleven. Does that make me a whore? Look at Mag Wildwood. Or Honey Tucker. Or Rose Ellen Ward. They've had the old clap-yo'-hands so many times it amounts to applause. Of course I haven't anything *against* whores. Except this: some of them may have an honest tongue but they all have dishonest hearts. I mean, you can't bang the guy and cash his checks and at least not *try* to believe you love him. I never have. Even Benny Shacklett and all those rodents. I sort of hypnotized myself into thinking their sheer rattiness had a certain allure. Actually, except for Doc, if you want to count Doc, José is my first non-rat romance. Oh, he's not my idea of the absolute finito. He tells little lies and he worries what people *think* and he takes about fifty baths a day: men ought to smell *some*what. He's too prim, too cautious to be my guy ideal; he always turns his back to get undressed and he makes too much noise when he eats and I don't like to see him run because there's something funny-looking about him when he runs." (p. 267)

Holly's rationalizations about her love affairs and her contemptuous attitude toward the man she expects to marry reveal the opportunism behind her idealism.

As the story closes, Holly is under criminal indictment because of her regular—and paid—visits to an imprisoned mobster, and she has been deserted by the conservative José. The writer visits her in the hospital, where she is recovering from a miscarriage brought on by wild horseback riding. She decides that getting out of the country is her best opportunity, since she already has a ticket to Brazil, courtesy of the departed José. The writer tries to dissuade her, but she sees her options narrowing and—predictably for a Seven—feels that motion equals progress.

The Seven's History

As children Sevens often feel disconnected from the nurturing figure and conclude that they must nourish themselves. Adult Sevens continue to fear that nourishment is scarce, and they can be aggressive in their pursuit of food, money, novelty, pleasures—not to mention options of all kinds. The "deadly sin" associated with Sevens is gluttony—not only in the original sense of excessive eating, but also in the extended sense of consuming experiences and continually seeking novelty.

Like Holly Golightly, Sevens often seek out others for the material resources they can provide. Holly's determination to marry a rich man is understandable, given a childhood so impoverished that she had to steal turkey eggs from local farmers.

Levels of Health

Seven is the last of the Enneagram styles in the head/thinking triad, which is associated with fear. While Fives cope with a threatening world by developing their mental capacities in isolation, and Sixes cope through constant vigilance and seeking trustworthy allies, Sevens manage their fears by staying continually in motion and distracting themselves with activities and pleasures. Few Sevens are aware of how pervasive their underlying terror actually is and how useless any attempt to outrun it will prove.

The psychological defense mechanism characteristic of Seven is *rationalization*. When defensive, Sevens try to explain away their conduct, see negative situations in a positive light and justify their aggressive drive to accumulate material resources. Meanwhile, they deny their underlying fears, avoid their inner pain and dodge responsibilities that frustrate their narcissism and the continual feeding of their appetites.

Average Sevens are preoccupied with activity and options, and are especially focused on the future and its stimulating possibilities. They find it easier to begin new projects than to complete old ones. Their natural charm, optimism, and energy make them appealing companions, but these same qualities can be a smoke screen for their underlying narcissism. Sevens at this level of health are subject to impulsive actions that may verge on recklessness.

In literature we see a wide range of average Sevens: Peter Pan, Holly Golightly in *Breakfast at Tiffany's*, Mercutio in Shakespeare's *Romeo and Juliet*, Gulley Jimson in Joyce Cary's *The Horse's Mouth*, Daniel Defoe's Moll Flanders, Patrick Dennis's Auntie Mame, Bridget Jones in Helen Fielding's *Bridget Jones's Diary*, Rodolphe in Gustave Flaubert's *Madame Bovary*, Dickie Greenleaf in Patricia Highsmith's *The Talented Mr. Ripley*, Isadora Wing in Erica Jong's *Fear of Flying*, the title character in Jong's *Fanny*, Leopold Bloom in James Joyce's *Ulysses*, Sabina in Milan Kundera's *The Unbearable Lightness of Being*, Odysseus in Homer's *Odyssey*, Sissy Hankshaw in Tom Robbins's *Even Cowgirls Get the Blues*, Gulliver in Jonathan Swift's *Gulliver's Travels*, Vronsky in Leo Tolstoy's *Anna Karenina*, Mark Twain's Huckleberry Finn, Voltaire's Candide, Mozart in Peter Shaffer's *Amadeus*, John Proctor in Arthur Miller's *The Crucible*, and Maxine in Tennessee Williams's *The Night of the Iguana*.

Healthy Sevens display immense vitality, passionately enjoy life, and are able to sustain commitments to projects and people. Often multi-talented, they are productive and fulfilled in their lives. They are especially adept at "brainstorming" ideas. Not only do they frequently display original thinking, but their enthusiasm inspires others to creative problem solving that, in the Seven's company, becomes fun and exciting.

Healthy Sevens in literature include Tertius Lydgate in George Eliot's *Middlemarch*, Henry Fielding's Tom Jones, Monica Szabo in Mary Gordon's *Spending*, and Prince Hal in Shakespeare's *Henry IV* parts 1 and 2.

Unhealthy Sevens are demanding, materialistic, excessive, and self-indulgent. They are prone to rages when their desires are not quickly fulfilled, and tend to escape into drugs, sexual activity, overeating, whatever will offer them temporary relief from their anxiety. Unhealthy Sevens can often be manic and subject to panic attacks when they exhaust their resources and have to confront their underlying terror.

Literary examples include Morris in Henry James's *Washington Square*, McMurphy in Ken Kesey's *One Flew Over the Cuckoo's Nest*, Francie Brady in Patrick McCabe's *The Butcher Boy*, Julian English in John O'Hara's *Appointment in Samarra*, Aunt Sylvie in Marilynne Robinson's *Housekeeping*, Phillip Dean in James Salter's *A Sport and a Pastime*, and Shannon in Tennessee Williams's *The Night of the Iguana*.

Place in Society

Although Sevens are found in all professions, they are especially prominent in the entertainment field as actors, comedians, singers, dancers, circus performers, rock musicians, talk show hosts, and TV news reporters. Behind the scenes they may be stage, screen and television producers and directors. Natural extroverts, they enjoy work that puts them in contact with people, and they often make successful careers in public relations, advertising, marketing, and sales.

Their ability to synthesize ideas often makes Sevens innovative scientists, inventors, and computer experts as well as unusually creative designers in a variety of professions. Their love of adventure may lead them to careers as pilots, race car drivers, or travel writers. Sevens are also visible as doctors, psychologists, sex therapists, chefs, venture capital specialists, telemarketers, and internet entrepreneurs. Very unhealthy Sevens can become drug dealers, pimps, and scam artists of various kinds.

Stress and Security Points

Seven has connecting links to One (in the gut/will triad) and Five (in the head/thinking triad).

It is interesting to note that Seven is the only Enneagram number that has no link to the heart/feeling triad, which seems to reflect this style's tendency to avoid emotions. Out-of-touch Sevens use thinking to spur themselves to action, and the activity itself may reassure them that all is well. In a way, a Seven's pursuit of novelty and adventure is a way to substitute adrenaline for emotion.

Under stress, Sevens often move to One, and exhibit the irritability, rigidity, and intolerance characteristic of unhealthy Ones. Sevens at the One stress point can be self-critical and compulsive, but they may also feel a need to defend their own goodness and rightness. When Sevens fail to get the nourishment they crave, they may express their frustration in tantrum-like explosions of temper.

When Sevens feel safe and in control of their lives they often move to their security point, Five. Sevens at Five are able to concentrate and apply their imagination to completing important tasks. In this frame of mind they are able to tolerate the solitude and lack of external stimulation that otherwise trouble them. They learn to confront the shadow side of themselves and focus on depth of understanding and accomplishment rather than seeking continual distractions.

Wings

There is a marked contrast between Sevens with a Six wing and those with an Eight wing. While Six is a compliant/dependent style—giving the Seven more ability to connect with others, Eight is an aggressive style that reinforces the Seven's own tendency to dominate others.

Average Sevens with a Six wing are more able to relate to others as equals. Sixes have a gift for choosing trustworthy allies and avoiding direct conflicts whenever possible. The Six wing's tendency is to avoid conflict and establish alliances, which softens the Seven's hyperactivity and impulsiveness. Sevens with a Six wing have a natural exuberance and humor that makes them extremely likeable. Professional comedians, for example, often display this wing.

In *Breakfast at Tiffany's*, Holly's Six wing reveals itself in her natural charm, her vulnerability, and her occasional ability to confront her fears. Unlike a Six, however, Holly has a generally upbeat quality and a short attention span. Sevens with a Six wing seem especially prone to Attention Deficit/Hyperactivity Disorder (AD/HD).

All Sevens feel that the world is a dangerous place; the issue is whether to flee, at Six, or confront, at Eight. Eights can be bulldozers who defuse potential threats by direct and immediate confrontation, and average Sevens with an Eight wing are usually more aggressive. They care less about being liked than Sevens with a Six wing, but they still are oriented toward enjoyable activities, unlike Eights, who are more centrally power-driven. Sevens with this wing tend to be more materialistic, more oriented toward things than people.

Peter Pan's Eight wing is evident in the way he resists committing to anyone for fear of limiting his freedom. He seems more comfortable fighting with Captain Hook than sitting by the fire with Wendy. He also takes more pleasure in playing his pipes than in talking, and finds it difficult to remember even people who have been close to him.

Fear of Flying

Isadora Wing, narrator and protagonist of Erica Jong's *Fear of Flying*, is a good example of a Seven with a Six wing. Throughout the novel, we see Isadora's preoccupation with loyalty to her husband—influenced by her Six wing—on a collision course with her Seven desire for freedom.

Isadora is also conflicted over her Sevenish need for many lovers and her need to be alone and write—at her Five security point. Her vision of the "zipless fuck" is a classic Seven fantasy:

> My response to all this [her need for many lovers and her need for solitude] was not (not yet) to have an affair and not (not yet) to hit the

open road, but to evolve my fantasy of the Zipless Fuck. The zipless fuck was more than a fuck. It was a platonic idea. Zipless because when you came together zippers fell away like rose petals, underwear blew off in one breath like dandelion fluff. Tongues intertwined and turned liquid. Your whole soul flowed out through your tongue and into the mouth of your lover.

For the true, ultimate zipless A-1 fuck, it was necessary that you never get to know the man very well. I had noticed, for example, how all my infatuations dissolved as soon as I really became friends with a man, became sympathetic to his problems, listened to him *kvetch* about his wife, or ex-wives, his mother, his children. After that I would like him, perhaps even love him—but without passion. And it was passion that I wanted. I had also learned that a sure way to exorcise an infatuation was to write about someone, to observe his tics and twitches, to anatomize his personality in type. After that he was an insect on a pin, a newspaper clipping laminated in plastic. I might enjoy his company, even admire him at moments, but he no longer had the power to make me wake up trembling in the middle of the night. I no longer dreamed about him. He had a face.

So another condition for the zipless fuck was brevity. And anonymity made it even better. (pp. 11-12)

Isadora's need for the safety and security associated with her husband, Bennett, reveals her Six wing, while her hunger for a fling with Adrian, a psychoanalyst she meets at a conference that she and Bennett attend, exposes the unhealthy side of Seven:

... I already felt as if I were being torn apart by the two of them. It was not their fault, of course. They only represented the struggle within me. Bennett's careful, compulsive, and boring steadfastness was my own panic about change, my fear of being alone, my need for security. Adrian's antic manners and ass-grabbing was the part of me that wanted exuberance above all. I had never been able to make peace between the two halves of myself. All I had managed to do was suppress one half (for a while) at the expense of the other. I had never been happy with the bourgeois virtues of marriage, stability, and work above pleasure. I was too curious and adventurous not to chafe under those restrictions. But I also suffered from night terrors and attacks of panic at being alone. So I always wound up living with somebody or being married.

... If I were really an exceptional person, I thought, I wouldn't spend hours worrying my head about marriage and adultery. I would just go out and snatch life with both hands and feel no remorse or guilt for anything. My guilt only showed how thoroughly bourgeois and contemptible I was. All my worrying this sad old bone only showed my ordinariness. (pp. 79-80)

Doubt and worry are characteristic of Sevens with a Six wing. If Isadora had an Eight wing, she might feel less guilty about her desires.

Once she gives in to her cravings and goes off with Adrian, Isadora enjoys the adventure and the danger of their trip. For some Sevens death is preferable to boredom:

> We were usually drunk from noon on, careening down the *Autobahn* in a right-hand-drive car, taking wrong turns everywhere, being tail-gated by Volkswagens going 80 miles an hour, by Mercedes-Benzes blinking their headlights aggressively and doing 110, by BMWs trying to outrun the Mercedes-Benzes. . . . There was part of me that was terrified by this, but another part of me which thrilled to it. We were living on the edge. It was likely we'd be killed in a horrible wreck which would obliterate every trace of our faces and our sins. At least I knew for sure I wasn't bored.
>
> Like all people who are preoccupied with death, who hate plane rides, who study their tiniest wrinkles in the mirror and are morbidly afraid of birthdays, who worry about dying of cancer or a brain tumor or a sudden aneurysm, I am secretly in love with death. I will suffer morbidly through a shuttle flight from New York to Washington, but behind the wheel of a sports car I'll start doing 100 without hesitation and love every terrifying minute. The excitement of knowing that you may be the author of your own death is more intense than orgasm. (pp. 195-196)

For the Seven the danger of driving recklessly produces an adrenaline rush—again, a physiological substitute for real feelings. This may also be why Sevens frequently seek the artificial "highs" of drugs, alcohol, and compulsive sex.

Middlemarch

The physician Tertius Lydgate in George Eliot's novel *Middlemarch* is another clear Seven with a Six wing. Lydgate sees his profession as intellectually stimulating as well as a means to economic success. His interest in his patients as people—and not simply as cases—is a mark of his Six wing. His undoing comes through a kind of materialistic narcissism that is common in Sevens: a sense that he must have only the best:

> Our vanities differ as our noses do: all conceit is not the same conceit, but varies in correspondence with the minutiae of mental make in which one of us differs from another. Lydgate's conceit was of the

arrogant sort, never simpering, never impertinent, but massive in its claims and benevolently contemptuous. . . . All his faults were marked by kindred traits, and were those of a man who had a fine baritone, whose clothes hung well upon him, and who even in his ordinary gestures had an air of inbred distinction. . . . Lydgate's spots of commonness lay in the complexion of his prejudices, which, in spite of noble intentions and sympathy, were half of them such as are found in ordinary men of the world: that distinction of mind which belonged to his intellectual ardour, did not penetrate his feeling and judgement about furniture, or women, or the desirability of its being known (without his telling) that he was better born than other country surgeons. He did not mean to think of furniture at present; but whenever he did so, it was to be feared that neither biology nor schemes of reform would lift him above the vulgarity of feeling that there would be an incompatibility in his furniture not being of the best. (pp. 141-142)

After he marries the beautiful Rosamond, Lydgate quickly accumulates debts, thanks to his wife's overspending. When he is finally forced to face the extent of his financial troubles, he pleads with Rosamond to economize:

"Of course you can dismiss the other two servants, if you like," said Rosamond; "but I should have thought it would be very injurious to your position for us to live in a poor way. You must expect your practice to be lowered."

"My dear Rosamond, it is not a question of choice. We have begun too expensively. Peacock, you know, lived in a much smaller house than this. It is my fault: I ought to have known better, and I deserve a thrashing—if there were anybody who had a right to give it me—for bringing you into the necessity of living in a poorer way than you have been used to. But we married because we loved each other, I suppose. And that may help us to pull along till things get better. Come dear, put down that work and come to me."

He was really in chill gloom about her at that moment, but he dreaded a future without affection, and was determined to resist the oncoming of division between them. (pp. 616-617)

Aware of Lydgate's need for her, Rosamond, a Three, feels confident enough to lecture him about what he needs to do to make a better appearance with people. His reaction reveals the resentment of a Seven under stress moving to One:

Lydgate's anger rose; he was prepared to be indulgent towards feminine weakness, but not towards feminine dictation. The shallowness of a waternixie's soul may have a charm until she becomes didactic.

But he controlled himself and only said, with a touch of despotic firmness—

"What I am to do in my practice, Rosy, it is for me to judge. That is not the question between us. It is enough for you to know that our income is likely to be a very narrow one—hardly four hundred, perhaps less, for a long time to come, and we must try to rearrange our lives in accordance with that fact." (pp. 617-618)

Notice that Lydgate's response is still tempered, more evidence of his Six wing. A Seven with an Eight wing would most likely be much more forceful.

Like many Sevens, Lydgate tries gambling as a means to clear his debts. But he loses more money, and is forced to apply for a loan from the banker Bulstrode. Bulstrode actually grants the loan because he fears that Lydgate may have learned some of his secrets from Raffles, a now-deceased patient of Lydgate's. People in the town, knowing of the loan, are already speculating that Lydgate may have played a part in Raffles's death in an effort to serve Bulstrode's interests. Facing loss of reputation, Lydgate moves to his One stress point and expresses his resentment:

He felt himself becoming violent and unreasonable as if raging under the pain of stings: he was ready to curse the day on which he had come to Middlemarch. Everything that had happened to him there seemed a mere preparation for this hateful fatality, which had come as a blight on his honourable ambition, and must make even people who had only vulgar standards regard his reputation as irrevocably damaged. In such moments a man can hardly escape being unloving. Lydgate thought of himself as the sufferer, and of others as the agents who had injured his lot. He had meant everything to turn out differently; and others had thrust themselves into his life and thwarted his purposes. His marriage seemed an unmitigated calamity; and he was afraid of going to Rosamond before he had vented himself in this solitary rage, lest the mere sight of her should exasperate him and make him behave unwarrantably. (p. 702)

Finding it increasingly difficult to surmount the local gossip, Lydgate is distraught, yet he is determined not to be forced to leave town. When he realizes that even Rosamond may believe he deserves his disgrace, his despair deepens.

The only person who believes in him is Dorothea, a rich and benevolent widow who is greatly respected in the town. A highly evolved One, she is the moral center of the novel, and her sympathy for Lydgate's situation and offer of help give him hope:

"I know the unhappy mistakes about you [she tells him]. I knew them from the first moment to be mistakes. You have never done anything vile. You would not do anything dishonorable."

It was the first assurance of belief in him that had fallen on Lydgate's ears. He drew a deep breath, and said "Thank you." He could say no more: it was something very new and strange in his life that these few words of trust from a woman should be so much to him. (p. 725)

Trust is a major issue for Sixes, and Sevens with a Six wing can also be powerfully concerned with it. At the end of *Middlemarch*, thanks to Dorothea's timely help, it is clear that Lydgate and Rosamond may find the way to resolve the difficult issues in their marriage.

Even Cowgirls Get the Blues

A Seven with an Eight wing is powerfully exemplified in Sissy Hankshaw, the heroine of Tom Robbins's comic novel *Even Cowgirls Get the Blues*. Sissy's independence and determination are typical of this wing. Her most distinctive physical characteristic is her enormous thumbs, and her standard mode of travel is hitchhiking. Sevens like to stay in motion, and hitchhiking for Sissy is a pleasurable recreation as well as a convenient way to travel. The way she practices it, however, amounts to a vocation, even an art form. Early in the story, people try to dissuade Sissy from hitchhiking by warning her of the dangers, but being free and staying in motion are worth the things drivers do to her:

"There's sick men who drive around in cars," they told her. "Sooner or later you're bound to be picked up by some man who wants to do nasty things to you."

Truth was, Sissy was picked up by such men once or twice a week, and had been since she began hitching at age eight or nine. There are a lot more men like that than people think. Assuming that many of them would be unattracted to a girl with . . . with an affliction, there are a lot of men like that, indeed. And the further truth was, Sissy allowed it.

She had one rule: keep driving. As long as they maintained the forward progress of their vehicles, drivers could do anything they wished to her. . . . She caused a few accidents, taxed the very foundations of masculine ingenuity and preserved her virginity until her wedding night (when she was well past the age of twenty). (pp. 17-18)

Young Sissy is arrested twice, first for trying to hitch a ride on an ambulance, and again for flagging down a fire engine. When the authorities brand her incorrigible and try to send her to reform school, Sissy is protected by a social worker, who regards Sissy's enormous thumbs as a handicap. When the social worker takes Sissy to a dance for handicapped people. Sissy rebels, protesting that she is not handicapped. She makes a scene and ends up hitchhiking home in her formal gown.

Offered an operation to make her thumbs a normal size, Sissy refuses. She grabs food from the family refrigerator and embarks on a hitchhiking odyssey. Ten years later, she has become a legend among hitchhikers. In her footloose lifestyle, one of her few stable connections is with a man who calls himself "Countess" and who occasionally offers her work as a model. Sissy maintains contact with him by checking for mail at particular post offices across the country. When he sends a message that he has a job for her, she heads for his elegant Park Avenue apartment in New York.

The Countess introduces her to Julian Gitche, a commercial artist and full-blooded Mohawk Indian who becomes her lover. Julian questions Sissy about her dedication to hitchhiking:

> "But why? Why bother? You've traveled your whole life without destination. You move but you have no direction."
> "What is the 'direction' of the Earth in its journey; where are the atoms 'going' when they spin?"
> "There's an orderly pattern, some ultimate purpose in the movements of Nature. You've been constantly on the move for nearly twelve years. Tell me one thing that you've proven."
> "I've proven that people aren't trees, so it is false when they speak of roots."
> "Aimless . . ."
> "Not aimless. Not in the least. It's just that my aims are different from most. There are plenty of aimless people on the road, all right. People who hitchhike from kicks to kicks, restlessly, searching for something: looking for America, as Jack Kerouac put it, or looking for themselves, or looking for some relation between America and themselves. But I'm not looking for anything. I've *found* something."
> "What is it that you've found?"
> "Hitchhiking." (pp. 80-81)

For Sevens, especially those with an Eight wing, pleasure in any activity justifies doing it as often as possible. For some the activity is eating, for others it is sex; for Sissy it is hitchhiking.

After living with Julian for several months, Sissy can stand the inactivity no longer, and she tells him she has to go. After she departs, he writes to her at the post offices where she collects her mail. Eventually, she returns and marries him, but their union is not happy:

> While her husband painted, Sissy would stare out the windows at traffic. Or she would leaf through the motoring magazines that she bought regularly at newsstands, although Julian, a nondriver, vowed he'd never own a car. Her thumbs ached, and in order to relieve them, she took to imaginary hitchhiking, the game she'd played as a small child. . . .

She was a ratty housekeeper. She hadn't the experience or the aptitude. So Julian, on top of his picture-making, his conferences with art dealers, collectors and advertising men, had to attend to domestic chores. When he washed dishes, Sissy, a bit embarrassed, would retire to the bedroom to chat with the birds. The birds and Sissy had real rapport. Was it an interest in "freedom of movement" that they had in common? (pp. 91-92)

Freedom is important to all Sevens, but the Seven with an Eight wing is more enamored with it than with relationships—which seem more vital to the Seven with a Six wing.

The Countess gives Sissy a modeling assignment at his Rubber Rose Ranch in North Dakota and asks her to report to him about the activities of the cowgirls there. The leader of the cowgirls at the ranch is Bonanza Jellybean, with whom Sissy immediately feels a strong rapport. After Sissy and Jelly become lovers, Sissy is confirmed in her Seven quest for thrills, freedom and motion.

The kingdom of formal ideas will always be a weak neighbor to the kingdom of thrills, and Sissy was a princess of thrill. Blood bunched in her head like grapes in a wig. It sang there like a popular ballad—even though the only radio station in the area played nothing but polkas. Jelly had promised to come to her room that night, with marijuana and new positions. (p. 159)

Here we see Sissy's delight in sexual indulgence, a major area of interest for some Sevens, especially those with an Eight wing, combining the Seven passion of gluttony with the Eight passion of lust.

After she returns to Julian in New York, Sissy learns that the Countess plans to inform the Secretary of the Interior about the whooping cranes nesting on a lake near his ranch. Sissy knows that the cowgirls are protecting the cranes—the last existing flock—and this threat to her beloved cowgirls incites her to violence against him. Under stress Sissy moves to One with an explosive anger that is intensified by her Eight wing:

Thumbs that not once in a lifetime had been raised in anger; thumbs that had known risk often but never violence; thumbs that had invoked and mastered secret Universal Forces without acquiring the faintest stain of evil; thumbs that had been generous and artful; thumbs that were considered so delicate and precious that their owner would not so much as shake hands for fear of damage; those same thumbs, wound 'round with the glory of a million innovative and virtuoso hitchhikes, are now smashing the face of a human being.

What are you doing, Sissy? I'll tell you what you're doing. You're swinging them like ballbats, like the legendary swatters of Babe Ruth,

246 The Literary Enneagram

socking flaming homers over the left-field fence of Hell. Beats of blood
land noiselessly upon the keys of the white piano. (p. 267)

Sevens with an Eight wing are more prone to violence than those with a Six
wing. In the aftermath of her assault on the Countess, Sissy takes stock of herself
and her situation:

> After that thumping she'd given the Countess, the authorities
> would say she was crazy for sure. And one thing she did not want, could
> not tolerate, was to be committed to the Goldman Clinic or its state-
> funded equivalent. She felt guilt, she felt sorrow, shame and confusion,
> but she did not feel that she owed society any accounting for her
> behavior, as bad as her behavior might have been. Society had never
> looked upon her with favor. It had been eager to write her off when she
> was just a little girl. Society might have institutionalized her way back
> then if she had cooperated. Society had neither liked her nor believed in
> her, but luckily she had liked herself and believed in herself, and
> although she recognized that she had floundered in recent years, erred
> in recent hours, she still liked and believed, and the reckoning she must
> make was with herself, not with society, especially not with a society
> that was willing to put a matter as delicate as this in the kitten-crusher
> hands of the police.
>   Thus, Sissy Hankshaw Gitche, a self-recognized ongoing system
> of uncommon abilities and unexpected vices, headed for New Jersey,
> for options, alternatives, choices. And didn't it feel sweet to be up to her
> armpits in traffic again, to be dancing cheek to cheek with traffic, to be
> charming the deadly snake of traffic, to be sticking her thumb into the
> pie of traffic. (pp. 273-274)

Sissy's ability to tolerate having minimal connections with other people
reflects her Eight wing, but her devotion to "options, alternatives, choices" is
pure Seven.

Appointment in Samarra

Another vivid Seven with an Eight wing is Julian English, the protagonist
of John O'Hara's *Appointment in Samarra*. An automobile dealer in 1930s
Gibbsville, Pennsylvania, Julian sets his downfall in motion by impulsively
throwing a drink in the face of a friend at a country club dance on Christmas Eve.
Here we see Julian, already fairly drunk, planning the act while listening to the
friend, Harry Reilly, tell a story:

> Julian English sat there watching him, through eyes that he
> permitted to appear sleepier than they felt. Why, he wondered, did he
> hate Harry Reilly? Why couldn't he stand him? What was there about

Reilly that caused him to say to himself: "If he starts one more of those moth-eaten stories I'll throw this drink in his face." But he knew he would not throw this drink or any other drink in Harry Reilly's face. Still, it was fun to think about it. . . . Yes, it would be fun to watch. The whole drink, including the three round-cornered lumps of ice. At least one lump would hit Reilly in the eye, and the liquid would splash all over his shirt, slowly wilting it as the Scotch and soda trickled down the bosom to the crevice at the waistcoat. The other people would stand up in amazed confusion. "Why, Ju!" they would say. Caroline would say, "Julian!" Froggy Ogden would be alarmed, but he would burst out laughing. So would Elizabeth Gorman, laughing her loud haw-haw-haw, not because she enjoyed seeing her uncle insulted, nor because she wanted to be on Julian's side; but because it would mean a situation, something to have been in on. (pp. 13-14)

Characteristic of bolder, more impulsive Sevens with an Eight wing, Julian is undeterred by the prospect of shocking others with his actions. Instead he anticipates the fun he will have seeing everyone's reaction.

Julian throws the drink at Harry and returns the following evening to another party at the club. He stations himself in the locker room with a bottle of bootleg Scotch, hoping Monsignor Creedon, a respected Catholic cleric, will arrive to use the men's room and help Julian resolve the social mess he has created by throwing the drink.

Two more kids looked at Julian and said hyuh, but they did not hover thirstily and wait for him to offer them a drink. He wondered about that again, and as it had many times in the last year and a half, Age Thirty stood before him. Age Thirty. And those kids were nineteen, twenty-one, eighteen, twenty. And he was thirty. "To them," he said to himself, "I am thirty. I am too old to be going to their house parties, and if I dance with their girls they do not cut in right away, the way they would on someone their own age. They think I am old." He had to say this to himself, not believing it for a moment. What he did believe was that he was precisely as young as they, but more of a person because he was equipped with experience and a permanent face. (pp. 112-113)

Although Julian is preoccupied with the question of youth, he seems to have no interest in the boys in the locker room as individuals—an attitude more characteristic of the Seven with an Eight wing than the Seven with a Six wing. The Seven with an Eight wing, less concerned with relationships, focuses on maintaining his options and remaining ready for action.

Sevens are generally concerned about money because it represents options—fun, adventure, distraction, a solution to the dire threat of boredom. Here Julian reflects on the money he has borrowed from Harry Reilly:

He had lent Julian twenty thousand dollars last summer, and that was a nice piece of change no matter how much Harry might be worth. It was enough to excuse any extraordinary interest Harry might be taking in Julian's business.

Twenty thousand dollars! Why in God's name had he ever asked for that much? He knew perfectly well why he had asked for that much: at the time he needed ten thousand, but he figured he might as well get a good hunk while he was at it. Ten thousand had gone in no time; it cost, even with the cheap labor and construction costs of last summer, about eight thousand to build the inclined driveway inside the building, which he had calculated would mean eventually a great saving in electric power bills through decreased use of the elevator. So far it hasn't made much difference, if any. (pp. 215-216)

Here we see a Seven's gluttony—Julian borrowed more money than he needed so he would be sure to have enough. Many Sevens find that money slips through their fingers easily. They also fear the lack of it because it represents deprivation.

Julian's relationship with his wife has been rapidly deteriorating, and he ponders his own outrageous behavior toward her and others, including a recent poisonous altercation with a friend named Froggy.

And then, a little before he was ready for it, he thought of the thing that in its way was more important than anything between himself and Caroline; that thing was the never-to-be-buried discovery that all this time Froggy Ogden had been his enemy. That was worse than anything he could do to Caroline, because it was something that did something to him. It made a change in himself, and we must not change ourselves much. . . . He thought and thought, and the last time there had been a change in himself was when he discovered that he, Julian English, whom he had gone on thinking of as a child with a child's renewable integrity and curiosity and fears and all, suddenly had the power of his own passion; that he could control himself and use this control to give pleasure and a joyous hiatus of weakness to a woman. He could not remember which girl it had been; to forget her had been a simple manifestation of his ego; the important part of the discovery, the change, had been a thing for himself, his own moment. (pp. 263-264)

Notice that Julian sees his discovery of Froggy's hostility toward him as something that changes *him*. He isn't personally hurt by it the way a Seven with a Six wing might be. The girl Julian remembers meant nothing to him—she was simply a mechanism for realizing his own sexual power. This passage is a fine example of the Seven's narcissism, flavored with the Eight drive for power over others.

Subtypes

Energetic and optimistic, Sevens of all subtypes evade their underlying anxiety by seeking life's pleasures, staying in motion and continually exploring new options.

Self-Preservation Sevens, whom Oscar Ichazo calls "defenders," are highly social, unlike the Self-Preservation subtypes of other Enneagram styles. Sevens with this subtype seek out like-minded people to share fun, information, and stimulation. They see their circle of friendships and family as a barricade against boredom, stagnation, and pain. Enthusiastic about acquiring possessions as well as having new experiences, Self-Preservation Sevens are often more materialistic than the other subtypes of Seven.

Examples include Peter Pan, Holly Golightly in *Breakfast at Tiffany's*, Beatrice in *Much Ado About Nothing*, Sissy Hankshaw in *Even Cowgirls Get the Blues*, Voltaire's Candide, the title character in Daniel Defoe's *Moll Flanders*, Morris in Henry James's *Washington Square*, Leopold Bloom in James Joyce's *Ulysses*, the title character in Mark Twain's *Huckleberry Finn*, the title character in Helen Fielding's *Bridget Jones's Diary*, and the title character in Patrick Dennis's *Auntie Mame*.

A Sport and a Pastime

A strong example of a Self-Preservation Seven is Phillip Dean in James Salter's novel *A Sport and a Pastime*. The character's materialism and narcissism are especially common in less healthy individuals with this subtype.

Driving through France in an elegant vintage car he has borrowed, Dean, a young American, hopes to use as his base a house that belongs to friends in Paris. Dean's love of speed and desire to impress a man who is staying in the house are quickly evident. During a brief conversation over drinks, Dean arranges to stay at the house and to borrow money from his new acquaintance, a Nine. As the two men discuss their backgrounds, Dean reveals that he went to Yale but quit before graduation. His companion, the novel's narrator, considers the implications of this:

> He quit. It was too easy for him, his sister told me, and so he refused it. He had always been extraordinary in math. He had a scholarship. He knew he was exceptional. Once he took the anthropology final when he hadn't taken the course. He wrote that at the top of the page. His paper was so brilliant the professor fell in love with him. Dean was disappointed, of course. It only proved how ridiculous everything was. He'd already been given a leave in his freshman year, now he took another. He went to see a psychiatrist. He lived with various friends in New York and began to develop a style. It lasted a whole year, but the university was very understanding. Finally he went back and did another year, but in the end he quit altogether. Then he began educating himself. (pp. 39-40)

Sevens often have difficulty following a course of action through to the end. Dean's refusal to commit to college—because it wasn't stimulating enough—is more likely for Self-Preservation Sevens. They have little tolerance for boredom, and usually need stimulation to come from outside; they are less capable than, say, Sexual Sevens of generating it internally.

Soon after his arrival, Dean meets Anne-Marie, a young Frenchwoman who lives and works in a nearby town, and they quickly become involved in a passionate love affair.

If money represents options to most Sevens, the Self-Preservation subtype is particularly focused on maintaining an ample supply of cash:

Dean feels a slight chill as he draws the bedspread over him. Perhaps it was the sun. He lies quite still. The room is bare. He recognizes nothing in it, not a color, not a line. Suddenly he becomes frightened. He begins to count his money mentally. He's left some of it behind, five hundred francs, and there was a garage bill for tuning the engine. They bought some clothes. He adds it up. He decides to put two hundred francs under the floormat of the car. That will leave about seven hundred—he adds it again—it will be close. It's forty or fifty every time they get gas. He tries to calculate the mileage. Perhaps they should not try to go so far.

His eyes open a little at the sound of the key. Anne-Marie has been taking a bath. She's wearing his cotton robe. When she stands near the bed she unties it. It opens, falls away. The sight of her fresh nakedness frightens him even more. Suddenly it is quite clear how acrobatic, how dangerous everything is. It seems not to be his own life he is living, but another, the life of some victim. It will all collapse. He will have to find work, pay rent, walk home every day for lunch. He is weak suddenly, he doesn't believe in himself. She slips into the bed. A virtual panic comes over him. He lies motionless, his eyes closed.

"*Tu dors?*" she says softly.

He doesn't know what to answer.

"No," he breathes. After a moment he adds, "I have a little headache."

"Poor child." She strokes his cheek. He manages a papery smile. (pp. 164-165)

Here we see Dean's panic at the possibility of having to live an ordinary life, paying rent, accepting the responsibilities of a married man.

The sex between them is powerful, and Dean marries Anne-Marie anyway. But on their honeymoon he is already restless and bored:

At the casino there's dancing and second-rate films. They haven't the money to gamble. Anyway, she's too young. It's on her identity papers. They sit in the empty salon of the hotel. In the evening darkness, it's like a great, abandoned liner. . . .

Along the dim corridor they walk, the floor groaning under their feet. There is no music from the closed doors, no voices. The sheets are damp. Nights of marriage. Dean is worried about the salt air ruining the chrome of the car. He should have coated it with something. There's no garage—it's parked behind the hotel, covered with moisture. In the morning the sun dries it off. . . .

They are like invalids. Their hours are long and uneventful. They eat three times a day. In the mornings, on the way to the W.C. the hall is lined with breakfast trays, napkins soiled, rolls broken, abandoned outside the doors. The patients have already gone out, walking slowly in the sunlight. Years of marriage. After breakfast is quite a long time until lunch, and after lunch, the whole afternoon. . . . (pp. 168-169)

Dean's anxiety about his beautiful car corroding represents his anxiety about marriage eroding his mobility.

Right after their honeymoon, a relieved Dean leaves Anne-Marie at her flat and returns to the house he shares with the Nine narrator. Dean tells him that he wants to go back to America and persuades him to lend him the money for a ticket:

"I don't have quite enough for the ticket." He pauses. "So, I was wondering . . . "

"How much would it be?" I ask.

"I'd leave you the car, you know, if anything happened . . ."

"The car? But it's not your car."

"Yes, it is," he says.

"I thought it belonged to some friend."

"No, no, he gave it to me. I can even get a letter from him if I have to."

I know it's not true. He's simply out of money, like a gambler, and he must be supplied. I hurriedly try to think of a phrase to help me refuse him, but I can't. If I were to deny him . . . anyway, it wouldn't make that much difference. He would go on. Besides, I cannot make such a decision. He isn't subject to judgments of mine—and I have the money.

"I need about three hundred dollars," he says.

"Three hundred."

"Can you let me have that much? I mean, against the Delage, of course."

"Well . . . Yes, I guess so."

"Oh," he says, his head falls back, "listen, you're a great guy."

Yes, and I find myself believing it even though I am helping prepare his escape. The act is somehow criminal. It is something I will be ashamed of later. I am only exchanging his disgust for my own.

"How long will you be gone?"

"I don't know," he says. "I honestly don't. Not long. Maybe a month or so, I'm not sure."

"Well, if you really go back to school . . ."

"That's right, it would be much longer. Of course, that's only a possibility."

" . . . you wouldn't be back."

"Oh, don't worry. If that happens, I'll send you the money. I mean, I can get it easily enough. Even if I had to take it out of tuition or something. It wouldn't make any difference."

"I'm not worried. It's not that. The whole thing surprises me, that's all."

"You thought I was getting married," he says.

"No."

"I might."

"Really?"

"I've thought about it," he says.

"I suppose so."

He jumps up. The promise of money has given him an appetite. (pp.176-178)

This is more of the materialism of the Self-Preservation Seven: for Dean the prospect of borrowing enough money to make him feel momentarily secure gives him a renewed zest for life. Note the charlatanism in his willingness to put up a borrowed car as security. Betraying his bride is a mere detail in Dean's larger plan to keep his life stimulating.

Bridget Jones's Diary

The title character in Helen Fielding's *Bridget Jones's Diary* offers a comic version of a Self-Preservation Seven. The book, which began as a newspaper column and went on to become an international bestseller, presents the fictional diary of the life of a young urban woman in London.

Bridget and her friends, Jude and Sharon, are single career women in their thirties who continually remind each other that a woman doesn't need a man in order to be a whole person. They also spend a lot of time planning to lose weight, cut down on alcohol and cigarettes, and improve their figures to attract the men they don't need. Then they spend even more time smoking and drinking as well as reading self-help books.

Bridget begins each day's diary entry with an accounting of the previous day, listing her current weight and the amount of alcohol, cigarettes, and calories she consumed. Her preoccupation with consumption is characteristic of Sevens:

SUNDAY 1 JANUARY
129 lbs. (but post-Christmas), alcohol units 14 (but effectively covers 2 days as 4 hours of party was on New Year's Day), cigarettes 22, calories 5424
Food consumed today:
2 pkts. Emmenthal cheese slices
14 cold potatoes
2 Bloody Marys (count as food as contain Worcester sauce and tomatoes)
1/3 Ciabatta loaf with Brie coriander leaves—1/2 packet
12 Milk Tray (best to get rid of all Christmas confectionery in one go and make fresh start tomorrow)
13 cocktail sticks securing cheese and pineapple
Portion Una Alconbury's turkey curry, peas and bananas
Portion Una Alconbury's Raspberry Surprise made with Bourbon biscuits, tinned raspberries, eight gallons of whipped cream, decorated with glacé cherries and angelica. (p. 7)

At a New Year's Day party Bridget meets Mark Darcy, who seems at first unprepossessing but later becomes a serious contender for Bridget's affections. Trying to make conversation with him, she describes her take on New Year's resolutions:

"I was at a party in London last night. Bit hungover, actually." I gabbled nervously so that Una and Mum wouldn't think I was so useless with men I was failing to talk to even Mark Darcy. "But then I do think New Year's resolutions can't technically be expected to begin on New Year's Day, don't you? Since, because it's an extension of New Year's Eve, smokers are already on a smoking roll and cannot be expected to stop abruptly on the stroke of midnight with so much nicotine in the system. Also dieting on New Year's Day isn't a good idea as you can't eat rationally but really need to be free to consume whatever is necessary, moment by moment, in order to ease your hangover. I think it would be much more sensible if resolutions began generally on January the second." (pp. 13-14)

Here we see Bridget's ambivalence about her appetites: alternately rationalizing them and then judging them from her One stress point. The Seven's defense mechanism is rationalization, and the "deadly sin" associated with this personality style is gluttony. When these are juxtaposed in a character who has no insight into her own psychology the result is comical.

Bridget decides to visit her parents, partly to stave off her anxiety about being humiliated on Valentine's Day and partly to shore up her self-image as a selfless and caring daughter. But there are obvious problems in her family, and when her father puts her off, her response is typically narcissistic:

SUNDAY 5 FEBRUARY . . .
2 p.m. remaining tiny bath mat of security has been pulled from under my feet. Magnanimous offer to pay caring surprise visit met by odd-sounding Dad on end of phone.
"Er . . . I'm not sure, dear. Could you hang on?"
I reeled. Part of the arrogance of youth (well, I say "youth") is the assumption that your parents will drop whatever they are doing and welcome you with open arms the second you decide to turn up. He was back. "Bridget, look, your mother and I are having some problems. Can we ring you later in the week?"
Problems? What problems? I tried to get Dad to explain but got nowhere. What is going on? Is the whole world doomed to emotional trauma? Poor Dad. Am I to be the tragic victim of a broken home now, on top of everything else? (pp. 37-38)

Bridget's strong attachment to her family and like-minded friends is characteristic of Self-Preservation Sevens.

After a night of sex with Daniel, her boss, Bridget decides that sex is a good substitute for her usual forms of indulgence:

SATURDAY 25 FEBRUARY
122 lbs. (miracle: sex proved indeed to be best form of exercise), alcohol units 0, cigarettes 0, calories 200 (at last have found the secret of not eating: simply replace food with sex). (p. 52)

But when Daniel fails to call immediately after leaving her on Saturday night, she copes with her anxiety by relapsing into appetite:

SUNDAY 26 FEBRUARY
126 lbs., alcohol units 5 (drowning sorrows), cigarettes 23 (fumigating sorrows), calories 3856 (smothering sorrows in fat-duvet).
Awake, alone, to find myself imagining my mother in bed with Julio. Consumed with repulsion at vision of parental, or rather demi-parental sex; outrage on behalf of father; heady, selfish optimism at example of another thirty years of unbridled passion ahead of me (not unrelated to frequent thoughts of Goldie Hawn and Susan Sarandon); but mainly extreme sense of jealousy of failure and foolishness at being in bed alone on Sunday morning while my mother aged over sixty is probably just about to do it for the second . . . Oh my God. No. I can't bear to think about it. (p. 53)

Bridget also displaces her anxiety by judging her mother and the mother's lover.

Self-Preservation Sevens can seem like Fours in the way they long for novelty and envy other people's apparently richer lives. Bridget's compulsive Seven need for options is particularly evident here:

SUNDAY 11 JUNE
125 lbs. (v.g., too hot to eat), alcohol units 3, cigarettes 0 (v.g., too hot to smoke), calories 759 (entirely ice cream).
Another wasted Sunday. It seems the entire summer is doomed to be spent watching the cricket with the curtains drawn. Feel strange sense of unease with the summer and not just because of the drawn curtains on Sundays and mini-break ban. Realize, as the long hot days freakishly repeat themselves, one after the other, that whatever I am doing I really think I ought to be doing something else. . . .
The more the sun shines the more obvious it seems that others are making fuller, *better* use of it elsewhere: possibly at some giant softball game to which everyone is invited except me; possibly alone with their lover in a rustic glade by waterfalls where Bambis graze, or at some large public celebratory events, probably including the Queen Mother and one or more of the football tenors, to mark the exquisite summer which I am failing to get the best out of. (pp. 128-129)

This passage shows the stress an average Seven can endure in the relentless pursuit of fun. Ultimately, Bridget can't enjoy the present because her attention is always jumping into the future, and her continual anxiety about missing out becomes more like torture than joy.

Social Sevens, the subtype that Ichazo associates with "social sacrifice," feel a particular tension between their ideals and their need to be free from the responsibilities their ideals impose. Sevens with this subtype can resemble Ones (Seven's stress point) in their dutiful behavior toward others.

Examples in literature include Tertius Lydgate in *Middlemarch*, Prince Hal in Shakespeare's *Henry IV* parts 1 and 2, John Proctor in Arthur Miller's *The Crucible*, and Aunt Sylvie in Marilynne Robinson's *Housekeeping*.

Housekeeping

In *Housekeeping*, Aunt Sylvie, an eccentric Social Seven, comes to care for her two orphaned nieces. Sylvie's decision to take responsibility for the girls seems to be motivated by idealistic duty, since she has had no contact with the family for decades.

Sylvie has lived most of her life as a transient, and her housekeeping skills are nonexistent. As she settles into life with the girls, she masks the increasing deterioration of the house by serving dinner in near darkness. One night Lucille, a One, turns on the lights and exposes the squalor around them. She confronts Sylvie with questions about her life, which Sylvie evades. Ruth, a Nine, narrates the scene:

> Lucille had startled us all, flooding the room so suddenly with light, exposing heaps of pots and dishes, the two cupboard doors which had come unhinged and were propped against the boxes of china. The tables and chairs and cupboards and doors had been painted a rich white, layer on layer, year after year, but now the last layer had ripened to the yellow of turning cream. Everywhere the paint was chipped and marred. A great shadow of soot loomed up the wall and across the ceiling above the stove, and the stove pipe and the cupboard tops were thickly felted with dust. Most dis-spiriting, perhaps, was the curtain on Lucille's side of the table, which had been half consumed by fire once when a birthday cake had been set too close to it. Sylvie had beaten out the flames with a back issue of Good Housekeeping, but she had never replaced the curtain. . . .
>
> In the light we were startled and uncomfortable. Lucille yanked the chain again, so hard that the little bell at the end of it struck the ceiling, and then we sat uncomfortably in an exaggerated darkness. Lucille began swinging her legs. "Where's your husband, Sylvie?"
>
> There was a silence a little longer than a shrug. "I doubt that *he* knows where *I* am."
>
> "How long were you married?"
>
> Sylvie seemed a little shocked by the question. "Why, I'm married now, Lucille."
>
> "But then where *is* he? Is he a sailor? Is he in jail?"
>
> Sylvie laughed. "You make him sound very mysterious."
>
> "So he isn't in jail."
>
> "We've been out of touch for some time."
>
> Lucille sighed noisily and swung her legs. "I don't think you've ever *had* a husband."
>
> Sylvie replied serenely, "Think what you like, Lucille." (pp. 101-102)

Sylvie's social connections have rarely been strong enough for her to commit to a person or a situation. In committing to care for her nieces, we sense that she may have taxed her psychological resources so severely that she has nothing left over for maintaining their house.

Later, we see the other side of this strained sense of duty in Sylvie's need to stay constantly ready to escape:

> There were other things about Sylvie's housekeeping that both-ered Lucille. For example, Sylvie's room was just as my grandmother

had left it, but the closet and the drawers were mostly empty, since Sylvie kept her clothes and even her hairbrush and toothpowder in a cardboard box under the bed. She slept on top of the covers, with a quilt over her, which during the daytime she pushed under the bed also. Such habits (she always slept clothed, at first with her shoes on, and then, after a month or two, with her shoes under the pillow) were clearly the habits of a transient. They offended Lucille's sense of propriety. (pp. 102-103)

As people in the town begin to disapprove of Sylvie's care of the girls, an uncomfortable Lucille moves in with a local family, leaving Sylvie and Ruth alone together.

Sylvie reacts by taking Ruth out for an adventure in a stolen boat on the local lake, keeping her out all night and returning to town by hopping a freight car. The townspeople respond by campaigning to put Ruth in a foster home. Sensing the possibility of a forced separation, Sylvie and Ruth agree that they need to put on a better appearance:

"I don't know what to think," Sylvie said. "We could fix it up around here," she said finally. "Some of this stuff could go out to the shed, I suppose."

The next day I combed my hair and went to school, and when I came home Sylvie had emptied the parlor of cans entirely and had begun to remove the newspapers. She had put a bouquet of artificial flowers on the kitchen table, and she was frying chicken. "Now, isn't this nice?" she asked, and then, "Did you have a nice day at school?"

Sylvie was pretty, but she was prettiest when something had just startled her into feeling that the world had to be dealt with in some way, and then she undertook the most ordinary things with an arch, tense, tentative good will that made them seem difficult and remarkable, and she was delighted by even partial successes. (p. 187)

The danger escalates when the sheriff notifies Sylvie and Ruth of a hearing about Ruth's legal status. Sylvie responds by trying harder to clean things up:

I loved to watch these bouts of zeal and animation—Sylvie flushed in the firelight, prodding her whole hoard into the quick of the fire, even the *National Geographic* with a fold-out picture of the Taj Mahal. "We'll buy some clothes," she said. "We'll get you something in very good taste. Maybe a suit. You'll need it for church, anyway. And we'll get you a permanent. When you fix yourself up, you make a very nice impression. You really do, Ruthie." She smiled at me across the fire. I began to imagine that Sylvie and I might still be together after the hearing. I began to think that the will to reform might be taken for reform itself, not because Sylvie could ever deceive anyone, but because her eagerness to save our household might convince them that it should not be violated. (p. 201)

After another visit from the sheriff makes it clear that Ruth will almost certainly be taken from her, Sylvie tries to burn the house down. She takes Ruth to the town's long railroad bridge, and in the middle of the night they walk across to freedom. Ruth becomes a transient like Sylvie.

In Robinson's story, Sylvie is portrayed as a free spirit unable to conform to society's norms, who manages to do her duty—important to a Social Seven— toward the niece who depends on her. While Sylvie's limitations prevent her from seeing a healthier way to take care of Ruth, it is difficult not to be touched by this Social Seven's quirky attempts at heroism.

The Crucible

A healthier Social Seven is John Proctor in *The Crucible*, Arthur Miller's play about witchcraft trials in 17th century Massachusetts.

The play focuses on Proctor and his wife Elizabeth, a One. John's adultery with Abigail, a young girl employed in their home, led some months earlier to her dismissal by Elizabeth. Word comes that Abigail has suddenly denounced various townspeople as witches. A court convenes to investigate the girl's charges, and Elizabeth urges John to disclose Abigail's secret confession to him that her charges of witchcraft are fabricated. Social Sevens can feel judged and condemned by Ones—and by society in general—for indulging their appetites:

PROCTOR: Woman. *She turns to him.* I'll not have your suspicion any more.
ELIZABETH, *a little loftily:* I have no—
PROCTOR: I'll not have it!
ELIZABETH: Then let you not earn it.
PROCTOR, *with a violent undertone:* You doubt me yet?
ELIZABETH, *with a smile, to keep her dignity*: John, if it were not Abigail that you must go to hurt, would you falter now? I think not.
PROCTOR: Now look you—
ELIZABETH: I see what I see, John.
PROCTOR, *with solemn warning:* You will not judge me more, Elizabeth. I have good reason to think before I charge fraud on Abigail, and I will think on it. Let you look to your own improvement before you go to judge your husband any more. I have forgot Abigail, and—
ELIZABETH: And I.
PROCTOR: Spare me! You forget nothin' and forgive nothin'. Learn charity, woman. I have gone tiptoe in this house all seven month since she is gone. I have not moved from there to there without I think to please you, and still an everlasting funeral marches round your heart. I cannot speak but I am doubted, every moment judged for lies, as

though I come into a court when I come into this house! (pp. 51-52)

Elizabeth believes that Abigail still fantasizes about marrying John, and she begs him to disabuse her of this possibility. Elizabeth's fears prove well-founded: Abigail denounces her to the court, and only Elizabeth's pregnancy prevents her from being hanged. After a frustrated John fails to persuade the court that Abigail is lying, he reveals his adultery with her.

Governor Danforth, the chief judge, orders Elizabeth brought in and questioned, to see if she will confirm John's accusation. But she lies, for the first time in her life, hoping to protect his honor. As a result John is condemned.

Now, in order to save his life, John's only recourse is to confess to being involved in witchcraft. A sympathetic minister persuades Elizabeth to plead with him to confess, and they are given time together just before he is to be hanged. We see a Social Seven wavering in his idealistic commitment to the truth:

PROCTOR, *with great force of will, but not quite looking at her:* I have been thinking I would confess to them, Elizabeth. *She shows nothing.* What say you? If I give them that?
ELIZABETH: I cannot judge you, John.
Pause.
PROCTOR, *simply—a pure question:* What would you have me do?
ELIZABETH: As you will, I would have it. *Slight pause.* I want you living, John. That's sure.
PROCTOR—*he pauses, then with a flailing of hope:* Giles' wife? Have she confessed?
ELIZABETH: She will not.
Pause.
PROCTOR: It is a pretense, Elizabeth.
ELIZABETH: What is?
PROCTOR: I cannot mount the gibbet like a saint. It is a fraud. I am not that man. *She is silent.* My honesty is broke, Elizabeth; I am no good man. Nothing's spoiled by giving them this lie that were not rotten long before.
ELIZABETH: And yet you've not confessed till now. That speak goodness in you.
PROCTOR: Spite only keeps me silent. It is hard to give a lie to dogs. *Pause, for the first time he turns directly to her.* I would have your forgiveness, Elizabeth.
ELIZABETH: It is not for me to give, John, I am—
PROCTOR: I'd have you see some honesty in it. Let them that never lied die now to keep their souls. It is pretense for me, a vanity that will not blind God nor keep my children out of the wind. *Pause.* What say you? (pp. 125-126)

After a tender moment with his wife, John announces that he wants his life. But, faced with actually signing the paper confessing to the lie, he cannot do it, knowing that it means giving up his good name. He refuses and is taken away to be hanged.

In this powerful story, a Social Seven's conscience ultimately wins out over his desire to live, and Miller shows us this subtype at its most heroic.

Sevens with a **Sexual** subtype, whom Ichazo associates with "suggestibility," are enthusiastic about new experiences, continually seeking new romantic partners and enjoying new ideas. They often have powerful imaginations, which they use to the full. Fascinated by their own flights of fancy as well as their fantasies about other people, Sexual Sevens can easily grow bored and often find it difficult to sustain commitments in love or work.

Literary examples of this subtype include Mercutio in Shakespeare's *Romeo and Juliet*, Fevvers in Angela Carter's *Nights at the Circus*, the title character in Henry Fielding's *Tom Jones*, Rodolphe in Gustave Flaubert's *Madame Bovary*, Isadora Wing in *Fear of Flying*, McMurphy in Ken Kesey's *One Flew Over the Cuckoo's Nest*, Odysseus in Homer's *The Odyssey*, Gulley Jimson in Joyce Cary's *The Horse's Mouth*, Julian English in *Appointment in Samarra*, Benedick in *Much Ado About Nothing*, Maxine in Tennessee Williams's *The Night of the Iguana*, and Monica Szabo in Mary Gordon's *Spending*.

Spending

In Gordon's novel, Monica, a painter, enters a passionate affair with a wealthy man she calls "B," who offers to subsidize her work. Although she has reservations about the arrangement, she allows B to pay for various things, buy her an apartment, and let her use his vacation home. Thanks to his support, she decides to do a series of paintings called "SPENT MEN, AFTER THE MASTERS," depicting post-coital men in poses echoing those of the dead Christ depicted in great paintings.

As Monica adjusts to having money for the first time in her life, she discovers the pleasure of material possessions:

Money slowed me down. I was becoming surrounded by things that were there for their fineness. They required, therefore, my attention. I was becoming a citizen in the world of things deserving of attention. Grapefruit. Knives. Silk pajamas. Caviar, or *caviars*. But I kept telling myself that that was what I did, as a painter; I did honor, paid homage to the physical world. It was part of my work. That's what he was telling me by giving me so much money. That anything was good if it enriched my work. So I had to think of my work in a new way too, and even that took time. (p. 75)

Monica's rationalization of her situation is an example of the Seven's defense mechanism. But the One side of her keeps criticizing her for being a kept woman.

When B develops a back problem, Monica feels pressure to care for him. We see her stress point come into play as she judges him and herself:

> I don't know what I wanted him to do, given his herniated disc. No, that's not true. I know exactly what I wanted him to do. I wanted him to be active. To *move*.
>
> Don't think I was proud of all this. I would like to have that combination of discipline and generosity that would allow me to do without sleep so I could shift from artistic creation to nursing my lover without a second's hesitation. Simply to go from this to that because I wanted to do both.
>
> But I couldn't. I was at that stage of making a painting that's so physical that the moral has no force in relation to it. When you're thinking about painting—no, not thinking, it's a much more physical thing—you're involved in the creation of shapes and color, and that relationship, in ideas of emptiness and fullness and the connections between the two, you're in a world that stops at the edge of the canvas, or does it? You enter a universe entirely absorptive, or centrifugal, pulling everything it needs into itself. I'm not saying this right because words don't serve; this isn't about language. It isn't a code for anything else, it's only itself, the thing and the appearance of the thing. Pulled as I was by the universe of my own canvas, how could I give it up to go with my lover to physical therapy, to be sure that he was really getting the abdominal exercises right?
>
> And of course, the nature of my agreement with B was that nothing was meant to stop me from working full out, the way I wanted to, anytime and for as long as I liked. How could I put his suffering body in the center of our agreement? (pp. 151-152)

Although aware of social pressure to take care of her injured lover, Monica's primary commitment is to her work and she rationalizes her choice.

Monica's dealer is ecstatic about her new paintings, and her first impulse is to call B to share the news. But she recognizes her own ambivalence about him:

> He'd watched me paint, but he hadn't seen anything finished. Why hadn't I shown him anything? I guess I felt no one painting was complete until the series was. I guess it's simple, I was scared.
>
> I was tempted to forget being with anyone, go down to the liquor store, buy a bottle of Merlot and a bag of salted cashews, leave a message for Michael [a homosexual friend] and sit in my bed with my quilt around me, eating and drinking till the phone rang. But that seemed like a posture of defeat rather than exaltation. It was a moment not for

cowering and furtive consumption, but for exaltation and display. (p. 157)

Celebrating with food and drink is usual for a Seven.

As a Sexual Seven Monica is especially conscious of how others—even loved ones—might impinge on her freedom:

> This was the problem. I loved waking beside him in the morning; I loved turning and fitting into his body in the middle of the night. I liked sex in the morning, and I knew it was best for him. But if he was there, I couldn't have those early-morning hours to myself. He was a light sleeper. If he stayed in bed, I knew he was doing it to give me time to myself, and I felt every breath he took. So even trying not to, he stole my freedom. I'd been living in his house because he was gone during the week, and also because I wasn't working on anything. But now that ideas were coming, I was simultaneously longing to share them with him—just a little, then to cut him off when he was asking me something it would have been dangerous to talk about before I tried it out. And, of course, when I was excited about working, I was randy and frisky as a colt. (p. 215)

Monica's show is a success. All her paintings sell, and more are commissioned. Suddenly B develops money problems, and she has an impulse to give him some of what she has:

> I wanted to give him the money I soon would get from Peggy [a commission]. It seemed right; it made me happy to be able to repay him in some way for the gift that had changed my life so dramatically. I kept telling myself that I didn't need Peggy's money; I owned an apartment, all I had to do was pay twelve hundred dollars a month maintenance. I had a sold-out show, a commission, a job at Watson I could go back to anytime. I had more money than I'd ever had, and even before that I'd lived perfectly well.
>
> But I felt the tooth of greed, the first hint of the idea that there was no such thing as too much money, that there could never possibly be enough. I didn't see the money, but I heard it. Coins clinking down a well. I heard a voice saying, "You're ruined." The words were from the mouth of someone in a Cruikshank illustration of Dickens, or the Charnel House painting of Géricault. I heard creditors on the phone, calling day and night, threatening me with jail. I heard the insults of the people who refused to hire me to work as a dishwasher; I heard the mad ravings of the woman I slept next to on the shelter floor.
>
> And his reluctance to take the money from me, his feeling that it was adding to his impotence, made it more tempting for me to forget the

whole idea, to keep the money for myself. (p. 240)

Monica's response reveals the Seven's underlying anxiety about being deprived and in pain. Her reaction also shows how Sevens can yo-yo between gluttony and the avarice of their Five security point.

As Monica prepares a celebration dinner party, we see her sensuous delight in food and tendency toward extravagance.

> But now, there was no single, identifiable mouth that my imagination yearned to please. I was creating a celebration in praise of prosperity. It had to be opulent, extravagant, an obvious tribute to a generous claque of gods. So I sat with my cookbooks spread out: the general now conquering hero who is offered, as spoils, the most inventive and most submissive of the eager harem. Try me, cried the Fava Beans with Peccorino. No, me, insisted the Sweet Fennel in Garlic. How could I not consider Priest Stranglers—twisted pasta with clams and squid— particularly since the writer, neglecting to explain what priest is being strangled and why, assures me that much of the work can be done ahead of time. (p. 294)

By now Monica has resolved her mixed feelings about B, and the purpose of the feast is both to celebrate the success of her painting show and to introduce him to her circle of family and friends. For a Sexual subtype, this kind of commitment is a major step toward achieving a balance that Sevens often lack.

The Horse's Mouth

Gulley Jimson in Joyce Cary's *The Horse's Mouth* is another vivid Sexual Seven. An eccentric and brilliant painter, 67-year-old Gulley lives from hand to mouth in London, cadging food, drink, and lodging from friends and acquaintances. He has had many relationships with women, none of them permanent, although he remains friendly with his ex-wives and lovers. His devotion to painting is the only stable aspect of his life; otherwise he is continually in motion, on the lookout for fun and opportunities. Something of a charlatan, his charm nevertheless allows him to stay afloat financially.

Here Gulley rationalizes his addiction to alcohol while resolutely maintaining the positive outlook common to his Enneagram style:

> The middle of the night is a good time for a man to study his picture because he can't see it then; and the new scheme worked out well. On Saturday morning it looked so good that I began to like it. I promised myself a bottle of whisky, if I could borrow the price. Whisky is bad for me. I hate the stuff. And so I only take it for the consequences, as a special reward for a lucky day's work. Yes, I said, admiring the fishes and already getting a little whiskified, by sympathetic magic; the fish are

good; I am good; life is good; whisky, though bad, is good. . . . (p. 35)

Gulley believes that his creativity is bound up with staying in motion, a common Sexual Seven illusion. Even after he has taken seriously ill, he refuses to stay in bed and be nursed by his friend Coker:

> She gave me orders to stay in bed and took away my trousers. But as soon as she was round the corner with the pram, I was out and about. I didn't need my trousers, with my long overcoat and a pair of long socks well pulled up, and though the people looked, I might have been a squire in plus fours, going round his estate.
>
> And I had to be out in the air. Even one day in bed was putting a cramp on my ideas, tucking them up in a tight parcel. My imagination was working inwards instead of outwards; it was fitting things into a pattern, instead of letting them grow together. If I stayed in the boat-shed for a week under Cokey, I said, I could say good-bye to my Creation— it would turn into a little square picture with four corners and a middle. However big I made it on the wall, it would be a piece of art work. A put-up job. A jigsaw of the back room. Whereas a real picture is a flower, a geyser, a fountain, it hasn't got a pattern but a Form. It hasn't got corners and a middle but an Essential Being. And this picture of mine, the Creation, had to be a creation. A large event. And no one can feel largely except in the open air. (pp. 231-232)

Although sleep-deprived, Gulley stays high on his own adrenaline. Renting a shack because it has the perfect walls on which to paint his Creation—which promises to be his masterpiece, he has premonitions of his death and senses he will have to move fast to get his vision on the wall.

Gulley is well aware that his anarchistic art is a threat to the social order. But when Nosy, his would-be acolyte, tells him that one of his supporters is really in league with his enemies, he is surprisingly tolerant. Gulley has no interest in setting the world right, as a One or even a Social Seven might do. He would rather celebrate the opportunities for creativity life has given him. He is undeterred, even when his last and best wall crumbles into dust, destroying his great Creation painting and seriously injuring him.

> 'It's not fair,' said Nosy. 'They're all against you.'
>
> 'There you go,' I said, 'getting up a grievance. Which is about the worst mistake anyone can make, especially if he has one. Get rid of that sense of justice, Nosy, or you'll feel sorry for yourself, and then you'll soon be dead—blind and deaf and rotten. Get a job, get that grocery, get a wife and some kids, and spit on that old dirty dog, the world. Why, I can tell you, as a friend, if it goes no further, that I once had a sense of justice myself, when I was very young. I resented seeing my mother

scrub the floor while her worsers went to take the air in Heaven-sent bonnets and shining two-horse chariots that were a glory to the Lord. Works of passion and imagination. Even when I was a young man older than you, I didn't like being kicked up the gutter by cod-eyed money-changers warm from the banquets of reason, the wine of the masters, and the arms of beauty, that hoor of paradise. I was a bit inclined to think it a raw deal. Yes, even the celebrated Gulley Jimson, the darling of fortune, much caressed by all classes except the ones that never heard of him, might have turned a bit nasty and given the dirty dog best, if it hadn't been for his fairy godmother sending him a wall. Walls have been my salvation, Nosy, not forgetting the new types of plaster-board. Walls and losing my teeth young, which prevented me from biting bus conductors and other idealists. But especially walls. And above all that wall which is now no more. Yes, I have been privileged to know some of the noblest walls in England, but happy fortune reserved the best for my last—the last love of my old age. In form, in surface, in elasticity, in lighting, and in that indefinable something which is, as we all know, the final beauty of a wall, the very essence of its being, Pepper-nose's wall was the crowning joy of my life. I can never forget the way it took the brush. Yes, boys, I have to thank God for that wall. And all the other walls. They've been good to me. . . .'

'Please don't talk,' said the nun. 'That's all right, mother,' I said, 'they can't hear me because of the noise of the traffic and because they aren't listening. And it wouldn't make any difference if they did. They're too young to learn, and if they weren't they wouldn't want to.' 'It's dangerous for you to talk, you're very seriously ill.' 'Not so seriously as you're well. How don't you enjoy life, mother. I should laugh all round my neck at this minute if my shirt wasn't a bit on the tight side.' 'It would be better for you to pray.' 'Same thing, mother.' (pp. 288-289)

Here, at the end of the novel, Cary suggests that, even as Gulley is about to die, his way of celebrating life is to enjoy it, to laugh at his own misfortune. As a Sexual Seven, Gulley has willingly paid the price for his life of freedom, creativity and self-indulgence. He has no regrets and accepts his death without fear. Gulley's joy in life, Cary seems to insist, is a form of prayer.

Sevens in literature rarely exhibit a wide character arc. Gulley Jimson, Peter Pan, Holly Golightly, Julian English, Bridget Jones, Isadora Wing, Sissy Hankshaw, Aunt Sylvie, and Phillip Dean all change little over the course of their stories. The only exception is John Proctor—whose heroism in *The Crucible* shows how a Seven can transcend his style.

Sources

Barrie, J.M., *Peter Pan* (London, Hodder and Stoughton Ltd., 1928)

Capote, Truman, *Breakfast at Tiffany's*, in *A Capote Reader* (New York: Random House, 1987). First published 1958

Cary, Joyce, *The Horse's Mouth* (New York: Grosset & Dunlap, 1944)

Eliot, George, *Middlemarch* (New York, Barnes & Noble, 1996). First published 1871

Fielding, Helen, *Bridget Jones's Diary* (New York: Penguin Books, 1996)

Gordon, Mary, *Spending: a utopian divertimento* (New York: Simon & Schuster 1998)

Jong, Erica, *Fear of Flying* (New York: Holt, Rinehart and Winston, 1973)

Miller, Arthur, *The Crucible* (New York, Penguin Books, 1976). First produced 1952

O'Hara, John, *Appointment in Samarra* (New York: Duell, Sloan and Pearce, 1934)

Robbins, Tom, *Even Cowgirls Get the Blues* (New York: Bantam, 1990). First published 1976

Robinson, Marilynne, *Housekeeping* (New York: Farrar, Straus & Giroux, 1980)

Salter, James, *A Sport and a Pastime* (New York: North Point Press, 1985). First published 1967

Eight: The Trail Blazer

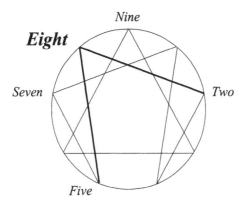

Nine

Eight

Seven

Two

Five

Meet Victoria Warshawski, the Eight hero of Sara Paretsky's detective series. In this scene from *Blood Shot* we see her interviewing Ed and Martha Dijak, the parents of her terminally ill friend Louise:

"Spell it out for me, Mr. Dijak," I said offensively. "What'd she do to make you suffer so?"

Martha made a little noise in her throat. "Victoria is working as a detective now, Ed. Isn't that nice?"

He ignored her. "You're just like your mother, you know. She used to carry on like Louise was some kind of saint, instead of the whore she really was. You're just as bad. What did she do to me? Got herself pregnant. Used my name. Stayed in the neighborhood flaunting her baby instead of going off to the sisters the way we arranged for her to do."

"Louise got herself pregnant?" I echoed. "With a turkey baster in the basement, you mean? There wasn't a man involved?"

Martha sucked in a nervous breath. "Victoria. We don't like to talk about these things."

"No, we don't," Ed agreed nastily, turning to her. "Your daughter. You couldn't control her. For twenty-five years the neighbors whispered behind my back, and now I have to be insulted in my own house by that Italian bitch's daughter."

My face turned hot. "You're disgusting, Dijak. You're terrified of women. You hate your own wife and daughter. No wonder Louise turned to someone else for a little affection. Who was it to get you so exercised? Your local priest?"

He sprang up from the table, knocking over his beer stein, and hit me in the mouth. "Get out of my house, you mongrel bitch! Don't ever come back with your filthy mind, your vile tongue!"

I got up slowly and went over to stand in front of him, my face close enough to smell the beer on his breath. "You may not insult my mother, Dijak. Any other garbage from the cesspool you call a mind I'll tolerate. But you ever insult my mother again in my hearing I will break your neck."

I stared at him fiercely until he turned his head uneasily away. (pp. 34-35)

Eights are one of the easier Enneagram styles to identify because they are often aggressive, comfortable with confrontation, and apparently spoiling for a fight. From their point of view, their stance of intimidation is an acid test of the people they meet, and those who fail to stand up to them lose their respect.

For all their bravado, Eights admire courage in others, particularly the elderly or the very young, and their instinct is often to protect those who are vulnerable. In the following scene Victoria has been told by the elderly Miss Chigwell that Miss Chigwell's brother is not home. Victoria vows to wait in her car outside until he returns. After a while Miss Chigwell goes outside to confront her:

I admired her courage: to be seventy-something and confront a young stranger takes a lot of guts. I could see the fear mingling with the determination in her pale eyes.

"I'm an officer of the court, ma'am. I would be happy to explain to the police why I want to speak to your—brother, is it?"

That was only partially true. Any licensed attorney is an officer of the court, but I much prefer never talking to the police, especially suburban cops, who hate urban detectives on principle. Fortunately, Miss Chigwell, impressed (I hoped) by my professional demeanor, didn't demand a badge or a certificate. She compressed her lips until they almost disappeared into her angular face and went back to the house.

I had barely settled back in my car when she returned to the walk and beckoned me vigorously. When I joined her at the side of the house she said abruptly:

"He'll see you. He was here all along, of course. I don't like telling his lies for him, but after all these years it's hard to start saying no. He's my brother. My twin, so I got into too many bad habits too long ago. But you don't want to hear all that."

My admiration for her increased, but I didn't know how to express it without sounding patronizing. I followed her silently into the house. (pp. 70-71)

Along with Ones and Nines, Eights are part of the triad at the top of the Enneagram symbol that is associated with gut impulses and will. While Nines retreat from overt contests of wills and Ones turn their wills inward to compulsive self-discipline, Eights channel their wills outward in a full-bore attempt to dominate the world around them. Being at the mercy of someone else's will is this style's ultimate nightmare.

Later in *Blood Shot*, Victoria has been badly injured and nearly killed by people trying to stop her investigation. She considers turning the matter over to the police:

As I lay still, letting images flow through my mind, I realized that this time, at least, wanting to give the powers-that-be a Bronx cheer wasn't what had kept me quiet. I was well and truly scared. Every time I tried sending my mind back to the three black-slickered men I shied away from the memory like a horse frightened by fire. There were a lot of parts of the assault I hadn't told Bobby, not because I was trying to hold back on him but because I couldn't bear to touch the memories. The hope that some forgotten phrase or cadence would give me a lead to who they worked for wasn't enough to force the memory of that terrifying near-suffocation.

Once I'd let that little piece of self-knowledge float to the top of my mind, a terrible rage began to seize hold of me. I would not be turned into a eunuch, be driven to living my life in the margins designed by someone else's will. I didn't know what was going on in South Chicago, but no one . . . was going to keep me from finding out. (p. 209)

In addition to having formidable wills, Eights can have prodigious appetites: for sex, money, power, sometimes alcohol and other drugs. They are champion carousers who can out-drink everyone at a party, perform amazing feats of sexual staying power, sleep an hour or two and then put in a full day's work with no apparent ill effects. This extraordinary energy is the key to Eights' immense success—and the key to their spectacular failures when they lose control of it.

The Eight's History

A siege mentality is at the root of the basic Eight attitude that "the best defense is a good offense." The Eight power game is played for keeps because most Eights have an underlying fear of annihilation. Some experienced childhood physical assaults or other attempts to crush their will by force. As a result, their central issue is survival: eat or be eaten. Other Eights may have grown up in a power vacuum, needing to compensate for or be responsible for passive or dependent parents. Given either of these scenarios, it's not surprising that adult Eights can come on too strong and be loud, hostile, and excessive.

Underneath an Eight's outer forcefulness is an inner vulnerability. The

Eight defense mechanism is denial: being unable to perceive danger or their own feelings of helplessness. Although Eights deny their vulnerability, when they see someone who is weak or helpless they are reminded of their own feelings. One reason they want to protect the vulnerable is that their own innocence was trampled when they were children.

In novels such as *Blood Shot*, Eight narrators rarely reveal the fear beneath their aggressiveness because they are unable to admit it to themselves. Still, we occasionally see unguarded moments, as in this exchange between Victoria Warshawski and Lotty, her friend and doctor:

> "I don't know how many times I have patched you up in the last ten years, Victoria. Many. And almost every time a life-threatening situation. Why do you value yourself so little?"
>
> I stared at the floor. "I don't want anyone solving my problems for me."
>
> "But you came here last night. You involved me in your problems, and then you disappeared without a word. That isn't independence— that is thoughtless cruelty. . . ."
>
> I rubbed my head tiredly. Finally I looked at her. "Lotty, I'm scared. I've never been this frightened, not since the day my dad told me Gabriella was dying and nothing could be done for her. I knew then that it was a terrible mistake to depend on someone else to solve my problems for me. Now I seem to be too terrorized to solve them for myself and I'm thrashing around. But when I ask for help it just drives me wild. I know it's hard on you. I'm sorry for that. But I can't get enough distance right now to do anything about it." (pp. 252-253)

Later in her investigation Victoria learns that a man who sexually abused his fifteen-year-old niece had been protected by the girl's parents, who blamed her for getting pregnant. Victoria feels both furious and helpless as she describes the case to Lotty:

> I swallowed some of the cognac. It washed the taste of bile from my throat. With Lotty holding my hand, I blurted out the story. How I'd seen the resemblance between young Art and Caroline, and thought his mother must have been related to Caroline's father. Only to learn that it was his father who was related to Caroline's grandmother.
>
> "That part wasn't so awful," I gulped. "I mean, of course it's awful. But what made me so sick is their horrible scrubbed piety and the way they insist Louise was to blame. Do you know how they raised her? How strictly those two sisters were watched? No dates, no boys, no talk about sex. And then her mother's brother. He molested the one girl and they let him stay around to molest the other. And then they punish her."
>
> My voice was rising; I couldn't seem to control it. "It can't be,

Lotty. It shouldn't be. I should be able to stop something that vile from going on, but I don't have any power."

Lotty took me in her arms and held me without speaking. After a time my sobbing dried up, but I continued to lie against her shoulder.

"You can't heal the world, Liebchen. I know you know that. You can only work with one person at a time, in a very small way. And over the individuals you help you have much effect. It's only the megalomaniacs, the Hitlers and their ilk, who think they have the answer for everyone's life. You are in the world of the sane, Victoria, the world of the limited." (p. 279)

Despite her grief over the abused child, Victoria is able to hear her doctor's reminder that violence cannot right the balance. Her control over her aggressive impulses is one marker that she is a healthy Eight.

Major Barbara

Andrew Undershaft, munitions manufacturer and father of the title character in George Bernard Shaw's *Major Barbara*, is another healthy Eight. A powerful and successful industrialist, Undershaft uses his wealth to improve social conditions. His daughter, Barbara, an officer in the Salvation Army, has devoted her life to converting the poor, confident that religious faith can alleviate their suffering. When Undershaft is asked by one of Barbara's cohorts, Adolphus Cusins, a One, if he has any religion, his answer reflects an Eightish philosophy:

UNDERSHAFT. Yes.
CUSINS. Anything out of the common?
UNDERSHAFT. Only that there are two things necessary to Salvation.
CUSINS *[disappointed, but polite]* Ah, the Church Catechism. Charles Lomax also belongs to the Established Church.
UNDERSHAFT. The two things are—
CUSINS. Baptism and—
UNDERSHAFT. No. Money and gunpowder.
CUSINS *[surprised, but interested]* That is the general opinion of our governing classes. The novelty is in hearing any man confess it.
UNDERSHAFT. Just so.
CUSINS. Excuse me: is there any place in your religion for honor, justice, truth, love, mercy and so forth?
UNDERSHAFT. Yes: they are the graces and luxuries of a rich, strong, and safe life.
CUSINS. Suppose one is forced to choose between them and money or gunpowder?
UNDERSHAFT. Choose money and gunpowder; for without enough of both you cannot afford the others.
CUSINS. That is your religion?

UNDERSHAFT. Yes. (pp. 384-385)

Toward the end of the play, Undershaft invites Barbara, an idealistic Two disillusioned by the hypocrisies of the Salvation Army's leadership, to leave the organization and save souls at his munitions works:

> UNDERSHAFT. . . . It is cheap work converting starving men with a Bible in one hand and a slice of bread in the other. I will undertake to convert West Ham to Mahometanism on the same terms. Try your hand on my men: their souls are hungry because their bodies are full.
> BARBARA. And leave the east end to starve?
> UNDERSHAFT *[his energetic tone dropping into one of bitter and brooding remembrance]* I was an east ender. I moralized and starved until one day I swore that I would be a full-fed free man at all costs; that nothing should stop me except a bullet, neither reason nor morals nor the lives of other men. I said 'Thou shalt starve ere I starve'; and with that word I became free and great. I was a dangerous man until I had my will: now I am a useful, beneficent, kindly person. That is the history of most self-made millionaires, I fancy. When it is the history of every Englishman we shall have an England worth living in. (p. 435)

In other words, an Eight's sense of social responsibility rests on having acquired power. Confident that he can dominate most situations, Undershaft can afford to be magnanimous.

Place in Society

The virtue of Eights is that they are ready and willing to take action. Their presence in the world offers an essential balance to the thinkers and feelers represented in other Enneagram styles. Eights are out there—putting themselves on the line, taking risks, starting businesses, blazing trails. We depend on them to be our pioneers, entrepreneurs and explorers. They may lack the psychological complexity of Sixes or Fours, but they get things rolling.

Eights can have notable success in politics; in the military; in business—as entrepreneurs and CEOs; in sports—especially boxing; in acting, film directing, law enforcement, and organized crime. Less visibly, they might also be rough-and-ready construction foremen, coaches, or social workers who specialize in working with gangs. They also make up a disproportionate percentage of the prison population.

Whether male or female, Eights personify the masculine principle: action, motion, energy directed outward, compelling respect and physical change in the world. The "deadly sin" associated with the Eight is lust—and the stereotype of Eight sexuality is that of an aggressive, insatiable, cocky, not-too-subtle charac-ter. In literature these qualities are more often assigned to male characters than to females.

In the movies, male Eights are often the heroes of westerns, war stories and action-adventure films. John Wayne, Charles Bronson, and Clint Eastwood have often played Eight characters. There are also many colorful Eight film villains, such as Marlon Brando in *The Godfather* and Lee J. Cobb in *On the Waterfront*. Whether inspiring or terrifying, Eights can seem like a force of nature—impressive in their energy and physical power.

Female Eights are not as visible in films as their male counterparts. The physical power and combativeness of Eight is at odds with many cultural ideals of femininity, and aggressive Eight women can be viewed as oddities if not aberrations. Some female Eight comediennes play on this and use comedy to defuse the threat of their power. Roseanne, who often plays Eight roles and prefers to be called "killer bitch" rather than "feminist," puts it this way:

> "It's like this: I gave birth to ya, and I can take ya out, too. I think that's what makes me a bit different from other women. Because I'll beat the shit out of them, and not just verbally. I'm not opposed to violence. In fact, I think it's great. I think women should be more violent, kill more of their husbands. I like the fight. If people are comin' at you, you don't just sit there and lay down and go, 'Oh, bless you.' That's not in the human arsenal. To say that women should do that is to say women aren't human."

Levels of Health

Average Eights take a pragmatic attitude toward life and seek to dominate the world they live in. Since they see society as filled with ruthless competitors, they often respond by being confrontative, intimidating, and excessive, as represented by such characters as Stanley Kowalski in Tennessee Williams's *A Streetcar Named Desire*, Jimmy Porter in John Osborne's *Look Back in Anger*, Michael Henchard in Thomas Hardy's *The Mayor of Casterbridge*, Antony in Shakespeare's *Antony and Cleopatra*, Petruchio in Shakespeare's *The Taming of the Shrew*, the Wife of Bath in Chaucer's *The Canterbury Tales*, Lady Bracknell in Oscar Wilde's *The Importance of Being Earnest*, Tom in David Hare's *Skylight*, and the Red Queen in Lewis Carroll's *Alice in Wonderland*.

Healthy Eights are archetypal leaders—magnanimous, protective of the weak, passionate, effective. They often have a vision of a better world and courageously use their extraordinary energies to make it a reality. In addition to V. I. Warshawski and Andrew Undershaft, we see examples in George Bernard Shaw's Saint Joan, Jean Valjean in Victor Hugo's *Les Miserables*, Mary Russell in Laurie R. King's *The Beekeeper's Apprentice*, and Kinsey Milhone in Sue Grafton's detective series (*A Is for Alibi*, etc.).

For Unhealthy Eights confrontation and intimidation have become a way of life. Often violent, abusive, ruthless and vengeful, they are visible in such books as Mario Puzo's *The Godfather* and *The Last Don* and Roddy Doyle's *The Woman Who Walked into Doors*.

Stress and Security Points

For all their power and protective force, even healthy Eights have problems in intimate relationships. When we look at the Eight's stress point, Five, and security point, Two, the reasons become clear.

To a stressed Eight other people look overwhelming, as though they might engulf the Eight if he or she were to allow any contact at all. Eights' solution is to retreat, to isolate themselves and regroup for another assault on the world. This strategy is characteristic of Fives, and so we say that under stress Eights move to Five.

When Eights feel more secure they become outgoing, generous and protective toward others—but from a position of strength: the powerful benefactor who can afford to give something away—with characteristic Two pride. This behavior is common in Twos, and Eights move to Two in security.

The "one up" or "one down" position—Two sociability versus Fiveish isolation—can be a conflict for Eights. Some have trouble sustaining intimate relationships because they don't relate to others as equals or peers.

The Mayor of Casterbridge

The Eight emotional compass is vividly on display in Thomas Hardy's *The Mayor of Casterbridge*. The title character, Michael Henchard, is so ill-tempered that one day, while drunk at a country fair, he sells his wife to the highest bidder. The following morning he ruminates on what has happened:

> "Did I tell my name to anybody last night, or didn't I tell my name?" he said to himself; and at last concluded that he had not. His general demeanour was enough to show how he was surprised and nettled that his wife had taken him so literally—as much could be seen in his face, and in the way he nibbled a straw which he pulled from the hedge. He knew that she must have been somewhat excited to do this; moreover, she must have believed that there was some sort of binding force in the transaction. On the latter point he felt almost certain, knowing her freedom from levity of character and the extreme simplicity of her intellect. There may, too, have been enough recklessness and resentment beneath her ordinary placidity to make her stifle any momentary doubts. On a previous occasion when he had declared during a fuddle that he would dispose of her as he had done, she had replied that she would not hear him say that many times more before it happened, in the resigned tones of a fatalist. . . . "Yet she knows I am not in my senses when I do that!" he exclaimed. "Well, I must walk about till I find her. . . . Seize her, why didn't she know better than bring me into this disgrace!" he roared out. "She wasn't queer if I was. 'Tis like Susan to show such idiotic simplicity. Meek—that meekness, has done me more harm than the bitterest temper!" (pp. 14-15)

Henchard fails to find his wife, and when we next see him, years later, he has sworn off drink, become a successful businessman and been elected Mayor of Casterbridge. Now at the height of his powers, he is affable and supportive, eager to help others. Yet even when he generously takes young Donald Farfrae into his business, it is always clear who is boss. As one character observes:

> Henchard's tigerish affection for the younger man, his constant liking to have Farfrae near him, now and then resulted in a tendency to domineer, which, however, was checked in a moment when Donald exhibited marks of real offence. (p. 87)

This is an average Eight feeling secure: moving to Two and seeking to control others through affection and personal favors.

Over the course of Hardy's novel, we see Henchard bring about his own downfall. This downward arc is first visible when he develops a sudden unfounded mistrust of Farfrae and drives the younger man out of his business. When Farfrae, a healthy One, responds by starting his own competing business, Henchard is enraged:

> Henchard, who had been hurt at finding that Farfrae did not mean to put up with his temper any longer, was incensed beyond measure when he learnt what the young man had done as an alternative . . . and his voice might have been heard as far as the town pump expressing his feelings to his fellow councilmen. . . .
>
> ". . . I'd have shared my last crust with that young fellow at one time, I liked him so well. And now he's defied me! But damn him, I'll have a tussle with him now—at fair buying and selling, mind—at fair buying and selling! And if I can't overbid such a stripling as he, then I'm not wo'th a varden!" (p. 109)

As Farfrae's business succeeds, Henchard tries to shore up his powers by cutting corners in his own business. When this tactic ultimately fails, he grows cruel and suspicious, alienating his family and closest allies with belligerent behavior. He also starts drinking again.

Late in the story he forces Farfrae into a life-and-death test of physical strength, where the loser of the contest is almost certain to be killed. In the struggle, Henchard overpowers Farfrae, who helplessly admits his defeat. The Mayor is unwilling, however, to fully press his advantage:

> "Now," said Henchard between his gasps, "this is the end of what you began this morning. Your life is in my hands."
>
> "Then take it, take it!" said Farfrae. "Ye've wished to long enough!"
>
> Henchard looked down upon him in silence, and their eyes met. "O

Farfrae!—that's not true!" he said bitterly. "God is my witness that no man ever loved another as I did thee at one time. . . . And now—though I came here to kill 'ee, I cannot hurt thee! Go and give me in charge— do what you will—I care nothing for what comes of me!"

He withdrew to the back part of the loft, loosened his arm, and flung himself into a corner upon some sacks, in the abandonment of remorse. Farfrae regarded him in silence; then went to the hatch and descended through it. Henchard would fain have recalled him; but his tongue failed in its task, and the young man's steps died on his ear. (pp. 266-267)

Henchard's reluctance to completely destroy a weaker person is a common impulse in Eights, reminiscent of the way a wolf will abandon an attack when another wolf bares its throat. After Farfrae leaves, Hardy tells us:

Henchard took the full measure of shame and self-reproach. The scenes of his first acquaintance with Farfrae rushed back upon him— that time when the curious mixture of romance and thrift in the young man's composition so commanded his heart that Farfrae could play upon him as on an instrument. So thoroughly subdued was he that he remained on the sacks in a crouching attitude, unusual for a man, and for such a man. Its womanliness sat tragically on the figure of so stern a piece of virility. (p. 267)

Eights rarely agree to a test of physical strength unless they are prepared to follow it through to the end. Thus Henchard feels humiliated by his own Twoish impulse toward Farfrae.

Bankrupt and estranged from everyone, Henchard quietly leaves Casterbridge. In another town he returns to his original menial job as a hay-trusser:

"Here and everywhere be folk dying before their time like frosted leaves, though wanted by their families, the country, and the world; while I, an outcast, an encumberer of the ground, wanted by nobody, and despised by all, live on against my will!" (p. 312)

In the end, he gets his wish and dies alone. Henchard's downward Eight character arc is complete, having moved by stages from a Twoish desire to help others—who in turn love him for his generosity—to a strong connection to Five, through which he ends up isolated and fearful.

Wings

The world views of Seven and Nine, the wings of Eight, are in many ways opposed. While Sevens are interested in physical pleasure, fun, new ideas, and seeking out a variety of options, Nines are preoccupied with seeing the big picture, avoiding conflict, and making connections between people and ideas.

An Eight with a strong Seven wing is likely to be exceptionally energetic, charismatic and lusty, as well as physically hefty, given Seven's appetite for food and drink. Both Seven and Eight are aggressive styles, and the combination makes for a distinct battle-readiness. In healthy individuals, a Seven wing often makes the Eight highly articulate, perceptive about relationships, and fluent with ideas.

Nine is a withdrawn type, and Eights with a Nine wing tend to be less aggressive, more tolerant of others, more philosophical, and more concerned with maintaining harmonious relationships.

Othello

At the beginning of Shakespeare's *Othello,* the title character, an Eight with a Seven wing, seems healthy. We first see him being threatened by followers of Brabantio, Desdemona's father, who are outraged that the Moor has secretly married her. But Othello has the personal authority and self-control to command the situation and avoid a violent confrontation with his bride's father:

> Keep up your bright swords, for the dew will rust them.
> Good signior, you shall more command with years
> Than with your weapons. (I, ii, 76-78)

When Brabantio accuses Othello of drugging Desdemona and using witchcraft to persuade her to marry him, Othello still refuses to take offense. He patiently explains how he wooed the lady—by telling her war stories:

> She loved me for the dangers I had passed,
> And I loved her that she did pity them.
> This only is the witchcraft I have used.
> Here comes the lady. Let her witness it. (I, iii, 193-196)

The character arc for Othello—the tragic downfall of a great-souled man— is especially dramatic because of the way he is manipulated by Iago, a sociopathic Three, to mistrust Desdemona, the person who loves him most.

The Eight obsession with justice and vengeance is powerfully depicted in the last act of the play when Othello comes into Desdemona's bedroom intending to kill her:

> It is the cause, it is the cause, my soul.
> Let me not name it to you, you chaste stars.
> It is the cause. Yet I'll not shed her blood,
> Nor scar that whiter skin of hers than snow,
> And smooth as monumental alabaster.

Yet she must die, else she'll betray more men.
Put out the light, and then put out the light.
If I quench thee, thou flaming minister,
I can again thy former light restore
Should I repent me. But once put out thy light,
Thou cunning'st pattern of excelling nature,
I know not where is that Promethean heat
That can thy light relume. When I have plucked [the] rose,
I cannot give it vital growth again.
It needs must wither. I'll smell [it] on the tree.
O balmy breath, that dost almost persuade
Justice to break her sword! (V, ii, 1-19)

Othello's conflict is between his love for his sleeping wife and his Eightish obsession with vengeance. His powerful intuition senses Desdemona's innocence, yet his will implacably pushes him to take action anyway, and he kills her.

At the play's end, seeing through Iago's lies and realizing his terrible mistake, Othello moves to his Five stress point. We see his ability to observe himself, to clearly see his value, and take upon himself what he considers an appropriate vengeance:

Soft you. A word or two before you go.
I have done the state some service, and they know't.
No more of that. I pray you in your letters
When you shall these unlucky deeds relate,
Speak of me as I am. Nothing extenuate,
Nor set down aught in malice. Then must you speak
Of one that loved not wisely, but too well. . . .
And say besides, that in Aleppo once,
Where a malignant and a turbanned Turk
Beat a Venetian and traduced the state,
I took by th' throat the circumcisèd dog,
And smote him, thus.
        (He stabs himself)
(V, ii, 397-417)

Othello's remorse, dignity, and sense of honor ultimately earn him the stature of a tragic hero and show an Eight redeeming himself by destroying the self who acted so unjustly towards his innocent wife.

The Last Don
An unhealthy Eight with a Nine wing, while less overtly aggressive than an Eight with a Seven wing, can be just as dangerous. Such people may talk softly,

but they are capable of forceful action. An excellent example is Don Domenico Clericuzio in Mario Puzo's *The Last Don*. Head of the most powerful Mafia Family in America, Don Domenico is planning to consolidate his power while seeming to relinquish it, by setting up his sons in legitimate businesses like banking, restaurants, construction, and legal gambling:

It was time to play a different hand; obvious power was too dangerous. But the relinquishing of power was dangerous in itself. He had to do it with the most skillful benignity and with personal goodwill. And he had to do it on his own base. . . .

Before the arrival of the guests, the Don and his sons sat around the white wrought-iron table in the trellised garden at the back of the mansion. The oldest, Giorgio, . . . was twenty-seven, saturnine, with savage wit and closed face. The Don informed Giorgio that he, Giorgio, would be applying to the Wharton School of Business. There he would learn all the intricacies of stealing money while staying within the law.

Giorgio did not question his father; this was a royal edict, not an invitation to discussion. He nodded obedience. . . .

"Giorgio," the Don said, "you will be my successor. You and Vinnie will no longer take part in that necessary part of the Family which invites danger, except when it is absolutely necessary. We must look ahead. Your children, my children, and little Dante and Croccifixio must never grow up in this world. We are rich, we no longer have to risk our lives to earn our daily bread. Our Family will now serve only as financial advisors to all the other Families. We will serve as their political support, mediate their quarrels. But to do this we must have cards to play. We must have an army. And we must protect everyone's money, for which they will let us wet our beaks."

He paused. "Twenty, thirty years from now, we will all disappear into the lawful world and enjoy our wealth without fear. Those two infants we are baptizing today will never have to commit our sins and take our risks."

"Then why keep the Bronx Enclave?" Giorgio asked.

"We hope someday to be saints," the Don said. "But not martyrs."

(pp. 1-3)

The Don's Nine wing is evident in his concern for maintaining harmony within his Family and in its future relationship to the outside world. Meanwhile, however, he keeps an absolute Eightish hold on power.

Following the christening of two infants in the Family, the Don watches the celebration from a balcony, pleased at what his plan will accomplish:

The Don felt a surge of joy that these two infants would grow up sheltered and safe and would never know the price that had been paid for

their happy destiny. . . .
The Don looked back on his life and marveled it had come to such glorious fruition. Certainly he had made monstrous decisions to achieve power and wealth, but he felt little regret. And it all had been necessary and proved correct. Let other men groan over their sins, Don Clericuzio accepted them and placed his faith in the God he knew would forgive him. . . .
His dear friend Virginio Ballazzo had appeared on the boccie court, the only man who could rival Pippi's skill. Ballazzo gave a great flourish as he let his ball go, and there was a loud cheer as he made the successful hit. He raised his hand to the balcony in triumph, and the Don clapped. He felt a sense of pride that such men flowered and prospered under his rule, as had all the people who had gathered together on this Palm Sunday in Quogue. And that his foresight would protect them in the difficult years to come. (pp. 13-14)

Mixed with the Don's sense of pride in his Family and trusted associates is his sense of absolute power over their lives. Even with a moderating Nine wing Eights see confrontation as an inevitable part of life, and very unhealthy Eights may even resort to murder to maintain their control over others. An essential quality of this power is an absence of guilt.

Subtypes

Self-Preservation Eights are preoccupied, in Oscar Ichazo's words, with "satisfactory survival." Average individuals with this subtype are especially materialistic. They tend to be highly competitive and driven to amass money, property and power for themselves and their families. Since Self-Preservation Eights' sense of personal security comes from controlling their material resources—as well as the people in their life—the threat of losing their wealth can throw them into a panic.

Literary examples of the Self-Preservation subtype include the Wife of Bath in Chaucer's *The Canterbury Tales* and Charlie Croker in Tom Wolfe's *A Man in Full*.

A Man in Full

Charlie Croker is a rich, aging real estate developer in Atlanta, married to a young second wife. Massively overextended and nearly bankrupt, Charlie exudes bravado and physical prowess while struggling to hide his health problems and his terror of public humiliation by the bank that has financed his huge, empty development complex.

In the novel's opening passage we see Charlie attempting to maintain an aura of physical vitality while playing the role of munificent host at his vast plantation, which he is at risk of losing. Here he and his guests are shooting quail:

Charlie Croker, astride his favorite Tennessee walking horse, pulled his shoulders back to make sure he was erect in the saddle and took a deep breath . . . Ahhhh, that was the ticket . . . He loved the way his mighty chest rose and fell beneath his khaki shirt and imagined that everyone in the hunting party noticed how powerfully built he was. Everybody; not just his seven guests but also his six black retainers and his young wife, who was on a horse behind him near the teams of La Mancha mules that pulled the buckboard and the kennel wagon. For good measure, he flexed and fanned out the biggest muscles of his back, the latissimi dorsi, in a Charlie Croker version of a peacock or turkey preening. His wife, Serena, was only twenty-eight, whereas he had just turned sixty and was bald on top and had only a swath of curly gray hair on the sides and in back. He seldom passed up an opportunity to remind her of what a sturdy cord—no, what a veritable cable—kept him connected to the rude animal vitality of his youth. (p. 1)

As a Self-Preservation Eight, Charlie's preoccupation with property and possessions seems to shore him up in a dangerous world:

And to think what he, Cap'm Charlie, had here! Second biggest plantation in the state of Georgia! He kept up 29,000 acres of fields, woods, and swamp, plus the Big House, the Jook House for the guests, the overseer's house, the stables, the big barn, the breeding barn, the Snake House, the kennels, the gardening shed, the plantation store, the same one that had been there ever since the end of the Civil War, likewise the twenty-five cabins for the help—he kept all this going, staffed, and operating, not to mention the landing field and a hangar big enough to accommodate a Gulfstream Five—he kept all this going, staffed, and operating year round . . . for the sole purpose of hunting quail for thirteen weeks. And it wasn't sufficient to be rich enough to do it. No, this was the South. You had to be man enough to deserve a quail plantation. You had to be able to deal with man and beast, in every form they came in, with your wits, your bare hands, and your gun. (p. 9)

After a humiliating meeting with the loan officers at his bank, Charlie impulsively flies down to his plantation in his Gulfstream. On the way, he ruminates about his situation, and his fears reveal the preoccupations of his subtype:

It was utterly, blatantly wasteful to crank up a ship like the G-5 and have two pilots and a stewardess hop to it in order to take two men down to Baker County, where they weren't going to do anything but talk, and then fly back. Well—so what! It underscored his rights, his power, his refusal to cave in to a lot of impudent threats. . . .

But there was something else also, something he fought to keep from becoming a conscious thought. The truth was, he had been afraid to return to the office immediately. He didn't dare return in a state of . . . of . . . of . . . agitation (he avoided the word panic) . . . to that grand space he had set aside for himself and Croker Global up on the thirty-ninth floor at Croker Concourse.

Why had he taken an army with him over to PlannersBanc? Eleven people he had brought along! Christ! By now the word was all over the office! Cap'm Charlie has just been humiliated! They ripped his eyeballs out and made him swallow them! Nothing like this had ever happened to Charlie Croker before. They had punched holes in his charisma and . . . right now he felt as if he was leaking fast, right down to charisma zero. He couldn't let them see him in this state. He had to regroup. He had to stop gimping around on an old rusting football knee. Tomorrow morning, when he took the elevator up to the top of Croker Concourse, he had to look, sound, make every move of his alpha lion body, as if nothing had happened. (pp. 69-70)

Some average Self-Preservation Eights try to bolster their self-esteem by imagining themselves a sexual force of nature. Here Charlie tries to pump himself up with sexual fantasies about a woman on his staff, but his thoughts keep returning to his crumbling empire:

He closed his eyes and thought about Peaches and hoped he'd feel a tingle in his loins. He had a theory . . . If you lost your sexual drive, you lost everything, your energy, your daring, your imagination. He kept waiting for the tingle. . . . Instead, he felt an electrical jolt in his solar plexus. Suppose it happened! Suppose they took everything from him! They could wipe him out. He was sixty years old, and this time they could wipe him out—utterly! (p. 79)

Later, awake in the middle of the night, Charlie thinks about his responsibilities and the people who depend on him, a common Self-Preservation Eight preoccupation:

Jesus Christ! What a menagerie! All these people to look after, support, pay for—all of them sleeping like tops, no doubt—while he has to wake up in the middle of the night with insomnia and go to the mat with phantom gains and a lot of other horrible nonsense. (p. 137)

When his young wife, Serena, acts sexually inviting, Charlie's latent anxieties about his potency come to the fore:

He was afraid. That was the word. Since he believed that his performance as a developer, as an entrepreneur, as a plunger, as a creative person, was bound up with his sexual vitality, then he also believed that if he ever lost that, he would lose his . . . power . . . in business and everything else. And now he was afraid that the pressure had rendered him exactly that: impotent. He could sense it; he could feel it; somehow he knew it. But he didn't want to have to take the test and find out for sure. Not tonight.

Serena took a seat in the easy chair near his, and he got an eyeful of the inside of her thigh as she crossed her legs. The slow, voluptuous way she had of crossing her legs and letting a half-slipper dangle on her toes had been enough to set him off all by itself . . . once upon a time. Now he stared and waited for the tingle, which never came.

Godalmighty . . . That was one of the ways he had worked it out in his mind that he was right to break up with Martha and marry Serena. He had had to. It had been necessary, in order to maintain his vitality. He had been fifty-five when he first started fooling around with Serena, and she had made him feel like twenty-five. (p. 227)

When a black Georgia Tech football player is accused of raping the daughter of one of Charlie's friends, Charlie is offered an opportunity to get the bank off his back in exchange for publicly supporting the football player. He is torn, but finds a way to deny that he is betraying his friend:

In spite of himself, Charlie could feel himself weakening, feel himself trying to believe all this arrant flattery pouring out of this slick black lawyer. So he fought back. His sense of loyalty, his sense of honor, his strength of character in the face of temptation—well, not counting sexual temptation, which a man really had no rational control over—his personal courage, which had never deserted him, not even in the deadliest moments on the field of battle in Vietnam—all of this would make him do the right thing, and—but of course at the same time it wouldn't hurt, would it, as a matter of curiosity, as a sheer experiment, to see if this lawyer dressed up like a British diplomat actually could control the workout department at PlannersBanc with a mere snap of his fingers, implausible as that sounded—it wouldn't hurt to see if such a stunt could be pulled, would it?—wouldn't compromise him in any way, wouldn't force him to support Fareek "the Cannon" Fanon if he didn't want to, wouldn't even force him to lay eyes on the man—

—and so before he knew it, he heard himself saying: "All right . . ." (p. 560)

The Eight defense mechanism—denial—and the defense mechanism associated with Charlie's Seven wing—rationalization—make a potent combination. As an average Self-Preservation Eight, maintaining a bulwark of money and possessions around himself allows Charlie to feel secure, and he will do almost anything to avoid losing that fire wall.

The Canterbury Tales

In *The Canterbury Tales*, Alison, the Wife of Bath, a lusty, earthy, practical woman who has survived five husbands, also has a distinct materialistic bent. In the "Prologue to the Wife of Bath's Tale," Alison describes her marriages almost entirely in terms of money and power, important subjects to a Self-Preservation Eight:

> May I never see another drop of ale or wine, if I say not sooth of my husbands; and three of them were good, and two of them were bad. The three men were good, rich and old, and by my faith, I set no store by them. They had given me their gold and their treasure; I needed no longer do my diligence to win their love or do them honor. They loved me so well that I set no value on their love. A wise woman ever alike will set her to win love where she has none; but since I had them under my thumb and had all their land, why should I take heed to please them, unless it were for my profit and pleasure? (pp. 159-60)

To other wives who may have strayed from their marriage vows, she offers this advice on how to control their husbands:

> O Lord! The pain and woe I did them, and full guiltless, by the rood! For I could bite and whine like a horse. I knew how to complain, though I were the culprit; else oftentimes had I been undone. He who first comes to the mill, first grinds; I complained first, and thus our war was ended. They were right glad to excuse themselves full hurriedly of things that they never had done in all their lives. I would accuse mine old husband of wenches, when he could scarce stand for sickness; yet it tickled his heart because he thought that I had so great fondness for him. I swore that all my walking abroad by night was to espy wenches whom he made merry with. Under color of that I had many a privy jest at him; for all such wit is given to us when we are born. Deceit, weeping, and spinning has God given to women by nature, so long as they live.
>   And thus I boast me of one thing: in the end I had the better in every way, by cunning, or by force, or by some manner of device, such as continual murmur or grumbling. And chiefest at night had they ill fortune; then would I scold and grant them no ease, till they had paid their ransom to me, whatever I would have. And therefore I tell this to every man: let him win who can, everything has its price. With empty hand men may lure no hawks. (p. 163)

By threatening to withhold sex, Alison extorts gifts from her husbands.

This kind of shrewd materialism comes easily to an average Eight with this subtype.

Alison marries her fifth husband, a scholar, for love rather than money—which leads to trouble. When he reads books at night instead of attending to her sexual needs, she tears pages out of his book and hits him. Here she parlays his angry response into a strategic advantage:

> I plucked three leaves out of his book, even as he read, and also I so took him on the cheek with my fist that he fell down backward into our fire. And he started up like a mad lion, and smote me on the head with his fist so that I lay as dead on the floor. And he was aghast when he saw how still I was, and would have fled on his way, till at last I came out of my swoon. "Oh, hast thou slain me, false thief, and hast thou murdered me thus for my land?" I said. "Ere I die, yet will I kiss thee." And he came nearer and kneeled down fairly and said, "Dear sister Alison, so God help me, I shall never smite thee again! Thou thyself art to blame for what I have done. Forgive it me; and that I beseech thee." —And yet again I hit him upon the cheek, and said, "Thief, thus much I am revenged. Now I will die; I can speak no more."
>
> But at last with great pain and grief, we fell into agreement betwixt ourselves. He gave into my hand all the bridle to have the governance of house and estate, and over his tongue and hands to boot. And I made him burn his book then and there. And then I had got unto myself all the sovereignty, through a master stroke, and when he said, "mine own faithful wife, do as you will the rest of your days; be you the guard of your honor, and of my dignity eke,"—we had never a dispute after that day. God help me so, I was as loving to him as any wife betwixt Denmark and India, and eke as true; and so was he to me. . . . (pp. 169-170)

Had Alison's spouse capitulated to her bullying, she would have lost respect for him, as she did for her previous husbands. At the same time, she sees her husband's scholarly interests as a threat to her "sovereignty." By forcing him to burn his book, she demonstrates her control over him. But his ability to fight back increases the odds of a successful marriage. Assured of a strong partner, Alison feels secure enough to abandon her combative stance and enjoy a match of equals.

Eights with a **Social** subtype, which Ichazo associates with "friendship," focus on being part of a group, usually as its leader. They are often devoted to social causes and play the role of protector of a chosen group, especially against other groups. Social Eights also have a complicit quality, of being willing to let their hair down among trusted friends. Because they feel more accountable to others, the anti-social tendencies of the Eight style are generally less evident in this subtype.

Examples of Social Eights include: Michael Henchard in *The Mayor of Casterbridge*, V. I. Warshawski in *Blood Shot*, Andrew Undershaft in *Major Barbara*, Jean Valjean in Victor Hugo's *Les Miserables*, Antony in Shakespeare's *Antony and Cleopatra*, Don Vito Corleone in Mario Puzo's *The Godfather* and Don Domenico Clericuzio in Puzo's *The Last Don*, and Merci Rayborn in T. Jefferson Parker's *The Blue Hour*.

The Blue Hour

Merci Rayborn, the thirty-four-year-old daughter of a veteran Sheriff's Department Investigator, is herself an Investigator in the same Department, in Orange County, California. As *The Blue Hour* begins she is assigned a new partner: Tim Hess, a Nine, an older man who is undergoing chemotherapy for cancer.

Through Hess's eyes, Merci initially seems unappealing:

> At first she was a department favorite, but the novelty of a second-generation deputy wore off fast. There were a half dozen of them. Hess had found her to be aggressive, bright, and a little arrogant. She'd told him she expected to run the homicide detail by age forty, the crimes against person section by fifty, then be elected sheriff-coroner at fifty-eight. She was twenty-four at the time, working the jail as all Sheriff Department yearlings do. In the decade since then, she had not become widely liked. She seemed the opposite of her soft-spoken, modest father. (pp. 4-5)

Merci's ambition to lead a group is typical of a Social Eight. But she has much to learn before she can be an effective leader, and over the course of the story we watch her mature.

Among the qualities she has to overcome are the characteristic Eight defensiveness and suspiciousness that show up in her attitude toward her new partner:

> "We need to get some ground rules straight," said Merci Rayborn. She walked half a step ahead of Hess, her hands on her hips and a pair of aviator shades on. This was their first time out of the building and earshot of other deputies. . . .
> "First of all, this is my case," she continued. Her voice was clear and certain but not loud. She was tall and big boned, dressed in chinos, a sport shirt and one of the ubiquitous black windbreakers of law enforcement, OCSD on the back in orange block letters. Black duty boots. Her hair was dark and pulled back.
> She slowed a step and looked directly at Hess. "So I make the calls. If you've got a problem with that, you should probably excuse yourself from this one."

"I need the benefits."

"I heard."

She was just ahead of him again and they continued walking. Merci Rayborn's head turned and her gaze fixed on her new partner. Hess wondered if he'd lost half a step or if Merci was just fast. His neck was stiff from his fall out of the oak tree.

"Here's my wish list," she said. "One, don't smoke in my car. I quit again two months ago and I'm prone to recidivism. Two, don't bother asking me to lunch because I don't take lunch hours. I eat fast food in the car or cafeteria food at my desk. . . . If you have things to say, just say them. I'm a big girl. But I don't owe you any favors, no matter how many mastodons you slew with my father. I don't need any action behind my back, the way things are round here."

"That's concise. I understand."

She stopped and guided Hess to a halt with a hand on his shoulder. "Last, if you want to play grab-ass and titty-pinch I'll have your dick on a plate immediately. There, that's my wish list. Now, can we all just get along!" (pp. 21-22)

Like many Eights, Merci has difficulty with even minimal social graces. She is also worried about what her colleagues might have heard about a sexual harassment lawsuit she has filed against her former partner. This makes her even more defensive and abrupt.

Tim takes her to visit a troubled man who fits the profile of a serial killer they're looking for. Her hot-headed reactions to the man interfere with her ability to gain psychological insights from this meeting that might help her solve their case. When Hess expresses his disappointment, what he says to her could apply to many Eights:

". . . I learned something about our man and you got a chance to understand something you don't understand yet."

"Yeah? *What.*"

"That other people don't think like you, so you have to think like them. They don't feel like you. So you have to empathize. They don't behave like you, so you have to get a feel for what they're going to do next. That goes for creeps, so you can catch them, and everybody else, so you can get along with them."

"And what if I just decide not to?"

"Then you won't make sheriff by sixty."

The rage hit her heart like a shot of speed. "Fifty-eight. And that's not a joke to me."

"I'm not joking. And you could handle that job, so long as you understood that the only person in the world who thinks like you is you. Being a good hunter isn't about being in touch with your feelings,

Rayborn. It's about being in touch with everyone else's. That's how you find the people you need, no matter what you plan on doing to them. Creeps or husbands, you find them the same way."

"I don't want a husband. And you picked a helluva time for a lecture on feelings."

"It was important." (pp. 116-117)

As they drive, Merci thinks about what Hess said. The fact that she's willing to consider his suggestions is a healthy sign. An unhealthy Eight would grow aggressive in the face of this kind of criticism:

She looked at his face in the rearview again and thought it looked pale. . . . He looked old and tired, but that's exactly what he was. She wondered what it felt like to sit there with cancer growing in your lung, watching the sky get light. She had no idea because she wasn't used to figuring what other people were thinking. Hess was right about that. So she tried to feel what he might feel, pretending she had the cancer too and she was heading down into Lake Elsinore to interview a speed freak who might be a murderer. But it was hard to feel what Hess felt because what she felt was already there. It was right in the way. So she sent her thoughts out around her own feelings, like birds flying around trees.

What she came up with was, if she was in the same position, every waking moment would scare the living piss out of her. (p. 143)

As Merci tries to feel what empathy means, we see her moving to her security point, Two.

When another woman is killed—probably by the serial killer they are pursuing—Merci feels guilty and angry about not following certain leads in the case. Her response is to drive herself physically while castigating herself. Working out with weights at a gym, she pushes herself beyond her abilities and spills the weights on the floor. Her Eightish focus is on will, in relation to both herself and others:

For just a moment she thought about who she was, and about how strong she was. She remembered the most important thing she had learned in her life thus far: you are powerful and you can make things bend to your will as long as you try hard enough.

Your will is the power to move the world.

So she set the resistance even higher than the first time. Effort was how things got moved. Effort was pain. Pain was strength.

She looked at herself in the mirror as she stood on the pedals to get them going. Pale as a sidewalk, she thought, and about as good looking. (p. 224)

Increasingly drawn to Hess, Merci fumbles for ways to show her interest in him, but she's so unfamiliar with the territory of personal relationships that she's inept. He seems to care for her, but is wary about assuming a role as her mentor:

> Hess studied her. He had a way of looking disapproving and tolerant at the same time. Maybe she was making it up.
> "Power," she said. "Everything comes from the power you have inside yourself. Your will."
> That look again.
> "You've got this look, like you think two things at once."
> "I guess I do."
> "Well, what are they?"
> More of the same look. "Can't I just say that I admire you a lot? Your youth and everything it implies. I like the way you wear it, what you're doing with it."
> "Even when I screw up?"
> "Yeah."
> She considered. "You're still thinking two things about me at the same time—things that don't go together except that you're making them."
> "I'm wondering how you can be so bright and so dull at the same time. How you'll either do really well for yourself or you'll fail big. Just notions."
> "Hey, I'm your commanding officer."
> "You asked." (p. 234)

Merci tells Hess about her sexual harassment suit and her regret that it has become so politicized. We see a Social Eight's conflict between remaining a loner and serving a system that she loves:

> "Truth, Hess? What I want most is to go back in time and not file the goddamned thing. I'm already sorry I did it."
> She hoped he wouldn't say just drop it, and he didn't.
> "But I'm not going to drop it, Hess. I'll chase Kemp all the way to court if I have to. He's gonna stop and he's gonna apologize or I'll ruin him. Guaranteed. And if fifteen other broads want to join in and wreck him with me, then they've got the right. They can do what they want. But I wish they'd quit treating me like some kind of leader. I got ten e-mails over the last three days, thanking me for stepping forward. For being courageous enough to stand up to the system. What they don't get is I love the system. I'm part of it. I'm going to run the whole thing someday. Put money on that. And it really infuriates me to have to file a suit to get this guy to stop asking me to suck his miserable dick. But what I want

to say to everybody else is, stay off my side." (p. 241)

Later, after Merci is gratuitously rude to a young reporter who asks a question about the lawsuit, Hess suggests that being civil to the press might someday pay off:

> "Thanks," she said.
> "You're welcome."
> "Do not tell me I should have felt what she was feeling, or thought what she was thinking."
> "Oh hell, no. She's just an ambitious young reporter who might be happy to help you someday. It would have taken about thirty seconds of your time to be civil."
> "So I screwed up again."
> "Why be a bitch all the time?'
> "I'll get the hang of good manners sooner or later."
> "I'm starting to think you don't want to."
> "Now you're thinking what I'm thinking."
> When they got into the car Merci exhaled and looked at Hess.
> "I'll tell you something, partner—bringing that suit was the dumbest goddamned thing I've ever done in my life. How can I get out of it now, after I've started all this?" (p. 282)

Merci has grown significantly by this point. She is able to hear Hess's criticisms without taking offense and is more honest about her mistakes and limitations. She understands that Hess is trying to help her rather than tear her down. The distance she has come with this unlikely partner has brought her closer to realizing her ambitions as a Social Eight: to move into a responsible leadership role for which she is fundamentally well-qualified.

The Last Don

Don Domenico Clericuzio in Mario Puzo's *The Last Don* is also a Social Eight. Even in his old age, the Don regards his Family as the center of his world and the focus of his personal responsibilities:

> Don Domenico Clericuzio, in his eighties, still commanded his Empire. A world he had created with great endeavor and at great cost and so therefore felt he had earned. . . .
> He was content that, at his advanced age, he had the will to pass the sentence of death on his enemies. Certainly he forgave them, was he not a Christian who maintained a holy chapel in his own home? But he forgave his enemies as God forgives all men while condemning them to inevitable extinction.

In the world Don Clericuzio had created, he was revered. His family, the thousands who lived in the Bronx Enclave, the Brugliones who ruled territories and entrusted their money to him and came for his intercession when they got into trouble with the formal society. They knew that the Don was just. That in time of need, sickness, or any trouble, they could go to him and he would address their misfortunes. And so they loved him.

The Don knew that love is not a reliable emotion no matter how deep. Love does not ensure gratitude, does not ensure obedience, does not provide harmony in so difficult a world. No one understood this better than Don Clericuzio. To inspire true love, one also had to be feared. Love alone was contemptible, it was nothing if it did not also include trust and obedience. What good was love to him if it did not acknowledge his rule?

For he was responsible for their lives, he was the root of their good fortune, and so he could not falter in his duty. He must be strict in his judgment. If a man betrayed him, if a man damaged the integrity of his world, that man must be punished and restrained even if it meant a sentence of death. There could be no excuse, no mitigating circumstance, no appeal to pity. What must be done must be done. (pp. 286-287)

Don Domenico is an unhealthy Eight, but his lack of sentimentality is not unusual. Even Social Eights, who are often less aggressive than other Eight subtypes, are aware that fear motivates people more than love does.

The **Sexual** subtype, which Ichazo associates with "possessiveness," is more intense and flamboyant. Eights with this subtype often defy social norms, and seem to delight in flouting the rules. In intimate relationships, they can be possessive and expect complete surrender from their beloved. If a Sexual Eight suspects that anything is being withheld, accusations and recriminations are likely. Very unhealthy Eights with this subtype are capable of physical abuse. Notable examples of Sexual Eights in literature are Stanley Kowalski in *A Streetcar Named Desire*, Shakespeare's Othello, Charlo Spencer in Roddy Doyle's *The Woman Who Walked into Doors*, Jimmy Porter in John Osborne's *Look Back in Anger*, Mary Russell in Laurie R. King's *The Beekeeper's Apprentice*, and Petruchio in Shakespeare's *The Taming of the Shrew*.

The Taming of the Shrew
Petruchio, who tames the shrewish Sexual Six Katharina, behaves with the disarming panache of a Sexual Eight. Warned about Katharina's violent temper, Petruchio is nevertheless confident from the beginning that he can control and marry her:

292 The Literary Enneagram

GREMIO: But will you woo this wild-cat?
PETRUCHIO: Will I live?
GRUMIO: Will he woo her? Ay, or I'll hang her.
PETRUCHIO: Why came I hither but to that intent?
Think you a little din can daunt mine ears?
Have I not in my time heard lions roar?
Have I not heard the sea puff'd up with winds
Rage like an angry boar chafed with sweat?
Have I not heard great ordinance in the field,
And heaven's artillery thunder in the skies?
Have I not in a pitched battle heard
Loud 'larums, neighing steeds, and trumpets' clang?
And do you tell me of a woman's tongue,
That gives not half so great a blow to hear
As will a chestnut in a farmer's fire?
Tush, tush! Fear boys with bugs. (I, ii, 199-211)

Practical about money and property, Petruchio discusses the details of a dowry with Katharina's father, Baptista, who makes it clear that he will not sanction the marriage unless Petruchio wins Katharina's love. Petruchio's description of the chemistry between a Sexual Eight and a Sexual Six is vivid and perceptive. He may be a rough wooer, but we sense that this couple is sexually well-matched:

PETRUCHIO: Why, that is nothing: for I tell you, father,
I am as peremptory as she proud-minded;
And where two raging fires meet together
They do consume the thing that feeds their fury:
Though little fire grows great with little wind,
Yet extreme gusts will blow out fire and all:
So I to her and so she yields to me;
For I am rough and woo not like a babe. (II, ii, 131-138)

Next Petruchio details his plan to win Katharina by complimenting her on behavior that is exactly the opposite of what she displays. This is an astute ploy to use with a Sexual Six, whose show of strength is based on fear:

PETRUCHIO: I will attend her here,
And woo her with some spirit when she comes.
Say that she rail; why then I'll tell her plain
She sings as sweetly as a nightingale:
Say that she frown; I'll say she looks as clear
As morning roses newly wash'd with dew:
Say she be mute and will not speak a word;

Then I'll commend her volubility,
And say she uttereth piercing eloquence:
If she do bid me pack, I'll give her thanks,
As though she bid me stay by her a week:
If she deny to wed, I'll crave the day
When I shall ask the banns and when be married.
(II, i, 169-181)

Petruchio puts his plan into action. Although he and Katharina argue
violently, Petruchio tells her father that his daughter has privately agreed to
marry him but will remain contrary in public. She does not contradict him—
perhaps because she is too startled to protest, or perhaps because she is attracted
to a man who is completely unintimidated by her antics.

Immediately after their wedding, Katharina asks Petruchio to postpone
their return to his house long enough to enjoy their wedding dinner. He says no,
and shows his determination to establish his control over her:

PETRUCHIO: It cannot be.
KATHARINA: Let me entreat you.
PETRUCHIO: I am content.
KATHARINA: Are you content to stay?
PETRUCHIO: I am content you shall entreat me stay;
But yet not stay, entreat me how you can.
KATHARINA: Now, if you love me, stay.
PETRUCHIO: Grumio, my horse.
GRUMIO: Ay, sir, they be ready: the oats have eaten the horses.
KATHARINA: Nay, then,
Do what thou canst, I will not go to-day;
No, nor to-morrow, not till I please myself.
The door is open, sir; there lies your way;
You may be jogging whiles your boots are green;
For me, I'll not be gone till I please myself:
'Tis like you'll prove a jolly surly groom,
That take it on you at the first so roundly.
PETRUCHIO: O Kate, content thee; prithee, be not angry.
KATHARINA: I will be angry: what hast thou to do?
Father, be quiet; he shall stay my leisure.
GREMIO: Ay, marry, sir, now it begins to work.
KATHARINA: Gentlemen, forward to the bridal dinner:
I see a woman may be made a fool,
If she had not a spirit to resist.
PETRUCHIO: They shall go forward, Kate, at thy command.
Obey the bride, you that attend on her;
Go to the feast, revel and domineer,

Carouse full measure to her maidenhead,
Be mad and merry, or go hang yourself:
But for my bonny Kate, she must with me.
Nay, look not big, nor stamp, nor stare, nor fret;
I will be master of what is mine own:
She is my goods, my chattels; she is my house,
My household stuff, my field, my barn,
And here she stands, touch her whoever dare;
I'll bring mine action on the proudest he
That stops my way in Padua. Grumio,
Draw forth thy weapon, we are beset with thieves;
Rescue thy mistress, if thou be a man.
Fear not, sweet wench, they shall not touch thee, Kate:
I'll buckler thee against a million. (III, ii, 201-240)

Once they arrive at Petruchio's house, he keeps her hungry by telling her that the meal that has been prepared is not fit for her to eat. Then he insists on carrying her to the bridal chamber. Rather than making love to her, he gives her a lecture on "continency" and later gloats about his successful strategy for taming her:

PETRUCHIO: Thus have I politicly begun my reign,
And 'tis my hope to end successfully. . . .
She eat no meat to-day, nor none shall eat;
Last night she slept not, nor to-night she shall not;
As with the meat, some undeserved fault
I'll find about the making of the bed;
And here I'll fling the pillow, there the bolster,
This way the coverlet, another way the sheets:
Ay, and amid this hurly I intend
That all is done in reverend care of her;
And in conclusion she shall watch all night:
And if she chance to nod I'll rail and brawl
And with the clamor keep her still awake.
This is a way to kill a wife with kindness;
And thus I'll curb her mad and headstrong humor.
He that knows better how to tame a shrew,
Now let him speak: 'tis charity to show.
(IV, i, 201-224)

Just as Petruchio intends, Kate's hunger and exhaustion begin to raise her level of anxiety. Next he announces that the two of them will visit her father, but he deliberately misstates the time of the visit. When she corrects him he immediately cancels the visit, in order to again assert his authority. He repeats this lesson in various forms, eventually wearing her down:

PETRUCHIO: Come on, i' God's name; once more toward our father's.
Good Lord, how bright and goodly shines the moon!
KATHARINA: The moon! The sun: it is not moonlight now.
PETRUCHIO: I say it is the moon that shines so bright.
KATHARINA: I know it is the sun that shines so bright.
PETRUCHIO: Now, by my mother's son, and that's myself,
It shall be moon, or star, or what I list,
Or ere I journey to your father's house.
Go on, and fetch our horses back again.
Evermore cross'd and cross'd; nothing but cross'd!
HORTENSIO: Say as he says, or we shall never go.
KATHARINA: Forward, I pray, since we have come so far,
And be it moon, or sun, or what you please:
An if you please to call it a rush-candle,
Henceforth I vow it shall be so for me.
PETRUCHIO: I say it is the moon.
KATHARINA: I know it is the moon.
PETRUCHIO: Nay, then you lie: it is the blessed sun.
KATHARINA: Then, God be bless'd, it is the blessed sun:
But sun it is not, when you say it is not;
And the moon changes even as your mind.
What you will have it named, even that it is.
And so it shall be so for Katharine.
HORTENSIO: Petruchio, go thy ways; the field is won. (IV, v, 1-24)

At Kate's father's house they join the celebration of her sister Bianca's wedding. While talking to some of the other guests, Petruchio wagers that, of three wives summoned by their husbands, Kate will come running the most quickly on command. He wins the bet, and the newly "converted" Kate offers advice to the two other wives: make themselves subservient to their husbands. Thus a Sexual Eight achieves his goal of dominating his spouse, and a Sexual Six comes to appreciate the truth of the old adage, "You catch more flies with honey than with vinegar."

The Woman Who Walked into Doors

Roddy Doyle's novel *The Woman Who Walked into Doors* features an extremely unhealthy Sexual Eight, described in the following passage by his Two wife:

—Where would you be without me? he said.
He put his hand on my shoulder.
I could never get past the door. There were too many things. Things

I didn't have. Money, somewhere to go. Too many things. The kids. The schools. People seeing me. All of them stopped me. It was all black out there. He said he'd kill me if I ever went. I knew he'd do it. He said he loved me and he couldn't live without me; he didn't care what happened to him after he'd done it, it made no difference to him, dead or alive, the rest of his life in jail, he didn't care—he'd kill me. I believed him. It was in his face and voice. He couldn't live without me, he said. He loved me. I couldn't go. He was sorting himself out. He'd come after me and kill me. (p. 209)

The Beekeeper's Apprentice

In Laurie R. King's *The Beekeeper's Apprentice*, Mary Russell is a healthy Sexual Eight. The premise of this novel is that Arthur Conan Doyle's Sherlock Holmes was an actual person, and that Mary Russell met him in 1915, when she was fifteen and he well into middle age. Although their relationship is not sexual, we see from the beginning how she insists that she is his mental equal. She becomes his apprentice, learning the fine points of the detective's profession under his tutelage. Her response to Holmes, a Five, is completely different from that of Dr. Watson, a Nine:

I think, however, that even if the world had not changed and even if I had met Holmes as a young man, my portraits of him would still be strikingly different from those painted by the good Dr. Watson. Watson always saw his friend Homes from a position of inferiority, and his perspective was always shaped by this. Do not get me wrong—I came to have considerable affection for Dr. Watson. However, he was born an innocent, slightly slow to see the obvious (to put it politely), although he did come to possess a not inconsiderable wisdom and humanity. I, on the other hand, came into the world fighting, could manipulate my iron-faced Scots nurse by the time I was three, and had lost any innocence and wisdom I once may have had by the time I hit puberty.
It has taken me a long time to find them again.
Holmes and I were a match from the beginning. He towered over me in experience, but never did his abilities at observation and analysis awe me as they did Watson. My own eyes and mind functioned in precisely the same way. It was familiar territory. (pp. xx-xxi)

Walking on the Sussex Downs with her nose in a book, Mary nearly trips over Holmes at their first meeting. He tells her he is watching bees, and as they talk it is clear that both have prodigious powers of observation and deduction. Mary softens her combative stance when she realizes who he is:

I was horrified: Here I was, standing before a Legend, flinging insults at him, yapping about his ankles like a small dog worrying a bear.

I suppressed a cringe and braced myself for the casual swat that would send me flying.

To my amazement, however, and considerable dismay, instead of counterattacking he just smiled condescendingly . . . and looked at me with tired eyes.

"Young man, I—"

"'Young man'!" That did it. Rage swept into my veins, filling me with power. Granted I was far from voluptuous, granted I was dressed in practical, that is, male, clothing—this was not to be borne. Fear aside. Legend aside, the yapping lapdog attacked with all the utter contempt only an adolescent can muster. With a surge of glee I seized the weapon he had placed in my hands and drew back for the coup de grâce. "'Young man'?" I repeated. "It's a damned good thing that you did retire, if that's all that remains of the great detective's mind!" With that I reached for the brim of my oversized cap and my long blonde plaits slithered down over my shoulders.

A series of emotions crossed his face, rich reward for my victory. Simple surprise was followed by a rueful admission of defeat, and then, as he reviewed the entire discussion, he surprised me. His face relaxed, his thin lips twitched, his grey eyes crinkled into unexpected lines, and at last he threw back his head and gave a great shout of delighted laughter. . . . I was totally disarmed. (pp. 9-10)

A natural loner, Mary is especially pleased to find an intellectual match. Her parents are dead and she lives with an aunt whom she loathes. The intensity of her connection with Holmes is characteristic of a Sexual Eight:

Three months after my fifteenth birthday Sherlock Holmes entered my life, to become my foremost friend, tutor, substitute father, and eventually confidant. . . . By our second meeting we had dropped "Mr." And "Miss." After some years we came to end the other's sentences, even to answer an unasked question—but I get ahead of myself. (p. 33)

Many Eights are physically courageous, and Mary is willing to take on difficult and dangerous tasks. Pursuing an early case, she volunteers to climb a telephone pole. Later, when they find themselves facing a pack of angry dogs, Holmes gropes in his rucksack for a chemical repellent, while Mary simply intimidates the dogs with the force of her personality. When Holmes gets involved in a case he considers too dangerous for Mary, she insists on being included:

"Russell, I am very sorry, but I cannot include you in this case."
"Why not, Holmes?" I was becoming really very angry. So was he.
"Because, damn it, it may be dangerous!"

I stood staring across the room at him, and my voice when it came was, I am pleased to note, very quiet and even.

"My dear Holmes, I am going to pretend you did not say that. I am going to walk in your garden and admire the flowers for approximately ten minutes. When I come back in we will begin this conversation anew, and unless you wish to divorce yourself from me entirely, the idea of protecting little Mary Russell will never enter your head." I walked out, closing the door gently . . . and in ten minutes I went back through the door.

"Good afternoon, Holmes. That's a natty outfit you're wearing [one of his disguises]. I should not have thought to wear an orange tie with a shirt that particular shade of red, but it is certainly distinctive. So, where are we going?"

Holmes looked at me through half-shut eyes. I stood blandly in the doorway, arms folded. Finally he snorted and thrust his violin into its disreputable case.

"Very well, Russell. I may be mad, but we shall give it a try." (pp. 106-107)

For this case, Mary performs a difficult and dangerous rescue of a kidnapped child from a heavily guarded house. When the child, an intelligent girl of six, confesses her fear that her parents might blame her for the kidnapping, Mary sets her straight. She might be giving advice on how to survive in the world as an Eight:

"You tried to get away, even though they hurt you for it, and when they had you in a place where you could do nothing, you waited. . . . And when I came you acted like the intelligent person you are, and you kept quiet and let me carry you away over those skinny branches, and you were absolutely quiet, even when I squashed your arm coming down the tree."

"It didn't hurt much."

"You were brave, you were intelligent, you were patient. And as you say, it isn't really over yet, and you're going to have to be brave and intelligent and patient for a while longer, and wait for the anger and the fear to settle down. They will. . . . Do you believe me?"

"Yes. But I'm still very angry."

"Good. Be angry. It's right to be angry when someone hurts you for no reason. But do you think you can try not to be too afraid?"

"To be angry and—happy?" The incongruity obviously appealed to her. She savoured it for a moment and jumped to her feet. "I'm going to be angry and happy." (p. 166)

Here we see a healthy Eight modulating her need to dominate when faced with a vulnerable individual. The Eight's link to Two is present as Mary empathizes with the girl's anger, and supportively coaches the child about how to survive in a hostile world.

On another case, Holmes is injured. Mary dresses his wound, but he refuses to eat anything, insisting that they need to set off for their destination as soon as possible. As they drive, we again see a Sexual Eight assert her right to be treated as an equal:

> I waited for Holmes to stop his silent fuming, which was not until we were south of Tower Bridge.
> "Look here, Russell," he began. "I won't have you—" but I cut him off immediately by the simple expedient of thrusting a finger into his face. (Looking back I am deeply embarrassed at the affrontery of a girl not yet nineteen pointing her finger at a man nearly three times her age, and her teacher to boot, but at the time it seemed appropriate.)
> "You look here, Holmes, I cannot force you to confide in me, but I will not be bullied. You are not my nanny, I am not your charge to be protected and coddled. You have not given me any cause to believe that you were dissatisfied with my ability at deduction and reasoning. You admit I am an adult—you called me 'woman' not ten minutes ago—and as a thinking adult partner I have the right to make my own decisions. I saw you come in filthy and tired, having not eaten, I was sure, since last evening, and I exercised my right to protect the partnership by putting a halt to your stupidity. Yes, stupidity. You believe yourself to be without the limitations of mere mortals, I know, but the mind, even your mind, my dear Holmes, is subject to the body's weakness. No food or drink and filth on an open wound puts the partnership—puts me!—at an unnecessary risk. And that is something I won't have." (p. 262)

Without argument, Holmes henceforth treats her as his peer.

Later in the case, closing in on their adversary, Holmes proposes that he serve as bait while Mary covers him, ready to rescue him if their would-be killer strikes. His trust in her is complete, and she accepts the dangerous challenge.

Mary's courage and quick reflexes are crucial in this final confrontation. Her drive for dominance is channeled into a life-saving heroic gesture and she proves herself the true equal of the great detective.

The range of literary Eights is enormous—from the brilliant, courageous Mary in *The Beekeeper's Apprentice* to the earthy, materialistic Wife of Bath in *The Canterbury Tales*; from Undershaft, the enlightened industrialist in *Major Barbara*, to the wife-battering husband in Roddy Doyle's *The Woman Who Walked into Doors*. Stories of Eights are invariably full of strong dramatic action, and Eight protagonists often lack the psychological complexity we find in other Enneagram styles. But their stories remind us what powerful forces people with this style can be for correcting injustices and making an impact on the world.

Sources

Chaucer, Geoffrey, *The Canterbury Tales*, in *The Complete Poetical Works of Geoffrey Chaucer*: Now First Put into Modern English by John S. P. Tatlock and Percy MacKaye (New York, Macmillan, 1952)

Doyle, Roddy, *The Woman Who Walked Into Doors* (New York: Viking, 1996)

Hardy, Thomas, *The Mayor of Casterbridge* (New York: Bantam, 1981). First published 1912

King, Laurie R., *The Beekeeper's Apprentice or The Segregation of the Queen* (New York: Bantam, 1996). First published 1994.

Lahr, John, *"Dealing with Roseanne,"* The New Yorker, V. 71, p. 42-8+, July 17, 1995, p. 58.

Paretsky, Sara, *Blood Shot* (New York: Dell, 1988)

Parker, T. Jefferson, *The Blue Hour* (New York: Hyperion, 1999)

Puzo, Mario, *The Last Don* (New York: Random House, 1996)

Shakespeare, William, *Othello*. First produced 1604

_____ *The Taming of the Shrew*. First produced 1593-4

Shaw, George Bernard, *Major Barbara*, in *Complete Plays with Prefaces*, Vol. I (New York: Dodd, Mead, 1962). First published 1907

Wolfe, Tom, *A Man in Full* (New York: Farrar, Straus & Giroux, 1998)

Nine: The Connector

Nine

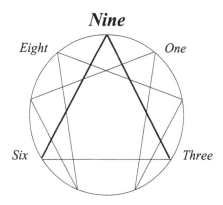

Eight — *One*

Six — *Three*

The title character in James Thurber's "The Secret Life of Walter Mitty" embodies several distinctive characteristics of the Nine style:

"We're going through!" The Commander's voice was like thin ice breaking. He wore his full-dress uniform, with the heavily braided white cap pulled down rakishly over one cold gray eye. "We can't make it, sir. It's spoiling for a hurricane, if you ask me." "I'm not asking you, Lieutenant Berg," said the Commander. "Throw on the power lights! Rev her up to 8,500! We're going through!" The pounding of the cylinders increased: ta-pocketa-pocketa-pocketa-pocketa-pocketa. The Commander stared at the ice forming on the pilot window. He walked over and twisted a row of complicated dials. "Switch on No. 8 auxiliary!" he shouted. "Switch on No. 8 auxiliary!" repeated Lieutenant Berg. "Full strength in No. 3 turret!" shouted the Commander. "Full strength in No. 3 turret!" The crew, bending to their various tasks in the huge, hurtling eight-engined Navy hydroplane, looked at each other and grinned. "The Old Man ain't afraid of Hell!" . . .

"Not so fast! You're driving too fast!" said Mrs. Mitty. "What are you driving so fast for?"

"Hmm?" said Walter Mitty. He looked at his wife, in the seat beside him, with shocked astonishment. She seemed grossly unfamiliar, like a strange woman who had yelled at him in a crowd. "You were up to fifty-five," she said. "You ought to know I don't like to go more than forty. You were up to fifty-five." Walter Mitty drove on toward Waterbury in silence, the roaring of the SN202 through the worst storm in twenty years of Navy flying fading in the remote, intimate airways of his mind. (p. 47)

While Thurber's story comically exaggerates the disparity between a Nine's inner life and his real-life situation, people with this style do tend to be extremely active mentally yet passive in the face they present to the world. While a Nine might enjoy fantasizing about being a courageous and decisive leader, he could be easily dominated by others in his daily life. Generally accommodating, serene, and self-effacing, Nines are driven if not controlled by a strong desire to maintain harmony in personal relationships.

One special attribute of Nines is their ability to make others feel "seen," accepted, and appreciated. Also, their open, empathetic, non-judgmental attitude can make them immensely likeable. I call this temperament "The Connector" because of its gift for making personal connections and facilitating understanding between people. In a very real sense, Nines are the connective tissue in the social body. Though the role of connective tissue is not as dramatic as that of the heart, liver or lungs, it is essential to the life and health of the body.

"The Love Song of J. Alfred Prufrock"
T.S. Eliot's poem "The Love Song of J. Alfred Prufrock" offers a succinct and elegant portrait of a Nine. Prufrock's vagueness, personal insecurity, and lack of decisiveness are common to unevolved Nines:

Do I dare
        Disturb the universe?
        In a minute there is time
        For decisions and revisions which a minute will reverse.

Prufrock understands well that he is not cut out for a heroic role in life, and his ironic humor about his own limitations makes him sympathetic:

        No! I am not Prince Hamlet, nor was meant to be;
        Am an attendant lord, one that will do
        To swell a progress, start a scene or two,
        Advise the prince; no doubt, an easy tool,
        Deferential, glad to be of use,
        Politic, cautious, and meticulous;
        Full of high sentence, but a bit obtuse;
        At times, indeed, almost ridiculous—
        Almost, at times, the Fool.

Fifth Business
At the beginning of his novel *Fifth Business*, Robertson Davies offers a definition of the title that also describes the role of his Nine narrator, Dunstan

Ramsay. It is a supporting role similar to Prufrock's:

Fifth Business . . . Definition
Those roles which, being neither those of Hero nor Heroine, Confidante nor Villain, but which were nonetheless essential to bring about the Recognition or the dénouement, were called the Fifth Business in drama and opera companies organized according to the old style: the player who acted these parts was often referred to as Fifth Business.

Ramsay's role in the novel is that of a catalyst, in that he reveals important information at a crucial moment and brings about the story's resolution, even though he does not participate in the climactic action. Earlier, Liesl, an acquaintance of Ramsay's, makes an astute assessment of his character that applies to many Nines:

"Listen, Ramsay, for the past three weeks you have been telling me the story of your life, with great emotional detail, and certainly it sounds as if you did not think you were human. You make yourself responsible for other people's troubles. It is your hobby. You take on the care of a poor madwoman you knew as a boy. You put up with subtle insult and being taken for granted by a boyhood friend—this big sugar-man who is such a power in your part of the world. You are a friend to this woman—Leola, what a name!—who gave you your congé when she wanted to marry Mr Sugar. And you are secret and stiff-rumped about it all, and never admit it is damned good of you. That is not very human. You are a decent chap to everybody, except one special somebody, and that is Dunstan Ramsay. How can you be really good to anybody if you are not good to yourself? . . . [T]here is a whole great piece of your life that is unlived, denied, set aside. That is why at fifty you can't bear it any longer and fly all to pieces and pour out your heart to the first really intelligent woman you have met—me, that's to say—and get into a schoolboy yearning for a girl who is as far from you as if she lived on the moon. This is the revenge of the unlived life, Ramsay. Suddenly it makes a fool of you." (pp. 225-226)

At the end of *Fifth Business*, after something Ramsay says indirectly causes the death of another character, he is so overwhelmed by the consequences of his actions that he has a seizure and is hospitalized. It is just the kind of scenario Nines dread—that some action of theirs may have dire consequences for others—and this possibility keeps them focused on maintaining harmony at all costs while avoiding purposeful action.

Nines' lack of assertiveness and their habit of mirroring others leads them, at different times, to display the qualities of several Enneagram styles, making their core style more difficult to identify. Like Threes—their security point—

Nines have a gift for taking on characteristics of the person they are with; automatically merging with others in an effort to keep the peace. When Nines feel secure, they are more likely to risk decisive action of the kind Walter Mitty is able only to fantasize about. Like Sixes—their stress point—Nines are often beset with many fears.

The Nine is part of the Eight-Nine-One triad, associated with gut impulses and will. As the central point in the "will" triad, the Nine is characterized by a disorder of will—just as the Three, the central point in the "feeling" triad, is characterized by a disorder of feeling, and the Six, the central point in the "thinking" triad, is characterized by a disorder of thinking. Where Eights try to dominate others and impose their will, and Ones turn their will inward to a compulsive self-discipline and perfectionism, Nines avoid an open contest of wills and maintain harmony with others through evading decisions and action. Their will sometimes manifests itself in passive-aggressive behavior, creating difficulties for others by failing to act or by saying one thing and doing another.

The great strength of Nines is their ability to accept others without either judging them—like Ones—or trying to control them—like Eights. Their generous spirit and non-threatening demeanor can make Nines appealing as friends, counselors or political leaders. Ronald Reagan and Dwight D. Eisenhower, for instance, were both Nines. Like Fives, people with this style like to collect information and are willing to do vast quantities of research before coming to conclusions about a subject. Far from rushing to judgment, they usually suspend it for as long as possible.

Nines' sins are generally those of omission: they neglect duties, forget their promises and make path-of-least-resistance choices. Sloth is the "deadly sin" associated with this style, but Nines are not lazy in the usual sense of the word. Rather, they are often so exhausted from the continuous push-pull of their thoughts and feelings that they become immobilized. The result is a mental, if not physical, lethargy and a desire for peace at any price.

The Nine's History

Nines often feel an unconscious longing to return to the state of the well-fed baby. Even though they may have been deeply bonded with both parents, they frequently felt their parents had little time to give them close attention and care. As a result, Nines are often willing to go to great lengths to feel stable and peaceful. They accommodate others, smooth over conflicts and make few demands, to avoid jeopardizing their relationships. While Nines are busy keeping others happy and maintaining a harmonious status quo, they pay little attention to their own desires and may feel hidden resentment about this sacrifice. Although they achieve a kind of safety and peace, unevolved Nines often have a resigned quality that suggests the price of peace may be too high.

Something Happened

In Joseph Heller's novel *Something Happened* we get important clues about the childhood roots of the Nine's sense of resignation from Bob Slocum, the Nine narrator:

Something must have happened to me sometime.
Maybe it was the day I came home unexpectedly with a fever and a sore throat and caught my father in bed with my mother that left me with my fear of doors, my fear of opening doors and my suspicion of closed ones. Or maybe it was the knowledge that we were poor, which came to me late in childhood, that made me the way I am. Or the day my father died and left me feeling guilty and ashamed—because I thought I was the only little boy in the whole world then who had no father. Or maybe it was the realization, which came to me early, that I would never have broad shoulders and huge biceps, or be good enough, tall enough, strong enough, or brave enough to become an All-American football player or champion prizefighter, the sad, discouraging realization that no matter what it was in life I ever tried to do, there would always be somebody close by who would be able to do it much better. Or maybe it was the day I did open another door and saw my sister standing naked, drying herself on the white-tile floor of the bathroom. She yelled at me, even though she knew she had left the door unlocked and that I had stumbled in on her by accident. I was scared. (pp. 3-4)

Slocum dislikes his life and continually searches for an explanation of the "something" that "happened" that caused him to become the man he is. A middle-level executive with a large company, he is suffering from the Nine version of mid-life crisis. During the first three-quarters of the novel, there are few changes in his life, although we see him considering divorce, ruminating about his relationships with his children, imagining how a promotion would affect his life, and trying to face the necessity of institutionalizing his retarded child.

Slocum is seeking a place to stand where he will be able to make decisions, but his endless rumination simply leads him from association to association and back to feeling frustrated at his lack of identity. Late in the book, Slocum finally realizes the source of his immobilizing anxiety:

Oh, my God—we go into torment long before we even know what suffering is. We are saddled with it before we can even see. There is so much inner fright. I was born, I was told, with a mashed face and red and blue forcep bruises on my shoulders and arms but felt not one message of pain because I had no nervous system yet that could register any. But I knew what loneliness was. I was already afraid of the dark. Or the light. If I knew what cold and sleet were I would have been afraid of those too. (Are we afraid of what we can't see or of what we will see when we do?)

I was afraid I would open my eyes and it would still be dark. (It was that way in that hospital the night they took my tonsils out.) I am afraid of that happening now. And no one would come. Fear. Loss of love, loss of the loved one, loss of love of the loved one. Separation. We don't want to go, we don't want them to go, we can't wait for them to leave, we wish they'd return. There seem to be conflicts. I was in need of whatever nipple succored me and whatever arms lifted me. I didn't know names. I loved the food that fed me—that's all I knew—and the arms that held and hugged and turned me and gave me to understand, at least for those periods, that I was not alone and someone else knew I was there. Without them, I would have been alone. I am afraid of the dark now. I have nightmares in strange beds, and in my own. I have apparitions underneath my bed waiting to stream out. I have spirits in my bedroom closets. I am anxious as a four-year-old child. I am afraid of the light. I am afraid I will open my eyes someday and it will still be dark. And no one will come. (pp. 555-556)

Slocum's terror of being separated from and abandoned by his parents has colored all the relationships in his life. His anger at them for leaving, his desire to punish them, and his fear of his own neediness are played out in his difficulties with his wife and children, mistresses, and co-workers. His reliance on food and women for comfort also has its roots in this childhood insecurity.

Slocum embodies the Nine inertia and resistance to change. In the large company he works for, he maintains an image as a competent middle-manager among his supervisors and subordinates, even though the job requires him to take almost no decisive action.

Whenever he is challenged by his job, Slocum enjoys it, and moves to his Three security point. But he also struggles with boredom and self-pity:

Actually, I enjoy my work when the assignments are large and urgent and somewhat frightening and will come to the attention of many people. I get scared, and am unable to sleep at night, but I usually perform at my best under this stimulating kind of pressure and enjoy my job the most. I handle all of these important projects myself, and I rejoice with tremendous pride and vanity in the compliments I receive when I do them well (as I always do.) But between such peaks of challenge and elation there is monotony and despair. (And I find, too, that once I've succeeded in impressing somebody, I'm not much excited about impressing that same person again; there is a large, emotional letdown after I survive each crisis, a kind of empty, tragic disappointment, and last year's threat, opportunity, and inspiration are often this year's inescapable tedium. I frequently feel I'm being taken advantage of merely because I'm asked to do the work I'm paid to do.) (p. 33)

Notice that Slocum never considers generating new challenges for himself. He disdains a more ambitious Three manager because his own sense of security lies in his limited ambitions:

> Near the very bottom of my Happiness Charts I put those people who are striving so hard to get to the top. I am better off (or think I am) than they because, first, I have no enemies or rivals (that I know of) and am almost convinced I can hold my job here for as long as I want to and, second, because there is no other job in the company I want that I can realistically hope to get. I wouldn't want Green's job; I couldn't handle it if I had it and would be afraid to take it if it were offered. There is too much to do. I'm glad it won't be (I'm sure it won't be).
>
> I am one of those many people, therefore, most of whom are much older than I, who are without ambition already and have no hope, although I do want to continue receiving my raise in salary each year, and a good cash bonus at Christmastime, and I do want very much to be allowed to take my place on the rostrum at the next company convention in Puerto Rico (if it will be Puerto Rico again this year), along with the rest of the managers in Green's department and make my three-minute report to the company of the work we have done in my department and the projects we are planning for the year ahead.
>
> It was downright humiliating to be the only one of Green's managers left out. The omission was conspicuous, the rebuff intentionally public, and for the following four days, while others had a great, robust time golfing and boozing it up, I was the object of expressions of pity and solemn, perfunctory commiseration from many people I hate and wanted to hit or scream at. (pp. 34-35)

Slocum's connection to his Six stress point is evident here in his paranoia. His basic bargain with life is to challenge no one in exchange for keeping his well-paying job. His only ambition is to gain a limited visibility, a timid man's move toward Three. Note, too, in his underlying rage at Green's slight, how Slocum's bonhomie continually masks his fear and anger. He actually longs to behave like an openly aggressive Three:

> [Green] is, I think, as big a coward as I am; yet, he is the only person in the company with enough courage to behave badly. I envy that: I am cordial and considerate to many people I detest (I am cordial and considerate to just about everybody, I think, except former girl friends and members of my family); I trade jokes convivially with several salesman who annoy the hell out of me and make me waste much of my time with their frantic and contradictory requests; I get drunk with others who bore and irritate me and join them at orgiastic parties with secretaries, waitresses, salesgirls, housewives, nurses, models from

Oklahoma, and airline stewardesses from Pennsylvania and Texas; I have two men in my department I'd like to fire and one girl, and there are days when I would truly like to be rid of them all; but I try not to show how I feel, and I'll probably never do anything about any of them, except keep hoping sullenly that they'll disappear on their own. . . . I know so many people I want to be mean to, but I just don't have the character. (pp. 40-41)

As Slocum moves deeper into his mid-life crisis, he has more trouble distinguishing fantasy from reality. Aware of how he looks to others, thanks to his Three connection, he also fears that he may be losing his moorings at his Six connecting point. Meanwhile he maintains the personable façade of a Nine:

I must remember not to smile too much. I must maintain a façade. I must remember to continue acting correctly subservient and clearly grateful to people in the company and at the university and country clubs I'm invited to who expect to find me feeling humble, eager, lucky, and afraid. I travel less, come home more. (I'm keeping myself close to home base, which isn't home, of course, but the company.) (p. 405)

Even though he's aware that he doesn't love his wife, Slocum wonders whether leaving her would make him feel any better:

I don't think I could (I would probably miss her). She wants me to tell her I love her. I won't. A reason I won't is that I know she wants me to. This is one advantage I have over her that I am still able to hang on to.
    She used to make me say it. It seems a silly, awkward thing for a sapient human being to have to say—especially if it's true. It might make some sense on occasion when it's a lie. Now she cannot make me say it, and I have my revenge. She doesn't ask me to anymore. And between us now there is this continual underground struggle over something trivial and nebulous that won't abate and has lasted nearly as long as the two of us have known each other. (p. 516)

Slocum's pattern of hurting others through what he fails to do—an aspect of passive-aggressive behavior—is characteristic of Nines. The reason Slocum can't leave his wife is that he depends on her for his identity.

Levels of Health

Nines generally have difficulty asserting their wills, and one key to how healthy they are is whether they can take purposeful and effective action.

Average Nines—pleasant, conventional, and self-effacing, but often immobile or indecisive—appear in many literary works. They are represented by such diverse characters as Bob Slocum in Joseph Heller's *Something Happened*, Walter Mitty in James Thurber's "The Secret Life of Walter Mitty," Billy Pilgrim in Kurt Vonnegut's *Slaughterhouse Five*, Sancho Panza in Miguel de Cervantes's *Don Quixote de la Mancha*, Harry "Rabbit" Angstrom in John Updike's four Rabbit novels, Yossarian in Joseph Heller's *Catch-22*, the narrator of Jay McInerney's *Bright Lights, Big City*, Dorothy in L. Frank Baum's *The Wizard of Oz*, Pollyanna in Eleanor H. Porter's novel, Catherine Sloper in Henry James's *Washington Square*, Sinclair Lewis's Babbitt, Mr. Micawber in Charles Dickens's *David Copperfield*, Celie in Alice Walker's *The Color Purple*, Cal in Judith Guest's *Ordinary People*, and Margaret Nathan in Cathleen Schine's *Rameau's Niece*.

When Nines are healthy, they transcend the style's natural sluggishness to act in decisive and positive ways but retain their peaceful, unselfconscious, comforting qualities. Healthy Nines in literature include Mrs. Moore in E.M. Forster's *A Passage to India*, the title character in Ernest Hemingway's *The Old Man and the Sea*, Nick Carraway in F. Scott Fitzgerald's *The Great Gatsby*, Bob Hampton in Carolyn See's *The Handyman*, Mr. Jarndyce in Charles Dickens's *Bleak House*, and Aliosha in Fyodor Dostoevsky's *The Brothers Karamazov*.

Unhealthy Nines can be willfully blind to the reality of their lives, enslaved by addictions or numb, disoriented and delusional. The rich fantasy life of an average Nine degenerates into an inability to distinguish reality from fantasy. Pathological Nines includes characters like Shakespeare's Macbeth, Chauncey Gardener in Jerzy Koszinski's *Being There*, Mary Tyrone in Eugene O'Neill's *Long Day's Journey into Night*, Elwood P. Dowd in Mary Chase's play *Harvey*, Humbert Humbert in *Lolita*, and the child molesters in both Paula Vogel's *How I Learned to Drive* and Miguel Pinero's *Short Eyes*.

Place in Society

Though Nines are found in many jobs and professions, their nonthreatening persona and acceptance of others make them natural therapists, teachers, ministers and helping professionals. Nines can also be notably successful in areas of the law such as mediation, estate planning, and negotiation of contracts. In business, they often do well in areas related to human resources. They are frequently attracted to work in civil service.

Their peacemaking skills make them excellent diplomats. Personable and trust-inspiring, they often succeed in politics. Their love of research and learning—as well as their appreciation of a settled, tenured position—makes them comfortable in academia, where they are often polymaths.

Professional sports teams have a high proportion of Nines among their players, partly because the Nine's ability to "merge" with a team effort has a powerful payoff. Many musicians are also Nines, especially drummers, backup musicians, and members of orchestras.

Stress and Security Points

The emotional compass of The Connector is seen in the tension between Nine's security point at Three (The Achiever) and stress point at Six (The Pessimist). Especially when they feel confident and secure, Nines can exhibit the energy, drive and decisiveness of Threes. They assert themselves and take purposeful action.

When under stress, Nines often behave like Sixes: preoccupied with worst-case scenarios, procrastinating, suspicious of others. They lose their comfortable, open stance and may even become paranoid.

Bob Slocum's indecisiveness stems from two opposing drives: to confront others—at his Three security point—and to avoid losing their allegiance—at his Six stress point. In both business and personal relationships, he is immobilized by the tension between the two, so taking no action becomes his option of choice, even if this means a stagnant career and a perfunctory marriage. This pattern is common in unevolved Nines.

Wings

Nine is located at the top of the Enneagram diagram between the Eight's strong outward expression of anger and the One's denial of anger. This metaphorically reflects the bind that Nines are in.

Nines with a One wing are usually more intellectual, more refined, more compulsive about work and ethics. Nines with an Eight wing tend to be less cultured, more spontaneous, and more pleasure-oriented.

In *Something Happened*, Bob Slocum's consciousness of his own anger marks him as a Nine with an Eight wing. But he rarely expresses this anger openly or confronts others. Even with his family, he is mainly passive-aggressive, sometimes deliberately causing damage by failing to act.

Rabbit, Run

John Updike's Harry "Rabbit" Angstrom is a Nine with more of a One wing. He is strongly aware of others judging him and wants to do the right thing—if only he could figure out what that is.

In *Rabbit, Run*, the first book in Updike's series, we see Rabbit, fresh from a fight with his wife, Janice, mulling over two tasks he needs to accomplish: 1) to pick up his car from his in-laws and 2) to pick up his son from his mother's house.

> He goes to the closet and takes out the coat he hung up so neatly. It seems to him he's the only person around here who cares about neatness. The clutter behind him in the room—the Old-fashioned glass with its corrupt dregs, the choked ashtray balanced on the easy-chair arm, the rumpled rug, the floppy stacks of slippery newspaper, the kid's toys here and there broken and stuck and jammed, a leg off a doll and

a piece of bent cardboard that went with some breakfast-box cutout, the rolls of fuzz under the radiators, the continual crisscrossing mess— clings to his back like a tightening net. He tries to sort out picking up his car and then his kid. Or should he pick up the kid first? He wants more to see the kid. It would be quicker to walk over to Mrs. Springer's [his wife's mother], she lived closer. But suppose she was watching out the window for him to come so she could pop out and tell him how tired Janice looked? Who wouldn't be tired after tramping around trying to buy something with you you miserable nickel-hugger? You fat hag. You old gypsy. If he had the kid along this might not happen. Rabbit likes the idea of walking up from his mother's place with his boy. Two-and-a-half, Nelson walks like a trooper, with choppy stubborn steps. They'd walk along in the day's last light under the trees and then like magic there would be Daddy's car at a curb. But it will take longer this way, what with his own mother talking slyly and round-about about how incompetent Janice is. It ruined him when his mother went on like that; maybe she did it just to kid him, but he couldn't take her lightly, she was somehow too powerful, at least with him. He had better go for the car first and pick the kid up with it. But he doesn't want to do it this way. He just doesn't. The problem knits in front of him and he feels sickened by the intricacy. (pp. 14-15)

Like many Nines, Rabbit has difficulty making decisions, even inconsequential ones. It seems there are always so many factors to be considered, and Rabbit is easily distracted. The thinking of Nines can have a convoluted quality, driven by an anxiety that is always threatening to break the surface of their placid exterior. Rabbit's interior monologue also reflects his One wing in his concern for orderliness, his simmering resentment, and his sense that others are continually criticizing him.

Nines generally do anything they can to maintain a peaceful atmosphere and avoid conflict. But in the above situation Rabbit is in a double bind: if he picks up the car first he risks a confrontation with his hated mother-in-law; if he picks up his son at his mother's house without the car he might be overwhelmed by his super-critical mother.

Unable to make this seemingly minor decision and feeling trapped by family responsibilities, Rabbit runs. He picks up the car, starts driving, ending up hundreds of miles away. When he returns several days later he avoids his family and instead goes to stay with his old basketball coach. Through the coach he meets Ruth, a prostitute, and begins an affair with her. Soon Rabbit leaves his wife, who is pregnant with their second child, to move in with Ruth.

When Janice goes into labor, Rabbit moves back home to take care of their son. Despite the ambivalence he feels toward his wife, Rabbit still prefers familiar surroundings and the security of family ties. But when Janice returns from the hospital with their new daughter Rabbit again quarrels with her and leaves her for Ruth. Distraught over being abandoned, Janice gets drunk and accidentally drowns their infant daughter while bathing her. At the funeral, Rabbit senses that everyone blames him for the baby's death:

"Don't look at me," he says. "I didn't kill her."
This comes out of his mouth clearly, in tune with the simplicity he feels now in everything. Heads talking softly snap around at a voice so sudden and cruel.
They misunderstand. He just wants this straight. He explains to the heads, "You all keep acting as if I did it. I wasn't anywhere near. She's the one." He turns to her, and in her face, slack as if slapped, sees that she too is a victim, that everyone is; the baby is gone, is all he's saying, he had a baby and his wife drowned it. "Hey it's O.K.," he tells her. "You didn't mean to." He tries to take her hand but she snatches it back like from a trap and looks toward her parents, who step toward her.
His face burns; forgiveness had been big in his heart and now it's hate. He hates her dumb face. She doesn't see. She had a chance to join him in truth, just the simplest factual truth, and turned away in horror. He sees that among the heads even his own mother's is horrified, blank with shock, a wall against him; she asks him what have they done to him and then she does it too. A suffocating sense of injustice blinds him. He turns and runs. (p. 293)

Again, Rabbit's need to defend the "rightness" of his actions is characteristic of his One wing. His attempt to blame his wife backfires. When he feels his anger welling up, he is too frightened to express it. Again he turns and runs, returning to Ruth, only to learn that she is pregnant with his child, a situation he is responsible for, since he refused to let her use birth control. Ruth tells him she considered an abortion but couldn't go through with it. When Rabbit urges her to have the baby, she questions him sharply about whether he will divorce Janice and marry her. As usual, he is indecisive, and she confronts him:

"Will you divorce her? No. You love being married to her too. You love being married to everybody. Why can't you make up your mind what you want to do?"
"Can't I? I don't know."
"How would you support me? How many wives can you support? Your jobs are a joke. You aren't worth hiring. Maybe once you could play basketball but you can't do anything now. What the hell do you think the world is?"
"Please have the baby," he says. "You got to have it."
"Why? Why do you care?"
"I don't know. I don't know any of these answers. All I know is what feels right. You feel right to me. Sometimes Janice used to.

Sometimes nothing does."
"Who cares? That's the thing. Who cares what you feel?"
"I don't know," he says again.
She groans—from her face he feared she would spit—and turns
and looks at the wall that is all in bumps from being painted over peeling
previous coats so often.
He says, "I'm hungry. Why don't I go out to the delicatessen and
get us something. Then we can think." (pp. 303-304)

Rabbit's sudden preoccupation with food is a Nine attempt to deflect the
pressure on him to make a decision. But Ruth refuses to be distracted and insists
that he deal with the issue at hand:

She turns, steadier. "I've been thinking," she says. . . . "Now I'd
like to marry you. I would. I mean whatever I said but if we're married
it'll be all right. Now you work it out. You divorce that wife you feel so
sorry for about once a month, you divorce her or forget me. If you can't
work it out, I'm dead to you; I'm dead to you and this baby of yours is
dead too. Now; get out if you want to." Saying all this unsteadies her and
makes her cry, but she pretends she's not. The sides of her nose shine but
she doesn't touch them.
He has nervously felt her watching him for some sign of resolution
inspired by this speech. In fact he has hardly listened; it is too complicated and, compared to the vision of a sandwich, unreal. He stands up,
he hopes with soldierly effect, and says, "That's fair. I'll work it out.
What do you want at the store?" A sandwich and a glass of milk, and then
undressing her, getting her out of that hot cotton dress harried into
wrinkles and seeing that thickened waist calm in its pale cool skin. He
loves women when they're first pregnant; they look so gentle. If he can
just once more bury himself in her he knows he'll come up with his
nerves all combed.
"I don't want anything," she says. (p. 304)

On his way to the deli, Rabbit thinks about his son and begins to have new
doubts about divorcing Janet:

He decides to walk around the block, to clear his head and pick his
path. Funny, how what makes you move is so simple and the field you
must move in is so crowded. His legs take strength from the distinction,
scissor along evenly. Goodness lies inside, there is nothing outside,
those things he was trying to balance have no weight. He feels his inside
as very real suddenly, a pure blank space in the middle of a dense net.
I don't know, he kept telling Ruth; he doesn't know, what to do, where
to go, what will happen, the thought that he doesn't know seems to make

him infinitely small and impossible to capture. Its smallness fills him like a vastness. It's like when they heard you were great and put two men on you and no matter which way you turned you bumped into one of them and the only thing to do was pass. So you passed and the ball belonged to the others and your hands were empty and the men on you looked foolish because in effect there was nobody there.
   ... His hands lift of their own and he feels the wind on his ears even before, his heels hitting heavily on the pavement at first but with an effortless gathering out of a kind of sweet panic growing lighter and quicker and quieter, he runs. Ah: runs. Runs. (pp. 306-307)

In these final paragraphs of the novel, Rabbit continues to struggle with conflicting desires and responsibilities, unable to decide what to do. Under pressure to make a commitment, he seeks distraction in food, sexual fantasies and memories of playing basketball—the only thing he has ever been really good at. Ultimately, though, he is too frightened to do anything but run.
   Apart from his roles—as a former basketball star, Janice's husband, his son's father, his parents' son—Rabbit doesn't know who he is: "in effect there was nobody there." Although the pregnant Ruth represents the good mother he never had, a soul-mate with whom he might find real happiness, he is too insecure about his own core identity to jettison the other roles that shore him up. Nines often cling to the familiar, even in extremely unhappy situations, because it reassures them that they exist, something about which they are deeply anxious.
   Rabbit's continual running under pressure is a common pattern in Nines: forcing others to bear the full brunt of uncomfortable situations by removing themselves from the picture. And Rabbit is rarely aware of his own anger, a familiar pattern when Nines have a One wing.

The Puttermesser Papers
   In Cynthia Ozick's comic fantasy *The Puttermesser Papers* we find a distinctly different example of a Nine with a One wing. Ruth Puttermesser, the novel's protagonist, is a lawyer working for the city of New York in the Department of Receipts and Disbursements:

> The truth was that Puttermesser was now a fathomer; she had come to understand the recondite, dim, and secret journey of the City's money, the tunnels it rolled through, the transmutations, investments, multiplications, squeezings, fattenings and battenings it underwent. She knew where the money landed and where it was headed for. She knew the habits, names, and even the hot-tempered wives of three dozen bank executives on various levels. She had acquired half a dozen underlings of her own—with these she was diffident, polite; though she deemed herself a feminist, no ideology could succeed for her in aggrandizing force. Puttermesser was not aggressive. She disdained assertiveness.

Her voice was like Cordelia's. At home, in bed, she went on dreaming and reading. . . .

Every day, inside the wide bleak corridors of the Municipal Building, Puttermesser dreamed an ideal Civil Service: devotion to polity, the citizen's sweet love of the citizenry, the light rule of reason and common sense, the City as miniature country crowded with patriots—not fools and jingoists, but patriots true and serene; humorous affection for the idiosyncrasies of one's distinctive little homeland, each borough itself another little homeland, joy in the Bronx, elation in Queens, O happy Richmond! Children on roller skates, and over the Brooklyn Bridge the long patchwork-colored line of joggers, breathing hard above the homeland-hugging green waters. (pp. 29-30)

Puttermesser's quiet capability, her idealism, her disdain for assertiveness, and her propensity to fantasize about ideal scenarios are all marks of a Nine with a One wing.

Single and in her forties, Puttermesser has a married lover, Rappoport. But when they are in bed together she continually shows more interest in reading than in sex. He finally leaves her in disgust.

"You have no feelings," Rappoport once told her: he meant that she had the habit of flushing with ideas as if they were passions.

And this was true. Puttermesser's intelligence, brambly with the confusion of too much history, was a private warted tract, rubbled over with primordial statuary. She was painfully anthropological. Civilizations rolled into her rib cage, stone after graven stone: cuneiform, rune, cipher. She had pruned out allegory, metaphor; Puttermesser was no mystic, enthusiast, pneumaticist, ecstatic, kabbalist. Her mind was clean; she was a rationalist. . . . What transfixed her was the kind of intellect (immensely sober, pragmatic, unfanciful, rationalist like her own) to which a golem ordinarily occurred—occurred, that is, in the shock of its true flesh and absolute being. The classical case of the golem of Prague, for instance: the Great Rabbi Judah Loew, circa 1520-1609, maker of that renowned local creature, was scarcely one of those misty souls given over to untrammeled figments or romances. He was, instead, a reasonable man of biting understanding, a solid scholar, a pragmatic leader—a learned quasi-mayor. What he understood was that the scurrilous politics of his city, always tinged with religious interests, had gone too far. (p. 44)

When Puttermesser is demoted from her job for political reasons and her letter of protest to the mayor goes unheeded, she is outraged but helpless. In her bed one day she finds a female golem: a creature that, according Jewish legend, can be artificially created through cabalistic rites. Puttermesser senses that she may have made the golem, half unconsciously, from the earth of the plants in her apartment. The golem represents Puttermesser's alter-ego, her liberated will—the opposite of the walled-off will common in Nines. The golem announces that her name is Xanthippe and immediately busies herself with cooking, cleaning, and developing a plan to get Puttermesser elected mayor of New York.

Fueled and supported by the golem's prodigious energy, Puttermesser is elected mayor, and a golden age begins in the city: crime vanishes, the streets become clean and safe, and good people find worthy employment. But Puttermesser grows uneasy about her relationship with the golem:

> The coming of the golem animated the salvation of the City, yes—but who, Puttermesser sometimes wonders, is the true golem? Is it Xanthippe or is it Puttermesser? Puttermesser made Xanthippe; Xanthippe did not exist before Puttermesser made her: that is clear enough. But Xanthippe made Puttermesser Mayor, and Mayor Puttermesser too did not exist before. And this is just as clear. Puttermesser sees that she is the golem's golem.
>
> In the newborn peaceable City, Xanthippe is restless. She is growing larger. Her growth is frightening. She can no longer fit into her overalls. She begins to sew together pairs of sheets for a toga. (pp. 78-79)

It is Puttermesser's fear of her own will that keeps her from asserting herself even to a reasonable degree. She senses that her will is actually enormous, and that the more she exercises it the more unruly it is likely to become. The symbol of her externalized will to power, the golem, represents both Puttermesser's deepest desires and her deepest anxieties.

Not only does Xanthippe keep getting bigger—as golems in legend always do, she develops outrageous sexual appetites that eventually decimate the ranks of Puttermesser's mayoral appointees and threaten to bring down her administration:

> The City is diseased with the golem's urge. The City sweats and coughs in her terrifying embrace. The City is in the pincer of the golem's love, because Xanthippe thirsts, she thirsts, she ravishes and ravages, she ambushes management level after management level. There is no Supervising Accountant or Secretary to the Minority Leader who can escape her electric gaze.
>
> Sex! Sex! The golem wants sex! Men in high politics! Lofty officials! Elevated bureaucrats!
>
> Mayor Puttermesser is finished. She can never be re-elected. She is a disgrace; her Administration is wretched. Distrust. Desolation. It is all over for Mayor Puttermesser and the life of high politics. The prisons are open again. The press howls. Mayor Puttermesser is crushed. The

golem has destroyed her utterly. (pp. 86-87)

Thus we see how a Nine with a One wing can fear that her appetites could totally destroy her and her world if given free rein.

Puttermesser is quick to assume responsibility for the golem's destructiveness. Finally, in despair and grief—for she has grown fond of Xanthippe—Puttermesser decides to destroy her alter ego. She persuades her old lover, Rappoport, to lure Xanthippe into a sexual situation, and together Puttermesser and Rappoport perform a ritual that destroys the golem. But it is too late for Puttermesser's political career; she loses her job as mayor and New York returns to its previous deplorable state.

Ozick's story of a Nine's gargantuan will and appetite running amuck is richly comic as well as flamboyant and horrifying. Rather than risk this possibility, most Nines—especially those with a One wing—keep a tight grip on their unruly desires, avoid conflicts, and live out their lives with few demands.

Subtypes

Self-Preservation Nines, whom Oscar Ichazo associates with "appetite," are creatures of habit, absorbed with food, television, reading, gardening and other simple pleasures. Although individuals of this subtype may be highly talented, they are rarely ambitious, preferring the reassurance of routine and physical comfort over significant challenges. Self-Preservation Nines also tend to be the most socially conventional of Nines.

Self-Preservation Nines in literature include Falstaff in Shakespeare's *Henry IV* parts 1 and 2, Sancho Panza in Miguel de Cervantes's *Don Quixote de la Mancha*, Catherine Sloper in Henry James's *Washington Square*, Dorothy in L. Frank Baum's *The Wizard of Oz*, Celie in Alice Walker's *The Color Purple*, Chauncey Gardener in Jerzy Koszinski's *Being There*, and the title character in Ernest Hemingway's *The Old Man and the Sea*.

The Old Man and the Sea

The Self-Preservation Nine preoccupation with physical survival especially drives the title character of this Hemingway novella. The story is simple: an old fisherman who has failed to catch anything for eighty-four days puts to sea and hooks an immense fish. He fights the fish for several days, finally succeeds in killing it, and lashes it to the side of his little boat. On the trip home sharks attack and, despite the old man's fierce attempts to fight them off, they devour the fish carcass, leaving only the bones.

Self-Preservation Nines continually think about what is necessary to survive. Once he has hooked the big fish, the old man sees his task clearly:

He is a great fish and I must convince him, he thought. I must never let him learn his strength nor what he could do if he made his run. If I were him I would put in everything now and go until something broke.

But, thank God, they are not as intelligent as we who kill them; although they are more noble and more able. (p. 63)

The old man has an Eight wing, and he is conscious of testing his strength against that of the fish. As a Self-Preservation subtype, everything the old man does is calculated to help him catch and keep the fish. He is not distracted by philosophical issues that can preoccupy the other Nine subtypes:

[H]e knew that he was not being clear-headed and he thought he should chew some more of the dolphin. But I can't, he told himself. It is better to be light-headed than to lose your strength from nausea. And I know I cannot keep it if I eat it since my face was in it. . . . You're stupid, he told himself. Eat the other flying fish.

It was there, cleaned and ready, and he picked it up with his left hand and ate it chewing the bones carefully and eating all of it down to the tail.

It has more nourishment than almost any fish, he thought. At least the kind of strength that I need. Now I have done what I can, he thought. Let him begin to circle and let the fight come. (pp. 85-86)

After the sharks attack, the old man fights them off with every weapon he has, including the tiller of his boat. But the struggle is useless:

He knew he was beaten now finally and without remedy and he went back to the stern and found the jagged end of the tiller would fit in the slot of the rudder well enough for him to steer. He settled the sack around his shoulders and put the skiff on her course. He sailed lightly now and he had no thoughts nor any feelings of any kind. He was past everything now and he sailed the skiff to make his home port as well and as intelligently as he could. In the night sharks hit the carcass as someone might pick up crumbs from the table. The old man paid no attention to them and did not pay any attention to anything except steering. He only noticed how lightly and how well the skiff sailed now that there was no great weight beside her. (p. 119)

Once the fish is irrevocably lost, we see the old man surrender to a resignation that comes easily to Nines. Devoid of feelings, he simply focuses on returning to his home port. Self-Preservation Nines are often more stoic, more accepting of inevitable losses than Nines with other subtypes.

The old man makes it back to port, pulls his boat up on the sand, staggers to his shack and falls onto his bed:

Up the road, in his shack, the old man was sleeping again. He was still sleeping on his face and the boy was sitting by him watching him.

The old man was dreaming about the lions. (p. 127)

Although exhausted by his epic battle, with a good night's sleep the old man will survive to successfully fight other fish. Hemingway's understated ending makes us appreciate the unpretentious heroism that healthy Self-Preservation Nines are capable of.

The Wizard of Oz

Dorothy in L. Frank Baum's book *The Wizard of Oz* is another clear Self-Preservation Nine. The familiar story opens with Dorothy living on a farm in Kansas with her Aunt Em and Uncle Henry. Left mostly on her own, she daydreams about fantastic lands she might visit. One day a big cyclone comes up, and Dorothy is knocked unconscious by a window frame blown into her bedroom. She dreams the house is lifted from its foundation and lands in the mythical world of Oz.

From the beginning of her adventure Dorothy is eager to get home. Attachment to familiar surroundings and comforts is a hallmark of Self-Preservation Nines. Glinda, the Good Witch of the North, advises her to walk to Oz and consult the Wizard about how she can return to Kansas.

On the road Dorothy acquires three companions: the Scarecrow, a Seven who hopes the Wizard will be able to give him some brains; the Tin Woodman, a Two who wants the Wizard to give him a heart; and the Cowardly Lion, a Six who hopes to acquire courage.

One obstacle on the journey is a huge field of poppies that puts Dorothy, Toto, and the Lion to sleep as they walk through it. This could be seen as a metaphor for how drowsiness and inertia can prevent Nines from reaching their destination, something that is especially true for Self-Preservation Nines.

Dorothy and her companions survive several attempts by the Wicked Witch to destroy them, arrive at the Emerald City, and find their way into the chamber of the Wizard, whom no one has ever seen. There is an impressive stage effect of smoke, and they hear the sonorous voice of the Wizard. He tells them that before he will grant their wishes they must prove their worthiness by bringing him the broomstick of the Wicked Witch.

When the four of them eventually return with the broomstick, the Wizard demands that they come back the following day. But Toto pulls aside a curtain, revealing the Wizard to be a man running all the machinery and stage effects. They realize the whole show is "humbug" and their wishes won't be granted, after all. A Three, the Wizard is a master at creating illusions.

But the Wizard gives the Scarecrow a diploma that attests to his brains, and once he believes he has brains, he does. The Lion, says the Wizard, is suffering from disordered thinking—a distinct characteristic of Sixes. All he needs to attest to his courage is a medal, and the Wizard produces one. The Tin Woodman, who needs a heart, is given a testimonial that might be a Two's motto: "A heart is not judged by how much you love, but by how much you are loved by others."

The Wizard agrees to take Dorothy back to Kansas in a balloon. Just as they take off, however, Toto jumps out of the balloon basket. When Dorothy runs after him, the balloon leaves without her.

Dorothy despairs of ever getting home, but Glinda appears and tells her she has always had the power to go home. All she needs to do is close her eyes, click the heels of her ruby slippers together three times and think three times, "There's no place like home." Dorothy wakes up in her bedroom, thrilled to be home, and vows never to leave again.

The theme of trying to return home is central to the Oz story and to the Nine's predicament in general. The dream of going "over the rainbow" to find beauty and excitement is a strong element in a Nine's fantasy life, and the implicit danger is that the Nine may lose her way and become "stuck" in the fantasy—the land of Oz. To find her way back, Dorothy needs to do more than simply drift, she needs to take purposeful action: go down the yellow brick road and find the help she needs to achieve her goal. Ultimately, she realizes that the power to find her "home"—and her true self—has always rested with her, but she has needed the challenge in order to come into her own.

Like most Nine protagonists—especially Self-Preservation Nines—Dorothy finds herself in a situation not of her own making. Unlike Sevens, Nines usually do not seek adventure or challenges; things simply happen to them. The way Dorothy meets the "tests" set before her earns her the right to "home" and a secure and valued personal identity. In fairy tales featuring Nines the "tests" are often "impossible" tasks that the Nine must accomplish. The task the Wizard sets Dorothy and her friends—to bring back the Witch's broomstick—requires their conquering fear in a situation that looks life-threatening. It is notable that Dorothy's destruction of the Witch is accidental—she throws water on the Scarecrow, whom the Witch has set on fire. While trying to save her companions, Dorothy acts decisively—and this action is crucial to achieving her goal of getting home.

A Self-Preservation Nine's instinctive reactions are nearly always reliable and effective, and have only to be translated into Threeish action to transform the Nine's situation.

When Dorothy repeats the phrase "There's no place like home" and clicks her heels together, her intention is clear and unambiguous. Like many Nine fairy tales, *The Wizard of Oz* is an allegory of self-transformation.

Social Nines, whom Ichazo associates with "participation," want to be liked by others and avoid conflict. They often become involved in groups but may resist taking large amounts of responsibility. Social Nines have a strong desire to "fit in," and avoid deviating too far from group norms.

Examples include Nick Carraway in F. Scott Fitzgerald's *The Great Gatsby*, Ruth Puttermesser in Cynthia Ozick's *The Puttermesser Papers*, Mr. Jarndyce in Dickens's *Bleak House*, Walter Mitty in James Thurber's "The Secret Life of Walter Mitty," the narrator of Jay McInerney's *Bright Lights, Big*

City, the title character in Eleanor H. Porter's *Pollyanna*, Aliosha in Dostoevsky's *The Brothers Karamazov*, Babbitt in Sinclair Lewis's novel, Elwood P. Dowd in Mary Chase's play *Harvey*, and Mrs. Moore in E. M. Forster's *A Passage to India*.

A Passage to India

Forster's story is set in the 1920s, when India was still a colony of Great Britain and beset by many cultural and racial tensions. Mrs. Moore arrives to visit her Three son Ronny, a Civil Magistrate in Chandrapore. The British colonials are a self-satisfied group, and Mrs. Moore is distressed by their insensitivity to the spiritual climate of the country. When her son smugly tells her that he is "not in India to behave pleasantly," she gently rebukes him:

"I'm going to argue, and indeed dictate," she said, clinking her rings. "The English are out here to be pleasant."

"How do you make that out, mother?" he asked, speaking gently again, for he was ashamed of his irritability.

"Because India is part of the earth. And God has put us on the earth in order to be pleasant to each other. God . . . is . . . love." She hesitated, seeing how much he disliked the argument, but something made her go on. "God has put us on earth to love our neighbors and to show it, and He is omnipresent, even in India, to see how we are succeeding."

. . . Mrs. Moore felt that she had made a mistake in mentioning God, but she found him increasingly difficult to avoid as she grew older, and he had been constantly in her thoughts since she entered India, though oddly enough he satisfied her less. She must needs pronounce his name frequently, as the greatest she knew, yet she had never found it less efficacious. Outside the arch there seemed always an arch, beyond the remotest echo a silence. And she regretted afterwards that she had not kept to the real serious subject that had caused her to visit India— namely, the relationship between Ronny and Adela. Would they, or would they not, succeed in becoming engaged to be married? (pp. 51-52)

After Adela, a Four, agrees to marry Ronny, Mrs. Moore feels that the purpose of her visit has been accomplished, and her thoughts turn to her responsibilities at home. In the following passage we see both her Social subtype—in her sense of responsibility for maintaining the social order—and her One wing's idealism:

"My duties here are evidently finished, I don't want to see India now; now for my passage back," was Mrs. Moore's thought. She reminded herself of all that a happy marriage means, and of her own happy marriages, one of which had produced Ronny. Adela's parents had also been happily married, and excellent it was to see the incident repeated by the younger generation. On and on! the number of such unions would certainly increase as education spread and ideals grew loftier, and characters firmer. . . . Ronny was suited, now she must go home and help the others, if they wished. She was past marrying herself, even unhappily; her function was to help others, her reward to be informed that she was sympathetic. Elderly ladies must not expect more than this. (p. 95)

Before Mrs. Moore can book her return passage to England, she travels with Adela and a group of English colonials to visit the caves at Marabar. The caves are famous for the quality of their echo but Mrs. Moore finds it terrifying and experiences a spiritual crisis:

The crush and the smells she could forget, but the echo began in some indescribable way to undermine her hold on life. Coming at a moment when she chanced to be fatigued, it had managed to murmur, "Pathos, piety, courage—they exist, but are identical, and so is filth. Everything exists, nothing has value." If one had spoken vileness in that place, or quoted lofty poetry, the comment would have been the same— "ou-boum." If one had spoken with the tongues of angels and pleaded for all the unhappiness and misunderstanding in the world, past, present, and to come, for all the misery men must undergo whatever their opinion and position, and however much they dodge or bluff—it would amount to the same, the serpent would descend and return to the ceiling. Devils are of the North, and poems can be written about them, but no one could romanticize the Marabar because it robbed infinity and eternity of their vastness, the only quality that accommodates them to mankind.

She tried to go on with her litter, reminding herself that she was only an elderly woman who had got up too early in the morning and journeyed too far, that the despair creeping over her was merely her despair, her personal weakness, and that even if she got a sunstroke and went mad the rest of the world would go on. But suddenly, at the edge of her mind, Religion appeared, poor little talkative Christianity, and she knew that all its divine words from "Let there be Light" to "It is finished" only amounted to "boum." Then she was terrified over an area larger than usual; the universe, never comprehensible to her intellect, offered no repose to her soul, the mood of the last two months took definite form at last, and she realized that she didn't want to write to her children, didn't want to communicate with anyone, not even with God. (pp. 149-150)

This tendency to ruminate over philosophical and spiritual questions is characteristic of Nines, particularly with a Social subtype.

Adela, too, has found the caves disorienting, so much so that she believes Dr. Aziz, their Indian guide, has attempted to rape her. When she announces this, the British authorities take immediate steps to bring Aziz to trial.

Mrs. Moore is so disillusioned at the lack of order and justice in the universe that she doesn't even offer an opinion as to Aziz's guilt until directly asked—another expression of Nine passivity. When she says "Of course he is innocent," her son is furious that his fiancée's word is being questioned. But Adela herself is no longer certain that anything actually happened with Aziz in the cave. Mrs. Moore then becomes impatient with the situation:

> "Oh, how tedious . . . trivial . . ." and as when she had scoffed at love, love, love, her mind seemed to move towards them from a great distance and out of darkness. "Oh, why is everything still my duty? When shall I be free from your fuss? Was he in the cave and were you in the cave and on and on . . . and Unto us a Son is born, unto us a Child is given . . . and am I good and is he bad and are we saved? . . . and ending everything the echo."
>
> "I don't hear it so much," said Adela, moving towards her. "You send it away, you do nothing but good, you are so good."
>
> "I am not good, no, bad." She spoke more calmly and resumed her cards, saying as she turned them up, "A bad old woman, bad, bad, detestable. I used to be good with the children growing up, also I met this young man [Aziz] in his mosque, I wanted him to be happy. Good, happy, small people. They do not exist, they were a dream. . . . But I will not help you to torture him for what he never did. There are different ways of evil and I prefer mine to yours." (pp. 204-205)

Here we see again a Nine's resignation, fatalism and indifference, even in someone relatively healthy. Mrs. Moore's solution to the conflict is not to attempt any kind of mediation—which she knows would be useless—but to simply walk away.

As a Social Nine her quality of "participation" has moved toward thinking about larger spiritual questions rather than being involved in the lives of actual people, even family members. Although Mrs. Moore remains aware of her social responsibilities, she is weary of doing her duty and prepared to jettison relationships that thwart her quest to answer her spiritual questions before she dies.

Harvey

In Mary Chase's play *Harvey*, the title character is an imaginary 6-foot-one-and-a-half-inch rabbit who is the best friend and constant companion of Elwood P. Dowd, a comical version of an unhealthy Social Nine. The story revolves around the efforts of Dowd's family to have him committed to a mental institution. At one point in the play, a nurse in the asylum, seeking to draw him out, asks him what it is he does.

ELWOOD: Harvey and I sit in the bars and we have a drink or two and play the jukebox. Soon the faces of the other people turn toward mine and smile. They are saying: "We don't know your name, Mister, but you're a lovely fellow." Harvey and I warm ourselves in all these golden moments. We have entered as strangers—soon we have friends. They come over. They sit with us. They drink with us. They talk to us. They tell about the big terrible things they have done. The big wonderful things they will do. Their hopes, their regrets, their loves, their hates. All very large because nobody ever brings anything small into a bar. Then I introduce them to Harvey. And he is bigger and grander than anything they offer me. When they leave, they leave impressed. The same people seldom come back—but that's envy, my dear. There's a little bit of envy in the best of us—too bad, isn't it? (p. 54)

Social Nines have a natural charm, apparent in the above speech, that arises from the their ability to accept others just as they are, whatever their illusions—or delusions—may be. The typical Nine "live and let live" philosophy is highly appealing in a world where many people feel judged and inadequate. People feel comfortable, safe, and appreciated around Nines, and Social Nines are especially adept at eliciting these feelings.

Sexual Nines, whom Ichazo associates with "union," are focused on merging with another person, connecting so completely with that person that their lives become inseparable. Sexual Nines are especially attracted to dynamic people and draw an energy from their partner that counters their own inertia. Nines with this subtype may be more aggressive than other Nines in seeking out a suitable life partner and doing whatever is necessary to preserve the relationship. This one-on-one intensity is also characteristic of Sexual subtypes in all Enneagram styles, but in Nines it can be particularly acute.

Examples of Sexual Nines include Bob Slocum in Joseph Heller's *Something Happened*, Shakespeare's Macbeth, Mary Tyrone in Eugene O'Neill's *Long Day's Journey into Night*, Humbert Humbert in Vladimir Nabokov's *Lolita*, and Margaret Nathan in Cathleen Schine's *Rameau's Niece*.

Rameau's Niece

Margaret Nathan is the scholarly author of an unlikely best-seller based on the life of Madame de Montigny. Married to Edward, a benevolently egotistical Seven college professor, Margaret has grown forgetful and dreams of overcoming this inadequacy by merging more completely with her husband:

I have forgotten even more than I ever knew, Margaret thought. Names and dates, faces, theories—she sought them with a kind of desperation. She could never possess them, not really, and so they had become for her precious, moving, full of wonder. Margaret had become a connoisseur of these treasures, they were so rare, so delicate, so easily destroyed. Insatiable, she had studied history in college and then in graduate school, plunging into dusty libraries and dreary indices as if they were pools of clear, cool water.

Margaret was considered an important new voice after the publication of her book. But by those who met her, at conferences or even at dinner, she was considered a mute, and so a fool. I don't want to be a mute fool, she thought. I want to be witty and wise. Like Edward. If only Edward were a ventriloquist. I could move my mouth and not worry about what came out. And I could sit on his knee! (p. 33)

Margaret's mental contortions about her relationship with Edward are characteristic of a Sexual Nine. Aware of her addiction to him, she is unable to move beyond ruminating about it:

Margaret watched Edward walk away and thought that he was like a drug, a dangerous, potent, exhilarating drug, that the more she had of him the more she seemed to need him and want him. Did that mean she had too little of him, or too much? (pp. 49-50)

When Margaret discovers a libertine novel in a library, she becomes obsessed by the idea of adultery. Moving to the paranoia of her Six stress point, she begins to imagine that Edward is having affairs with his students. Next she fantasizes about affairs of her own, for instance while sitting on an airplane next to a sleeping Frenchman:

I want, I want, I want, Margaret thought. I want to sleep with him. I want to forget I am married and drown myself in an affair with a stranger. No. I want, I want, I want to forget this stranger and drown myself in marriage. No, no, that's not right either. No drowning. I want to observe, to experience, to know! I am in search of truth and beauty. I am a scholar! That's why I want to fuck the French fellow.

Margaret watched him as he slept. Here was beauty, anyway. A beauty of sorts. If debauched Frenchmen were to your taste. He breathed softly but audibly. Edward, she thought, Why aren't you here? You are my husband. You're meant to protect me, to shelter me, to surround me, to make me forget everything and everyone else.

Edward engulfed the world; he held out his arms in an irresistible embrace, a gesture of supreme self-love and supreme largess. Margaret admired this ability to co-opt existence, to make it his. She loved Edward for that embrace. She had married him in anticipation of it; then, soothed and warm, she had lived among Edward's enthusiasms, swept up in the wave, the nurvanic swoon of living someone else's life.

Hey! Drowning again, Margaret, she thought. Waves indeed.

Wake up. Smell the flowers. Fuck the Frenchman. (p. 135)

Many Nine themes are visible here: wanting two incompatible things at once; longing to merge with a loved one; vague, undefined bodily desires; a free-floating anger; tamped-down feelings that keep rising up.

Margaret becomes more and more involved with fantasizing about possible affairs: with her editor, a woman friend, even her dentist. Here we see her sleepless and ruminating about the nature of love:

> I am in love with three people and married to another, Margaret thought. But what is love? How do I know I'm in love? To "know" what love, or anything else, is, first I must ask, What is knowledge? Okay: "What is knowledge?" I don't know.
>
> And then there are the three propositions. That is, (1) I'm in love with my dentist, (2) I want to sleep with a Belgian hi-fi manufacturer, (3) I am a lesbian. How can I be sure of their validity? Do they correspond to facts? Are they internally logical? Does certainty exist? Why can't I fall asleep? What is sleep? Does sleep exist? Not for me. I must demonstrate the validity of these three propositions. I must demonstrate the validity of sleep. I must verify the three propositions, but first the proposition of sleep. On the other hand, maybe I am asleep, and my inability to fall asleep is a dream.
>
> The last idea relaxed her, and Margaret thought no more about it, or about anything at all, drifting peacefully into unconsciousness. (p. 203)

Using philosophical discourse to solve a personal problem is comically inappropriate, and Margaret's ruminations have the disordered quality of most confused Nines, especially when they are under stress.

Meanwhile, her fantasies become more absorbing and detailed:

> Sometimes she would gaze in fascination at one of her mind's eye's lovers, at Dr. Lipi, or the pursed, moist lips of Martin, or Lily sighing seductively, her big, bright eyes shaded by dark lashes, and then Margaret would suddenly see before her what was before her, and she would realize where she was, on the toilet facing the green tropical birds of the shower curtain; crossing the street against the light; accepting change from the square-faced butcher. She wandered from vision to vision, and from these daydreams of bodies to secret, minute observations of bodies, real bodies, strangers, the bodies of strangers.
>
> I'm out of control, she thought. But she felt strangely in control, powerful. If she was at the mercy of her desires, those desires were hers, and they swept away all obstacles before them, slashing and burning and building their own fantastical cities. (p. 207)

By now Margaret has fully convinced herself that Edward is having affairs and she punishes him with passive-aggressive sulking. When he withdraws—largely because of her hostility—she assumes that this proves her suspicions about his unfaithfulness:

Margaret lay in bed watching *Claire's Knee* on Channel 13 and thinking of Lily's knee, Dr. Lipi's knee, Martin's knee. She turned the TV off, unable to concentrate on French witticisms. I'm not making sufficient progress, she thought. I'm stagnating. That's because I'm suffocating. Because Edward is always here, in this apartment, always around, always talking to me, at least he used to always talk to me, always listening to me when I talked, attentive, bringing me coffee, giving me encouraging kisses when I worked. No wonder I'm making so little progress! He has no consideration. And now, he's never even around! Just because I barely speak to him does not mean it's right for him to come home late, to devote so much time to his students and his sordid little didactic love affairs with pretty girls.

It was no one's fault. That's just the way it was, irresponsibility and betrayal on his side; the simple search for independence on hers. She would have to stop fooling around and tell him. The fruit was ripe, ready to fall from the tree. Quit standing around in the shade palms up, waiting. Shake the branches, Margaret. (pp. 217-218)

Of her four fantasy lovers, only her dentist, Dr. Lipi, actually accepts her sexual overtures. But when the actual lovemaking begins, Margaret dissociates from it:

[T]his is probably not truth, Margaret thought, pressing her lips to his neck, running her hands over his back. It can't be, can it? Pleasure, yes. But also the distinct opposite of pleasure. I hardly know this man. He's my dentist, not my lover. I am disgusted, actually, with this absurd man who has wrapped himself around me, not without encouragement, I admit, but still—if I am disgusted, and I am, then Dr. Lipi, logically speaking, cannot be the only thing desirable, can he? He cannot be truth.

"I'm sorry, Dr. Lipi." She stepped away.

Fool, she thought, looking at him in all his considerable glory. Margaret, you're a fool. Who cares if he's an idiot? And a stranger? Men sleep with idiots and strangers all the time. Yes, but I'm not a man. If Edward wants to sleep with nubile idiots with long silky hair and nearly middle-aged former lesbian idiots with short black, tousled hair, that's his problem. Dr. Lipi, Dr. Lipi, if only the reality of you had not interfered with the idea of you, the idea of you as mere physical being. You are a mere shadow of yourself, Dr. Lipi.

"Margaret, what's wrong?" He put his hand gently on her face and stroked her cheek. "Don't clench your jaw, darling," he whispered. "Your lovely jaw."

His voice startled her. He stood before her, magnificent and now quite naked, his clothes in a puddle at his tanned feet. Oh, fool, fool. Look at this gorgeous creature, as beautiful as any statue, a man of truly heroic proportions. But statues, bless them, do not speak. And Dr. Lipi does speak. And when Dr. Lipi speaks, I remember that he and not just his perfect body and overcharged eyes exists. I remember that Dr. Lipi's personality is one of his parts.

"Margaret," he said, taking her hands and putting them on his flat stomach, then pushing them down, and then down some more.

On the other hand, she thought, "Dr. Lipi," after all, is just a name, a linguistic convenience. There is no Dr. Lipi over and above his various parts, and Margaret contemplated his various parts with increasing interest and enthusiasm.

This is not real, she thought finally. This is just an illusion of perfection. But what an illusion! She held the illusion. Dr. Lipi's hands were pushing down her jeans. The illusion was pushed between her legs.

"This is just an illusion," she said.

"Yes. It's all a wonderful dream." (pp. 246-248)

Thus Margaret, unable to cope with her own desires, turns reality into fantasy even when actually having sex with the dentist. Sexual Nines can resemble Fours in this focus on fantasy and in their longing for lovers they can't have.

The episode with the dentist shocks Margaret into realizing that it is her husband whom she really loves. After rationalizing her fantasies and adulteries as a search for knowledge, she resolves to win Edward back:

All this time away from Edward, wandering—her mind wandered, at least—had left Margaret more and more homesick for him. Her shamed anger simply grew at first, becoming grander and more intense; and then it stopped growing and seemed to blossom and flower into something else entirely: determination. How dare Edward leave her? He had no right. She loved him, and she would have him. She would get him back. He was hers. She had sought friendship. She had sought lovers. She had sought knowledge, she had sought the truth about things. Now, she would seek Edward. (p. 264)

Here Margaret moves to her Three security point and takes action. She finds Edward in his office, dismisses some students he is advising, clears up the misunderstandings between them, and seduces him. They make love on top of his desk.

They lay quietly, wet with sweat, uncomfortable, their position absurd, their pleasure infinite.

In light of this critical discussion, in light of this severe testing, this ingenious testing, this modification of knowledge, this redemption, this remarriage, this lesson, this search for truth, this fucking on a desktop in an airless office, you seem by far to be the best, Edward, the best tested, the strongest. You seem to be the one nearest to truth.

"You're the best," Margaret whispered to her husband. "Of all my theories, Edward, you are the best." (pp. 276-277)

At the end of *Rameau's Niece* Margaret recommits to "union" with her husband. Her indecision has been resolved, at least for the time being. But we sense that her sexual fantasies will return, as they do for many Sexual Nines.

Lolita

A distinctly unhealthy Sexual Nine is Humbert Humbert, the sad pedophile of Vladimir Nabokov's *Lolita*. Humbert, a Nine with an Eight wing, narrates the story of his love affair and lifelong obsession with the "nymphet" Lolita, who is twelve years old when he meets her.

Humbert traces his obsession with pubescent girls to his experience with Annabel, his first love, who died when both he and she were thirteen. In his adult life, Humbert has suffered from mental illness severe enough for him to be treated in a sanatorium. He first sees Lolita when he rents a room in a college town from her mother. Soon he is recording his fantasies about her in his journal:

Friday. I long for some terrific disaster. Earthquake. Spectacular explosion. Her mother is messily but instantly and permanently eliminated, along with everybody else for miles around. Lolita whimpers in my arms. A free man, I enjoy her among the ruins. Her surprise, my explanations, demonstrations, ullulations. Idle and idiotic fancies! A brave Humbert would have played with her most disgustingly (yesterday, for instance, when she was again in my room to show me her drawings, school-artware); he might have bribed her—and got away with it. A simpler and more practical fellow would have soberly stuck to various commercial substitutes—if you know where to go, I don't. Despite my manly looks, I am horribly timid. My romantic soul gets all clammy and shivery at the thought of running into some awful indecent unpleasantness. (p. 53)

When Lolita's mother, Charlotte, leaves a note for Humbert declaring her passion for him, he marries her so he can have continued access to Lolita. He even uses his fantasies of the girl as a sexual aid with the mother. When Charlotte decides that Lolita should be sent away to school, Humbert can't protest, for fear of revealing his feelings for the child.

Later Charlotte is horrified when she discovers Humbert's journal, in which he describes not only his fantasies but his tentative sexual explorations with Lolita. Charlotte threatens to expose him, but is killed by a runaway car before she can. Humbert immediately takes Lolita on a long trip, away from the eyes of concerned neighbors. They stop for the night at a hotel, where he plots to seduce her. But before he can take any action, the sexually aggressive twelve-year-old makes the first move—a development that a passive Nine appreciates:

Frigid gentlewomen of the jury! I had thought that months, perhaps years, would elapse before I dared to reveal myself to Dolores Haze; but by six she was wide awake, and by six fifteen we were technically lovers. I am going to tell you something very strange: it was she who seduced me. (p. 133)

Humbert is shocked to learn that Lolita is not even a virgin, having had her first sexual experience while at camp, with Charlie Holmes, the 13-year-old son of the camp mistress.

Fearing exposure, Humbert rationalizes his continuing sexual activities with Lolita and threatens her with terrible consequences if she tells anyone:

"... I am not a criminal sexual psychopath taking indecent liberties with a child. The rapist was Charlie Holmes. I am the therapist—a matter of nice spacing in the way of distinction. I am your daddum, Lo. Look, I've a learned book here about young girls. Look, darling, what it says. I quote: the normal girl—normal, mark you—the normal girl is usually extremely anxious to please her father. She feels in him the forerunner of the desired elusive male ('elusive' is good, by Polonius!). The wise mother (and your poor mother would have been wise, had she lived) will encourage a companionship between father and daughter, realizing— excuse the corny style—that the girl forms her ideals of romance and of men from her association with her father. . . .

"Finally, let us see what happens if you, a minor, accused of having impaired the morals of an adult in a respectable inn, what happens if you complain to the police of my having kidnapped and raped you? Let us suppose they believe you. A minor female, who allows a person over twenty-one to know her carnally, involves her victim into statutory rape, or second-degree sodomy, depending on the technique; and the maximum penalty is ten years. So I go to jail. Okay. I go to jail. But what happens to you, my orphan? Well, you are luckier. You become the ward of the Department of Public Welfare—which I am afraid sounds a little bleak. . . . In plainer words, if we two are found out, you will be analyzed and institutionalized, my pet, c'est tout. You will dwell, my Lolita will dwell (come here, my brown flower) with thirty-nine other dopes in a dirty dormitory (no, allow me, please) under the supervision of hideous matrons. This is the situation, this is the choice. Don't you think that under the circumstances Dolores Haze had better stick to her old man?" (pp. 150-151)

Typical of the pedophile's pathology, Humbert combines persuasion and threats—also a mark of his Eight wing—to insure continued sexual access to the object of his desires.

Humbert arranges for Lolita to attend a private school, though the threat of exposure causes him continual anxiety. When summer comes, Humbert and Lolita are back on the road. Then, suddenly, she disappears.

For three years Humbert searches for her fruitlessly, brooding about taking revenge on whoever has abducted her. When he finally tracks her down, she is married, hugely pregnant and worn out at seventeen. Still obsessed, Humbert tries to persuade her to leave her husband, but she refuses.

During their conversation, Humbert learns that Lolita abandoned him for the playwright Clare Quilty, whom she had met when she performed in his play at school. Humbert later searches out Quilty and kills him. In Enneagram terms, the murder expresses both the vengeance of Humbert's Eight wing and the purposeful but not always healthy action that Nines can take at their Three security point. After Quilty is dead, Humbert gets back in his car and starts driving:

The road now stretched across open country, and it occurred to me—not by way of protest, not as a symbol, or anything like that, but merely as a novel experience—that since I had disregarded all laws of humanity, I might as well disregard the rules of traffic. So I crossed to the left side of the highway and checked the feeling, and the feeling was good. . . .

I was soon to be taken out of the car (Hi, Melmouth, thanks a lot, old fellow)—and was, indeed, looking forward to surrender myself to many hands, without doing anything to cooperate, while they moved and carried me, relaxed, comfortable, surrendering myself lazily, like a patient, and deriving an eerie enjoyment from my limpness and the absolutely reliable support given me by the police and the ambulance people. And while I was waiting for them to run up to me on the high slope, I evoked a last mirage of wonder and hopelessness. (pp. 306-307)

Here we see Humbert retreating back into Ninelike resignation, passivity, and hopelessness. He is taken for observation to a psychiatric facility, where he is judged sane enough to stand trial for Quilty's murder. He writes his story—the text of Nabokov's novel—as he awaits his trial.

To the end, Humbert resists any real self-awareness and fantasizes that the book will confer immortality on both him and Lolita. His idealization of a sick and sordid relationship is further evidence that he is extremely unhealthy; while

Sexual Nines are generally focused on merging with their beloved, sexual activity with an underage girl is a clear mark of pathology. Although the reader is horrified by Humbert's pedophilia and self-delusion, the wit and complexity with which Nabokov relates his story have made *Lolita* a comic classic. Most of the stories I have discussed in this chapter have a comical aspect: *The Wizard of Oz, Harvey, Fifth Business, Something Happened, The Puttermesser Papers, Rameau's Niece,* "The Secret Life of Walter Mitty," and *Rabbit Run.* Combining as they do qualities of all Enneagram styles, Nines express the contradictions and complexities of human nature. Unexpected and paradoxical combinations of qualities are a major ingredient of comedy, and when we laugh at the struggles of Nines we laugh at the human condition.

Sources

Baum, L. Frank, *The Wizard of Oz* (New York: Crown, 1961). First published 1900

Chase, Mary, *Harvey* (New York: Dramatists Play Service, 1943)

Davies, Robertson, *Fifth Business* (New York: Penguin Books, 1970)

Forster, E.M. *A Passage to India* (New York: Harcourt Brace Jovanovich, 1924)

Eliot, T.S. "The Love Song of J. Alfred Prufrock," in An Oxford Anthology of English Poetry (New York: Oxford University Press, 1956), pp. 1268-1270

Heller, Joseph, *Something Happened* (New York: Alfred A. Knopf, 1974)

Hemingway, Ernest, *The Old Man and the Sea* (New York: Simon & Schuster, 1952)

Nabokov, Vladimir, *Lolita* (New York: Putnam, 1958)

Ozick, Cynthia, *The Puttermesser Papers* (New York: Alfred A. Knopf, 1997)

Schine, Cathleen, *Rameau's Niece* (New York: Ticknor & Fields, 1993)

Thurber, James, "The Secret Life of Walter Mitty," in *The Thurber Carnival* (NY: Harper & Brothers, 1931), pp. 47-51

Updike, John, *Rabbit, Run* (New York: Alfred A. Knopf, 1979)

About the Author

JUDITH SEARLE is the author of *Lovelife*, a novel; *Getting the Part*, a book for actors and *In the Teeth of Time: Poems 1971-2004*. Her authorial credits also include *Sex, Love and Your Personality: The Nine Faces of Intimacy* by Mona Coates, Ph.D. and Judith Searle and *Sleep Talk* by Lois Haddad with Patricia Wilson and Judith Searle. Many of her articles have appeared in *Enneagram Monthly*. A former Board Member of the International Enneagram Association, she teaches workshops around the country. She lives in Santa Monica, California. Her website is www.judithsearle.com.

Bibliography

Books

Baron, Renee and Elizabeth Wagele, *The Enneagram Made Easy: Discover the 9 Types of People* (New York: HarperCollins, 1994)

Condon, Thomas, *The Enneagram Movie & Video Guide: How to See Personality Styles in the Movies* (Portland, OR: Metamorphous Press, 1999)

Daniels, David N., M. D. and Virginia A. Price, Ph.D, *The Essential Enneagram: The Definitive Personality Test and Self-Discovery Guide* (San Francisco: HarperSanFrancisco, 2000)

Horney, Karen, *Neurosis and Human Growth* (New York: W. W. Norton, 1950)

_____ *Our Inner Conflicts* (New York: W.W. Norton, 1945)

Naranjo, Claudio, M.D., *Character and Neurosis: An Integrative View* (Nevada City, CA: Gateways/IDHHB, Inc., 1994)

_____ *Ennea-Type Structures: Self-Analysis for the Seeker* (Nevada City, CA: Gateways/IDHHB, Inc., 1990)

_____ *Transformation Through Insight: Enneatypes in Life, Literature and Clinical Practice* (Prescott, AZ: Hohm Press, 1997)

Palmer, Helen *The Enneagram: Understanding Yourself and the Others in Your Life* (New York: HarperCollins 1991)

_____ *The Enneagram in Love & Work: Understanding Your Intimate & Business Relationships* (New York: HarperCollins, 1995)

Riso, Don Richard with Russ Hudson, *Personality Types: Using the Enneagram for Self-Discovery* (Revised Edition) (Boston: Houghton Mifflin, 1996)

Riso, Don Richard and Russ Hudson, *Understanding the Enneagram: The Practical Guide to Personality Types* (Revised Edition) (Boston: Houghton Mifflin, 2000)

_____ *The Wisdom of the Enneagram: The Complete Guide to Psychological and Spiritual Growth for the Nine Personality Types* (New York: Bantam, 1999)

Wagner, Jerome, Ph.D., *The Enneagram Spectrum of Personality Styles: An Introductory Guide* (Portland, OR: Metamorphous Press, 1996)

Journal

Enneagram Monthly ($40 year): Tel. (877) 428-9639 or (518) 279-4444. E-mail: EnneaMonth@aol.com. Web site: http://www.ideodynamic.com/enneagram-monthly

Software

Character Pro is professional character development software that uses the Enneagram in a basic way. Designed to help writers, actors, editors, and directors create story characters. Website: http://www.characterpro.com

Index

Copyright Permissions

Every effort has been made to trace copyright holders of the material in this book. The author apologizes if any work has been used without permission and would be glad to be told of anyone who has not been consulted.

Excerpts from MEDICINE MEN by Alice Adams, copyright © 1997 by Alice Adams. Used by permission of Alfred A. Knopf, a division of Random House, Inc.

Excerpts from THE SWEET HEREAFTER by Russell Banks, copyright © 1991 by Russell Banks. Reprinted by permission of HarperCollins Publishers, Inc.

Excerpts from PETER PAN by J.M. Barrie. Copyright © 1928 by J.M. Barrie. Reprinted by permission of Great Ormond Street Hospital for Children, London.

Excerpts from A MAN FOR ALL SEASONS by Robert Bolt. Copyright © 1960, 1962 by Robert Bolt. Reprinted by permission of Random House, Inc. Caution: Professionals and amateurs are hereby warned that A MAN FOR ALL SEASONS, being fully protected under the Copyright Laws of the United States of America, the British Empire including the Dominion of Canada and all other countries of the Berne and Universal Copyright Conventions, is subject to royalty. All rights including professional, amateur, motion picture, recitation, lecturing, public reading, radio and television broadcasting, and the rights of translation into foreign languages, are strictly reserved. Particular emphasis is laid on the question of readings, permission for which must be secured by the author's agents in writing. All inquiries in the United States should be addressed to the author's agents, Harold Freedman, Brandt & Brandt Dramatic Department, 101 Park Avenue, New York, NY; and in England to Margaret Ramsay, Ltd., 14 Goodwin's Court, London W.C.2.

Excerpts from THE STRANGER by Albert Camus, translated by Stuart Gilbert, copyright © 1946 and renewed 1974 by Alfred A. Knopf, a division of Random House, Inc. Used by permission of Alfred A. Knopf, a division of Random House, Inc.

Excerpts from THE HORSE'S MOUTH by Joyce Cary, copyright © 1944. Reprinted by permission of the trustees of the Joyce Cary Estate.

Excerpts from "Family Portrait," "In the Counting House," "No Oil," "Cadillac," "EK," "In the Garden," "'Do You Remember…?'" and "Joy to the World" from MR. BRIDGE by Evan S. Connell. Copyright © 1959 by Evan S. Connell. Reprinted by permission of North Point Press, a division of Farrar, Straus and Giroux, LLC.

Excerpts from BREAKFAST AT TIFFANY'S by Truman Capote, copyright © 1958 by Truman Capote. Reprinted by permission of Random House, Inc.

Excerpts from FIFTH BUSINESS by Robertson Davies, copyright © 1970 by Robertson Davies. Used by permission of Viking Penguin, a division of Penguin Putnam Inc.

Excerpts from THE WOMAN WHO WALKED INTO DOORS by Roddy Doyle, copyright © 1996 by Roddy Doyle. Used by permission of Viking Penguin, a division of Penguin Putnam Inc.

Excerpts from THE COCKTAIL PARTY. Copyright ©1950 by T.S. Eliot and renewed 1978

344

by Esme Valerie Eliot, reprinted by permission of Harcourt, Inc. and Faber and Faber Ltd.

Excerpts from BRIDGET JONES'S DIARY by Helen Fielding, copyright © 1996 by Helen Fielding. Used by permission of Viking Penguin, a division of Penguin Putnam Inc.

Excerpts from THE GREAT GATSBY ("Authorized Text") by F. Scott Fitzgerald, copyright © 1925 by Charles Scribner's Sons. Copyright renewed 1953 by Frances Scott Fitzgerald Lanahan. Copyright © 1991, 1992 by Eleanor Lanahan, Matthew J. Bruccoli and Samuel J. Lanahan as Trustees under Agreement Dated July 3, 1975, Created by Frances Scott Fitzgerald Lanahan. Reprinted with permission of Scribner, a Divison of Simon & Schuster, Inc.

Excerpts from A PASSAGE TO INDIA by Edward Forster, copyright © 1924 by Harcourt, Inc. and renewed 1952 by E.M. Forster, reprinted by permission of the publisher.

Excerpts from FINAL PAYMENTS by Mary Gordon, copyright © 1978 by Mary Gordon. Used by permission of Random House, Inc.

Excerpts from SPENDING by Mary Gordon, copyright © 1998 by Mary Gordon reprinted with the permission of Scribner, a Division of Simon & Schuster.

Excerpts from ORDINARY PEOPLE by Judith Guest, copyright © 1976 by Judith Guest. Used by permission of Viking Penguin, a division of Penguin Putnam Inc.

Excerpts from THE SILENCE OF THE LAMBS by Thomas Harris, copyright © 1988 by Thomas Harris. Reprinted by permission of St. Martin's Press, LLC

Excerpts from SOMETHING HAPPENED by Joseph Heller, copyright © 1966, 1974 by Joseph Heller. Used by permission of Alfred A. Knopf, a division of Random House, Inc.

Excerpts from THE OLD MAN AND THE SEA by Ernest Hemingway, copyright © 1952 by Ernest Hemingway. Copyright renewed © 1980 by Mary Hemingway. Reprinted with permission of Scribner, a Division of Simon & Schuster, Inc.

Excerpts from THE GLASS BEAD GAME by Hermann Hesse, © 1943 by Fretz and Wasmuth Verlag AG Zuerich. English translation © 1969, 1990 by Henry Holt and Company. Reprinted by permission of Henry Holt and Company, LLC.

Excerpts from TURTLE DIARY by Russell Hoban, copyright © 1975 by Russell Hoban. Used by permission of David Higham Associates representing Russell Hoban.

Excerpts from "The City" and "The Sea" from SMILLA'S SENSE OF SNOW by Peter Hoeg, translated by Tiina Nunnally. Translation copyright © 1993 by Farrar, Straus and Giroux, LLC. Reprinted by permission of Farrar, Straus and Giroux, LLC.

Excerpts from FEAR OF FLYING by Erica Jong, © 1973 by Erica Mann Jong. Reprinted by permission of Henry Holt and Company, LLC.

Excerpts from GOOD BEHAVIOUR by Molly Keane, copyright © 1981 by Molly Keane. Used by permission of Alfred A. Knopf, a division of Random House, Inc.

Excerpts from ONE FLEW OVER THE CUCKOO'S NEST by Ken Kesey, copyright © 1962, 1990 by Ken Kesey. Used by permission of Viking Penguin, a division of Penguin Putnam Inc.

Excerpts from THE BEEKEEPER'S APPRENTICE by Laurie King, copyright © 1994 by Laurie King. Reprinted by permission of St. Martin's Press, LLC.

Excerpts from THE POISONWOOD BIBLE by Barbara Kingsolver, copyright © 1998 by Barbara Kingsolver. Reprinted by permission of HarperCollins Publishers, Inc.

Excerpts from THE SPY WHO CAME IN FROM THE COLD by John le Carré, copyright © 1963 by John le Carré. Reprinted by permission of the author and Random House, Inc.

Excerpts from THE GOLDEN NOTEBOOK by Doris Lessing, copyright © 1962 by Doris Lessing. Copyright renewed © 1990 by Doris Lessing. Reprinted with permission of Simon & Schuster.

Excerpts from THE GIANT'S HOUSE by Elizabeth McCracken, copyright © 1996 by Elizabeth McCracken. Used by permission of The Dial Press/Dell Publishing, a division of Random House, Inc.

Excerpts from CHARMING BILLY by Alice McDermott, copyright © 1998 by Alice McDermott. Reprinted by permission of Farrar, Straus and Giroux, LLC.

Excerpts from THE CRUCIBLE by Arthur Miller, copyright © 1952, 1953, 1954, renewed © 1980, 1981, 1982 by Arthur Miller. Used by permission of Viking Penguin, a division of Penguin Putnam Inc.

Excerpts from DEATH OF A SALESMAN by Arthur Miller, copyright © 1949, renewed © 1977 by Arthur Miller. Used by permission of Viking Penguin, a division of Penguin Putnam Inc.

Excerpts from GONE WITH THE WIND by Margaret Mitchell, copyright © 1936 by Macmillan Publishing Company, a division of Macmillan, Inc. Copyright renewed © 1964 by Stephens Mitchell and Trust Company of Georgia as Executors of Margaret Mitchell Marsh. Reprinted by permission of William Morris Agency, Inc. on behalf of the Author.

Excerpts from LOLITA by Vladimir Nabokov, copyright © 1955 by Vladimir Nabokov. Used by permission of Vintage books, a division of Random House, Inc.

Excerpts from APPOINTMENT IN SAMARRA by John O'Hara, copyright © 1934 and renewed 1962 by John O'Hara. Foreword copyright 1953 by John O'Hara. Used by permission of Random House, Inc.

Excerpts from THE PUTTERMESSER PAPERS by Cynthia Ozick, copyright © 1997 by Cynthia Ozick. Used by permission of Alfred A. Knopf, a division of Random House, Inc.

Excerpts from BLOOD SHOT by Sara Paretsky, copyright © 1988 by Sara Paretsky. Used by permission of Dell Publishing, a division of Random House, Inc.

Excerpts from THE BLUE HOUR by T. Jefferson Parker, copyright © 1999, 2000 T. Jefferson Parker. Reprinted by permission of Hyperion.

Excerpts from "Swann's Way," from REMEMBRANCE OF THINGS PAST VOL 1 by Marcel Proust, translated by C.K. Scott Moncrieff and Terence Kilmartin, copyright © 1981 by Random House, Inc. and Chatto & Windus. Used by permission of Random House, Inc.

346

Excerpts from KISS OF THE SPIDER WOMAN by Manuel Puig, translated by Thomas Colchie, copyright © 1978, 1979 by Manuel Puig. Used by permission of Alfred A. Knopf, a division of Random House, Inc.

Excerpts from THE LAST DON by Mario Puzo, copyright © 1996 by Mario Puzo. Reprinted by permission of Random House, Inc.

Excerpts from EVEN COWGIRLS GET THE BLUES by Tom Robbins, copyright © 1976 by Thomas Robbins. Used by permission of Bantam Books, a division of Random House, Inc.

Excerpts from HOUSEKEEPING by Marilynne Robinson, copyright © 1981 by Marilynne Robinson. Reprinted by permission of Farrar, Straus and Giroux, LLC.

Excerpts from A SPORT AND A PASTIME by James Salter, copyright © 1967, copyright renewed 1995 by James Salter. Reprinted by permission of North Point Press, a division of Farrar, Straus and Giroux, LLC.

Excerpts from RAMEAU'S NIECE, copyright © 1993 by Cathleen Schine. Reprinted by permission of Houghton Mifflin Company. All rights reserved.

Excerpt from "The Secret Life of Walter Mitty" from the book MY WORLD—AND WEL-COME TO IT © 1942 by James Thurber, copyright © renewed 1971 by Helen Thurber and Rosemary A. Thurber. Reprinted by arrangement with Rosemary A. Thurber and The Barbara Hogenson Agency. All rights reserved.

Excerpts from ANNA KARENINA by Leo Tolstoy, translated by Joel Carmichael, copyright © 1960 by Bantam Books, a division of Random House, Inc.

Excerpts from RABBIT, RUN by John Updike, copyright © 1960 and renewed 1988 by John Updike. Used by permission of Alfred A. Knopf, a division of Random House, Inc.

Excerpts from THE WITCHES OF EASTWICK by John Updike, copyright © 1984 by John Updike. Used by permission of Alfred A. Knopf, a division of Random House, Inc.

Excerpts from "Death of a Traveling Salesman" from A CURTAIN OF GREEN AND OTHER STORIES, copyright 1941 and renewed 1969 by Eudora Welty, reprinted by permission of Harcourt, Inc.

Excerpts from A STREETCAR NAMED DESIRE by Tennessee Williams, copyright © 1947 by University of the South. Reprinted by permission of New Directions Publishing Corp.

Excerpts from THE GLASS MENAGERIE by Tennessee Williams, copyright © 1945 by University of the South and Edwin D. Williams. Reprinted by permission of New Directions Publishing Corp.

Excerpts from "Cap'm Charlie," "Turpintine," "Hello Out There, 7-Eleven Land," "The Superfluous Woman," and "The Deal" from A MAN IN FULL by Tom Wolfe. Copyright © 1998 by Tom Wolfe. Reprinted by permission of Farrar, Straus and Giroux, LLC.

Excerpts from MRS. DALLOWAY by Virginia Woolf, copyright 1925 by Harcourt, Inc. and renewed 1953 by Leonard Woolf, reprinted by permission of the publisher.

Lightning Source UK Ltd.
Milton Keynes UK
UKHW04f0736180918
329097UK00001B/420/P